Why Doesn't God Heal Me?

by Robert Scott

Why Doesn't God Heal Me?
by Robert Scott

Copyright © 2004 by Robert Scott

Cover Design: Thomsen, Germany/Nova Art Explosion

Published by Impact Christian Books, Missouri, USA

ISBN 0-89228-188-X

Unless otherwise noted, Scripture quotations are from *The New American Standard Bible* (NASB), Copyright © 1995 by The Lockman Foundation. Used by permission. Other translations are generally named in full the first time; they are cited and abbreviated thereafter.

Translations and Abbreviations

NIV – New International Version
NKJV – New King James Version
KJV – King James Version
AMP – Amplified Bible
NLT – New Living Translation
TCNT – Twentieth Century New Testament
RSV – Revised Standard Version
MOF – Moffatt Translation
CEV – Contemporary English Version
MSG – Message Bible

All rights reserved. No part of this publication may be reproduced, stored in a retrieval system, or transmitted in any form or by any means – electronic, photocopy, recording, or any other – except for brief quotations in printed reviews, without the prior permission of the publisher.

Printed and bound in the United States of America.

The desert and the parched land will be glad;
the wilderness will rejoice and blossom.

Like the crocus, it will burst into bloom;
it will rejoice greatly and shout for joy. …

Then will the eyes of the blind be opened
and the ears of the deaf unstopped.

Then will the lame leap like a deer,
and the mute tongue shout for joy.

Water will gush forth in the wilderness
and streams in the desert.

The burning sand will become a pool,
the thirsty ground bubbling springs.

In the haunts where jackals once lay,
grass and reeds and papyrus will grow.

Isa. 35:1-2, 5-7
New International Version (NIV)

*By His rivers of healing, God can change
your wilderness wasteland and
your desert of death and disease into a lush garden
of health and abundance.
What Jesus prophesies for all during
His soon-coming reign on earth,
He promises today for all
who believe.*

IN THE LOVE OF OUR FATHER GOD

The human family pictures God s Family.
Our Father of Love gave His Son Jesus
so that we could be saved and healed.
He doesn t want any of His Children hurting or sick.
He wants them to live long and happy lives, just like
any human father desires for his sons and daugthers.
If you are in pain or know someone who is,
keep reading and find out what may be hindering
the healing your loving Father has already
provided for you in the passion of Jesus,
your Brother of Love.

CONTENTS

Dedication vi
Acknowledgments vii
Ten Reasons why *EVERYONE* Needs This Book viii
Prologue ix

PART I
The Truth about Healing

1. Why Have We Not Understood Divine Healing? 1
2. Man's "Sick" Choice – the Way of Curses and Death 9
3. What *God* Says about Divine Healing 19
4. An Awesome Atonement 25
5. Healing in a Nutshell 37

PART II
How YOU Can Be Free from Hindrances and Be Healed and Blessed!

6. The Healing Process 51
7. "Not against flesh and blood" – the Shocking Truth about Demons and Illness 59
8. Our Secret (and Most Powerful) Weapon 71
9. Our Awesome Identity in Christ 81
10. The Key That Unlocks All God's Blessings 97
11. What You *Say* is What You Get 107
12. The Mighty Name of Jesus 117
13. Claiming All the Rights of Salvation 129
14. Defeating the Power of Sin 135
15. Hate Sickness like You Hate Sin! 143
16. God Has No Favorites – Only Intimates 153
17. Hindrances to Healing: Understanding the Concept ... 159
18. The Hindrances 169
19. Hindrances Checklist 233

PART II
SHALOM! To Your Health!

20. Walking in Divine Health 241
21. *Shalom* – Receive it and Share It! 247
Epilogue 251

Appendix 253
Healing Scriptures 295
Index 299

Dedication

I dedicate this book to the honor and glory of the great God who inspired it. He is the One who healed me of a deadly disease in 1986 when I had, according to a Quebec City doctor, only three hours to live. After my family and I endured living hell during twelve tragic years of two incurable, devastating illnesses, this awesome God healed me instantly on October 31, 1998. He gave me the grace to eliminate my major hindrance to healing.

I lost everything a man holds dear, and I almost lost my life. In spite of everything, God never forsook me.

My prayer is that all of you who suffer physically, mentally or emotionally will finally discover through these pages, sooner than I did, why God hasn't healed you. And I yearn for you to be healed by the loving, healing hand of God.

The following autobiographical verse traces my path through the morass of sickness to divine healing. For this book that the Holy Spirit has lovingly inspired, and for Jesus' beatings that paid for our healing two millennia ago, to God be all the glory!

Saved By His Stripes

How long, O God, will you hide Your face?
How long deny Your warm embrace?
My orphaned mentor's nails have held me
Fast to the tree of scorn and disgrace.

In prayer I groan, I flow with tears,
Father! Do You hear? Do You hear? Do You hear?
My deafening sin must surely reveal me
I'm losing all the things I hold so dear.

I hear a song of life gone wrong
Abounding grace, brings light – new dawn
I'm overwhelmed, demons flee me
You heal me, God; I will go on.

Jesus, restore my treasures lost
As my new eyes behold Your cross
Heartfelt thanks to You from me
May all be blessed by heaven's host.

Let His candle burn within you
Fill darkness with His light of truth
Praise You, Jesus, God within us
Your healing glory's wealth enough!

Acknowledgements

My manifold thanks to friends looked like the eternal kudos on Oscar night, so I will have to thank them personally. I will limit my thanks to the following people who have been tools of God's enabling power of grace to change my life: Benny Hinn, whose anointing affected me powerfully on stage in my native South Carolina and even via the television set!; Bob Brasset, who encouraged me more than he knows; Dennis Wiedrick, who ministered to me when I was in need and showed me the Father's heart; Creflo Dollar, whose deep and lively teachings have blessed me immeasurably; Sharon Curtis, the gentle healing servant; Mary Glazier, who showered her motherly love on us, her Edmontonian "children"; Willard Thiessen, the refreshingly humble TV host, whose program so blessed me; Steve Bell, whose song about Psalm 32 changed my life in October 1998; James Robison, who prayed for me in Fort Worth with the Father's love; Kenneth Copeland, a fellow Southerner who edifies me while tickling my funny bone; Tamara Winslow, whose deep, Spirit-breathed teachings have inspired me. Thanks to all y'all (this must be a Yankee computer – that last word doesn't pass the spellchecker)!

Thanks to the late F.F. Bosworth *(Christ the Healer)*, as well as T.L. Osborn *(Healing the Sick)* and Hugh Jeter *(By His Stripes*, out of print*)*, whose books helped ground me in the basics of healing. I believe the Holy Spirit has inspired this book, which adds much new healing revelation, for the purpose of releasing God's people into all His blessings – especially healing – in this exciting and miraculous time of the end.

Ten Reasons Why EVERYONE Needs This Book

1.   **Everyone gets sick and needs healing, that is, until they apply this book!**

2.   **The cost of medical and/or natural treatment can be excessive and pro-hibitive.** Although God does not condemn, per se, using "healing" practitioners, trying to get well can be expensive! The best deal going is the best healing by the best Healer. He created natural healing substances and a body that helps heal itself, but He offers to heal you supernaturally. This book is for thirsty and sick folks who come to healing waters, whose remedies are without price (and side effects!).

3.   **Almost *everyone* knows someone near or dear who is chronically ill.**

4.   **This book reveals *never before* understood hindrances to healing that show how anyone can be healed.** The Holy Spirit has supernaturally revealed these blockages to healing for the purpose of a powerful end-time healing revival. God wants the full gospel preached. Jesus came to save our bodies as well as our souls. The stripes on his back paid for our healing 2,000 years ago!

5.   **Everyone needs to know disease is the Devil's doing, not God's.** Parents, would you cause *your* children to be sick? While it is true that our heavenly Father does at times discipline His own, it is rarely by sickness, and then only a tempo-rary, corrective measure. Like us parents, God wants His Children well. It was Satan who introduced sin and sickness. They glorify him – not God!

6.   **If you are not a Christian, this book could lead you to accept Jesus Christ as Savior and Healer.**

7.   **If you are a real Christian, you will want to share the gospel with the spiritually and physically sick around you.** You can be a healing and saving balm by lending or giving this book to a sick person who can be physically healed and know the greatest miracle of all – salvation.

8.   **This book reveals essential keys to spiritual growth —most Christians are totally unaware of 99.9% of them!**

9.   **This book, by the grace of God, finally answers the haunting question "Why?" Why are a staggering number of Christians not healed?** Larry King asked a healing evangelist that question before millions. At last, millions can hear the answer.

10.   **Almost *all* of these hindrances (over 200!) are ones that keep us from receiving ALL of God's blessings,** whether physical, spiritual, relational, mental, emotional – even financial! If you're broke, this book can fix your finances. It can heal your marriage, your body, your soul, your mind, and your emotions. You can know *shalom,* the peace that comes from being whole or complete in every area of your life.

Prologue

Her name was Sonia. She was only seven. So innocent. She and her mother, originally from the French West Indies, attended our church in Paris. We met in the Palais de Chaillot, virtually in the shadow of the Eiffel Tower.

As many before and since, we found ourselves in another shadow – the valley of the shadow of death. We looked to Jesus, our High Tower, seeking to dwell in His shadow. But death's threatening shadow cast its ugly darkness over sweet Sonia.

It was the early seventies and I was young in my pastoral ministry. And she was young, too young. Too young to suffer. Too young to have a deadly cancer ravaging her petite body. She was a little darling, black and beautiful – only a child. And nothing plucks on the strings of our hearts more than watching the young and innocent suffer.

In her simple childlike faith she trusted in *le bon Dieu* (literally, "the good God"). And so did her mother. And so did I. At least, I thought so.

The doctors at Kremlin-Bicetre gave her no hope.

Doctors are good. But they are not God. With their medicine and skills, which come from the earth God made and from the brains God gave them, they can help. But even they only work within natural, God-ordained laws.

Some are humble. Some are haughty. Some few think they are God Almighty.

But all soon realize, as did these French doctors, that they are only dealing with natural healing, aided by some of man's medical prowess.

When there are no doctors or when doctors finally admit they can do nothing more, we turn to God. He is the only One who heals supernaturally.

And this healing is not a paltry cure with countless side effects. It is not a trade-off that leaves us half-sick in other ways or dependent on expensive pills for the rest of our lives.

Medical science could not heal Sonia.

When doctors shrugged their shoulders and lifted their hands in a French gesture of helplessness, we lifted up our hands to God in prayer.

I held her little hand. But I wanted more than comfort for her. I wanted Sonia well.

I prayed. I trusted in God. I hoped. At one point Sonia rebounded dramatically. A few days later her mother called full of tears and hopes dashed, sobbing the dreadful words," Sonia est partie." ("Sonia is gone.")

I would see many other Sonias suffer and die over the years. In France, in Quebec and in Edmonton, Alberta. The names changed – but the stories were the same.

I hate death. I hate funerals. And as a pastor it has been my sad lot to preach at many of them.

Why Doesn't God Heal Me?

On September 11, 2001, I awoke to tragic news like many of you. That was also the day I had to travel to perform the funeral of a young church member for whom I had a special affection. He had been the victim of a cruel murder, and the murderers got off Scott-free. This Scott was not free from tears as he preached that day – crying for his friend and his nation.

I saw a young man in Quebec City almost every day for a month before he died. We knelt together on his hospice bed that last night, only hours before cancer claimed him.

Life is so much more beautiful than death. My daughter Lisa was born in that same city, and my unprejudiced eyes saw her as the most beautiful baby I had ever laid eyes on – cuter than the Gerber baby-food ads. She was born in the same hospital where I almost died.

My son Paul's life began in a hospital in Trois-Rivieres, Quebec. Shortly before that, in the same hospital, I was only several feet away from a dear lady when she breathed her last. Life is beautiful, but death is ugly.

That's why God says, "Choose life!" He doesn't want the good to die young. And He doesn't even want the old to taste physical death before they live out a full life like Moses.

As many of you, I agonized as I watched good people that I loved die. As I watched death swallow them up, this question gnawed at me: "Why didn't God heal them?"

That question became even harder to deal with when years later it was I who was the victim – languishing with Legionnaire's disease. A Quebec City doctor told my wife I had three hours to live, but I miraculously escaped death. Nevertheless, a lack of oxygen to the brain and the stress of a near-death experience spawned two incurable illnesses, one hereditary.

During a period of twelve years I lost my wife, my family, my health, my wealth and my ministry. And the brain injury caused by the deadly disease Legionnaire's almost killed me – this time by suicide.

Now, getting an answer to the question I had asked so many times during those years took on a greater urgency: "Why doesn't God heal *me*?" Finally, the Holy Spirit revealed the answer to me through a Christian friend.

A false understanding of healing had hindered my faith, a condition to God's promise of healing. As a result of that revelation, I learned that a promise could be absolute, even though it is conditional.

But there was another important hindrance, which I will reveal later in this book. After dealing with it, God instantly healed me of two incurable illnesses on October 31, 1998.[1]

I am among a blessed few who are healed. The vast majority of Christians who

---

[1] As a help to those unfamiliar with the healing process and the proper way to pray for healing, I have included the actual prayers said over me on that day in the Appendices under "Prayers."

Prologue

ask God for healing do *not* get healed! And yet many of them ask in faith.

Even those who understand what this book reveals – that healing is a promise by God – do not understand why God has not healed many sincere Christians.

Ironically, Christians resemble those French doctors. They shrug their shoulders and lift up helpless hands to God for answers.

Today a desperate cry ascends to heaven from God's people. Their heart cry is "Why?" Millions feel betrayed by God. From the least to the greatest, the cry is the same.

Benny Hinn, whom I love and respect, is the most famous healing evangelist in the world today. I have been to a number of his crusades. I have seen with my own eyes awesome and undeniable healings. I have seen many get up out of their wheelchairs and walk.

But for every empty wheelchair on stage that brings hallelujahs, many more in the audience remain filled with people whose hearts groan with the bewildering question: "Why not me? I guess this wasn't my day – or my year. But why not?" But no one answers – not even God.

In 1999, before an audience of millions, talk show king Larry King fired the inevitable question at Benny Hinn. "Why are so many, including your own Christian mother, not healed?"

Hinn humbly admitted, "Larry, I'm not God. I don't have the answers."

I'm not God either. And it is only through His amazing grace and mercy that He has allowed me to receive some answers He wants me to share.

I can take no credit: this is the work of the Holy Spirit. You will see by the fruits of this book that this is not of man. That may sound pretentious to some, but it is true.

Except for the mention of a few hindrances by Bosworth in 1924 and one or two others since, these hindrances to healing have never before been revealed. God's time has come to vindicate Himself. This is undeniably the time of the end. Jesus wants an unblemished bride – healed spiritually and physically.

We ask why – as if it were God's fault. Why don't we look at *ourselves*? The answers to our question are in God's Word. And thanks be to God and God alone for revealing those answers to us in these last days.

As this book shows, healing is not a hapless hope. It's a **promise** – absolute but **conditional**.

We must first understand the truth about divine healing – from *God's* Word, not from the ideas of men.

Then we will come to the guts of this book (and it will take guts to practice what it says) – the answer to why you, or those you know and love, have not been healed.

We live in a sick world – in more ways than one. And this dark world needs a light.

And yet the supposed light of the world, the church, has been, alas, a fizzled-

xi

out sparkler. We Christians are sick – both physically and spiritually. We are a lukewarm, disunited church that is not preaching and living the full gospel of salvation and healing that Jesus preached.

How can the church preach that gospel if we are not living it? How can we share with the world what we have not experienced ourselves? Jesus sent His disciples – all the believers – to lay hands on the sick and said they would be healed (Mark 16:18). How can we be instruments of healing if we ourselves haven't been healed?

How can we bless others if we have not been blessed?

This book will be a small part of an end-time reformation and revival that will eclipse all others. The revelation of our identity as the righteousness of God – a vast subject this book can only briefly introduce – will revolutionize the church. When we begin to walk in the power and glory of our true identity as God-class beings on this earth, our healing will only be the beginning.

We will heal the sick and raise the dead! And much more!

Most of the hindrances explained in this book are hindrances to **all of God's blessings**! We need to discover why God has not blessed us physically, spiritually, emotionally, mentally, relationally – and even financially. This is not simply a book about healing!

The answer is not, as the movie title says, *Back to the Future*. Instead, it's "back to the beginning." It's more like *Return to Eden*.

As you will see, there was no sin and sickness in Eden, where all was "very good." Sin and sickness entered when man sinned. Before then, mankind was walking in intimacy with God and in obedience to Him.

Jesus, the "last Adam," came to restore that intimacy and make a way for sinful, sick man to be redeemed from sin and sickness.

God's time for explosive reformation has come. The Holy Spirit will be poured out in a powerful way so the Bride can be ready for the Bridegroom. Healing is a part of that revival.

The Holy Spirit is revealing these hindrances so we can walk as obedient Children blessed in every way by our Father. He wants us to be intimate with God – to know Him. And He wants us to finally realize the fullness of **who we are in Jesus** – knowledge that can eliminate all hindrances to receiving God's blessings.

He wants us to know *shalom* – the multi-faceted Hebrew word for "the peace that comes from being whole." He wants us whole in every way – even physically.

The song says, "Let there be peace on earth, and let it begin with me."

Shalom – the peace that comes from being whole or healed in every way – can begin with *you*. It can extend to the Sonias in your life. It can even one day include the sad, sick people of this sad, sick world, whom God can heal through *you*.

Prologue

We have entered the days of sorrow that Jesus foretold – and later some may read this book during a time of tribulation and even Great Tribulation, such as this world has never seen. Terrorist attacks, biological terror and widespread epidemics and pestilence will mount to a crushing crescendo before Jesus comes back to rescue this world. You need to know His healing power. Your life depends on it!

This book could change your life – and your world. I pray that what our God is revealing in these pages will help bring the day when the Bride of Jesus will walk in health, blessings, prosperity, harmony, power and resplendent glory.

Shalom! To your health!

– Robert Scott

Why Doesn't God Heal Me?

God's Book of Love – the Bible – is the foundation of this book. Every chapter will begin with a verse or verses that attempt to encapsulate the meaning of the chapter. A partial list of healing Scriptures is included in the very back of the book.

The book itself is full of Bible references that invite you into a fascinating study of God's Word on this vital subject. My prayer is that you, the reader, will come to love, cherish and obey the living and active Word of God.

It is written...

"Heaven is my throne," says the Eternal, "my footstool is the earth. Where would you build a house for me, where would you rear me a home? Such buildings I have made myself already, they are my own," says the Eternal.

"What I care for are humble, broken creatures, who stand in awe of all I say."

Isa. 66:1-2, Moffatt translation

PART I
The Truth about Healing

CHAPTER 1
Why Have We Not Understood Divine Healing?

As we live out these catastrophic last days, you need to understand divine healing. Your life and the lives of those you love depend on it. The answer has always been in The Book. It's in the bestseller that few – even Christians – have ever read. Please don't read this book without The Book by your side.

Please get a copy of God's Instruction Book of Love – the Bible. His Book is all about life and death, just as this book is that God inspired. And healing is a life-and-death matter. If you want to live – and live the abundant, healthy life – open the Word of life.

But be sure to open it and read it with the right attitude – humbly, prayerfully. Discard what men have taught you about healing and be willing to see what God actually says in His Word.

What the Bible really says will probably surprise you. It may pop a few pious and popular paradigms. It may not suit your fancy, especially if you're looking for fancy theological words to interpret – or more often misinterpret – what God's Word plainly says.

1 Why Doesn't God Heal Me?

Don't get me wrong. Using outside historical material or knowledge of Hebrew or Greek to better understand the Bible is fine. The scholarly, humanistic approach, however, isn't God's way. Higher criticism and hermeneutics use human and demonic reasoning that leaves our Teacher out of the picture. We need to ask the Holy Spirit to open our understanding as we approach with a sense of awe God's infallible Word.

Many today do not consider God's Word infallible. Even after the discovery of the Dead Sea Scrolls in 1947, people scoffed. Although Christian explorers have found the true Mount Sinai in Saudi Arabia, some will still scoff – despite astounding proof in uncanny detail that this was the scene of Bible history.[2] Mock and scorn though they may, the Bible is the only book ever written where One who calls himself God predicts the downfall of nations and the events of Jesus' life with pinpoint accuracy. And yet even some theologians still don't believe. Only those who have lived this book, putting it to the test in faith, see how inspired it is and how it works in a supernatural way. Only humble minds guided by the Holy Spirit believe and understand it.

The truth about healing may be too simple for some to grasp. Jesus said that to enter the Kingdom of God we must have humble, teachable, childlike hearts (Mat. 18:3).

Even that stalwart scholar Paul feared Satan would corrupt believers' minds from the simplicity of Christ (II Cor. 11:3). To understand this simplicity, how must we approach God's Word? The answer is simple: approach God's Word as you would God Himself – with awe (Isa. 66:2).

Higher criticism and exalted scholarship tend to look down on God, interpreting His words with carnal minds, watering down and explaining away what they can't understand or don't like to hear.

Instead, we need to look up to God, to lift up His Word with reverence.

Most of the basic truths of the Bible are surprisingly simple. You don't need a degree in theology to understand them. In fact, in most cases it will hinder you. I have a college degree in theology, but I had to unlearn much of the knowledge I acquired. Seminaries are more often cemeteries that need the Holy Spirit to make the Word come to life.

Jesus – the living Word who dwells within us through the Holy Spirit – spiritually discerns how we implement His words in our lives. Erudite though we may be, if the Holy Spirit is not our principal guide, we might as well be in a cemetery! God needs to raise the dead in more ways than one!

Paul, unlike the twelve, was a man of letters. He was able to use some of that scholarly learning once converted. But it wasn't the best theological school of his day that opened his mind to understand the Word of God and the gospel. It was the Holy Spirit!

---

[2] See the exciting story of two explorers who risked their lives to find Mount Sinai in the video entitled *In Search of the Real Mount Sinai*, available from John Haggee Ministries.

Read I Corinthians 2 in a modern translation and you will see what scholar Paul thought of human scholarship and reasoning versus the power of God. The things of God are foolishness to those without the Holy Spirit.

Theological arguments are full of maybes, speculations and reasoning, and often render the Word of no effect like the Pharisees did. At best they water down the truth to a comfortable and humanly acceptable error. Jesus did not speculate like the scribes. He spoke with authority.

The Link Between Carnality and Healing

I can say with authority that carnality is a major hindrance to understanding healing. In an important healing verse, Peter slips in an interesting concept: we must die to sin and live for righteousness (I Pet. 2:24).

The law of sin, sickness and death died with Jesus. He took the curse for us. The lifting of the curses, however, depends on our dying to sin or carnality.

Sadly, we have listened to teachers who take the carnal approach. They eat of the tree of the knowledge of good and evil – and feed us garbage. They use fleshly reasoning to determine truth – not revelation from God.

I myself swallowed their lies. I reasoned that since many Christians, including me, weren't healed, it must not be God's will.

What abysmal logic! Since when does what happens to men and human reasoning about their lacks or hindrances determine what God's will is? God's will is in His Word!

And His Word says, "For you were like sheep going astray, but have now returned to the Shepherd and Overseer of your souls" (I Pet. 2:25). Whom do you choose to believe and worship? Your pastor? Or your real Shepherd and Pastor? If there is a conflict, choose Jesus! He wrote the Book! He wrote the *whole* Book!

The Whole Thing!

That brings up an important point – and an important reason why people don't understand healing or any major Biblical doctrine.

"That's Old Testament!" That's a common excuse for not obeying the truth. But you can't understand the Bible unless you understand the beginning. Ever try to read a novel by beginning in the last 30% of the book?

Just because we no longer need to sacrifice bulls doesn't mean the first part of God's Word is a bunch of bull! Jesus' sacrifice paid for the disobedience of the principles in His Word. The foundational moral principles of Christianity are contained in what men have dubbed "Old Testament."

God revealed and elaborated His principles of love for Him and one's own neighbor (Deut. 6:5; Lev. 19:18) in that part of His Word that men like to call "old."

God's Word is eternal – as eternal as Jesus. It endures forever (Isa. 40:8;

Why Doesn't God Heal Me?

I Pet. 1:25). It is His Instruction Book – His Book of Love. It reveals Him — as who and what He is – and He *is* Love (I John 4:8).

The oracles of God were contained in 49 scrolls. Seven is God's number of completion and perfection, and 49 equals seven times seven. It's a complete and perfect Book in its original form.

God gave nine major covenants in His Word, and He will add a final tenth covenant when the earth and the heavens are made new. Eight of those covenants are contained in what men call the Old Testament. The ninth is the New Covenant in Jesus' blood, which is also a testament or will. That covenant enables us to claim all the promises of God's entire Word.

Except for mistranslations like in the King James Version, the terms "Old Testament" and "New Testament" do not occur in the Bible.

Almost three-fourths of the Bible, commonly referred to by translators as the Old Testament, was written primarily in Hebrew. God employed the Jewish people to preserve it. The rest was primarily written and saved in Greek.

While it is awkward to avoid the common terms men use, I will endeavor to do so in this book. Why? Because Satan has used the "that's Old Testament" nonsense to virtually throw out three-fourths of God's Word. When Jesus said to live by every word of God (Mat. 4:4), the last fourth of His Word had not been written!

It's a long story, but I suggest you carefully read Hebrews 9 and 10. God shows clearly in those verses that it was rituals and sacrifices that foreshadowed Jesus that are no longer necessary, not the principles of the Hebrew Scriptures. You can learn a great deal about Jesus by studying the sacrifices and rituals, even though His sacrifice makes them unnecessary to actually practice.

I prefer to be accurate and avoid man's frequently used terms. The Old Testament is not old. It is the living and active Word of God (Heb. 4:12). Paul refers to the Hebrew section of God's Instruction Book of Love as "the sacred writings which are able to give you wisdom that leads to salvation" and says: "All Scripture is inspired by God ..." (II Tim. 3:15-17).

Undermining any part of God's Book of Love is a serious offense. If Christians today would allow the Holy Spirit to unveil to them the vast riches embedded in the Hebrew section of God's Word, great power would be released. Dr. Creflo Dollar is a good example of an anointed preacher who teaches out of Part I of the Word of Love.

Jesus was the God who dealt with men in the first part of the Bible (read the proof under "Jesus" in the Appendix). And He put His stamp of approval on the words He spoke in Hebrew (Luke 24:44-45). The "Old Testament" could actually be called "The First Words of Jesus" and the New Testament "The Last Words of Jesus." You can't understand His last words without His first words – and the reverse is also true.

Without "that Old Testament stuff" you can't prove that Jesus is your Savior. And you can't claim 90% of the promises of God. Ever tried to fight with one-fourth of a sword? God's Word is our sword (Eph. 6:17).

The last fourth of the Bible shows us who we are in Jesus, but the first three-fourths show us who Jesus is! That Hebrew section is a gold mine – and we need to start digging!

When part of the instructions for fixing a household appliance is missing, are you able to fix it? If you knew bombs were coming tomorrow and you only found Part II of the instruction manual for building a fallout shelter, where would that leave you?

The Word of Love is also a Book of Life. Jesus said, "… if you [desire] to enter into life, keep the commandments" (Mat. 19:17). But the Ten Commandments are only fully enumerated in the Hebrew Scriptures!

When we frown on, fear, minimize or limit any part of God's Word of Love, we limit our God of Love. And when we deny any part of the Word of Love, we deny Love Himself. Do you want all of Love, or only part of Him?

To understand His healing, we need to understand His love. We need to embrace all of Him and all of His Book of Love.

The Pastors' Part of the Problem

The Book of Love, in Acts 28, gives us a clue as to why we haven't understood healing and haven't been healed. Luke, the beloved physician, after having recounted how God employed Paul (not doctor Luke himself!) to heal the Maltese leader Publius, writes of how Paul invited the leading Jews at Rome to hear him teach about Jesus from the Hebrew Scriptures. Some did not believe. Paul, inspired by the Holy Spirit, quoted to them Isaiah 6:9-10:

"Go to this people and say to them, You will hear and hear with your ears but will not understand, and you will indeed look with your eyes but will not see [not perceive, have knowledge of or become acquainted with what you look at, at all]." They had a different perception or paradigm when it came to spiritual things. And where did they get it?

"For the heart [the understanding, the soul] of this people has grown dull [stupid, hardened, and callous], and their ears are heavy and hard of hearing and they have shut tight their eyes, so that they may not perceive and have knowledge and become acquainted with their eyes and hear with their ears and understand with their souls and turn [to Me and be converted], that I may heal them" (Acts 28:26-27, *Amplified Version*).[3] Healing is a part of salvation, and it is the same

---

[3] The italics and bold type within Bible quotations, as well as the brackets and parentheses found therein (except for quotations from the *Amplified Version*), have been inserted by the author of this book. The best translation of the Bible would be a combination of the NASB and the NIV, each of which is written in a different style. The NASB is the one most reliable translation, with only about 3% error. The lovely King James that many swear by has 8% error. Some have as much as 50% error. Modern translations and paraphrases can be helpful if used wisely. Modern believers, however, having adopted many traditions of men, would do well to put accuracy ahead of beauty or readability in establishing doctrine.

Why Doesn't God Heal Me?

Greek word. This also applies to physical healing.

Jesus used exactly the same verses when explaining to His disciples why He spoke to the Jews of His day in parables. He told the disciples these Jews did not understand and believe the gospel for the same reason as those in Rome. In Acts 28:28, Paul goes on to say that Israel was blinded but that the Gentiles would listen. How and why were they blinded?

They were blinded by Satan and by their religious teachers, the Pharisees, "the blind who lead the blind." Jesus called their teaching leaven, their sinful doctrine spreading like yeast. Leaven puffs up and decays, as does the heady knowledge of false teaching. The Pharisees were blind shepherds, as are many today. The Jews at Rome had been lulled to sleep. Some themselves teachers had in turn been soothed into slumber by those who had taught them.

The Jews had a different paradigm than what Paul and Jesus were explaining to them from the Word. As the *Fiddler on the Roof* song says: "Tradition!" Jesus said their traditions "invalidated" or "made void" the Word of God. The religious leaders or shepherds of that day were responsible for being Satan's agents to void the Word through tradition, staid orthodoxy and human reasoning. How history repeats itself!

In pointing the finger at pastors, I'm looking in the mirror. God called me to pastoral ministry over thirty years ago, and I know how easy it is to try to be an "almighty pastor."

Respect for pastors has too often, however, become "pastor worship." Thank God the "one-fold ministry" is about to fold! The Ephesians 4 five-fold model will be restored as the spotless Bride of Jesus readies herself for the wedding. Pastors will still have a key role nonetheless. But God will judge us overseers and teachers with stricter judgment.

He had strong words for Israel's religious hierarchy, the spiritual shepherds of their day. Those words also apply to our modern pastors, who have been the influential ones responsible for leading the flock astray on healing. Space prohibits quoting Jeremiah 23, Ezekiel 34 and Malachi 3, but I can't resist quoting Hosea, a prophecy for "the latter days" (3:5). God bemoans the fact that there is no truth or knowledge of God in the land (4:1).

And whom does God blame? The priests! (4:7; 5:1) God blames the clergy, who should be teaching the truth!

In Hosea 4:6 God charges: "My people are destroyed for lack of knowledge." He said they had forsaken His law. Pastors have not told the truth about healing or about God's law.

"The prophet is [considered] a crazed fool and the man who is inspired [treated as if] mad or a fanatic, because of the abundance of your iniquity ..." (9:7, AMP). It doesn't pay to speak out about God's truth and His law today.

It hardly pays to preach and teach and practice the truth about healing. Some – indeed some Christians – consider even genuine healing evangelists who do what

Why Have We Not Understood Divine Healing? 1

Jesus did to be "Holy Roller" sideshow embarrassments!

On the contrary, it's the shepherds who should be embarrassed! They have fooled the sheep with foul fodder. Instead of the pure forage of liberating truth, they have enslaved the sheep by feeding them falsehood. Rather than making them lie down in green pastures, their pastors have pastured them in the stubble of black lies. Some of those false shepherds may not even know Jesus, and they are probably less guilty. But even the real Christian leaders have watered down God's truth on healing to a comfortable level of error.

In so doing, they've made a sick choice, so to speak – and in more ways than one. It's the same choice Adam and Eve made. Before we see what God says about healing, let's look at that choice.

1 Why Doesn't God Heal Me?

It is written...

I call heaven and earth to witness against you today, that I have set before you life and death, the blessing and the curse. So choose life in order that you may live, you and your descendants, by loving the [Eternal] your God, by obeying His voice, and by holding fast to Him; for this is your life and the length of your days ...

Deut. 30: 19-20a

CHAPTER 2
Man's "Sick" Choice – the Way of Curses and Death

Adam and Eve chose curses and death instead of the eternal life and spiritual and physical blessings made possible by intimacy with God. They rejected the tree of life, representing the way that would lead to eternal life and abundant joy and health in this life. They chose to fall under the curse that would be carried out by Satan. In the garden they weren't sick, spiritually or physically.

Like comic Flip Wilson, the Devil made them do it! They were responsible for their wrong choice, but Satan gave them the idea to sin, and he inflicted upon them the curse God warned them would be their lot if they sinned. That curse involved sickness and death.

They chose the only tree God said not to touch. That was the tree of the knowledge of good and evil. It is not wrong to know the difference between good and evil. But that was not what it was all about. Instead of letting God tell them what was good and what was evil and believing Him, they chose to believe Satan's lie. And what was that?

Satan convinced them that they, apart from the revelation of God and simply

Why Doesn't God Heal Me?

using their human reasoning, could decide what was good and evil. As the song says, "I'll do it *my* way." It's like a little boy who insists on doing it by himself, not in the way Mama or Daddy said. The result? A big mess, at best. And sometimes even death.

For Adam it wasn't a matter of maybe dying or maybe being cursed. On the contrary! In Genesis 3 God said, "You will *surely* die [and you will surely be cursed]." My sweet Southern grandmother used to warn us with: "I don't mean maybe!" But – unlike my dear grandmother – God really meant it!

Here's the gist of what He said: "You two and the rest of you afterwards will be cursed in the ground, cursed in the field, cursed in your childbearing." God never intended that women should suffer the way they do now in delivery, which should show us that bodily suffering and pain are not God's perfect will for His Children. At creation God said everything was "very good." Pain is not good. Sickness only came when Satan and sin entered the world.

God basically said, "Now you have chosen death and sin instead of life and blessings, the Kingdom of Darkness over the Kingdom of Light. I warned you but you didn't listen. Since you have chosen sin's dark realm over the law and its way of life and blessings, you fall under the curses of the King of Darkness, Satan the Devil. You will be cursed – with sin and death." Sickness is part of the curse.

Some of you logical people, playing devil's advocate, may be thinking of a possible flaw in reasoning. If God caused a dramatic increase in childbirth pain after Eve's wrong choice, then Christian women today shouldn't suffer birth pains as unbelievers do. Is it possible for believers to be delivered from bad deliveries?

We have not because we ask not. I know of Christian women who have claimed release from the curse of excessive birth pains, and were blessed with virtually painless deliveries. Jesus' bodily pain broke the curse of physical pain and sickness – including the childbirth curse. Women of God, claim it!

A Curse-Destroying Sacrifice

Jesus' sacrifice takes away all curses, if we accept Jesus and renounce the curses in His name. The major curses of sickness and death, perpetrated by Satan, are eliminated by God's grace in the price Jesus paid through His broken body (suffering pain for us) and His bloody death (tasting death in our place).

What a tragic shame that many, if not most Christians today are still under the curse of sickness! We have accepted the blood Jesus shed for our sins – but not the bloody stripes that took away our sicknesses.

We've watered down the blood of Jesus. We've changed the communion wine into water and made the stripes of Jesus of no effect!

We have watered the wine of gospel truth, turning it into gospel half-truth. It's about time the church heard the full gospel truth – the good news of our physical

Man's "Sick" Choice 2

salvation, the healing of our bodies. We have preached a so-so gospel instead of a *sozo* gospel. That's Greek for *save*. As we shall see, it means *heal* as well.

Christians are the body of Christ as well as His Bride. And Christ's body is gravely, physically ill. But that also means Christ's Bride is too, so she definitely is not without blemish.

Why? Because she hasn't heard the full gospel.

Furthermore, she has accepted the curse of sickness. She has tolerated it to the tomb. But Jesus' time has come to release His church from curses – including the curses of Deuteronomy 28.

The Curses of Deuteronomy 28

The New Living Translation gives more life to Deuteronomy, or more curses and death, depending on what we choose. In verse 15 God says if His people refuse to obey Him thus rejecting life and blessings, "all these curses will come and overwhelm you." Verses 20-22: "The [Eternal, or Jesus – the correct translations of the Hebrew YHVH] Himself will send against you curses, confusion and disillusionment in everything you do ..." Have you ever seen a more mixed-up, emotionally distraught, confused and cursed society than in our supposedly advanced Western nations today?

One clarification is in order about curses. God allows Satan to carry out most curses while God still claims responsibility for them as the sovereign God. There are many cases in the Bible, however, where God issues a curse and carries it out Himself in order to bring us to repentance for our own good. God is always love, even when He disciplines or chastens His created or "born again" Children (Heb. 12:10).

"The [Eternal] will send diseases among you until none of you are left in the land you are about to enter and occupy. The [Eternal] will strike you with wasting disease, fever, and inflammation, with scorching heat and drought, and with blight and mildew. These devastations will pursue you until you die" (Deut. 21-22).

In verse 27: "The [Eternal] will afflict you with the boils of Egypt and with tumors [as with cancer], scurvy, and the itch, from which you cannot be cured. The [Eternal] will strike you with madness [mental illness, which can be a worse nightmare than most physical ailments, for the ill and especially for his or her family], blindness, and panic [panic attacks and other illnesses affecting the emotions]."

Jesus said that if we wouldn't obey Him, the diseases of Egypt would be our lot (Ex. 15:26). SARS may not be Egyptian, but you can't get much more Egyptian than West Nile virus! But if you've been redeemed by Jesus' blood from the Egyptian bondage of sin and sickness, West Nile virus can't touch you. So don't fear it!

Don't be afraid of any sickness! In verse 59-62, God warns of "indescribable plagues" that will overwhelm the disobedient. "The [Eternal] will bring against

11

you every sickness and plague there is, even those not mentioned in this Book of the Law, until you are destroyed." Cancer, venereal diseases, AIDS – and now even deadly anthrax and smallpox genetically altered by terrorists to murder their victims – are modern-day realities.

But terrorist attacks do not surprise God. His healing power is not limited – He heals anthrax too. And we needn't fear death from a sabotaged water supply. Read Exodus 23:25 and Isaiah 33:14-16 and claim them! But before you do, get to the chapter on the key that unlocks all blessings – **knowing you are the righteousness of God**. Get established in Jesus' righteousness. Then you'll know you have a right to be protected!

Combining Genesis 3 with Deuteronomy 28, this is what God was saying: "You and your descendants will live a life of curses and death, in the hope that those curses will bring you to repentance, so your children can turn to me and live. I want to bless you, not curse you. But it may take the tragic results of a cursed life to bring you back to me. I will come to redeem you from your sins and your curses. And I, the Eternal Healer, will come to be beaten by humans. By my stripes you will be healed."

That's fine and dandy, you may think, for those who know Jesus. But what about those who don't know Him as Savior and Healer?

God is Fair

Some may think that because most have never had a chance to accept Jesus' sacrifice for sin and sickness, God is unfair. That's a lie!

It only appears that way because the church doesn't have the whole story. And so our good God is made to look extremely bad.

It seems that everybody, even Christian evangelists, paint God out to be the bad guy. God is perfectly just, but He is perfectly merciful. It isn't God's fault that we are sinful and sick. It's our fault. As we shall see later, when Adam sinned, Satan became the god of this age. And he's done a naughty number on both the unsaved and the church. He has brought in deceptions and hindrances that have kept the unsaved as well as many of the saved in poor health.

Satan has concealed the saving and healing knowledge from the world – and even from many in the church.

But for those who want to dig for it, the knowledge has been there all along – in God's Word. In Hosea 4:6 Jesus laments, "My people die for lack of knowledge." Yes, even Christians, even innocent children like Sonia have died because knowledge about God and healing was missing. I know some dear friends who have been chronically sick or who have died because they did not understand the hindrances to healing in this book.

Even I myself lost everything because of a sickness and almost died because I didn't fully understand and eliminate a hindrance. And I was more sinful than ignorant. Christians can be sick, nevertheless, and even die of a disease because of ignorance. But that needn't affect their eternity.

Others, the majority, endure the curses of sin, sickness and physical death without ever even hearing the name of Jesus. And yet God says plainly in Acts 4:12, "And Salvation comes through no one else, for there is no other Name in the whole world, given to men, to which we must look for our salvation" (TCNT – *Twentieth Century New Testament*). Most fire-and-brimstone preachers would have us believe that all these innocent people will go to hell.

What? You mean our Father of Love and mercy and fairness would send a family to hell because some missionary had a flat tire? God says He is not willing that any should perish, but that all should be saved, or at least have a fair chance for salvation. God tells us what He is like in II Peter 3:9: "… He is longsuffering [*extraordinarily patient*] toward you, not desiring that any should perish, but that *all* should turn to repentance" (AMP).

Furthermore, I Timothy 2:4 says God desires all men to be saved. Verse 6 says Jesus died for *all*. Is God so powerless that He would die for all human beings and yet not be able to find a way to tell them about it so they could be saved? The question is not *if* He is able – but *when*.

Most of the world has never heard the gospel truth. That's the gospel truth – or at least a fact of history. And yet God so loved the *world* – not only a handful of favored ones – that He sent His Son Jesus to die so "that whosoever believes in Him should not perish but have everlasting life" (John 3:16). And how do they believe unless someone preaches to them (Rom. 10:14)? And what if you never heard His name so you could believe in Him? "Tough luck. Go to hell!"

That, unadorned, is what these preachers of hell – and supposedly of grace – are saying. The God of fairness and grace never says that in the Bible. He is Love, and that would be against His nature. If God convicted people without a fair trial, He would be neither believable nor worthy of our trust.

God is not a harsh judge who condemns you to the electric chair before reading you the riot act and giving you a chance to change. He will not condemn you without first introducing you to your Advocate – who even died in your place. Exactly how He will do it in detail is not clear in the Bible, but more than 600 Bible verses support the controversial truth I am introducing here. That is another subject for another time, but now that I have challenged a cherished false idea, I will briefly explain.

A *First* Chance for the Ignorant and/or Deceived

Revelation 20:5 speaks of the resurrection of "the rest of the dead" after the Millennium, which begins with Jesus' return and the resurrection of the righteous dead, i.e. Christians who died before His return. What about dead Buddhists? What about someone who never heard the name of Jesus?

2 Why Doesn't God Heal Me?

Suffering in sickness and curses in this life is one thing. Being eternally damned due to ignorance is quite another. That's not fair! And God is always perfectly fair, both in His mercy and in His judgment.

Revelation 20:12 speaks of the "great white throne judgment," which occurs after the Millennium. Judgment does not always imply condemnation (I Pet. 4:17). How can those who never heard the gospel in this life be judged fairly if God does not preach the gospel to them as He raises them for this period of judgment? Notice that "the Book of *Life*" is opened at this time, meaning an opportunity to receive eternal life.

Ezekiel 37, fertile fare for revivalists and for Negro spirituals, is also a prophecy for the future. Verses 12 and 13 are talking about more than revival – God means it literally! To ancient Israel God says, "I will open your graves and cause you to come up from your graves, and bring you into the land of Israel." It doesn't take an Einstein, even without God's Spirit, to figure out that God is talking about a resurrection from the grave. God says this no less than three times.[4] This is a resurrection of Hebrews who never had the Holy Spirit. Only the leaders and prophets had the Spirit. The Book of Revelation shows that these leaders will be in the first resurrection, that of the righteous dead just before the thousand-year rule of Jesus on earth. Only the "dead in Christ" rise at Jesus' return.

If God Himself says He is giving these Israelites another "chance," then He obviously feels they did not have a fair chance the first time without the Holy Spirit. It is the first fair chance for these people, even though they did at least know of God, unlike many others.

Since the resurrection of the righteous is the first resurrection mentioned, this would be the second one, a resurrection to physical life as opposed to the glorious and incorruptible body of the righteous (I Cor. 15). These physical people will live a second life – this time free of Satan's influence. Although this is the second general resurrection, it is, of course, the first time these people will be resurrected. So it is the second resurrection – not a second chance.

For the unmerciful Christians who argue that this is a second chance, I ask this question: Have you sinned this last month? Have you not stumbled and failed miserably at times? Did God not give *you* a second chance – and a third chance, and a fourth chance, and … What if God was as hard on you as you are on people who haven't been called and had their minds opened to Jesus yet? Would you like God to curse you to hell as easily as you curse the unsaved?

God has a merciful plan. His Holy Days depict several harvests of souls.

---

[4] *The New Living Translation* renders it "graves of exile." Peter says Scripture is of no private interpretation. This version of the verse in Ezekiel is some scholar's own interpretation as he apparently tries to make this verse make sense to his way of thinking. It contradicts the other translations and is nowhere found in the Hebrew.

Israel offered the wave sheaf, or the first of the first fruits of the spring barley harvest, during the Feast of Unleavened Bread. This symbolized Jesus, the "firstborn of many brethren" (Rom. 8:29). The rest of the first fruits were harvested at Pentecost, 50 days later. That is the church of this age, called to be Jesus' Bride and the first harvest of God's Children glorified at the first resurrection (Rev. 20:4-6; 5:10).

The later and bigger harvest was at the time of the Feast of Tabernacles, which prefigures the time when Jesus will rule over the whole earth and bring everyone into the knowledge of Him.

The last of God's feast days is the Last Great Day. It depicts the time after the Millennium (represented by the Feast of Tabernacles) when all will begin to have a chance for salvation, through a resurrection to hear the name of Jesus or understand the meaning of His gospel for the first time.

It was on the Last Great Day that Jesus said in John 7:37 that *anyone* could come and drink of the living waters of eternal life. Israel had been blinded and couldn't taste of that life, as is the case for many today (II Cor. 4:4; Mat. 13:11-13). That Last Great Day in prophecy will take place after Jesus' 1,000-year reign on earth. That is the appointed time for everyone else including the many Moslems, Hindus and Buddhists. Only God, of course, can truly judge when a person has indeed received a fair chance for salvation.

Although the greatest harvest ever is about to occur as we enter these very last days, only those who have "been appointed to eternal life" accept Jesus in this age (Acts 13:48). You can hear about Jesus and not be appointed to receive eternal life now.

Of course, people must first hear of Jesus before they believe (Rom. 10:14). "And how shall they hear without a preacher?" So if the preacher has a flat tire and never shows up, does that mean the people he was trying to reach will go to hell when they die?

Even of blinded and rebellious Israel, Romans 11:25-36 says, "all Israel will be saved ..." How can all Israel be saved if they are not resurrected? And Ezekiel 37 says they will be. The plan of God pictured by His Holy Days says they will. And God is no respecter of persons. If Israel will, then everyone else – the rest of humanity – will also be resurrected to receive salvation. God's desire for all men to be saved is not some weak, futile hope. It is His firm assurance that all will be given an opportunity for salvation.

Some say that because God gave everyone a conscience and they know right from wrong in a general way, God judges them now in this life. Not so. They will indeed have to answer for their evil deeds when they are resurrected, just as we must acknowledge our sin when we come to Jesus. And our fair and just Jesus will deal with them as He does with us. They will finally have the opportunity to accept Jesus and be cleansed by His blood. And like us, they will be judged and rewarded according to their works after they accept Jesus.

Why Doesn't God Heal Me?

Doesn't that make more sense than the lie about them going to hell? They can't live eternally *anywhere* – with Jesus or in eternal torment – until they accept Life Himself. As we shall see, our spirit is dead until we accept Jesus and eternal life. Where we spend that eternal life depends on our choice. But since the Father is the One who draws us to Jesus (John 6:44) and Jesus said He chose us (John 15:16) – not the other way around – our only initial choice is to respond to God's call.

"Shall not the Judge of all the earth deal justly?" inquires Abraham in Genesis 18:25.

What about the poor lady who died never hearing Jesus' name because a missionary never reached her with the only Name under heaven by which men can be saved? She will rise up and at last have a fair chance – her first chance to know Jesus Christ and be with Him for all eternity.

That's fair. And that's love – the mercy and justice of our awesome God.

Dead Spirits versus Live Spirits

How can God condemn unsaved people to eternal life in hell when they have not yet even received eternal life by the Holy Spirit? They are sons and daughters of Adam, who never took the tree of life representing the Holy Spirit and salvation.

Jesus, the One who created Adam, gave him the Holy Spirit as a Guide. The Holy Spirit was with him or upon him yet not *in* him as He is in Christians today. But there's more. With the breath of God Jesus actually breathed into Adam a part of Himself. Yet He gave Adam free will.

God meant what He said when He warned Adam that he would die on the day he ate the fruit of the forbidden tree. He only died physically some 900 years later. But he died spiritually that day. His spirit died. And all humans have inherited that dead spirit. "The wages of sin is death, but the gift of God is eternal life" (Rom. 6:23).

Contrary to the popular "once saved, always saved" teaching, only live spirits, Christians enlivened by the eternal Holy Spirit, are now alive eternally. It is only they who have now begun to live forever. Their only choice now is to live forever – with God or without God. The Bible indicates that only a small minority of Christians will probably be stupid enough to forfeit eternal "heaven" (which will eventually be on earth, as Revelation 21 and 22 teach) and opt for an eternal hell.

This is a big subject. Suffice it to say that many Bible passages are clear on this topic (Heb. 6:4-6; II Pet. 2:17-22; I Cor. 9:27). God plainly says Christians can "fall away" or fall permanently from grace. God does not take away human free choice once we are converted. We must choose to walk in the Spirit, in the way of life and blessings, every day of our lives (see "Daily Declarations" in the Appendix). When we choose that way, by God's grace our burden is light and we can feel eternally secure.

Man's "Sick" Choice

But we do have a choice. Eternal security is not automatic. We have it only if we choose it on a continual basis. God will not force an eternal, heavenly life on anyone, including Christians.

The point of this sidelight is this: the billions of people who died in sin and *sickness* without knowing God will be given a future opportunity for wholeness and salvation. Even some who have been deceived, even by false religion, yes, and even false "Christian" religion (II Cor. 4:4; Rev. 12:9), will be resurrected and will have their first chance to know Jesus as Savior and Healer. They did have to suffer in this present life in Satan's sick world, but the great news is this: they will be healed!

The Law of Sin and Death versus the Law of Life in Christ

But now back to the "sick" choice man made. It *was* sick. Satan, that sick, perverted seducer, inspired it. It made for a sick world, in every possible way. Mankind – the majority, that is, that followed the "broad way" – rejected the way of life and blessings for the "law of sin and death." But a minority of first fruits has had their eyes opened by God to be able to choose "the law of the Spirit of life" and enter in at the "narrow gate" of life and freedom (Rom. 8:2, AMP).

We need to yield to God so we can soar like the eagle sailing on the winds high above the law of gravity The law of sin and death pulls us into a downward spiral of curses, sickness, and a messed-up life leading to the final crash of death below. The Holy Spirit is like the wind – the literal meaning of the Biblical words for *spirit*.

We glide on the wind of God's grace, as we recognize who we are in Jesus and choose life daily. Fleshly efforts create drag and we fall. Powerful Holy Spirit gusts lift us up above the circumstances and the curses, soaring to blessings now and forever.

The law of spiritual aerodynamics gives us a lift. Thanks to the motor of the Holy Spirit we have lift-off. As long as the motor works, the law of gravity can't pull us down to crash. The operation of the law of life in Jesus, the law and way of life and blessings, will prevent the law of sin, sickness and death from pulling us down for a cursed, tragic fall and eventual death.

2 Why Doesn't God Heal Me?

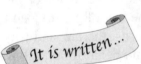

When evening came, they brought to Him many who were demon-possessed; and He cast out the spirits with a word, and healed all who were ill. This was to fulfill what was spoken through Isaiah the prophet: "HE HIMSELF TOOK OUR INFIRMITIES AND CARRIED AWAY OUR DISEASES."

Mat. 8:1-3; 16-17

CHAPTER 3
What *God* Says about Divine Healing

A prayerful attitude is essential in approaching this subject. I think there is something even more important – prayer itself!

Since the subject of healing is so controversial, let us pray this prayer, getting our own opinions out of the way and humbly asking the Holy Spirit to guide us:

"Father of grace and truth, I come as a little child before You to seek the simplicity of Jesus my Savior. Guide me with Your Spirit to discern whether this is a message from man or from You. Let anything that is not of You pass over me, in Jesus' name. Help me prove all things and hold fast that which is true. Holy Spirit, convict me of the truth. Thank You, dear Father, for I know You have heard and answered my prayer. In Jesus' name, Amen."

Now we should be ready to put our own ideas aside, and see what God says about divine healing. It doesn't really matter what *people* think about healing. It doesn't matter what *men* say, even if they are pastors, famous evangelists, theologians with letters after their names, or eminent authors of commentaries – or even if they have papal authority.

Why Doesn't God Heal Me?

Millions of religious people believe an untruth about healing because of what respected Christian leaders say. And many Christians, laymen and leaders alike, have serious questions about healing.

But what does **God** say?

Seven "Power Passages" on Healing

Hebrews 4:12 thunders for all who will hear: "For the word of God is living and active and sharper than any two-edged sword ..." God can be emphatic, and some of His words are more powerful than others. Some are a little vague and hard to be understood, as Peter said some of Paul's subjects were. But many of them are loud and clear. We can't establish doctrine on some private interpretation of an isolated verse.

The following passages are abundantly clear and cannot be misinterpreted by an honest seeker of truth. They are only a few of many Bible passages on healing, but they are a good foundation. I call them the seven "power passages" on healing.

1. Exodus 15:26 – God promised Israel on the condition of obedience that He would give them divine health – freedom from Egypt's diseases. He called Himself *Yahweh* (or *Yehovah*) *Rapha*, the *Eternal* Healer. Some don't understand that *Eternal* means *now* too.

"… and He said, If you will give earnest heed to the voice of the [Eternal] your God, and do what is right in His sight, and give ear to His commandments, and keep all His statutes, I will put none of the diseases on you which I have put on the Egyptians, **for I, the [Eternal], am your Healer**."

The Hebrew word *rapha* implies Health, Healer and Doctor. James Strong, who gives an overview of the meaning of Hebrew and Greek words in his concordance, provides this definition for *rapha*: mend, heal, cure, physician, repair, thoroughly make whole. *Rapha* contains the idea of *shalom*, the peace which comes from being whole. And the Greek word for salvation, *soteria*, applying to both spiritual salvation and physical healing, also conveys the idea of wholeness.

The word *right* in this verse has manifold meanings in the Hebrew, as revealed by lexicons and the Holy Spirit. *Yashar* implies all the following: to be with the Healer, to have healing medicine, to obey with your heart and will, to be in God's favor, to be blessed by God, to be put at the right hand of God, and, most importantly, **to meet the conditions set out by God**.

This last meaning, as connected with the stipulation of keeping all of God's laws, is extremely important. It is the **centerpiece of this book**. We don't set the conditions for healing. God does!

It may surprise you that an absolute promise of God has conditions. Yet this verse is clear. If you are knowingly compromising with God's commandments, you are blocking your healing.

If there are **hindrances to healing**, you must eliminate them. A full explanation of hindrances follows later in the book.

What God Says about Divine Healing

The first use of a word in the Bible is significant, and the first time healing is mentioned by name is important for understanding hindrances. God showed He was sovereign by healing a pagan king and his wife whom He had afflicted for trying to take Abraham's wife (Gen. 20:17). God can decide to heal in His mercy in spite of a hindrance.

This second mention of healing in Exodus 15 shows how believers can be healed. We are healed and we are blessed as we realize we are the **righteousness of God** because of what Jesus did for us. That realization causes us to be established in that righteousness, to exercise the right to be cleansed from sin, and to walk in obedience to God's commands. Stay tuned for much more on that key to unlock all God's blessings later in the book!

God is *Yahweh Rapha,* which means He is Healer yesterday, today and forever. God healed Israel many times of all their diseases.

Jesus made it clear in numerous passages that He was the God who dealt with men in the Hebrew part of His Instruction Book of Love (see "Jesus, God of the 'Old' Testament" in the Appendix). He was the member of the God Family who was *Yahweh Rapha.* Hebrews 13:8 says He never changes. He's the same – forever!

2. Psalm 103:3 – "Who forgives *all* your iniquities, who heals *all* your diseases." Psalm 103:2-3 (NLT): "Praise [Jesus], I tell myself, and never forget the good things he does for me. He forgives all my sins and heals all my diseases."

That means what it says, even though an evangelist friend in a respected denomination tried to tell me the words "heals" and "diseases" don't really mean that in the Hebrew. Sorry, but the word is *rapha* and the word "disease" here is elsewhere translated as a sickness that caused a king to die. The word comes from the same root as the word "diseases" in Exodus 15:26. The idea of illness can be spiritual in Hebrew as in English, but that is not the case here.

This psalm is one of the strongest verses on healing in the Bible. It is from the pen of a man after God's own heart. Did David believe with all his being that God forgave every one of his heinous sins, including adultery and murder? You bet he did!

We believe God forgives our sins too, don't we? If we didn't, we wouldn't be saved. We would be dead in our sins – with no promise of eternal life, ever!

In Psalm 103, did the man after God's own heart, a man who knew God's will, say, "He just might forgive *some* of your sins and He just might heal *some* of your diseases?" No! God is not a liar! Let God be true.

The truth is clear: God says He forgives **all** our sins and heals **all** our diseases. You can't get any plainer! This is *not* taken out of context.

And it is not invalid because of being in what man has dubbed the *Old* Testament. Every word of God's Book of Love is divinely inspired.

And Psalm 103:3 is *not* Old Covenant! It is as "New Covenant" as the bread and wine, the broken body and shed blood of our Savior! It is only the Old *Covenant* that is an old deal. Healing existed *before* the Old Covenant.

Why Doesn't God Heal Me?

We understand the Hebrew section of the Instruction Book in the light of Jesus, who is still the *Eternal* Healer. Verse 3 is the epitome of His atonement, a complete sacrifice including the bread – the broken body of Jesus mentioned in Isaiah 53 and I Peter 2:24 ("stripes" referring to something totally physical).

So physical healing is included in the atonement! The wine is the blood of Jesus, which pays for our sins. He bore our sins *and* our sicknesses.

Remember that Israel not only shed the lamb's blood at Passover. They ate the flesh, which gave them physical strength for their journey, showing the health aspect of Jesus' sacrifice. We need strength for our "journey," so that we may abound in God's work. That is hard to do when we are sick, feel miserable and only want to stay in bed. Health and healing are precious blessings or benefits from God.

David was blessing or praising God for all His benefits. What is David's definition of benefits? Some have said these benefits are simply vague, general blessings. But David says they include more than merely a general type of benefit. David includes *promises* in those benefits.

Is forgiveness not a promise? If not, then you and I are dead in our sins!

And since forgiveness of sin is a promise, so is the corresponding clause, which is by its very structure, as equally true as the first clause. Satan wants us to "spiritualize" this verse away. There is no other correct way to read it. God views the forgiveness of sin exactly the same as the healing of our diseases!

The two promises have something else in common: they are both conditional (Mat. 6:15; Ex. 15:26).

There are two phrases in Psalm 103:3. Why do so many Christians believe the first and not the second? Why do we believe the first and spiritualize or explain away the second?

There is no honest way of getting around the fact God is talking about physical healing here. It says the same thing in English, French, Swahili and Hebrew! Physical healing is a promise in which we can have faith.

True faith is not saying, "God can heal." It is a matter of acknowledging and believing that we already have what we ask for. Even though the Adversary causes symptoms to persist, we say in faith, "It is done." And when we persevere in that God-given faith, the symptoms soon go away too, and even the doubters see we're healed.

Finally, and most importantly, how can we fail to believe that He who died for our sins was also horribly beaten to atone for our sicknesses? I am beating this subject to death because people beat Jesus to death – and Christians let themselves get beat up by the Devil by not claiming Jesus' stripes. There is no excuse, especially for a Christian, not to believe that "by his stripes we were healed!"

3. Isaiah 53 – Passage number three turns out to be a three-in-one version. Since Mathew 8:17 and I Peter 2:24 basically quote it, I have combined them. It's too bad a number of translations have drained this passage of its power-packed, Hebrew intensity. My favorite version is that of the French rabbis, which brings out clearly the concept of Jesus bearing our sicknesses, becoming sickness for us, just as He became sin for us – as our substitute. I will quote verses 4, 5 and 10 from the *Revised Standard Version* (RSV): "Surely he has born our griefs [margin: or *sicknesses*] and carried our sorrows [margin: or *pains*]; yet we esteemed him stricken by God, and afflicted, But he was wounded for our transgressions, he was bruised for our iniquities; upon him was the chastisement that made us whole, and with his stripes we are healed. ... Yet it was the will of the [Eternal] to bruise him; he has put him to grief [margin: Heb *made him sick*] ..."

Matthew 8:16-17 – "... they brought to Him many who were under the power of demons and He drove out the spirits with a word and restored to health all who were sick and thus He fulfilled what was spoken by the prophet Isaiah, *He Himself took (in order to carry away) our weaknesses and infirmities and bore away* **our** *diseases*" (Isaiah 53:4, AMP). (If He fulfilled verse 4, He also fulfilled verse 5. His stripes healed us. Take heed, you who would spiritualize away I Peter 2:24.)

Commentators who give their own interpretation of Isaiah 53 should read how the greatest Commentator – the Holy Spirit – interprets it. He plainly says Isaiah's words include physical healing.

I Peter 2:24 – "Who Himself bore our sins in His own body on the tree, that we, having died to sin, might live for righteousness – by whose stripes you *were* healed." (This is quoted from Isaiah 53 in Matthew 8:16-17. The Holy Spirit related this section of Scripture to *physical* healing as well as spiritual.)

God is plainly saying you have **already** been healed 2,000 years ago! It's a done deal. As with the forgiveness of sin, we simply have to claim it.

Too many Christians, even some who mentor others, believe they must suffer like Jesus suffered by being sick. We may suffer persecution for righteousness' sake, but Jesus suffered the poisoning of illness through His beatings as a substitution for us. And He suffered much more than sickness in our place so we could be set free (see "Jesus' Substitionary Sacrifice" in the Appendix).

4. Mark 16:17-18[5] – "These signs will accompany those who have believed: in My name they will cast out demons, they will speak with new tongues; they will pick up serpents, and if they drink any deadly poison, it will not hurt them; *they will lay hands on the sick, and they will recover.*" One important lesson of this verse is this: although there are special gifts and anointings of healings, Jesus here shows that *every believer* should show love and compassion by laying hands on

---

[5] Some dispute the inspiration of these last verses of Mark. Although it seems evident that God employed someone other than Mark to pen these lines, they were accepted as Scripture by the early church. In the late second century, Irenaeus used these verses to defend the faith against heretics. James Hastings, in *Dictionary of Christ and the Gospels*, confirms what history shows. He stated that no church writer before Eusebius ("Christian" emperor Constantine's ecclesiastical historian) and no manuscript after him disputed this text. Eliminating these verses also interrupts an astounding numerical pattern throughout the Scriptures, based on numerical values of Hebrew and Greek letters of the alphabet. Nothing in these verses mentions any sign that was not mentioned in either the Gospels or the book of Acts.

Why Doesn't God Heal Me?

the sick and expecting God to heal them. We have all been made the righteousness of God, and that is our right!

5. Acts 10:38 – Jesus *"healed (NIV) all who were harassed and oppressed by (the power of) the **devil**"* (AMP). Although God did discipline Miriam temporarily with leprosy and did send pestilence upon His disobedient people, it was Satan who brought sickness into this world through sin. And it's almost always the Devil's doing. And Jesus came to destroy the works of the Devil (I John 3:8).

6. I Corinthians 11:23-30 – Many were sick because they did not "discern" the body of Christ that was broken to pay the penalty for our sickness (see Chapter 18, Hindrance No. 32).

Verse 24 in the RSV (taking the bread of the Passover): "… He broke it and said, 'Take, eat; this is my body which is broken for you …'" with verse 30 adding "… for this reason ('not discerning the Lord [Jesus]'s body') many are weak and *sick* among you, and many sleep ('and some have died')."

7. James 5:14-16 – These last two passages reveal the importance of hindrances. James shows the importance of declaring to the sick as Jesus did that their sins are forgiven (John 20:23). As these verses show, sin is not always the reason we are not healed. Some hindrances are curses and witchcraft prayers from others. Most of the hindrances in this book, however, involve missing the mark by omission or commission.

Further validating the concept of hindrances, verse 16 reveals that confession of sin, often to our Christian brothers, is sometimes necessary for both physical and spiritual healing.

The Holy Spirit has revealed certain truths that make this passage more understandable. First, anointing with oil is not always a necessity. The oil was added as encouragement because of the waning faith of those who had been disappointed because Jesus had not come back as expected. Also, "raise him up" implies a serious illness where the help of elders was needed. In many cases, as the righteousness of God we can reject Satan's lying symptoms ourselves and claim healing without the intervention of others.

It is written …

> Surely He has borne our griefs (sicknesses, weaknesses, and distresses) and carried our sorrows and pains [of punishment], yet we [ignorantly] considered Him stricken, smitten, and afflicted by God [as if with leprosy]. But He was wounded for our transgressions, He was bruised for our guilt and iniquities; the chastisement [needful to obtain] peace and well-being for us was upon Him, and with the stripes [that wounded] Him we are healed and made whole.
>
> Isa. 53:4-5; 11-12 – AMP

CHAPTER 4
An Awesome Atonement

I love the story of the man who made a transatlantic trip by ship. He had scrimped and saved to pay his ticket and had brought along enough crackers and cheese in his sack to eat along the way. While he made do on meager rations, every night he would see wealthy passengers reveling in gourmet meals in stately dining rooms. At the end of the voyage, the captain said to him, "Why haven't I seen you at dinner during our cruise?"

"I couldn't afford those fancy dinners. I ate cheese in my room," the poor fellow replied.

"What?" said the captain, "you didn't know? Everything was included in the price of your ticket!"

Our Savior Jesus Christ paid the price of our sins and sicknesses 2,000 years ago. He not only paid the price in our place for our spiritual salvation. He also paid the price by His stripes – by His broken body – for our physical healing. Yes! Healing is in the atonement! It is already paid for in our "ticket." We don't have to suffer – eating crackers and old cheese while others feast on filet mignon. Healing is included in our ticket – the ticket Jesus actually paid for us.

Many are not healed because they don't think it's part of the "deal."

Oh, yes it is! Healing is indeed part of the deal – the agreement between God and us – the New Covenant. It's part of the Old and part of the New. But the Christians who believe and claim it are few.

The Healing Aspect of the Atonement in the Hebrew Scriptures

While the New Covenant looks back to what Jesus did for us, the Hebrew part of God's Book of Love looks forward to His sacrifice. The Hebrew word for the atonement literally means "covering." And in fact, as Hebrews 10:4 says, the blood of bulls and goats only covered sins symbolically, looking forward to Jesus shedding His blood and actually blotting out our sins.

Nevertheless, all the many sacrifices in the Hebrew Scriptures prefigured in minute detail Jesus' future sacrifice. It is clear that the wine of the New Covenant Passover in I Corinthians 11 and Matthew 26 represented Jesus' blood shed for us – thus forgiving our sins and giving us, by grace, spiritual salvation. The shedding of animal blood under the Old Covenant foreshadowed the spilling of Jesus' blood.

What many do not realize is that the Hebrew Scriptures speak of both the promise of healing and the healing aspect of Jesus' atonement (Gen. 20:17; Deut. 7:15). As we have seen, they ate the Lamb's flesh, representing physical healing.

Healing was a promise in the Old Covenant (Ex. 23:25). And as we shall see a little later, God foreshadowed Jesus' sacrifice with many types of His healing atonement in the Hebrew Scriptures.

Healing glorifies God and enables us to glorify Him in active, healthy service – even being His tools to heal others.

"Without Blemish"

We are *living* sacrifices. By Jesus' blood and His life in us we can present ourselves "without blemish" (Rom. 12:1; Eph. 5:27). It's the same with His body broken for us. He wants every member of the body of Christ healed – without blemish or physical defect. It's part of the ticket to salvation. Many Christians, however, are in wheelchairs or chronically ill – and some think God wants it that way!

Nonsense! God wants you well! He wants you to get rid of every hindrance to healing so you can abound in His service. He does not want others to see how righteous and courageous you can be in illness, although shining in character while enduring illness is commendable. But God's *perfect* will is that you be healed and show others how to be healed! And that doesn't mean that every chronically ill or handicapped Christian is self-righteous. It is nonetheless easy to be spiritually proud without fully realizing it.

I was. Terminally ill, I was later mentally ill for 12 years. Although at times I came close to suicide, I thought I was a mighty good Christian to endure such suffering. And I sometimes thought, "Nobody knows the trouble I've seen ... Look at all I'm enduring. Look how righteous I am!" I tried to forget the dumb, outrageously unrighteous things I did in acute mania. No one could understand suffering like I did – or so I thought.

The perfect Lamb of God was righteous – not self-righteous. And He never had a trial involving illness until He suffered for us on His last day.

We have trials of many kinds; God even promises us trials. But not sickness! Jesus paid for it. Our trials of physical illness should be either short-lived, as we learn the lesson of persevering faith – or non-existent. God's perfect will is that we walk in divine health (Ex. 15:26; III John 2).

If we are not healed, it is because there are hindrances we need to shed. He shed His blood so we could shed our hindrances.

Exchange is God's system. He told Israel, "None shall appear before Me empty-handed" (Ex. 34:20). We surrender our sins and our sicknesses, which are actually not ours but gifts from Satan. We lay them down at the foot of Jesus' cross and exchange them for His righteousness and health.

Healing and health – not hindrances – are God's will for us. Jesus would never have endured such hellish torture for us if healing were not His will.

Would a doctor sweat through years of medical school, qualify as a licensed physician – and then not practice? Jesus went through the literal school of hard knocks, enduring the most unbelievable, demon-devised torture ever seen. He thus qualified to be our Healer. Would He go through all that and then refuse to practice as our Physician?

When we refuse to call on our Doctor, we are actually mocking Him – and trampling underfoot His precious sacrifice! Don't refuse His services. He's on duty "twenty-four-seven." He even makes house calls. No bills to pay – He's already footed the bill. And Hallelujah! No side effects!

Yahweh's Redemptive Names

Yes, Jesus is our Doctor – our Healer. He was the YHVH of the Hebrew Scriptures in God's Book of Love (see "Jesus" in the Appendix). In addition to being called *Yahweh*, the Eternal reveals Himself in seven redemptive names. They describe the atoning work of our Savior and God. The following Hebrew names of God follow the hyphen after the name *Yahweh*, showing who the Eternal is, what He would do for us to redeem us and who and what He will always be.

Shammah means "the Eternal is there" or "present" (Ezek. 48:35). Because Jesus reconciled us to God, and we are now pure through Him, God can dwell with us and in us. And Jesus said He would therefore never forsake us.

Shalom means "He is our Peace" (Judges 6:24), and much, much more since

Why Doesn't God Heal Me?

this vast word has over fifty meanings. Through His atonement we have peace with God as well as the peace of God. We also have the peace that comes from being whole, the root meaning of this word. It means "nothing broken, nothing missing." Jesus' body was broken for us, so we need not be broken, even physically. In fact, that is an important part of the atonement.

Raah means "the Eternal is our Shepherd" (Ps. 23:1). He gave His life for His sheep.

Jireh means "the Eternal will provide" (literally, *has seen* – Gen. 22:14). God the Father has seen ahead – has foreseen and provided for a sacrifice for sin and sickness in His Son Jesus. All provision is in the name and person of Jesus, who has seen ahead our every need and provided for it (an offering). That was the word used in Genesis 22 when God provided a ram, symbolizing Jesus, to replace Isaac as the offering. Jesus is our Provision (see "Finances" in the Appendix).

Nissi means "Jesus is our Banner" (Ex. 17:15), our Victor and Victory, our Champion. Through the atonement He conquered Satan and all he brings, including sin and sickness. Through that atonement we claim victory over sin and illness.

Tsidkenu means Jesus is "our Righteousness" (Jer. 23:6). By His death our unrighteousness is miraculously erased, and by His resurrection and His grace we miraculously become **"the righteousness of God"** (II Cor. 5:21). The perfect Jesus now lives in us. Don't miss Chapter 10, which explains this important key to unlock all God's blessings!

Yahweh-Rapha is "Jesus who heals you" (Ex. 15:26) or "Jesus your Health, Healer and Physician." Jesus said of the Passover bread, "This is My body which is broken for you" (I Cor. 11:24). And "by His stripes" (cuts and bruises caused by lashings of a whip) we were and are healed. Healing is in the atonement!

The Passover bread is unleavened in order to represent the perfection of Jesus Christ living in us. Jesus even commanded, "You shall not offer the blood of My sacrifice with leavened bread …" (Ex. 34:25). Taking Passover or communion with leavened bread contaminates it with sin. And since sin and Satan go together, we're putting the Devil in the dough. Leaven symbolizes sin, so unleavened means without sin (I Cor. 5:7-9). The blessed bread becomes in a real spiritual sense the resurrected body of Jesus, the resurrected life of the "Bread of Life" (John 6) living in His body – the church (Eph. 5:23).

These are redemptive names. And redemption is salvation. The Greek word for save, *sozo*, refers to both spiritual and physical salvation. It is used in cases of physical healing by Jesus, with the meaning "made whole" (Luke 8:36). We will explore later the powerful meaning of salvation.

Jesus came to save us – all of us – body, soul and spirit (I Thes. 5:23). As these seven names signify, He did a complete work of atonement – a perfect work of redemption and salvation. We can and should claim it all. It's paid for in the ticket!

Jesus' Complete and Perfect Atonement

At the very end of His life, Jesus shed His blood seven times to fulfill completely and perfectly His blood-sacrifice atonement for us.

First, the gospel accounts indicate that He shed blood twice in the garden before He died. His emotional stress and trauma were so great that He actually sweat blood. This is a blood sacrifice for your emotional healing.

Whatever your emotional problems, claim Jesus' healing! You may have anxiety or panic attacks or even traumatic stress disorder. You do not have to accept the symptoms Satan has brought upon you because of past or present emotional stresses. Jesus did not sin, yet all of our emotional suffering weighed upon Him in that garden. You need not go through such emotional illness. Plead Jesus' blood for your emotional healing. Realize that the communion cup is not only for spiritual healing.

Even though we can claim emotional healing under the atonement, unlike the other aspects of healing, it is a process. That may change as God begins to do mighty miracles in this end-time.

In the second trauma Jesus bore for us, He was mocked and beaten, even by the religious leaders (Mat. 26:57-68; Luke 22:63-71). Although no blood was shed in this beating, this Roman torture method was the most horrible way used to break the toughest of the tough – excruciatingly painful blows to the kidneys from the rear.

In the third shedding of blood and third trauma, they ripped His head open by forcing on it a crown of thorns (Mat. 27:29; John 19:2). These were no little thorns. They were sharp, three-inch long projectiles that rammed into His head and into the skull!

This sacrifice is dear to me, for it symbolizes His atonement for those who have had brain injuries and illnesses. It is the Bible pill for any and every illness in the DSM, the psychiatrist's diagnostic bible. And if yours is a lifelong, incurable illness like mine was, it will most probably be an instant healing as in my case. In a trice, Jesus' crown of thorns took away the crown of thorns that pierced my brain and bludgeoned my wife and children. While God leads some to stop medicine abruptly, I decided to taper off medication for a period of several weeks so as to avoid withdrawal reactions.

Severe emotional and mental illnesses can involve demonic strongholds. Because I had not truly forgiven from my heart a superior in the ministry, I opened doors for demons to influence me. The spirit of unforgiveness had allowed other evil spirits to affect me and had prevented the Holy Spirit from growing and flowing in me. By the laying on of hands, I had to be delivered first from the demonic strongholds. Then I had to invoke Jesus' beaten body for healing of the physical brain.

So if you are emotionally or mentally ill, you may have to seek a qualified

Why Doesn't God Heal Me?

counselor to discern demonic strongholds and have them dealt with, in addition to physical healing (see "Prayers for Healing" in the Appendix). Although God can and has healed in a sovereign way, He often requires us to deal with demonic strongholds so we can recognize them in the future in order to refuse them entry.

Probably fourth in the order of events, they ripped out Jesus' beard (Isa. 50:6) – a severe trauma and shedding of blood. Jews traditionally wore beards, which represented their authority. They shamed Him by robbing Him of His symbol of manhood. The ripping of His beard disfigured Him so much that He was "marred more than any man" (Isa. 52:14). Portraits and movies – even *The Passion of the Christ* – give a sanitized version of Jesus on the cross. His face was disfigured and unrecognizable – a bloody mess.

In the fifth shedding of blood and fifth trauma, they stripped Him and flogged Him with whips, so that "by His stripes" we might be physically healed (John 19:1). Once again He shed blood in extreme pain. Yet the silent Lamb of Love never cried out until sin caused Him to be separated from His Father. All He ever said was, "Father, forgive them, for they do not know what they are doing." He felt every unspeakable pain, but love lifted Him above the hurt. He endured because of the joy of seeing all mankind set free (Heb. 12:2). What love!

Then they drove nails into His hands and feet as they put Him on the cross. This sixth blood shedding and sixth trauma is the actual blood He shed on the cross for our spiritual sins, represented by the Passover wine.

Jesus' seventh trauma was the greatest. For the first time He cried out, forsaken and separated from His Holy Father because of the sin He bore (Mat. 27:46). In all eternity, it was the first time He had not felt the presence of the Father He loved. It was the blackest moment of His life.

The seventh and last shedding of blood actually occurred after Jesus' death (John 19:32-34). A soldier pierced His side with a spear and out spilled blood and water, falling on the very land that had been at the beginning cursed by sin. By this act He released His people from blood curses. As we take communion, we can orally reject these curses in Jesus' name.

And so by the fulfillment of these seven blood offerings – the number seven symbolizing completion and perfection – Jesus completed His perfect atonement for us. What an awesome God – and what an awesome atonement!

Alpha and Omega

Let's get a deeper understanding of that atonement as revealed in the communion ceremony. Let's see how the body and the blood relate. Then let's grasp the significance of the two pieces of bread or – after they are blessed – the two parts of the broken body of Jesus.

Both the blood and the body are part of the same atonement, and yet there is a difference. They are both elements of a covenant. And aspects of

30

An Awesome Atonement **4**

a covenant can have different applications.

Jesus' body was broken for us – in a general and in a specific way. We are healed physically by His stripes. And yet His body was broken *for* us. By His body we can claim all Biblical promises.

The blood is the seal of the covenant. Jesus said, "… This cup is the new covenant in My blood …" (Luke 22:20). There is power in the blood. By Jesus' blood we can seal the promises that we claim in His body.

Although different, a close connection and unity exist between the body and the blood. All seven sheddings of Jesus' blood involved stress on His body. And conversely, blood flowed from His broken body.

The meaning of the two parts of the bread or body of Jesus is a long story for another book. Here's a brief foretaste of the amazing story of the Bread of Life we eat in communion.

In Genesis 15, Jesus "cut" a covenant with Abraham. The Hebrew word for covenant implies the shedding of blood. An animal was sacrificed and the body was broken into two parts, just as with the unleavened bread of communion.

Picture this exciting scene: The God who made the universe comes down surrounded by fire and walks in a figure eight fashion through the two parts of the broken body of the animal (Jer. 34:19), which represented Jesus' sacrifice. Jesus leads Abraham through the figure eight.

How appropriate. Jesus is the Alpha and the Omega, the beginning and the end. Mathematicians did not invent the figure eight sign of infinity. Jesus did! Here we see the Eternal, Infinite One walk through the sign of infinity.

The first body part of the sacrifice through which they walked – the Alpha part – represented the covenant promises agreed upon. The second – the Omega part – stood for the covenant conditions.

Too many Christians want to receive the Alpha part of Jesus – the covenant promises, including healing, without fulfilling the covenant conditions of obedience – the Omega part. They don't go full circle – or full figure eight – with the Alpha and the Omega. They want the promises Jesus shows them in the beginning, but they don't want to follow through with the obedience part. And yet Jesus laid down conditions.

When they bless the bread and wine at communion and then break Jesus' body, they don't realize what it means. They hold in their hands the Alpha and the Omega, and He holds them intimately in His hands. But they don't want to fulfill the conditions, even though the Alpha and the Omega promises to lead them by His power through the obedience part and celebrate with them in the covenant blessings.

We are children of Abraham. Jesus led Abraham through the center of the Alpha and Omega figure eight. That center formed a cross. They walked together through the blood at the cross.

That's where we meet Jesus. As with Abraham, we are covenant blood brothers

Why Doesn't God Heal Me?

with the Most High God who made the universe! The God of all creation comes down and meets us at the cross. He meets us as a human – as a Brother – and as our God.

But we cannot claim the promises of the covenant unless we are willing to fulfill the conditions. That's what communion is all about. And that's what this book is all about.

Jesus says to us: "I am the Alpha and the Omega. When I died for you, I had both My hands extended and nailed to that cross. In one hand I hold the power to give you all the covenant promises. In My other hand I hold the power to lead you through your part of obedience – the covenant conditions. But you have free will. You must choose to obey. If you choose to obey and let Me lead you through the figure eight of eternity, you become one with Me, the Alpha and the Omega. We will walk together through the conditions and through the promises in this life. And you will take this body and this cup with Me throughout all eternity, enjoying the covenant blessings with Me. How badly do you want to be one with Me – forever?"

Do you want to take the walk of love? Jesus is Love. As with father Abraham, Love will lead you through. Love is your Shepherd. He will guide you and help you. As you and Jesus walk through the figure eight of an eternal covenant, as Abraham did, you will walk in traces of blood all the way. The blood of Jesus paves the way to eternity and to the blessings of the covenant in this life.

But you must be willing and obedient if you want the covenant promises – the best of the Promised Land (Isa. 1:19). That blessed walk in the loop of love – led by Love Himself – is for those who make a covenant of sacrifice (Ps. 50:5). That sacrifice is a life surrendered to Jesus. It includes a willingness to lay your life on the altar and to lift your praises to God's altar in heaven.

Are you sold out for Jesus? Have you truly decided to obey Him?

This is a book about being healed and blessed in this life, which most Christians don't presently enjoy. But it's much more. It's a book about what is required to walk through infinity with Jesus.

It's not "greasy grace." It is the oil of Jesus' anointing to strengthen us in our obedience. It is not license to sin. Too many Christians become mired in sin. They feel unworthy of being cleansed by Jesus' blood. They fall and refuse to get up and follow Jesus. They meet Him at the cross but refuse to follow the path traced in His blood. They refuse to let Love fulfill the commandments through them.

If God should count our sins against us, none of us could stand. "But there is forgiveness with You, that You may be [obeyed out of respectful awe]" (Ps.130:3-4).

The figure eight covenant walk of infinity is the blessed loop of love, now and forever. Jesus pledges His love to you and expects you to do the same. If your covenant of love is based on John 14:15, you will make good your pledge of love by obeying the Master. His awesome atonement of love requires proof of love on your part.

An Awesome Atonement

The Importance of Communion

We have just introduced a subject of the most extreme importance. And yet this subject seems so unimportant to many Christians today. Some churches don't have communion even once a year (see more in the Appendix under "Communion"). And how few Christians practice what the early church practiced: daily communion (Acts 2:42, 46).

Maybe it's because we are so far removed from the Hebrew concept of blood covenant. Covenants today must be written down and legalized, and even then you can't always trust the other party to keep his word. The days when a man's word was his bond seem like a fairy tale today.

When golfer Arnold Palmer and promoter Mark McCormick closed a multi-million dollar deal with a simple handshake years ago, it was one of those rare moments of loyalty to a covenant. It actually worked.

In ancient Hebrew culture, it had to work. The two covenant partners would sacrifice animals and make a binding, blood covenant. If one partner did not keep his word, the offended party would come and slaughter the man and every member of his family, along with his animals. This was no casual matter. You either kept word or you had to die!

And covenants are not a casual matter with Jesus, who invented them. When He made a blood covenant with someone, they had to keep it in order to live. And the promise He made may surprise you. He said, in effect, "If I don't keep My covenant word, I, the Father and the Holy Spirit will have to die!"

Now we know that God can't die, so how firm do you think a blood covenant with Him proves to be? It's unshakeable (Heb. 6:11-20). It's impossible for Him to die, and it's impossible for Him to lie. Wow! Our God is faithful – faithful to His covenants.

But none of the eight major covenants that preceded the New Covenant, the cross or Passover covenant, became valid for us today until Jesus' shed His blood. Without blood, no firm covenant exists.

God sometimes heals out of mercy, but look at what is happening among Christians today. Christian cowards abound. They don't boldly claim the healing promise in the covenant, and they don't take Jesus' blood in communion to seal it! And they ask, "Why doesn't God heal me?"

If you have only taken communion once in your Christian life, you are bound before God by a covenant of life and death. You have bound yourself, under penalty of eternal death, to fulfill the conditions of the covenant. You may have forgotten or ignored the covenants, but God hasn't!

What follows may be shocking, but it illustrates how serious Jesus is about blood covenants. One of the ten major Biblical covenants, now included in a spiritual sense in the New Covenant, was the covenant of circumcision.

When you read between the lines of Exodus 4:20-26, you realize how this

Why Doesn't God Heal Me?

leader had failed to keep this covenant with Jesus. How could he be trusted to lead Israel if he himself could not keep his covenant promise to God?

Jesus was about to kill him! When you don't keep a blood covenant, you have to die! Moses had refused to circumcise his son, and thus had removed the covenant protection off himself and his family. His wife stepped in, cut off her son's foreskin and thus saved her husband's skin.

History could have been rewritten because of failure to keep a covenant. Your personal health history and that of your family can be rewritten because you claim the blood covenant and keep it.

No covenant can be claimed without the blood of Jesus. We must take communion! And no healing can take place unless we claim the covenant that applies. We must claim healing in the New Covenant in Jesus' blood – the covenant of the cross. And we must seal it in communion!

A lackadaisical attitude toward communion can be a major hindrance to healing. "Pleading the blood of Jesus" only lasts for 24 hours.[6] Communion seals in the covenant promise. All hell cannot alter it. God *must* perform it.

You can actually go boldly before God and say, "I have sealed this healing covenant promise in Jesus' blood by communion. You must either keep your Word or you must die! Since you can't die, You have no choice but to come through! Thank You, Father. I praise You for my healing, in Jesus' name."

After your communion, go immediately into a song of praise and worship. Praise activates and intensifies faith. It releases faith into the covenant. The more you praise, the quicker you see the covenant promise manifested. Rejoice that you have what you asked for!

After all, you have a covenant of love with the Father of Love – sealed in the blood of Jesus! No promise can be fulfilled outside of the covenant. Not even the protection Psalm 91 promises. But all the promises come to us when we claim the covenant and trust Jesus to walk us in His righteousness through that loop of love pictured by the Alpha and Omega figure eight of eternity.

Believe, trust and surrender like Abraham did. Lay all your burdens, pains, weights, sins, human works, hopes and expectations on Jesus.

The covenant of the cross is your covenant of protection for you and your family. In Exodus 12, one lamb was slain for each family. You have the covenant promise of family salvation! Claim it! Claim it in the covenant!

The Passover covenant, the New Covenant in the blood of the Lamb, is your covenant of defense, purification and victory in Jesus' blood over all mental, emo-

---

[6] This is a revelation from the Holy Spirit proven by our experience in deliverance ministry and indicated by certain Scriptures. On the positive spiritual side, we are renewed daily (II Cor. 4:16). The same applies with negative thoughts, which if left unrepented, invite corresponding evil spirits (Eph. 4:26-27). In a spiritual sense, blessed communion wine or juice becomes the blood of Jesus. Pleading the blood of Jesus with the mouth only does not carry the same sealing and renewal power as the spiritual lifeblood of Jesus activated by the communion prayer.

tional and physical illness. Anything missing or broken must be restored, or God must die! That's how sure the promise is!

As the Appendix on communion states, cite the name of God that applies to what you are claiming. Call on *Yehovah* or *Yeshua Rapha, Jesus the Healer*. Name His name. Name the covenant. Name it! Claim it! Be steadfast in keeping your word – your part of the covenant. And seal it! Seal it in the blood of Jesus!

Types of the Atonement

This awesome blood atonement is revealed in several types found in the Hebrew part of God's Instruction Book of Love.

Jesus sent a plague on the Israelites because of rebellion (Num. 16:46-50). There were 14,700 who died before Aaron the high priest – physical forerunner of Jesus, our High Priest – made atonement for the healing of the remaining people, or at least the removal of the physical plague. As Aaron did, so our High Priest atones for us – even for physical illness.

God sent poisonous snakes to punish Israel (Num. 21:4-9). Many died. This sickness was a curse God put on them. When they followed God's order to lift up a bronze snake on a pole, He healed those bitten ones who looked to the serpent.

That serpent was a type of Jesus who was lifted up on a pole, stake, or cross. The poisonous snakes symbolized the first serpent, Satan, and the sin of which he is the author. Bronze signifies suffering. Jesus became sin – a sin offering for us. He took the curse of sickness and death upon Himself (Gal. 3:13). This also foreshadows Jesus putting on our coat of sin and entering undercover into hell to defeat Satan, as we will see in Chapter 10.

Sickness and death represent two objects of the atonement. He paid for our diseases and our sins, which brings death.

He also took upon Himself all our curses, including those involving sickness. You name it – voodoo, witchcraft, or even curses producing illness, spoken by those who hate us – all are covered by Jesus' sacrifice. He became a curse in our place and He shed His blood to break blood curses (see "Curses" in the Appendix).

God required atonement for the ceremonial cleansing of the leper (Lev. 14:18). Although it did symbolize sin, leprosy was a physical illness. Physical illness is involved in Jesus' atonement for us.

Isaiah 53, often called the Redemption Chapter, foretells Jesus' dual atonement. The Hebrew *choli* and *makob* (verse 4) are elsewhere translated to refer to physical illness and pain.

Jesus paid a high, "first class" price for our healing! So why settle for crackers and stale cheese? Why travel second class when your first class ticket is paid for in full? As you will learn later, you're not only traveling first class – you're traveling God class!

4 Why Doesn't God Heal Me?

Creative Miracles

God class means more than the healing of stuffy noses. Being made in God's image as the righteousness of God entails God-class, creative power – in Jesus' name.

Among the signs and wonders that God will release in this end-time will be a tidal wave of creative miracles. Creative miracles occur when a missing body part grows or when a brand new organ is created to replace a diseased one.

A good friend of mine whose word I trust implicitly saw an astounding miracle. A skeptical non-Christian woman had come to a healing crusade after being involved in a terrible accident. Her face was marred terribly and almost all her teeth had fallen out by the blow of the car accident. The evangelist prayed for her and instantly her face became as new and all the missing teeth grew back! My friend was only three feet away. It was not a trick – it was a miracle! A creative miracle.

Creative miracles were definitely a part of the atonement when the Israelites ate the lamb. After the terrible treatment from Egyptian taskmasters, missing limbs were certainly common. And yet the millions of Israelites came out of Egypt completely whole (Ps. 105:37).

The same promise of *shalom* – nothing missing, nothing broken – awaits in an even greater way God's people today. God has spare parts in the waiting for this exciting time of the end. And yet there's more. On a larger scale than ever, the dead will be raised! God has already worked through David Hogan to raise 200 people from the dead![7] Raising the dead is possible because of Jesus' death and resurrection. We are one with Him – and He *is* the Resurrection and the Life!

A century ago, God worked mightily through English evangelist Smith Wigglesworth (1859-1947). The wife of a dying man called him to come pray for her husband's healing. When he arrived the man was dead. That didn't stop Wigglesworth. Three times he lifted the corpse against the wall, commanding him to rise in Jesus' name. The third time it worked!

Jesus promised that we would do even greater works than He. When Christians begin to know who they are and the rights they have, they will not only be healed themselves. They will heal others – and raise the dead!

...by His wounds you were healed.
I Pet. 2:24

---

[7] Hogan was personally involved in about twenty of those miracles. More information is available at www.fuegodedios.com.

CHAPTER 5
Healing in a Nutshell

It seems everything today comes in a nutshell. Cable headline news. Bite-size, impacting ads. "In a Nutshell" was the title of a hot, end-of-century country tune (and even nuts still come that way). Since this is mainly a book on why some Christians aren't healed, I must condense divine healing into the proverbial nutshell. It's not as hard a nut to crack as some have made it. Healing and nuts aren't so different after all. While the nut sometimes requires powerful intervention to break open, the insides are not so complicated. But there is a lot to chew on – here's some food for thought.

Is Healing God's Will?

Why do we even ask if healing is God's will? Is it God's will that we be saved? Can you see someone coming to Christ and saying, "Jesus, save me, if it is your will"?

Remember the man who came to Jesus and asked Him to heal him if He was willing (Luke 5:12-13)? Jesus plainly said He was willing. It is His will.

Why Doesn't God Heal Me?

Look how many times it says in the gospels that He "healed them all" (Mat. 12:15; Luke 6:19; Acts 10:38; etc.). He never refused to heal anyone. Would He have healed all that came to Him if it wasn't His will?

Ted Williams made baseball history by batting over .400. That's only a 40% success rate. God bats a thousand! His perfect will is to heal 100% of those who ask. He is a perfect hitter. The problem is that our hindrances keep Him from stepping up to the plate and going to bat for us.

The only place Jesus was hindered from healing all was in His hometown (Mark 6:5). They couldn't believe anything good could come from the "local yokel." So even though our Healer is a perfect hitter, He rarely goes to bat for those who refuse to believe.

Does Sickness Glorify God?

When I played little league baseball, I got in some tight situations at bat. I would have loved to have my boyhood idol Mickey Mantle step in and pinch-hit for me.

You would think that people who get in tight spots health-wise would like nothing better than to see Jesus come to bat for them and save the day.

Doesn't every sick person want to be made well?

I always thought the answer to that question was an obvious yes. But since I have been serving in healing ministry, I found that many people don't answer yes to that question.

That revelation came as a shock to me. I thought everyone would welcome the good news I related: God promises to heal every one of our diseases. Wow! What great news!

But what a shock I got! Many sick Christians don't even want to be healed! What a sick way of thinking!

From the least to the greatest, many Christians today think their illness glorifies God! **And God is not going to heal those who are happy to be sick!**

When someone dares say it is God's will they be healed, that offends some. How dare insinuate that these righteous sick people might be imperfect in any way? I guess they would prefer to blame God, who supposedly uses sickness to glorify His name.

All this confusion makes God "sick"! He never intended His Children to be ill or that sickness should become a badge of righteousness.

Those, like me during my illness, who feel holier than the healed, are not the sweet-smelling savor in God's nostrils they think they are. Their attitude stinks to high heaven!

Some Christians in wheelchairs justify God not healing them by saying it helps them understand others who are sick. That may be, but that's not God's perfect will.

38

Healing in a Nutshell

Do we sin so we can understand sinners? We may use our past life of sin to minister to sinners, but Jesus warns us: "Go, and sin no more!" It's the same with sickness.

Jesus never once told lame people it was better if they stayed lame to minister more effectively to the lame. He told them instead, "Get up and walk!" Jesus treats sin and sickness the same. He hates both! Do we?

God's will is that Christians in wheelchairs get up and walk! Then they can really minister to others in wheelchairs: they can heal them (Mark 16:18)!

Admittedly, it is true that illness can sometimes draw us closer to God. Sin can too, if we turn back to God in heartrending repentance. But God doesn't want us to sin or to be sick. It is indeed rare that He directly uses sickness to further His plans for us. And, of course, He never tempts us to sin. The Devil does that.

I will rejoice when paralyzed Christians finally realize it's the *Devil* that wants them handicapped. God wants them healed! I can think of one precious, paralyzed sister in singing ministry who can one day sing out as she kicks her wheelchair aside, "Ta-dah! I'm healed!"

We must not confuse God's permissive will with His perfect will. God meets us where we are in our spiritual walk and understanding. He meets us in our mediocrity in order to lead us into His perfection.

He can turn our lemons of sin and sickness into lemonade. But His perfect will for us is more than lemonade in a paper cup. Our Father wants to pour us some bubbly Dom Perignon vintage in a crystal glass. He wants to bless His Children with the best.

Jesus can redeem anything. Even sin teaches us bitter lessons and thus works for good as we use our mistakes to help others and empathize with them. But sin is not good of itself, is it?

Sin and sickness are bed partners. They both, sooner or later, bring death. Sickness puts you to bed and sin puts you to sleep – permanently. They are part of the curse that came upon man after his wrong choice. Sin and sickness would not be around if the Devil had not entered the world.

Sickness may sometimes work for good, but sickness, like sin, is not good of itself. It does not come from God – except as a rare judgment upon us when we have hardened our hearts and need help to repent. Jesus disciplined Miriam with leprosy (Num.12:10), judged some careless Corinthians by allowing them to get sick and even die (I Cor. 11:27-32), and warns His idolatrous people of Thyatira, "I will throw her on a bed of sickness … and I will kill her children with pestilence" (Rev. 2:22-23).

Sickness never glorifies God, even when it comes as discipline from Him. He wants us rid of all sin and sickness. Healing and health glorify God.

What I shared earlier may sound heretical, but it is Biblical: God allows trials of all sorts to build character in us, but He does not want us to be sick. As we grow from glory to glory and faith to faith, perseverance in faith for a short time may be necessary before we actually see and feel the manifestation of the healing promise in the natural realm. If the healing manifests instantly, we no longer need faith to believe in it.

One famous evangelist sincerely misled millions on a talk show in 1999. He shared with Larry King a common misconception about Paul's thorn in the flesh that many Christians accept without serious study. This Christian leader basically said his illness was God's will, as was Paul's, so he could be humble. This book clearly debunks that idea.

I understand how easy it is to believe that error. I did. And I don't intend to judge the motivation of those who believe it. I believed it because it encouraged and even justified me as I faced the humiliation and shame of two devastating illnesses. As with Paul, or so I thought, it was God's will, and so it was good.

Good? What are we, masochists? I lost my health, my family, my money, my ministry, my reputation, and I came close to losing my very life. And that's supposed to be good? I could do without the "blessing" of sickness. Death is our enemy. And sin and sickness bring death.

Would you want your children to be in pain and die of an illness? Why do so many accuse our perfect Parent of such a sadistic approach? Would you "bless" your daughter with terminal cancer? Think about it!

Trials, in a general sense, are indeed good for us. But Jesus paid for our sins and our sicknesses. He suffered pain and death for us – in our stead. That's the covenant He made with us.

Is Healing for Today?

Is this covenant binding today? Is healing for today? What a question! God is the "high noon" God, as the Greek of James 1:17 reveals, with "no variation or shifting shadow."

Some think God is a fickle God like Baal who keeps His promises whenever He feels in a merciful mood. One pastor said that from the pulpit! It is not God's will to heal only 5% of His people today. It is His perfect will to heal all today as He did 2,000 years ago.

Jesus' name is *Yahweh Rapha* – the *Eternal* Healer. He is not – as some think – the "Has-been Healer." *Yahweh* means "*I am*." To those who say He doesn't heal today, He thunders, "**I am the HEALER!**" (Deut. 32:39-40). He hasn't changed His mind about *who He IS*! Unlike some people today, He's not trying to "find Himself." He has no identity crisis. He's not on strike.

Strikes were frequent in the years I lived in Paris. "I love Paris in the springtime," and all the time. It's beautiful. But when the garbage men strike, it stinks! And the garbage that some preach – that God is on strike – is a stench in God's nostrils!

Healing servant Rodney Howard-Browne says it best. In a little story he tells, he mocks the idea that healing ended with the apostles – an idea disproved by church history. The last living apostle, gasping for breath – near death – reaches a dying man who had called him for healing. Just before the apostle can lay hands on the poor man, the last apostle keels over and dies. "Sorry, fellow. You're out of luck!" The last apostle is dead. Too bad for that man and for all the other Christians down through the ages. Tough luck!

How ludicrous! Jesus said that we, His disciples, would do greater works. We should be seeing more healing – not less.

There have been healings throughout the history of the church, with powerful healing revivals at certain times. The coming end-time revival promises to be the greatest of all as God pours out His Spirit to prepare His Bride. Jesus said the gospel – the whole gospel – would be preached throughout the world.

"You gotta go sometime!"

The full gospel involves a full life. While it is true that we have an appointed time here on earth, Satan the Terminator wants us to die before our time. Nobody should die of disease. The "you gotta go sometime" fallacy has "gotta go"!

God promises long life to the righteous (Ps. 91:16; 118:17; Ex. 20:12). He's the One "Who redeems your life from the pit [of destruction, terminality – referring to a ditch or grave, meaning untimely death]" (Ps. 103:4). Since the flood, God has allotted us a life span of 120 years (Gen. 6:3).[8] That's how long Moses lived. Sin and speaking death over ourselves have shortened it, but it doesn't have to be that way (see "Prayer" in the Appendix: Psalm 91 and Prayer of Protection and Long Life).

God doesn't want us to die sick. It is possible to die of old age – simply to peacefully breathe your last breath. God wants us to die in peace – not suffering from one of Satan's gifts! Read how Moses was feeling when he died: "… his eyesight was clear, and he was as strong as ever" (Deut. 34:7 – NLT). Way to go, Moses! Indeed, I can't think of a better way.

It is true, of course, that our body may weaken considerably with age (Eccl. 12). But that is because of the ravages of sin and is not God's perfect will. And illness, whether it comes in our youth or in our golden years, is definitely not God's will for us. If you have arthritis or a heart condition, don't blame God. He wants you

---

[8] The reference in Psalm 90:10 of seventy to eighty years as a life span is better understood by reading this psalm in the *Amplified Bible*, which adds the following footnote: "This Psalm is credited to Moses, who is interceding with God to remove the curse which made it necessary for every Israelite over twenty years of age (when they rebelled against God at Kadesh-barnea) to die before reaching the Promised Land (Num. 14:26-35). Moses says most of them are dying at seventy years [of age]. This number has often been mistaken as a set span of life for all mankind. It was not intended to refer to anyone except those Israelites under the curse during that particular forty years. Seventy years never has been the average span of life for humanity. When Jacob, the father of the twelve tribes, had reached 130 years (Gen. 47:9), he complained that he had not attained to the years of his immediate ancestors. …"

to get rid of your hindrance and be healed. Then you can die when your appointed time comes – in peace and without suffering. God is good all the time – even when you're old.

If we declare daily in faith that our youth is "renewed like the eagle's" (Ps. 103:5), it will be!

One Christian lady in her eighties appeared on TV and gave an astounding testimony. Speaking out in faith God's promise of youth repeatedly on a daily basis transformed her lame frame into youthful splendor. She looked like an extremely attractive 35-year-old. At the time our house of healing was a house for abused and abandoned teenagers and some young adult males stayed here as well. The managing director asked them if they would date this lady. They didn't hesitate. "Sure!" was their enthusiastic answer. When he told them she was in her eighties, that didn't matter!

Paul's Thorn and Other Thorny Questions

Some believe that if we don't die early, we must suffer in the flesh – do penance – in order to please God. They say we need some "thorn in the flesh" like Paul's to keep us humble.

It never ceases to amaze me how people can take one or two verses to come to a conclusion that the whole Bible soundly contradicts. The Bible does not contradict itself. If you think a verse contradicts the rest of the Bible, you're mistaken. As Peter warned us in II Peter 3:16, Paul's writings are "hard to be understood." And those are the ones people twist the most. His explanation of his "thorn in the flesh" (II Cor. 12) is a blatant example.

Paul had just boasted of his "infirmities," better translated in the NASB and NIV as weaknesses. Not once did he mention sickness as a part of the many sufferings he endured. In the problematic verse 7, the above translations both render the word "buffet" as "torment." It means to beat back and forth. Note that God does not use the word "afflict" here, which would refer to a physical illness.

And who did the buffeting? "A messenger of Satan." I decided to cut through the hermeneutical heresy by asking the ten-year-old child of a Christian what a messenger of Satan was. He simply answered in two words: "A demon." The truth comes out of the mouth of babes. This word is translated 100 times in the Greek Scriptures as "angel." An angel of Satan is a demon. It takes a doctorate in theology to miss that obvious fact.

The infirmities or weaknesses or torments Paul was referring to were the result of a demon buffeting him, as explained in chapter 11. With all the talk about shipwrecks, beatings and a host of other trials, one phrase is missing: "in sicknesses often." God does not send sickness to humble us, even though sickness may affect us in that way. He uses other methods. Paul's thorn had nothing to do with illness.

God would be contradicting Himself if He had said that He gave Paul an ill-

Healing in a Nutshell

ness that He would not heal. He wants us free of hindrances – healed and completely whole.

We find the only other time "thorn in the flesh" is used in the Bible is in Numbers 33:55. It refers not to illness, but to people – the inhabitants of the land whom the Israelites refused to drive out. The demon that buffeted Paul used people to beat him and persecute him.

Verse 7 does not refer to illness, but Galatians 4:14-15 and 6:11 do indicate that Paul suffered from a physical ailment, probably an unsightly eye condition that resulted from the temporary blindness God used to call him when on the Damascus road. This is decidedly **not** what God is referring to in the "thorn" verse, since it is always God's will to heal.

The thorn in the flesh was a demon God allowed to pester Paul with persecutions and calamities. Thorns never have a positive connotation in the Bible. Although He may allow them, they always come from Satan. The common assumption that the phrase, "there was given me" (II Cor. 12:7), means God gave the thorn to Paul is simply not true. The thorn was a "messenger of Satan," so Satan sent it – not God.

The full meaning of this chapter would take several sermons to explain. Although the risk of being misunderstood is great, space allows only a brief explanation.

As Chapter 9 explains, Paul did not fully understand his identity in Christ until near the end of his life. He is exposing his own mistakes and weaknesses so we can learn from them, and even he probably did not fully understand at the time what God meant when He said that His grace was sufficient.

Some of the trials or "weaknesses" mentioned, such as imprisonment and persecution, were indeed God's will for Paul. He wrote some of his greatest epistles in prison and he rightly rejoiced in persecution. Many of those trials, however, were attacks from Satan that Paul did not have to endure.

Although there are 25 graces that come from God, the most important meaning of grace is the concept of empowerment. "My grace is sufficient" is not permission from God to let the Devil beat up on us. He gives us the grace or empowerment to overcome. Paul didn't have to spend a night hanging to a plank from a shipwrecked vessel. If he had known who he was in Jesus, he could have done like Jesus (and even Peter in his pre-Pentecost state) by walking on the water and rescuing his partners. He was hungry and thirsty because of demonic backlash from cursing Barnabas and Mark. God allowed certain of these problems so Paul would settle some issues in his life that he had not been willing to turn over to Jesus.

Jesus was saying to him, "You can handle all these situations, even eliminate some of them, by My empowering grace. Why are you asking me to take away the thorn of Satan? I have already given you the power and authority in My name to defeat Satan. Don't whine. Don't beg Me to do something I have already given you the power to do! You have My name, My blood, My gifts, My

Why Doesn't God Heal Me?

righteousness and My glory. What else do you need?"

God allowed these "weaknesses" or troubles – this opposition from Satan – to make Paul strong. And the apostle was "boasting" in Jesus' power to endure necessary hardship, as well as to overcome what the Devil was throwing at him.

Many have stumbled over these verses because of the way they have been translated. And yet when we rightly divide the Word of truth, comparing Matthew 13 with Isaiah 28, we realize that just as the Word in human flesh was a stone of stumbling, so the written Word is a test. Many – even believers – fail to pass. What the Word seems to say in the translation is not always what it truly means.

Satan wanted to buffet Paul so he would give up on his visions and revelations – not praying them out and causing them to come to pass – so he would not be able to fulfill his anointing. The demon's plan was to keep Paul busy with attacks so he would not exalt himself in a proper way above Satan and exert his apostolic authority. Satan wanted to shame him so he wouldn't fight back.

God endured Paul's whining prayer three times. Finally, God had enough of Paul shaming himself in this crying mode. "And He said to me, 'My grace [empowerment] is sufficient for you [I've got all you need, Paul], for power is perfected in weakness [troubles, buffeting].' Most gladly, therefore, I will boast about my weaknesses [the buffeting Satan tries to give me], so that the power of Christ may dwell in me [I will boast about Jesus' power in me to be victorious in these difficulties]" (verse 9).

Suffering shame for the cause of Jesus is praiseworthy, and God's grace can empower us to endure that gracefully. Allowing Satan to rob us of our joy and bring shame upon us is a different matter altogether. By the grace of God we don't have to put up with Satan's shaming tactics.

The important point to remember is that God never wants us to put up with Satan's lying symptoms of illness. That was not even the question in this thorny verse.

The eye condition in Galatians 4 was what I call in this book the "halter hindrance." A halter is a restraining rope, as used on horses. Since God requires more of leaders, in rare cases He refrains from healing a physical condition that restrains or limits one of His servants. He has every intention of healing it when the leader corrects the spiritual problem (see Chapter 18, Hindrance No. 14).

The "eye halter" was put on Paul to correct the pride of the former eminent pupil of Gamaliel. Paul said with his mouth that he no longer had this pride. But God wanted it destroyed down deep in his heart.

We don't' know for sure exactly when or if Paul learned the lesson and his halter was thus lifted. It does seem from II Timothy 4:7 that Paul finished his course with success. So it is likely that God healed the eye condition before Paul's death. But that is between God and Paul.

It is God's Word and His promises that are infallible, not men – not even great men of the Bible. David and Elijah were men of "like passions" as we are (James 5:17; Ps. 51).

Healing in a Nutshell

"Sick" Excuses

Elisha, who died of an illness, was also quite human. Some use his death from an illness in II Kings 13:14 as justification for the fact that some servants of God today die of illnesses. They believe it must be God's will. It isn't.

The Holy Spirit has shown that God allowed Elisha to die from an illness because he was an angry man. Elisha had not chosen to ask God to rid him of this hindrance of anger, as seen in II Kings 13:19. To whom much is given, much is required. Elisha had double the anointing of Elijah, so God expected much from him. Although healing was God's perfect will for him, Elisha did not follow God's perfect will in eliminating his anger problem. Obviously anger got in the way of healing.

Hindrances are common to humans. So everything that happened to them was not necessarily God's perfect will. Jesus was the only perfect person in the Bible, and nowhere does it say He got sick. Satan tried, but his gifts couldn't land on righteous Jesus.

The Bible says it is folly to compare ourselves with others. And yet Christians today compare themselves with great men of God, modern and Biblical, who for various reasons were sick for extended periods. Only God knows the heart. And He says, "Work out your own salvation with fear and trembling" (Phil. 2:12).

Epaphroditus was sick but was later healed (Phil. 2:25-30). Trophimus fell ill (II Tim. 4:20). Maybe he had a hindrance with which he had to deal. Maybe he never did. The self-imposed limitations of men of God don't do away with the promise of God. But if you're looking for excuses to call God a liar, you can twist a number of passages. God wants us to learn from people's mistakes (I Cor. 10:11).

What if Timothy *was* sick? It is highly possible, since Paul told him to stir up a faith that was apparently lacking at the time (II Tim. 1:6). He may have had other hindrances. Rather than encourage us to be sick, his example should encourage us to shed our hindrances and get healed!

"The Doctor Doctrine"

Just as it is not a sin to use natural remedies – as long as they are not more important than Jesus – it is not a sin to use the services of a physician, whether conventional or holistic.

Holistic practitioners may be closer to God's paradigm. They emphasize natural remedies and focus on cause and effect and prevention. Most medical practitioners tend to treat the effects with pharmaceutical drugs that alter and tamper with natural substances. Both deal with the natural realm as opposed to the supernatural, and they mutually excel each other in different areas of expertise. If they could only get together!

Choosing one or the other is not necessarily a more "righteous" decision. Holistic therapists admit that medical treatment may be necessary in some critical situations. It is a personal decision determined by wisdom and the level of faith and understanding.

Both camps have their incompetents. The decisions of both an arrogant doctor and an incompetent naturopath would have cost me my life had it not been for the hand of God.

Whatever route you choose, don't ever put a doctor before God. That includes chiropractors, naturopaths and pharmacists. That's idolatry! God doesn't tend to heal idol worshippers. According to your faith (and conscience) be it unto you. The Holy Spirit is our Guide.

The Bible commands us not to judge each other (Mat. 7:1; Rom. 14:10). We are all at different levels of faith and understanding. Also, we may have unresolved hindrances that may even make doctors and medicine necessary until we come to conviction and repentance. It's a personal matter. Busybodies, beware! Mind your own body!

Luke was a beloved Christian doctor, probably more "naturally" oriented than most modern doctors. He was most likely similar to some doctors today who are humble and gentle and treat the body and soul, emphasizing the "binding of wounds" and diagnosis.

Non-Christians do need doctors more than believers. They have not accepted Jesus' sacrifice for their salvation and healing and do not yet know the Eternal Healer. Doctors are their only recourse. That should not be the case for Christians.

Doctors of all sorts may have their role and their place in the balanced life of a believer. Benny Hinn's personal physician is an example. Dr. Don Colbert has studied nutrition extensively and has written a number of books, including *The Bible Cure For* ... series.

To teach that going to a doctor for any reason is a sin is unwise. It is picky legalism. Although such a "doctor doctrine" is not in the Bible, King Asa did die because he sought the physicians *instead* of God (II Chron. 16:12).

The last fruit of the Spirit mentioned in Galatians 5:22 can be translated temperance, moderation or balance. It balances or controls with wisdom all the other qualities we can bring to our lives. Prevention of sickness and taking supplements to bolster our health are fine, but let's remember who our Healer is. His name is Jesus!

And as Christian nutrition specialists know, you can be doing everything right and still be sick. Hindrances leave open doors for Satan to attack our bodies.

Although we cannot legislate what kind of medical services and interventions Christians may employ, let's remember this: God does not need doctors to perform His miracles. He does quite well, thank you, in primitive areas where no medical services are available.

To be sure, He has at times done miracles in cases where surgery and drugs

Healing in a Nutshell

been used. He meets us where we are, leading us from glory to glory, eventually to glorious health.

His permissive will and mercy notwithstanding, God has no limits. We are the ones who limit Him. He can heal anything and perform any creative miracle He desires. He alone can do the impossible. Neither conventional nor natural health professionals can compete with or replace our God. He operates in the supernatural. Whether under the Old Covenant or the New, Jesus has always done the impossible.

Denying the New Covenant and the Name of Jesus!

Some can see, as Exodus 15 shows, that healing is part of a special covenant between God and His people. But they argue: "That's Old Testament!" – as if close to three-fourths of the Bible whose every word we are to live by (Mat. 4:4) meant nothing.

Then what about the New Covenant?

The sign of that covenant is communion – the taking of the body and blood of our Savior and Healer. And that's exactly who Jesus is. Denying Jesus is *Yahweh Rapha* – the Eternal Healer – is denying who He is. That is tantamount to blasphemy against His very **name**!

Jesus was and is the Savior and Healer. And that's what He did and still does. When physically here on earth He said over and over again, "Your sins are forgiven," and healed people every day. He forgives and He heals. He has covenanted with His people to do that. And He promises to keep His part of the covenant.

Matthew 8:17 clearly shows that the redemptive power of Jesus definitely includes healing. The rest of God's Word shows the Holy Spirit continued to heal after Jesus left the earth.

God gave the conditional yet sure promise of healing to His physical people even before the Old Covenant was made. "… he brought his people safely out of Egypt, loaded with silver and gold; there were no sick or feeble people among them" (Ps. 105:37 – NLT).

Something is wrong with today's picture. Instead of a healthy church, we see myriads of feeble people under our steeples.

If God gave such health and wealth to His physical people, how much more would He bless His spiritual people under a new and "better" covenant?

Would God promise in the Old Covenant that He heals all our diseases and then heal only a few of our diseases under the better covenant?

Grace and love are definitely New Covenant. And healing is a powerful demonstration of God's grace and love. By the grace of God and Jesus' sacrifice, we are freed from Satan's yoke of sin and sickness. God saves and heals because of His great love for us. How often we read that Jesus was

47

Why Doesn't God Heal Me?

"moved with compassion" before He healed someone.

In the Garden of Eden, everything was "very good." There was no pain and no curse. The same will be true at the end (Rev. 21:4; 22:3). And in the interim, Jesus took the pain and the curses for His New Covenant people (Isa. 53; Gal. 3:13). If you are not healed, God desires to teach you something about your hindrances before healing you, so you can fulfil His perfect will for you.

Jesus called healing "the children's bread" (Mat. 15:26). How much more for us, the children of the New Covenant? *If healing is not New Covenant, then* **salvation** *isn't either!*

The "How" of Healing

We have examined the "what" of healing and, from a limited point of view, the "why." Now we will deal, also in a limited way, with the "how," which we will cover extensively in Part II of this book. How did God administer healing in His Word and how does He administer it today?

God is sovereign and He can heal in any way He chooses. Jesus healed by laying hands on the sick, by using His authority to speak to the sickness and by casting out the demons causing the illness. He even used in some cases physical substances such as mud in the practice of healing. And yet some think it strange when some healing evangelists blow on people as a healing method. Jesus used spit!

He said that believers – not only pastors and ministers – would lay hands on the sick and they would be healed (Mark 16:18). That is the principle method, but God is not limited to that.

God heals some people by simply answering their prayer (or even better, by their faith-filled demonic rebuke and declaration of healing). Praying and/or praying and fasting in agreement with another Christian is a powerful method of healing (Mat. 18:19).

Communion, which represents healing and salvation, can produce healing (I Cor. 11:23-30). Some are sick because of not properly taking communion. And on the positive side, it is an anointed ceremony that packs supernatural power – the power of the blood of Jesus.

As with the casting out of some demons, simply using the name of Jesus can sometimes produce healing.

God can simply touch people by His sovereign healing power, as I have seen in healing crusades. The healing evangelist does not have to touch them.

As mentioned earlier, anointing oil was added to encourage the church. The oil symbolized the power and comfort of the Holy Spirit, sorely needed by those early Christians who had seen Jesus delay His coming. The oil also symbolized consecration to God. It can be used at the discretion of the person administering the healing to encourage the sick and add special emphasis for particular cases.

The Biblical oil was olive oil, but God can heal with salad oil when that's all

48

there is. I know. That's all I had to anoint a sick person on a transatlantic flight to Europe years ago. God does have specific ways to do things, but He does make exceptions. David broke a ceremonial rule when he and his men were famished (Mark 2:25-26).

A word of caution to pastors from a pastor. God does not condone "pastor worship." I have seen it from both perspectives – pastor and laity. We need to delegate, realizing that Jesus said believers could lay hands on the sick. James says elders anoint. Early church tradition indicates that a growing member in good standing automatically became an elder after seven years. Elders could be ordained earlier if they fulfilled the Biblical requirements.

Some pastors burn out because they think they have to do everything. God gives gifts to all the body of Christ and we all serve in our particular ministries (Eph. 4:12; I Cor. 12:4-30).

Some in Christ's body have been endowed with special gifts of healing (I Cor. 12:9). Some even specialize in certain parts of the body. God gives Christians gifts of healing for the body, mind, emotions, relationships and even the land. He also gives gifts for group healings.

Jesus once healed a whole crowd of about 15,000. Peter's shadow healed people as he walked along busy streets. In anointed meetings, some have used a "tunnel of fire": Christians lift joined hands in a row as the sick pass under them.

God can even use objects to heal. In Acts 19, Paul sent out cloths that had touched his body to the distant sick for healing. Unlike some TV evangelists who make you pay for such substances as "holy water," Paul gave freely. Some use prayer shawls and other objects or substances, yet God is always the Healer. Trusting in an object or a place can be a hindrance to healing.

Some have been healed by simply hearing God's Word preached or by declaring it over themselves. "He sent His word and healed them ..." (Ps. 107:20).

Simply stretching out their hands to their television set as an anointed healing servant preaches has been the healing method for some people.

The methods that have produced healing are too numerous to mention. They simply show that God can use any method He pleases. After all, He is God.

We Can Share the Joy of His Healing Love

God is God because of His infinite love. Neither His love nor His healing power has changed.

God heals because He loves. And when we walk in His love, we receive healing and we give it out in love to others.

Our God of Love derives great joy from seeing people healed – and He wants us to share that joy. We become instruments of His love and mercy. Our hands are instruments of His compassion, and our hearts share His joy. God could do it all by Himself, and sometimes He does, but He loves to work through human

5 Why Doesn't God Heal Me?

instruments to manifest His power and glory.

And yet He does not want us to take the glory. That is one of the reasons Jesus sent His disciples out in pairs to heal and cast out demons. No one person gets credit. What's more, the two can complement one another and be an effective team.

James 5:14 speaks of "elders" in the plural. As I know by the experience of being a pastor in isolated areas, there are times when it is impossible to work in pairs. Also, you may be alone when God leads you to minister to a sick unbeliever on the street. Nevertheless, it is the general Biblical pattern to follow. There is power in agreement, and God blesses us when we take even the "iotas" of His Word seriously.

It is written...

> I pray that God, who gives peace, will make you completely holy. And may your spirit, soul, and body be kept healthy and faultless until our Lord Jesus Christ returns. The one who chose you can be trusted, and he will do this.
>
> I Thes. 5:23-24 – CEV, Contemporary English Version

PART II
How YOU Can Be Free
from Hindrances and Be Healed and Blessed!

CHAPTER 6
The Healing Process

We have explored in detail the *"what"* of healing – the truth about the promise of healing in the Word of God. Now we will begin to discover the answer to the question most readers are eager to discover – the **how** and **why** of healing. Why have you or your loved ones not been healed? And how do you go about being healed?

Being faced immediately with all the possible hindrances to healing could easily be discouraging. That's why I will first of all show how these hindrances can be eliminated. When you understand these important keys, the list of hindrances will seem less ominous. You will know the way and have the power available to conquer any hindrance. *You will be able to break through to freedom and walk unhindered in healing and all of God's blessings!*

First, understand that healing is a **process**. And that process begins on the *inside*. Studies have revealed that about 80% of illnesses stem from our emotions. So claiming our emotional healing by Jesus' sweating of blood in the garden can eliminate many physical illnesses as well. In any case, God promises to heal physical illness even if the illness is caused by emotions.

51

Why Doesn't God Heal Me?

The ideal, of course, is to walk in divine health, as we shall see in Chapter 20. As we know more and more who we are in Christ, that becomes more of a reality.

In most cases physical healing involves a spiritual element. Notice how often Jesus said to people seeking healing, "Your sins are forgiven." This is indeed our responsibility when God works through us to heal people. We have authority to forgive sin, as Jesus told His disciples (John 20:23), and God expects us to use it. What we bind on earth, He binds in heaven.

James 5:14-16 shows us that sin is often a factor in illness, although not always. We must, nevertheless, reassure and comfort the sick with authoritative words of forgiveness, as Jesus did. Sometimes God may withhold healing, even when people pray and fast for the sick, when we do not declare this.

We have seen that God's healing promise is based on the condition of obedience. Hindrances occur generally when we disobey. If sin is involved, we need to confess it and forsake it – to repent or change direction.

Remember the paralytic? "Which is easier, to say," asked Jesus, " 'Your sins have been forgiven you,' or to say, 'Get up and walk'?" (Luke 5:23). Christ discerned the sin hindering his healing, but He did not require this unsaved man to acknowledge and repent of what he did not know. He looked on his heart and his faith and used his "authority on earth to forgive sins" (verse 24), expressing the Father's love and opening a door so the man could come to repentance. It is Jesus' nature to forgive – and He gives us His nature and authority.

When sin is not involved, it may be the breaking of a natural law or a demonic attack, often because someone cursed us. Some headaches result from lack of sleep or stress, but they can also come because of curses. Any sudden, unexplainable pain can easily be demonic (i.e. caused by a demon, not necessarily implying demon manifestation). Whatever the cause, all illnesses fall under the promise of healing.

That promise is a done deal. We have *already been healed* 2,000 years ago by Jesus' stripes. So any symptoms that manifest in our bodies are a **lie**! And those lies come from the father of lies – Satan and his demons. We must rebuke those symptoms as lies, as we will find out in detail later. Then we claim our healing. Finally, we simply start **thanking** Jesus that we are healed!

I realize that some criticize the truth about Jesus' stripes healing us 2,000 years ago, as if we're denying the reality of the symptoms. The symptoms may be a fact in the natural, but the truth is more powerful and will win out if we are unwavering in persistent praise.

It's like mail orders. You have already paid for the item – you're simply waiting on it to arrive and manifest itself before your eyes. "The check's in the mail" is another way of saying it. Faith is indeed the evidence of things not yet seen in the natural realm (Heb. 11:1).

For our faith to be vindicated, however, we must be prospering in our soul or spiritual life. If we have not accepted Jesus' righteousness and are not

The Healing Process 6

defeating the power of sin in our life, as we shall see later, these words will be to no avail.

The good news, however, is that the Holy Spirit will reveal in this book how to defeat that power of sin. If we submit to God and choose to obey Him, our healing *will* become manifest.

The Process

When sin is involved in the life of a Christian, healing is a process. The physical and spiritual are closely linked. Spiritual wholeness must precede physical wholeness. Jesus exhorts us to seek the Kingdom first and He will add the rest (Mat. 6:33).

The apostle John relates the prosperity of our bodies and our worldly affairs to the prosperity of our souls (III John 2). As our spiritual life prospers – and we're not talking only about faith – our bodies prosper.

The opposite is also true. Sin opens doors for Satan, the author and instigator of sickness, to attack our bodies. After all, sin is what caused sickness to come on mankind in the first place. No illness existed in Eden.

Adam's sin called for Jesus to come for the redemption of our spirits and souls – but also for the redemption of our bodies! As we have seen, Jesus shed blood for our sins. He also shed blood for the healing of our emotions, our minds and brains – and our bodies.

Jesus thus made a blood covenant between Him and His people – His physical people Israel under the Old Covenant and His spiritual people – also called Israel – under the New. "The children's bread" is especially for the children of the New Covenant.

He did, however, make exceptions, as with the persevering Gentile woman who asked for "crumbs" from the children's bread. And He makes exceptions today. God is a big and merciful God. He often calls people to Him today by first healing them, showing them His power and love.

Kenneth Copeland relates the story of an intoxicated unbeliever who was touched by the anointing outside the meeting hall on the street. The man staggered into the hall and confessed his healing (which was a physical problem other than alcohol).

Jesus extended mercy to the people of His day since they did not yet have the Holy Spirit and were in ignorance. He holds us to a higher standard. James says knowledge is a big element in the determination of the responsibility for sin. "To Him who *knows*," it is sin (James 4:17). It may be sin before we know it to be, but we are held *accountable* the moment God opens our mind to see it.

We, the converted, do not have to be *perfect* to be healed. That's obvious. We must, nevertheless, accept and walk in Jesus' righteousness. Our heart is not perfect, but it is single and pure, and by grace we are spiritually *whole*.

6 Why Doesn't God Heal Me?

Holistic Healing – the Divine Kind

To understand how God heals us by healing the whole man, we must know what the soul is. The Hebrew *nephesh* or soul is used in a general sense to refer sometimes to a person or individual (Ezek. 18:20). And yet there is a more precise meaning to this word.

God's Word of Love in Greek shows that God wants soul and body healthy. John 10:28 says you can kill the body, but not the soul.

Hebrews 4:12 declares that the Sword of the Spirit penetrates deep, "even to the dividing asunder of soul and spirit." So there is even a distinction between soul and spirit, though both have a spiritual element.

We are made in God's image – a trinity of body, soul and spirit. The soul itself is a trinity of mind, heart (or emotions), and will.

We *are* spirits who *have* souls and who *live in* bodies. God made mankind after the *God* kind. God is a trinity – and so are we!

Adam, as do all of us, had a spirit – a spirit that died as God said it would, the day Adam sinned. Every human since has been born "dead in our transgressions" (Eph. 2:5). David said, "The wicked are estranged from the womb; These who speak lies go astray from birth" (Ps. 58:3). Children are born sinners, with dead spirits, because of forefather Adam. Jesus said to become like little children because their souls have not yet been corrupted by Satan's influence.

Paul says, "And you were dead in your trespasses and sins … even when we were dead in our transgressions, [God] made us alive together with Christ …" (Eph. 2:1, 5a). When we are born again, we – our spirits – become alive in Jesus (Rom. 8:10). The Spirit witnesses with our spirits that we are sons of God, no longer sons of the dead Adam.

But remember: we are spirits who have a soul. Our soul is alive from the moment of conception. Satan, the power of sin and the world negatively influence our soul. The Father calls a few of us to receive Jesus in this life. Jesus' life in us creates a new spirit and begins to heal our sin-sick soul.

Our spirits are sealed in the blood of Jesus. The evil one cannot touch us – i.e. our spirit (I John 4:18). He does, however, have access to our souls. As we allow our spirit man to take priority over our souls, we deny him that access. This resistance to sin denies him access to our bodies as well. He thus has no legal right to afflict our bodies. The sin and sickness link is inescapable.

A Personal Illustration

This book is not about me. It's about the loving God who healed me and promises to heal you. I can nevertheless best illustrate the healing process and the sin factor by using my own example.

I accepted Jesus in 1967 at the age of 16 and was baptized by immersion in

54

The Healing Process

1969. The Holy Spirit began to flow and grow in me. After four years of theological training, including a pastoral trainee post in 1972, I was called by God to the full-time pastoral ministry and began to serve in Paris, France in 1973. I experienced some difficult situations that deeply wounded my sensitive soul. I thought I had forgiven a superior for wrongs done to me, but I finally came to the belated realization that I had not forgiven from the heart.

God says He won't forgive us if we don't forgive others. I learned that the hard way.

As I discovered only in 1998 by revelation from the Holy Spirit, my wounded heart had hardened in unforgiveness 25 years earlier. The Holy Spirit had not flowed and grown in me for 25 years. He was grieved because of my refusal to forgive.

God never forsook me, but I was severely limited, even though God did bless my ministry in many ways in spite of me.

Jesus said we would be delivered to the tormenters – the demons – to bring us to forgive from the heart (Mat. 18:34-35). God allowed me to go through hell so I would wake up and forgive. I came within three hours of death from Legionnaires' disease when I was a pastor in Quebec City in 1986. My wife was making funeral plans – but God had other plans for me.

I did not feel righteous enough to claim healing as a promise. Coughing up blood with a 106° F degree fever, I lifted my hands to God and cried the following words to Him: "I can't ask You like Hezekiah did to extend my life because I'm righteous. I have so much to overcome. I need more time. I'm too young to die. I just plead for your mercy. Please don't let me die!"

David had asked God not to take him away "in the midst of my days" (Ps. 102:24), which was about 70 at that time. I was only 35 and did not want to be taken away in the middle of my life.

At this writing God has given me 15 years like Hezekiah and has promised me many more.

I was in a crowded emergency room in a Quebec City hospital before severe complications, including cardiac arrest, got me a bed in the intensive care unit. Thank God I was in His intensive care, even though I had only a marble-size worth of oxygen left in one lung. Doctors had no idea what I had, wondering if it was some deadly African disease.

The diagnosis came too late. But God was on time, even if the doctor was dangerously negligent. Miracles do happen. God saved my life.

This near-death experience brought on hereditary manic depression and a bruise or insult to the brain, exacerbating the mental symptoms and causing several organic personality disorders. After several years, I lost everything I held dear – my wife and family through separation and then divorce, my health, wealth and my ministry, which was my life. I even came perilously close to suicide on four occasions.

I could sanitize it by saying I had the spirit of unforgiveness, but in reality it

Why Doesn't God Heal Me?

was a demon of unforgiveness that invited other demons who played on my weaknesses, giving me the severe and embarrassing symptoms of mania. I realized later there were other demonic strongholds involved.

I had the Holy Spirit, so my spirit was sealed and could not be possessed by demons. Nevertheless, unforgiveness had a hold on my mind, so my soul had to be healed before my body or brain could be healed.

Too many Christians, even pastors, think they are somehow immune from demon activity. Don't be fooled! Satan has the world in the palm of his hands. It is in the Christian community where he and his demons work the hardest. They attack leaders, especially if they falsely think they are safe in Jesus while denying the authority He gave them over demons.

I may have given thousands of sermons in my life to a precious flock of French-speaking people who looked to me for leadership. And yet I was ignorant of the fact that I was beleaguered by demons.

God spoke directly to me through a Christian friend for five hours, telling me things about my past that only God could know. He even told me what my wife and daughter had told me in vain: I had not forgiven my boss (and a host of others). This time I knew it was from God and He had prepared me to receive it.

I acknowledged the reality of the offenses and the terrible hurt and anger I felt. I laid it all at the foot of the cross and received the grace to forgive. And since one of the sins committed against me was so serious it required Jesus Himself to forgive, I asked Him to forgive that sin for me.

It was a special sin that I had to forgive, the rejection of my status as a son of God. It grieved the Holy Spirit in me. He was similarly blasphemed when demons (bulls of Bashan, Psalm 22) used people to deny Jesus' Sonship on the cross when the Father was abandoning Him. He felt total rejection, as you have if you have been disfellowshipped from a church without real cause. It takes Jesus Himself to forgive that Satanic, blasphemous sin.

Tears fell and sobs gripped as the hurt came out and by Jesus' doing, I finally forgave – from the heart.

Seven believers laid hands on me for the healing of my soul and for the casting away of the demons involved in my illness. The list was so long that afterwards I had to renounce some of them specifically in Jesus' name. The main demon that blocked my healing was expelled and now I was ready for the physical healing. Unforgiveness gone, they laid hands on me again for the healing of my brain.

The method may vary with different ministries, but Doctor Jesus did the job – healing me of at least two incurable illnesses. The healing was an instant one, although it took me a while before I learned to walk in my healing. Curses from church people didn't help.

I know that everything will be restored, and God revealed that I would have

56

The Healing Process

restoration like Job, who according to tradition was also ill for 12 years. The big difference was that Satan could find plenty of reason to accuse me.

Someone said that when you "backmask" a country and western song, you "git" back your wife, children, job, money, respect – and your " pick-up." God has started restoring what Satan stole from me, beginning with my ministry, and I'm claiming seven-fold return (Prov. 6:31). The free will of individuals can nevertheless sometimes prevent or delay complete restoration.

The Holy Spirit gave the name for the church I now pastor, just as He did for the title of this book – and the one to follow this one. *Freedom Church of God* is the name – and "freedom" says it all. I am free – and called to set others free. To God be the glory!

A Biblical Bipolar?

God wants us free from the demonic influences that, despite what many religious people think, often represent the roots of illness.

King Saul was a prime example. He gave "access to the Devil" by his insane jealousy, hatred and anger directed at David. He was in a manic frenzy! A demon would trouble and torment him in his depressive phase, and David's music would help soothe his mind and soul.

If Saul were to have been permanently healed of his mental illness, he would have had to repent of the sins that opened the door for the demon and thus the condition. But he did not obey God and forgive Him for saying through Samuel that his line would not carry on the throne. It seems clear that Saul was manic-depressive or bipolar.

The Holy Spirit has revealed that bipolar illness is a diabolical duo. Satan likes to divide and conquer. He pits one demon against another.

The number two demon in authority directly under Satan is betrayal, who induced Judas to betray Jesus after he felt betrayed by Jesus' rebuke. Satan himself possessed Judas at the end. Betrayal has many demonic henchmen under him who are out of control in bipolar illness. Mockery, who was number two before the flood, fights with betrayal – a bipolar brawl.

Drugs simply dull the brain so demons have less power over it. Drugs mask. God heals. He's the Psychiatrist par excellence.

Doctors deal out drugs. That's because they don't know the root causes. The enemy is not flesh and blood. It's the demonic world!

Here comes one of the most controversial parts of this book – and a vital one. I have heard Christians angrily say, "The Devil makes me sick!" They usually aren't speaking literally. You will be shocked, however, when you hear the truth of how often those dirty little devils make us sick – literally!

Why Doesn't God Heal Me?

It is written...

How God anointed and consecrated Jesus of Nazareth with the [Holy] Spirit and with strength and ability and power; how He went about doing good and, in particular, curing all who were harassed and oppressed by [the power of] the devil, for God was with Him.

Acts 10:38 – AMP

CHAPTER 7

"Not against flesh and blood" – the Shocking Truth about Demons and Illness

In today's churches, "anti-supernatural bias" permeates the pews of the pious. If you dare mention demons in some religious circles, they think *you're* the one who has demon problems. The idea is this: don't use the dastardly dirty *demon* word and those devils will leave you alone. If you seem bedazzled by demons or "bogey-eyed about the bogeyman," they label you unbalanced.

Paradoxically, our secular world is talking more and more about such things as demons, witches, and mediums. This world of the last days is awakening to the supernatural as Satan and his cohorts attack ferociously, knowing their time is short. When will the religious crowd, "the people of the steeple," catch up to those "heathen people" who know demons are real? It's about time, church.

But churchianity and religiosity are blinded to powerful demons that have them in their clutches. In their deceptively comfortable pews they are sitting targets for demons that simply love to hear them talk of how secure they are in Jesus. Their "hear no evil, see no evil" demon defense makes them easy prey for deadly demon marksmen.

Why Doesn't God Heal Me?

Safe in Jesus? They don't have the slightest inkling of who they are in Christ (and many aren't in Christ at all). They don't use the authority Jesus gave them to tell demons where to go.

Demons "Out of the Closet" Today

Satan and his demons have deceived "the whole world" (Rev 12:9). And God Himself calls Satan "the god of this world" or age (II Cor. 4:4). That includes its religions – oh yes, even Christianity! While the greatest deception is the popular counterfeit – thousands of doctrines of demons in Christian churches taught by the "angel of light" – open and blatant demon activity abounds.

We have "progressed" from *The Exorcist* to *Malediction* (the word the French use for *curse*) to *The Blair Witch Project*. And through the popularity of a major book and movie series, a wily witch's broom has swept the Devil's dark dust into young, innocent minds. And many Christians have fallen into this deceptive witch's cauldron.

Witches are no longer secret folklore or something out of *The Wizard of Oz*. The broomstick bunch is as unabashed as gay activists. Psychic hotlines and astrology are "in." New Age teaching – first-century Gnosticism dressed up for a party – says "we know things you don't." Supernatural knowledge and power from questionable sources are in vogue. Youth are biting into TV shows about vampires. Openly Satanic and occult video games target young children.

Demons in Disease?

Amid such devilish doings, it seems strange that demonic involvement in illness, especially mental illness, should be regarded by anyone as a radical and unbalanced idea – especially by Christians!

Christians pooh-pooh the demon/disease connection: "That's medieval malarkey! Step into the twenty-first century!" Demons *have* kept up with the times. They're adapting and using their heads. Why can't Christians?

Christians, have you read the gospels? Have you ever read Acts 10:38? It plainly says Jesus went around *healing* those who were *"oppressed of the devil."* The Devil could not have done it all. *Demons* were involved! That is Bible teaching. The gospels are full of examples of demonic involvement in sickness.

Many seem to be as blind and dumb as the man with the blind and dumb demon whom Jesus encountered – unseeing and speechless when it comes to understanding demonic involvement in illness. It's as plain as can be for those with spiritual eyes to see.

God has inspired this book to open eyes dimmed by devilish deception. Some may be turned off because this subject is new to them and controversial. For some, new = untrue. That's messy math. It doesn't add up. Yet the Holy Spirit adds to

Biblical truth. "… He will guide you into all the truth …" (John 16:13) – even truth about demons and illness.

Don't close your mind. Open the Book and pray for discernment.

A discerning Christian friend gave me a powerful witness to the reality of demons dabbling in disease, especially the mental kind. As an intern for a year in Edmonton's psychiatric hospital, he saw clear evidence of demons in the psychiatrist's diagnostic handbook. He saw in a medical report the following diagnosis of one patient, penned by *two* psychiatrists: "demon-possessed."

C.A.T.S. – Christians Against The Supernatural

That's a surprising admission from psychiatrists! Too bad Christians can't admit it. They're naïve. And the demons are rubbing their hands in glee. They want the children of light to be in the dark when dealing with demons.

They don't want us Christians to know who we are in Christ. And you'll be surprised in Chapter 9 to find out how many Christians are devoid of this demon-defeating knowledge.

The Devil does not want us to know about the authority we have in Jesus to command demons to the pit in His name. He wants us to be nice, namby-pamby parishioners who think they don't have to acknowledge and confront the demonic world. "Be nice to them and they'll be nice to you." We're not talking about Chihuahuas. We're talking about Doberman pinchers that haven't eaten in a week! Was Jesus nice to them?

No! He declared all-out war on them! And He did what most Christians avoid like worms in a candy bar. He *talked* to them. God calls them enemies – His and ours.

Have you not read the good news in God's Word? Jesus won! Satan lost! The Devil is a defeated foe – a toothless lion. And "greater is He who is in you than he who is in the world" (I John 4:4). He gave us authority over the Devil and the demons. But we must use it!

He said we would do the works He did, which included casting out demons, and would do even greater works! He wants us to tell demons to get lost in the mighty name of Jesus.

On the other hand, the Devil wants us devoid of knowledge of his devices, ignorant both of demonic *manifestation* in illness and in demonic *causation* of disease, which are *not* synonymous. Causing an illness and displaying their personalities by manifesting through people are two different demonic activities.

Remember that Lucifer was a created angelic being with great, miracle-working powers. Although God took away his creative powers, he did not take his miracle-working power away when he rebelled.

Demons can indeed work miracles. After all, they are supernatural beings with supernatural powers enabling them to work miracles in the natural world. (By the way, Christians have much more power than demons. We simply haven't used it.) Some things demons do are unexplainable in the natural. Other things they do can be explained – even diagnosed.

Psychiatrists, for instance, diagnose demons all the time. Oh, they think they're diagnosing chemical imbalances. But who caused those chemical imbalances? Do you think demons are incapable of messing up a physical body? If they can cause blindness and deafness, can they not cause cancer and other diseases?

In fact, researchers know that the rapid growth of viruses follows no natural law. It is astounding and supernatural. Cancer cells go on a wild path of rapid destruction that is medically and scientifically unexplainable.

God, of course, is not generally in the business of destroying and killing. That's the Devil's doing. He's the one who comes to plunder and destroy. So the incredible rate of multiplication of viruses is a clear demonstration of demonic involvement in illness.

Demonic involvement does not always mean demonic manifestation. Demons can supernaturally cause a problem in a physical body and go on their wicked way, or they can stay and manifest, infest, influence or in rare cases possess. Don't downplay demonic power. And don't downplay the power Jesus gave us over them!

"If it's good enough for Jesus and Paul ..."

Once I talked to a Carolina Christian who attended a church that used the old King James Bible exclusively. I said jokingly to her: "Well, I guess if it's good enough for Jesus and the apostles, it's good enough for me!" My jaw dropped when she said: "Amen!"

As a matter of fact, when it comes to Biblical teaching and practice on demons: "If it's good enough for Jesus and the apostles (including Paul), it's good enough for me."

What, may I ask, did Jesus do on practically a daily basis? He dealt with demons! He healed many whose illnesses were caused by *demons*! He plainly talked about spirits (*demons!*) of *infirmity* (sickness, illness, disease).

Demon-induced Illness in the Gospels

Luke 13, cited below,[9] is properly translated in the NASB. It speaks of a woman who had a "*sickness caused by a* **spirit**." The NLT makes it clear it was an evil

---

[9] Luke 13:11-16:

v. 11 - And there was a woman who for eighteen years had had a sickness caused by a spirit; and she was bent double, and could not straighten up at all.

v. 12 - When Jesus saw her, He called her over and said to her, "Woman, you are freed from your sickess."

v. 13 - And He laid His hands on her; and immediately she was made erect again and began glorifying God.

v. 14 - But the synagogue official, indignant because Jesus had healed on the Sabbath, began saying to the

"Not against flesh and blood"

spirit or demon.

This was not, however, as the KJV incorrectly translates, a "spirit of infirmity," although such a spirit does exist. God has revealed that there is a crippling spirit or demon called "bent," who has access to people because of unconfessed sin. Instead of walking spiritually and physically upright, the burden of sin weighs them down and literally bends them over. The spirit of bent caused her sickness.

And notice in verse 16 who had bound her – Satan (through the demon). Demons haven't changed their methods. Yet humanistic doctors – biased against the supernatural – put fancy names on illnesses. Surprise! Demons did it.

Mainstream Christianity would like to label this view unbalanced. Well, if it's good enough for Jesus and Paul, it's good enough for this author too!

Why not go with the flow of Jesus – the narrow way – rather than the broad, popular flow of the mainstream?

Do you really know the real Jesus? Do you know the balanced, joyful Jesus who drank wine – in moderation? Do you think they saved the best *grape juice* for the last at that party in Cana? Do you think they would accuse Him of being a winebibber if He never touched the stuff?

Do you know the miracle-working, demon-defying, righteously angry Son of God who took a whip to run the moneychangers out of the temple, overturning their tables? Those tables weighed hundreds of pounds. He was a strong man – and He's an even stronger God!

Do you know the loving Healer who wants you to be like Him? Do you know Him who wants you to do even greater works? Do you know the Demon-basher who wants to employ you to destroy the works of the Devil – including sickness?

It was Jesus who cast out demons of infirmity. It was *Doctor* Luke who wrote that sickness involved *demonic oppression* (Acts 10:38)! Why don't Christian doctors today believe that? It was the apostle Paul who wrote Ephesians 6:12: "For our struggle is *not against flesh and blood*, but against the rulers, against the powers, against the world forces of this darkness, against the spiritual forces of wickedness in the heavenly places."

In earning my Bachelor of Arts in theology 30 years ago, I had a facility for memorizing Scriptures in an unconventional way. An insect repellent bearing the same numbers as Ephesians 6:12 reminded me of those flying critters "in high places." Paul says demons are our real but unseen enemies.

In other words, "don't sweat the small stuff" (human beings, or the physical, natural world). It's the ultimate reality – the spirit world – that is behind everything

crowd in response, "There are six days in which work should be done; so come during them and get healed, and not on the Sabbath day."

v. 15 - But the Lord [Jesus] answered him and said, "You hypocrites, does not each of you on the Sabbath untie his ox or his donkey from the stall and lead him away to water him?

v. 16 - And this woman, a daughter of Abraham as she is, whom Satan has bound for eighteen long years, should she not have been released from this bond on the Sabbath day?"

and everyone we think we are fighting in the natural. And, surprise, surprise! That includes physical illness.

Don't sweat the big stuff either. Jesus is bigger! The invisible is not invincible.

Our Invisible Battle or Spiritual Whaaat?

I love the story of the non-Baptist who attends a Baptist church and asks to join the choir. I should explain first that some use the term "invisible church" to mean those true, "born again" Christians who are known to God across "brand-name," denominational lines. The choir director asks the poor fellow if he's a Baptist. "No," he answers, "I'm in the invisible church."

"Well, then," says the director in a huff, "you can join the invisible choir!"

Why do we minimize the invisible? We can't see the wind, but we surely respected hurricane Hazel in South Carolina in 1954. She downed the biggest tree I had ever seen. We can't see electricity, but it can kill us in an instant. And what about the invisible energy in the atom?

Paul says our real battle is not with what we see as the real world. It's not our mate. It's not our boss. And our physical or mental illnesses are not always the result of physical causes, even though there may be a natural explanation that tells us what demons have done to mess up our bodies. And often demons will be behind our desire to eat, or say or do the wrong thing – the thing that will cause an illness or make it worse.

There is more to our Christian battle than we can see. And there is more to demons than meets the eye. Actually, there is more truth about the devices of the Devil and demons than is revealed in the Bible. The additional truth the Spirit gives only builds on the truth revealed by the foundation of all knowledge, the Word of God. The Spirit never contradicts that Word. After all, He wrote it!

The Holy Spirit has worked with many deliverance ministries (including our own) who have added to the understanding of the nature and devices of demons. This knowledge empowers us to do battle with the demonic world.

Did I say "battle"? That's a word some Christians don't like. One term provokes their ire: *spiritual warfare.*

"Spiritual whaaat?" That's the reaction of some.

But look how often the Bible uses the analogy of warfare. Actually, it's more than an analogy. It is the reality of a spiritual battle.

What in the world is spiritual warfare? Some Christians think it's singing "Onward Christian Soldiers"!

The all-too-frequent version of spiritual warfare for many Christians is a gutless, watered-down, gentleman's version. The Holy Spirit may be gentlemanly in many ways, but when our God fights, He really fights. Jesus is a Warrior (Ex. 15:3). And He wants us to be warriors.

As we saw earlier, Jesus didn't daintily rearrange the moneychangers' tables

"Not against flesh and blood"

from the temple, neatly stacking them in a row and apologizing for upsetting everything. He snapped a whip. And there is no indication that He used gentle, tactful words.

He will soon come back, not as a Lamb, but as a mighty Warrior to punish the Devil and those who follow him. And I hope to ride with Him. How about you? Are you a warrior? Or do you think serious spiritual warfare is for the unbalanced and weird?

Admittedly, some may go to the extreme of worshipping spiritual warfare rather than worshipping God. Some also worship the act of worship itself.

Such excesses do not mean we should refrain from worshipping or taking our God-given responsibility to exercise Jesus' authority over an already-defeated foe. He is defeated for us only if we declare with our mouths that he is defeated in Jesus' name.

If we ignore demons and don't fight them, they have us in their hands without a fight. And if we don't think they figure in illness, we may remain under attack with their lying symptoms. This is an important hindrance to healing. If we ignore demons, they won't go away. And we will be their prey.

If we are truly secure in Jesus, we will use His name and His authority to tell them where they belong – in the pit of hell. They are God's enemies. And God's enemies are our enemies. Pussyfoot with the demons – and you will be under *their* feet. They're supposed to be under *yours*!

As we shall explore in greater detail later, the Hebrew word *shalom* has an important connection with healing. One of its manifold meanings is "nothing missing, nothing broken." When Satan tries to steal our *shalom*, we can add, "Nothing doing, Devil!" We must do battle with supernatural forces. The Lion of Judah in us must enforce His victory – already won 2,000 years ago – over the wily, feline foe named Satan.

Who are the C.A.T.S. – Christians Against the Supernatural? Actually, Satan is called a lion, a cat – but a toothless one. Demons are like cats. They put up a big front, as if Jesus had not defeated them. When we Christians stand up to them with Jesus' authority, they run like "scaredy-cats," "fraidy-cats," as we called them in my boyhood Carolina. James says to draw near to God, resist the Devil and demons – and they will *flee*!

Demons may not be involved initially in our illnesses, but more often than not they are. They do attack, nevertheless, once we step out in faith. They go to war. So must we!

So many fine Christians give up when they don't see their healing manifested. They settle for second best, thinking maybe God doesn't want to heal them. Or they think they glorify God by enduring forever in faith. They may indeed have faith in God to help them endure – and He will. But they don't believe what He says. He says His will is to heal. And that means you!

And it doesn't mean in 30 years! And it doesn't mean at the resurrection! Get real! *Satan* is. And he wants to discourage you by making symptoms persist to wear you down.

Winston Churchill once gave a speech to a group of students. For several eternal minutes, he said nothing at all. At last he spoke these simple but stirring words: "Never give up! Never give up! Never give up!" Then he sat down.

Bulldog Churchill spoke truth. When it comes to healing, don't give up. Set your face "like a flint" and shoot *your* flaming arrows at the Devil!

If the healing does not manifest in a relatively short time, you may need to pray and fast. You may need to ask God to show you– with guidance from this book, if necessary – the hindrance or hindrances that are blocking you.

That's not giving up! That's seeking God. That is not resigning ourselves to accepting something short of God's perfect will for us.

One of the main reasons many Christians are not healed today is not realizing the involvement of demons to cause our illnesses and/or to make symptoms persist or recur. Satan wants to discourage us and sap our faith. To make symptoms disappear, we need to exercise confident spiritual warfare.

Confident warfare does not mean repeated commands to the enemy for the same illness. Jesus did not talk twice to demons. He told them to get lost – once!

Constantly repeating commands to the demons is like a harassed mother screaming orders at rebellious children who have no intention of obeying. A parent who knows his or her authority speaks firmly and doesn't have to constantly repeat commands. The demons will interpret the repetitive approach as worship. Let's use our authority in Jesus Christ!

The Practical Solution to Sickness

How should we use our authority to get a practical solution to sickness? What follows may be new and seem strange to you. It was new and surprising to us as well when the Holy Spirit revealed it. But it works!

Lest what follows appear to be a meaningless mantra – superstitious animism – remember this: Satan is a legalist. If we do not use his weapon against him, we're not being "wise as serpents." Let's beat him at his own game.

I know this discussion is distasteful to conservative Christians unfamiliar with spiritual warfare. It seemed strange to me as well when I first heard about it and began to practice it. But it does the job. Try it! You will see the fruits.

If you don't want to include the foreign concept of spiritual warfare into your healing paradigm, that's your choice. Stay sick!

My psychiatrically trained friend chooses to be healed by dealing with the demons. If they can miraculously make a big truck break down, or do other feats in other domains, why can't they make cells go berserk and start destroying bodies through cancer?

Just because there is a physical explanation doesn't mean nothing is happening

"Not against flesh and blood"

supernaturally. Demons can create reality in the natural world by supernatural means.

A person dear to me had a schoolteacher who was a witch (a real one!). She had her pupils levitate her desk three feet in the air! And you think they can't provoke sudden pains in the body?

When God said sickness was from the Devil (Acts 10:38), He was giving us a key to being healed. It may not be fashionable or agreeable to the natural mind, but it is true.

In most cases, we should deal with the cause of the illness first – the demonic realm (see "Satan" in the Appendix).

Here is a guideline to follow when symptoms of sickness or disease appear: *"In Jesus' name, I bind all spirits of fear and doubt and send them back to the pit."* If you discern any specific demons causing the illness, such as the spirit of bent, blight (causing almost all flu symptoms), infirmity, etc., bind them as well.

Then say something like this: *"I take authority over all demons and their agents enforcing these lying symptoms. I bind you in chains of confusion, cut you off from all support, burn up your demonic slime,[10] and command you to go back to the pit, in Jesus' name! Thank You, Father."*

In cases of mental illness, where not only the physical brain is affected but also the mind, the following addition would be useful: *"Satan and the demons, in Jesus' name, I forbid you from influencing my mind in any way, shape or form."*

"In any way, shape or form" may seem like a useless cliché, but not in the world of demons. They use ways, shapes and forms (people) to deceive and hurt. This is not a book on deliverance, so I will not go into detail.

Once we have dealt with the demonic cause, we need to make some scriptural declarations. Here are some examples:

It is written: I was healed by the stripes of Jesus 2,000 years ago (I Pet. 2:24). I claim my healing! **I am the righteousness of God, and no sickness has the right to exist in me!** *(II Cor. 5:21) No weapon formed against me shall prosper (Isa. 54:17). I cover myself with the blood of Jesus. I stand in my righteousness and claim the promise that none of the diseases that came upon Egypt will come upon me, for Jesus, You are My Healer (Ex. 15:26). Jesus, You took my infirmities and carried away my diseases (Mat. 8:17; Isa. 53:4). I claim Your promise, Jesus, that You will remove from me all sickness (Deut. 7:15).*

Jesus, You became a curse for me and have delivered me from the curse of the law, including all the sicknesses mentioned in Deuteronomy 28 and every sickness and plague that are not written in the book of this law (Deut. 28:61).

Satan, I am the temple of God (I Cor. 6:19-20). You have your eviction notice. Get off God's property! You're a loser and you're under my feet!

---

[10] Demons often call in support from other demons to take over where they left off. They will also leave demonic slime – spiritual, not physical slime – behind to cause minor symptoms.

Why Doesn't God Heal Me?

Bless Jesus, O my soul, and all that is within me, bless His holy name. Bless the Eternal, O my soul, and forget none of His benefits, who forgives all my sins and heals all my diseases (Ps. 103). When the believers drank the blood of the Lamb and ate His body, they went out of Egyptian bondage and there was none feeble among them (Ps. 105:37).

I prosper and am in good health, just as my soul prospers (III John 2). You sent Your Word and healed me (Ps. 107:20). Jesus, You healed all who were oppressed by the Devil, including me (Acts 10:38). Jesus, You have redeemed me to be just like the first Adam before sin, in Your perfect image, without sin or sickness, with all authority in heaven and earth (see Chapter 10). The Son of God appeared for this purpose, to destroy the works of the Devil (I John 3:8).

Satan, the blood of Jesus is against you. You are finished! Greater is He who is in me than he who is in the world (I John 4:4). Go, Satan! (Mat. 4:10) I will tread upon the lion and cobra, the young lion and the cobra I will trample down (Ps. 91:13). Toothless, defeated lion (or filthy snake), you are under my feet!

I am redeemed from sickness by the blood of Jesus, because My Father loves me.

That last sentence packs power that the bold type cannot begin to portray. When we say those words with conviction, tremendous power and anointing are released. We are combining in one breath the dynamite weapons of the blood, name and Word of Jesus with the love of God. The combination is unbeatable.

And you can apply those words to basically any sin or hindrance in this book or in your life that stands between you and the victorious life. You fill in the blanks: *I am redeemed from _____ by the blood of Jesus, because my Father loves me.* You'll be surprised how quickly you begin to live up to the name of overcomer.

Our Father's love for us is so awesome that He gave His precious Son Jesus to suffer and die for us. And together they made this colossal sacrifice so that we would be redeemed – redeemed from every deceptive gift from Satan that messes us up and deprives us of the abundant life. Our Father of Love wants the best for us. He wants us healed and blessed.

If symptoms persist after claiming healing by Jesus' stripes, simply keep *thanking and praising* God for your healing. If you **celebrate** your healing, you won't have to celebrate for long. And actually, the Christian life should be a continual celebration.

The warfare of Psalm 149:6-9 involves the "two-edged sword" of the Word *and* the "high praises of God." The kings bound in chains refer not only to physical rulers but also to the spiritual rulers or demons as well.

After you have waged spiritual warfare, the demons will often try to test your resolve by persisting with the lying symptoms. They want you to be so beleaguered by their attack that you will *speak the symptoms into law by claiming them as yours, by speaking them into existence with your mouth.* You have the godlike

"Not against flesh and blood"

power of the word: *what you **say** becomes law!*

Don't speed read that last paragraph. Let it sink in. Ponder it. It is so important I have dedicated all of Chapter 11 to the expounding of this vital subject.

In some cases, symptoms may persist for a day or even several days – especially if you are being cursed continually by a group of people and you don't possess or practice the information about curses revealed later in this book. Whatever you do, *don't claim the symptoms*! Don't say, "*I have* the flu." Change that to, "I am fighting some flu symptoms." Or even better, "I am under *attack*," or "Satan is *attacking* me with flu symptoms."

If the symptoms do not disappear in a reasonable amount of time, then you may have to examine yourself in the light of these hindrances to see if there is a reason God has withheld healing. If you are correct in finding no hindrance, it may simply be a test of your faith. If you persist in asking God's wisdom in the matter, He will be faithful to show you what you need to do.

Adopting the practice of spiritual warfare may involve surrendering your religious pride and saying no to the spirit of religiosity that doesn't want you healed. It may not fit a conservative, pious paradigm – but try it! You'll like it!

Put the Devil and the demons under your righteous heel – and be healed! God wants the best for you. Don't limit Him.

Don't underestimate His love for you. That's what Chapter 9 is all about. It expounds in detail one of the most important truths contained in this book. Without that truth spiritual warfare is an empty phrase. You have no authority over Satan until you know who you are.

But first, we need a whole chapter to explain the most powerful form of spiritual warfare. It's great importance deserves more than a few lines in Hindrance No. 53. The chapter you just read mentions it briefly. Can you guess what it is? It is God's secret weapon. But if you read on, it won't be a secret to you.

It is written...

Heal me, O [Jesus], and I will be healed; Save me and I will be saved, For You are my praise.

Jer. 17:14

CHAPTER 8
Our Secret (and Most Powerful) Weapon

To supplement our teachings in Freedom Church of God, we play video-tapes of anointed men and women of God. Some of the tapes offering the deepest teachings (and at the same time the most entertaining) are the ones of Dr. Creflo Dollar.

Recently Pastor Creflo stopped in the middle of a phrase, took off his quality suit jacket, and began to run around the room in jubilant exaltation. The Holy Spirit led him to do it, just after he had described how David took off more than Dr. Dollar did and celebrated before God. Such childlike exuberance makes Satan's evil spirits flee and the overly proper "religious" people extremely uncomfortable. But it gives great pleasure to God.

For many years I was part of the normal, staid religious crowd, singing stale hymns with little joy and no bodily movement. Then God healed me. Now as worship leader and especially when I'm in the audience, I can't help praising Jesus with all my heart and all my body. I jump and dance and spin around in boyish glee.

I just can't help it. God saved my life when I had three hours to live. He healed me of a dreadful illness men call incurable. My God twirls around in a dance of joy over me (Zeph. 3:17), so I can't help spinning around in joy for what He's done for me.

Children do it so naturally. They rejoice when Daddy blesses them. And they trust so completely in their father that they celebrate after they have asked Daddy for something. They know it's as good as done. Next to praising God in the spirit (in tongues), the most perfect praise comes out of the mouths of little children (Mat. 21:16, KJV).

God has not revealed this powerful weapon to the world. For one thing, praising God when bad things happen to you defies worldly logic. Celebrating something that hasn't yet happened is folly to the world. It is a secret He has revealed to those called-out ones who become like little children. Not even all Christians understand this secret. It is God's secret weapon. And what a powerful weapon it is!

The Power and Benefits of Holy Hoopla

The Hebrew concept of praise is foreign to most Christians today. God does not respond to unenthusiastic religious posturing. He wants you to raise a holy, hallelujah hoopla. Looking foolish is part of the concept of one of the Hebrew words for praise.[11]

People dance and holler in foolish frenzy at sports events. But when they enter church, they check their coats and their garments of praise at the door and quietly fold their hands. That's religion. It kills excitement and passion for Jesus. He must think, "So you love your football heroes more than Me?"

The benefits of praise are enormous. It releases and preserves God's blessings, unleashes His miracles, activates His scepter of authority in our lives, destroys pride and releases supernatural joy and peace.

The United States guarded a secret weapon and unleashed it at the end of World War II. The secret weapon God gives us is much more powerful (and certainly more beneficial) than the nuclear bomb.

Used properly, this secret weapon can defeat any foe, obliterating all their plans. That's why Satan hates it with a passion. It stops him in his tracks. Its spiritual mega-tonnage blows away sin, failure, addictions, poverty, lack and pain. And when we persist in praise, we defeat the cause of our pain. *Persistent praise can eliminate the hindrances to your healing!*

When you discover your hindrances in the following chapters, confess them

---

[11] "Hallelujah" comes from the word *halal*. The original idea was to be clear or shine, from which came the idea of making a show or boasting in foolish-looking celebration. Even the idea of raving is included, a term used today for night club revelry. Christian expression of excitement in praise should exceed in intensity but not imitate the worldly kind of celebration.

Our Secret (and Most Powerful) Weapon 8

first. Then start immediately praising Jesus for giving you the victory over them. He's *Yehovah-Nissi*, your Banner and Victory. Praise Jesus' name for redeeming you from your hindrance by His blood.

When you are healed, keep making praise a daily habit. Even on a physical level, praising Jesus prevents sickness. Praise extends your life, releases tension, changes your attitude, causes the body to dispose of poisons and (especially when accompanied by dancing) releases those feel-good brain chemicals.

But praise is not simply about feeling good. Praise can single-handedly defeat the enemy. The original passage on children's praise is Psalm 8:2. It says that their praise is strength. It defeats the enemy. Praise from the lips of "the weak things of the world" can crush the most powerful foe.

When we begin to praise Jesus for the victory, we recognize the Source of our victory. Our praise invokes Jesus' pledge to fight for us. The battle is no longer ours. In II Chronicles 20, Judah did not even have to fight. They simply sent out people to praise and worship God, and the various enemies started slaughtering each other!

When we are passive, Satan instills fear in us. When we go on the praise warpath, we are the ones that instill fear in Satan. And Satan cannot put up barriers where praise abounds. Do we cower in fear before Satan's waves, or do we release a tsunami of praise that sweeps him away?

Praise contains explosive power. It is the most powerful form of spiritual warfare. It is your greatest weapon against evil and demonic blockages. Praise automatically releases angels to go to war. And there's more: demons can't stand that sound of joy. They can't stick around where praise abounds. They skedaddle.

Read Psalm 149 and you will see the power of praise as warfare. The high praises mentioned here are when we speak out God's promises in His Word and praise Him for how He accomplished them in our lives.

And here is a surprise for many churchgoers. It's right here in the Bible: God says to dance in church! And He says praise should not be reserved for church. It should be a way of life. And yet sad to say, many churches have song services that are more like funerals than parties.

Praise and worship is the most important part of a church service. God inhabits – and Satan inhibits – the praises of the believers (Ps. 122:1-4). That's precisely why Satan inhibits praise. He doesn't want God to show up. If God doesn't show up, what good is the sermon? Things happen when God's people abandon their pride and sing and dance for joy before Jesus.

Dirges don't let you merge more completely with the One who inhabits your praises. Dead songs don't let the life of God flow through you. But the God of Love dwells in praise, releasing the giving spirit and compassion for others. Praise shows your love for God and it opens you up to receive His love and His power to change you.

Praise unleashes power for miracles. Jesus thanked the Father for always answering Him. Praise released the power to raise the dead! When we begin to praise God for raising the dead before we raise them, then we'll begin to see the

73

dead raised on a scale never seen. Praise activates faith and produces growth in your faith level (see "Faith, levels of" in the Appendix). Repeating the Word and rejoicing in it builds faith (Ps. 56:4; Rom. 10:17).

If we take time to praise God before we pray for someone's healing, we will see more healings!

Praise brings answers from the Holy Spirit. When we ask Him questions and thank Him in advance for the answers, the answers flow.

Expect God to move every time you pray. Thank Him before, during and after the answer.

Praise allows you to walk in the righteousness of God when you focus your attention on God and not on yourself or your own problems. When you're in the praise mode, compromise with sin does not pollute your purity in Jesus. When you get out of that worship mode, self-justification and legalism enter.

Praise releases your hope and joy. Some dances express joy. Other dances actually generate a special, anointed joy.

Praise establishes God's dominion. Judah means praise, and it was Judah that God called to go first into battle and into the land (Judges 1:1-2). Praise led the way and everyone and everything else followed to establish God's rule. Praise and joy is contagious. God employs the light of His people of praise to attract others into the joy of the Kingdom.

Praise activates all the aspects of your inheritance. It dramatically speeds up the harvest. The more you praise, the faster the promised blessings will come – and the better they will be. God wants you to rejoice in your blessings so He can give you more. Eventually you will begin to receive desired blessings before you ask!

Why stay a beggar when you can be blessed by being a "praiser"?

Christian Beggars?

With such benefits accompanying praise, you would think praise would be popular among Christians. Sadly though, many Christians go to God in prayer as beggars. They beg, whine, snivel, lament and complain. That's no way to get answers. We do want answers, don't we? Isn't prayer all about results?

Begging is no way to get results. Jesus' warning against vain repetitions includes repeated requests for the same thing (see "Prayer, Ten Steps to Heartfelt Prayer" and "Adversity" in the Appendix).

Did Jesus ask twice for Lazarus to be raised from the dead? No. He first thanked His Father for always hearing Him. His praise brought forth power! He simply said, "Lazarus, come forth!"

Jesus didn't beg His Father. He expected results and thanked His Father for those results.

None of the great men of God needed to beg Him for results. God does have His timing for fulfilling certain requests, but begging cancels the answers.

Elijah prayed about rain and the results rained down. He prayed a 20-second prayer and fire came down from heaven! Baal's prophets, on the other hand, begged and begged their god all day to answer (I Kings 18:26). Repetitious petitions are fruitless – even when praying to the true God (Mat. 6:7).

God repeatedly tells us to bathe our prayers in thanksgiving, from beginning to end (Col. 4:2; Eph. 5:20; I Thes. 5:16-18; Heb. 13:15; Col. 2:7; Ps. 95:2; 100:4; Phil. 4:6).

Prison doors miraculously opened when Paul and Silas prayed and sang praises (Acts 16:25).

Jesus says that obedient Christians can receive anything from God if they fulfill certain conditions. They must harbor no doubt about their request, which must be made according to the will and Word of God and in the name of Jesus (I John 3:22; 5:14-15; John 14:13; 15:7). We can even ask that mountains be moved – if we believe it (Mark 11:23). Jesus said, "… all things for which you pray and ask, believe that you *have received* them, and they *will* be granted to you" (Mark 11:24).

Ask Once! Then Praise!

Your Father has said in His Word that He would give you what you asked. When a little boy asks his daddy for a new bike and Daddy says yes, does the boy ask again? No! He's already jumping for joy. He can visualize the bike. He knows his daddy doesn't lie.

So why, why do we Christians have to ask our Father for the same thing again and again? Biblically or logically, it makes no sense! If we truly believe we have already received our request, why ask twice? Like that little boy, God simple wants us to celebrate and thank Him until we actually see with our physical eyes the request granted.

If we believe we have received the answer, asking again is mocking God and being double-minded (James 1:5-8).

Admittedly, because of the need for daily renewal, some prayers do need to be repeated daily, such as our daily bread (Mat. 6). But even then, we should be in a spirit of thanksgiving about our request.

Let's not misunderstand some isolated verses and establish our doctrine from them. In Luke 18, Jesus gives a parable to teach us perseverance in prayer. And as in Luke 11, the lesson is this: if even unjust humans give in to perseverance in prayer, how much more will our loving Father answer us (Luke 11:13). Fathers, what would you deny your children when they tell you how much they love you?

Asking, seeking and knocking – the words Jesus used – are not all necessarily referring to prayer. We seek first the Kingdom of God by tithes and offering, for instance. What's more, they're not even in sequence, since knocking normally precedes asking. Persistence does not mean asking the same question twice. God emphasizes that He is not deaf (Isa. 59:1). Persist in praise.

Why Doesn't God Heal Me?

Interestingly, Luke 18 refers to a widow's request for victory over an adversary. That's part of our daily prayers in Matthew 6, since our enemy is always on the prowl. There again, we can thank God daily for delivering us from the Adversary.

For other than daily requests, we need ask only once, unless the situation changes and requires new prayers. And realize that God doesn't always bring the answer immediately (Dan. 9:23; 10:2-4). But praise and celebration will bring the answer much more quickly. God never tempts us, but He does test us to see if we really believe Him (II Chron. 16:9; Ps. 11:4-5).

Jesus tested the Canaanite woman who wanted her daughter healed (Mat. 15:21-28). Jesus hailed her great faith. But what supplemented – and yes, even activated – that faith so strongly that Jesus could not refuse her? She bowed down before Him in praise and worship! Praise pays. Praise touches God's heart and unleashes His power.

But if theologians have convinced you that you are a beggar who needs to approach God exactly like you would plead your case before an unjust judge, do a little test. Take two prayer requests. Use repeated requests for one. For the other, ask once and then pour on the praise. Compare. If God's Word won't convince you, maybe experience will.

Rejoice! Again I say, "Rejoice!"

We have two ladies named Joyce in our church. I sometimes tease them by calling them Joyce and "Rejoice." It reminds me of Paul's exhortation: "Rejoice in [Jesus] always; again I will say, rejoice!" (Phil. 4:4). Must be an important concept!

A computer analogy may help. Those of you who send e-mails know about a little button called "Resend." You don't need to push that button unless something goes wrong. When you send a prayer "e-mail" request to heaven, it's faster than any server. And unless you have no faith or are full of unforgiveness or pride, God always hears and answers. You never need to hit "Resend."

You do, however, need to push the praise button. Don't resend. Rejoice! Again I say, rejoice!

Look at a Bible analogy – the seed. Prayer is a seed you plant in God's mind. No need to replace the seed. Just water it. Water it with praise!

The world praises Satan. Why can't we praise Jesus?

One Edmonton nightclub markets its revelries with the following ad: "Praise heaven. Raise hell." And I'm sure they do – I mean the latter.

Home games in sports give advantage to the home team because the local fans raise a "you-know-what of a hullabaloo." The local boys have the praise advantage.

When Christians start raising a heaven-of-a hullabaloo about Jesus, all heaven's blessings and power are going to break loose! And hell has as much

76

Our Secret (and Most Powerful) Weapon 8

staying power as a snowball within its fiery gates!

Even when the going gets tough – and especially when the going gets tough – the tough will press in with praise.

Praise Isn't Always Easy

In case you wondered, in this book I am often preaching to myself. And I know by experience that sometimes praise can be the last thing you want to do. But I'm learning.

A number of years ago, when my walk with Jesus left a lot to be desired, I was traveling by bus around the U.S. attending healing crusades to learn more about my calling of healing evangelist. Sadly, my belongings were stolen and I ended up in some homeless shelters and had to literally count my pennies. When I was able to access a few funds, they were stolen. But sin on my part was involved.

This time, however, I quickly repented. I went into a praise dance and looked like an Apache on the warpath. I spun around in a dance of victory, asking Jesus for provision and thanking Him for it. I was attending a prayer conference, and would have slept on the ground had God not blessed me with a few kind ladies who let me sleep in their car. The morning after my worship dance, I attended a church service where the pastor invited international visitors to come up on stage.

As I stood there, a young man approached me and said, "[God] told me to give you this." He put in my hand a wad of cash, $100 U.S. that looked gold – not green – to me. He drove me to a cell group meeting and meal that blessed me greatly. After one more homeless shelter, I made it back to Canada, tired but thankful.

I had been under much attack during my trip. A complaining spirit and lack of praise always leaves the door open for attack from Satan.

And when Satan buffets and afflicts us, it's not easy to lift up holy hands of praise.

When that happens, what occurs is a praise test.

I had a seventh grade teacher who would announce a pop test several days before the test. It was not a true pop quiz. Pop tests "pop up" on us unawares. God sometimes allows Satan to afflict us, and in so doing He is testing us. Can we praise Him when bad things happen? Can we pass the praise test?

We can, if we do like David. David primed himself with praise pauses. He praised God seven times a day (Ps. 119:164). If we are in the habit of the holy hoopla, as well as the quiet time of thanksgiving, we will be able to pass the praise tests that come.

If we don't get in the habit of jumping for joy in the good times, in the bad times we may jump off a cliff.

In the good times and bad, we need to praise Jesus by name. "... Let the afflicted and needy praise Your name [so they won't stay that way!]" (Ps. 74:21). If you're down in pain and in need of funds, have fun praising Jesus. Expect victo-

77

Why Doesn't God Heal Me?

ry. Thank Him for some future fun – and funds.

When it seems nothing is going right, and adversity is no longer knocking on the door but barging in, turn your back on what comes natural and turn to Habakkuk. The last few verses of that book will be the last thing your flesh wants to do, but do it. Rejoice in Jesus! Sing! Dance! Twirl around in celebration. It can make the attack stop quickly. Adversity is a spirit and he can't stay around when you're praising Jesus.

Praise makes your feet "like hinds' feet." You will move quickly into the high places with God. Your growth will speed up. Breakthrough will come.

After all, you're no beggar. You have a covenant with the Most High! Unlike the wicked, you have a right to remind God of His covenant (Ps. 50:16, 22-23). Rejoice that you are part of the covenant people.

When you do, the covenant promises will come quickly. Healing is part of that covenant. Complete healing will come speedily when you celebrate before you see it.

This book is all about healing, prosperity and all of God's covenant blessings. He has given nine covenants in His Word, as well as a tenth to come later.

"Gather My godly ones to Me," He says to us, "Those who made a covenant with Me by sacrifice" (Ps. 50:5). We lay ourselves on God's altar, and part of that sacrifice is what comes out of our mouths, which reveals what is deep in our hearts.

Verse 23 describes that sacrifice. It is part of our covenant promise to God. It releases the quick fulfillment of all God has promised in His covenants. "He who offers a sacrifice of thanksgiving honors Me; and to him who orders his way aright I shall show the salvation of God."

Will you pass the praise test? Will your praise pauses cause Satan to pause – and turn and run? Pausing to praise will keep that lying lion's paws off of you. Victory is in the celebration. Celebrate before the victory and you'll be sure to celebrate afterwards.

I added this chapter because I felt it was tremendously important. Satan did too. He attacked the book with a computer worm that threatened to ruin it. Fear knocked on my door, and I began to answer. Here I was, writing about praise and failing a praise test!

I quickly got into a rejoicing mode, using some of the twelve tools against adversity. Jesus quickly squashed the worm. That wily worm of a Devil slithered away – defeated. The high praises of God filled my mouth. I had claimed the verse that says that if this work was of God, it could not be destroyed. I knew it was God's book and He would defend it. He did.

When you begin to make praise a part of your life, you will see power unleashed as never before. You will bathe in God's love and your faith level will rise dramatically.

As you read God's Word and rejoice in it, those words will begin to evoke a

Our Secret (and Most Powerful) Weapon

new image of you that will also increase your faith. You will begin to act like the One in whose image you were made. That's the exciting subject of the next chapter. You've probably never read anything like it.

Why Doesn't God Heal Me?

It is written...

[accused of blasphemy] Jesus answered them, "Has it not been written in your Law, 'I SAID, YOU ARE GODS' [Ps. 82:6]? If he called them gods, to whom the word of God came (and the Scripture cannot be broken), do you say of Him, whom the Father sanctified and sent into the world, 'You are blaspheming,' because I said, 'I am the Son of God'?"

John 10:34-36

CHAPTER 9
Our Awesome Identity in Christ

Christians – 99.9% of them, to be specific – do not know who they are in Christ! Yet next to our knowledge of God, our knowledge of who we are in Jesus is by far the most important truth we can possess. It is the basis of our Christian walk. It is the very foundation stone of our Christian edifice. And more importantly, for the purposes of this book, it is the sure way to *freedom from hindrances to healing!*

Whether in the carnal or Christian realm, *identity precedes behavior*. No one can consistently behave in a way that is inconsistent with the way he perceives himself. In other words, if you don't know who you are, you will end up acting like someone else. Do you know who you are?

Forty years ago one TV program fascinated me. On *To Tell the Truth*, a panel asked questions of three guests, two of them imposters. The goal was to guess who was in fact the real "John Doe" – the guest whose feat was famous but whose face was not. I always hung on the host's final words: "Will the real John Doe please stand up?"

And now I ask a similar question. Will the real *you* please stand up? Who *are* you?

Why Doesn't God Heal Me?

A family friend asked a young child what his name was. He answered, "Johnny stop it!" He thought that was his name! Those words always accompanied his parents' nagging rebukes. They never told him he was precious to them, leaving him cursed with a negative identity.

I can almost hear a proud father in the South saying to his son, "Hold your head up high, son. You're a McCoy!" The son will most likely act like a McCoy. That could imply fighting with a rival clan or it could indicate noble deeds. Do you know "the real McCoy"? Do you know who you are?

In the carnal realm, we moderns talk much – too much – about self-esteem. We even have a magazine now called *Self*. What a commentary on our selfish society! God prophesied in II Timothy 3 that in the last days men would be "lovers of themselves." Too often self-esteem becomes self-glorification. Jesus said we were to die to self and let Him live in us. Self-esteem can include killing someone you esteem less than yourself, standing up for *your* rights, being selfish and a host of other carnal pursuits.

Self-worth is the proper word. When you value and love yourself, you can value and love others. That's Biblical teaching.

Even self-worth, however, is a paltry and carnal substitute for who we *become* when we accept Jesus Christ as our Master and Savior. That's right. We actually become someone different. An awesome miracle takes place at conversion that few Christians realize in its depth and splendor. If they did, they wouldn't act the way they do.

Tiger Wood's father did not teach Tiger he was a weekend "hacker." He was a golfer worthy of the name. He knew it. He believed in the positive truth of who he was. He became established in that truth – and practiced it. How much greater is our knowledge of who we are in Christ!

A friend of mine asked a seven-year-old boy who had accepted Jesus that simple question, "Who are you?" He didn't say his name. He said, with gusto, "I'm a son of God!" He knew. Do you?

Lies Satan Wants Christians to Believe

Most Christians have not internalized their identity as believers. Ask some Christians who they are and here's what you hear: "I'm a wretched sinner saved by grace, a hunk of junk, unworthy, weak and always messing up, constantly sinning, just hangin' on for dear life, hoping to somehow squeak into heaven. I don't see how God could love someone like me." If that's what you think of yourself and more importantly, what you *say* over yourself, it's no wonder you have become that kind of Christian!

Some Christians are defeated Christians. Their lives are perpetual pity parties. They are Christian killjoys – baptized in lemon juice! They sing sad songs about how bad and weak they are. They are constipated Christians who don't know the

Our Awesome Identity in Christ **9**

joy of Jesus. They are not living joyfully and victoriously in Christ! They have become what they perceive themselves to be.

And they live in the past! They believe Satan's lie that they are not new creations in Christ.

Satan wants us to believe a lie – that we are who we used to be. He tries to convince us we are not acceptable to God and will never amount to anything. He tries to convince us we really want his way instead of God's way.

Satan's lies about our identity block maturity and growth. They block our prayer life and our communion with the Father. Yes, we do occasionally sin, but what we *do* does not determine who we *are*. We get up, brush ourselves off and quickly remember who we are. We do not listen to the guilt trip the Devil wants to put on us. We refuse to listen to the "accuser of the brethren" and those, sometimes even Christians, who work for him.

New Life in Jesus

The moment we say "yes" to Jesus we are born anew – new creations. In water baptism by immersion we say good-bye for good to the old self, our old ways and habits and the power of sin in our life. That's why God commands baptism (see Hindrance No. 183).

At conversion Jesus begins to live in us. We receive the seed of eternal life. Although our souls still need renewal, in this seed form and in our spirits we become all that Jesus is. We are new creations. That is no empty phrase. It's a miracle!

Born as dead spirits in Adam, we're made alive in Jesus. That life is in the form of a seed, like a down payment of eternal life. God plants that seed and we show Him we are truly committed to Him by being baptized. The baptism begins to make that seed sprout or germinate. From that moment on, we are eternal! We have eternal life.

And we are new creations! "Therefore, if anyone is in Christ, he is a new creation; old things [our pasts] have passed away; behold, all things have become new" (II Cor. 5:17). God has buried and removed from His mind all our confessed sins, even the past sins we committed yesterday or two minutes ago!

We had a teacher in our school named Skinny Love. God's love is not skinny. It's extravagant! God is an encouraging teacher who erases all the mistakes we made yesterday from His heavenly blackboard. Clean slate. Clean feeling. Every day you start fresh and new.

As Willard and Betty Thiessen's Canadian TV program proclaims: "*It's a New Day!*" Every day is a new day for a Christian.

Our past is gone. In God's eyes, we have no past! We can learn from it, but we are not slaves to it. And God holds our future in His hands. Yet He wants us to change our present by showing us who we are.

9 Why Doesn't God Heal Me?

Paul, in the latter part of his letter to the Ephesians, tells them how to behave. But he spends the first three chapters telling them *who they are*! God also gives us a big dose of our awesome identity in the first two chapters of Hebrews and I Peter. Identity changes everything.

In the movie *King Ralph*, a boisterous, inept American (having lived in Europe, I know our reputation!) became king of England and made a mess of it. He finally asked one of his advisors, "What's a king supposed to *do*?" Most kings are groomed from infancy to be king. They *act* kingly because they know who they are. They have a dignity and bearing born of kingly identity. So should we.

God calls us kings and priests. We are part of a royal priesthood (I Pet. 2:9). We will act like it only when we realize who we are.

Who We Are in Christ

If you have truly accepted Jesus as your Savior, the following applies to you. Many Christians don't want to believe the truth the Bible reveals about them as Children of God. They do not want to accept the anointing of the Anointed One in them. Let's believe, speak and internalize what follows, showing who you and I are in Christ.

* * *

I am a Child of God, Jesus' Brother (Sister), a divine masterpiece, a child of light and not of darkness, a citizen of heaven, a precious jewel in God's eyes, a saint (not a wretched sinner but a saint who sometimes sins), a holy one, a minister of reconciliation, an enemy of the Devil, a living sacrifice to the glory of God, a warrior who stands in the breach, a wrestler who wrestles not against flesh and blood but against invisible spiritual beings, the salt of the earth, Jesus' witness on earth (and He is my Advocate in heaven before our Father), His ambassador, a king and a priest (this becomes a reality upon baptism), the apple of God's eye,[12] a unique creation, uniquely gifted by God to show forth His glory.

I am special in God's sight, accepted in the Beloved and secure in Him, filled with a Spirit of power, love and a sound, disciplined mind. I am Jesus' friend and my best Friend on earth is the precious Holy Spirit. I can now call God "Father." I am beloved of God, the pride and joy of my Father. He twirls around in a lively dance as He sings over me – with shouts of joy (original Hebrew, Zeph. 3:17). His eyes light up when He sees me. He has chosen a unique personal name for me and has given me a unique ministry and commission that allow me to work with God's gifts. I don't need to copy anyone. I am who I am by the grace of God and I rejoice in and celebrate my uniqueness. My calling was special. God called and justified me at a special time in my life and my sanctification is

---

[12] In Hebrew the idea is that of a father whose son has brought honor to him. He cherishes his son with fatherly pride and bestows great honor upon him.

Our Awesome Identity in Christ

following a unique course God designed just for me.

I am crucified with Christ and have suffered much in common with Him. He is embedded in me, so the Father will always accept me. When He looks at me, He sees the perfect Jesus – pure and holy. And God is bringing my soul in line with my perfect spirit. God hasn't finished with me yet! I am a precious piece of clay in the Potter's hands. God is working out for good everything that happens to me.

More than a conqueror, I can do all things through Christ who strengthens me. I am not a defeated, depressed Christian, sautéed in vinegar and baptized in lemon juice! I am a joyous victor, a winner, a success, an overcomer by Jesus' blood. I am more powerful than the Devil because He who lives in me "… is greater than he who is in the world" (I John 4:4). No weapon formed against me by Satan shall prosper (Isa. 54:17). An enemy of the Devil, I cast out demons and tell them where to go! I am no longer a slave to sin – praise God! I am free.

As Martin Luther King, Jr. said, "Thank God Almighty, we are free at last!" I am forgiven of all my sins and free forever from condemnation. I am free from people accusing me for things I did in the past. *I have no past!* I am dead to sin – yet alive in Jesus. He is living His resurrected life in me by the Holy Spirit. I live with excitement and joy *today*. And God holds my future in His loving, capable hands. I am delivered – and a deliverer.

Lincoln's Emancipation Proclamation declared slaves free. Many Southern masters did not want their slaves to know about it. Satan, our former slave driver, doesn't want us to know about our freedom either. He wants us to keep being his "cotton-pickin'" slaves and say "Yassuh, massuh" ("Yes sir, master") for the rest of our "cotton-pickin'" lives. A slave to sin? That's a lie! I reject it in Jesus' name! I am free from sin's slavery.

I will not die before I live a full life (Ps. 91:16; Ps. 118:17). Because I walk in Jesus' righteousness, no one can take my life unless I choose to lay it down as Jesus did.[13] I have the authority to bind any demons influencing them by saying, "Satan and demons, you cannot influence these people in any way, shape or form, in Jesus' name!" One young Christian boy, a first-grader, when confronted by a gang of big older boys who came to beat him up, simply said, "Be gone in Jesus' name!" They tore off running.

---

[13] God has made a law that sin brings death (Rom. 6:23). If we are walking in sin, Satan has a legal right to take our life. When we are repenting of sin, walking in righteousness and daily praying for angelic protection, unless we have the calling of a martyr and choose to lay our life down, Satan cannot take our life. Too many Christians – even leaders – speak fatalistically of dying in a plane crash because it may be their "time to go." That may be their choice, but it is not God's choice. When you know your authority in Jesus, though Bin Laden himself and all his top brass hijack your plane, you will not die. You may die, however, if you are speaking fear and death over yourself instead of life. The above example is a worse-case scenario, of course, and would be a severe test of faith and of your ability to remain steadfast in praise. The best-case scenario would have you interceding (standing in the gap) for all the other passengers and saving the day for everyone. On the other hand, thank God for I Corinthians 10:13!

Why Doesn't God Heal Me?

I am empowered and authorized by Jesus to do even greater works than He did on earth. I am an instrument of God's healing power. I lay hands on the sick and they recover. The lame walk, the deaf hear, the incurable are healed, the blind see – through Christ in me! I can even command stubs to grow out in Jesus' name. I can also, if need be, move mountains (which, while literal, can also mean governments or strongholds).

I have authority over the weather. Satan is "the prince of the power of the air" and has evil powers that cause phenomena such as storms and tornadoes. God is sovereign, of course, and I am His son (daughter). When the wisdom of Jesus dictates, I can rebuke the weather in Jesus' name! Jesus spoke peace to a storm – and proceeded to lie down and go to sleep! Hurricanes have inexplicably changed course because of what God's people declared.

If necessary, I can walk on water (and I'm not talking about the frozen kind). Peter did. And I have the Kingdom keys he didn't have at the time.

I can ask God to translate me miraculously to where I need to go to minister. Not many of us have ever done such things, but why limit ourselves? The time is coming when our intimacy with God and our knowledge of our identity is going to lift us up to heights we have never reached before.

I flow in the anointing of the Anointed One, with wisdom, knowledge, counsel and quick understanding. Through His Spirit I break burdensome yokes and set captives free. I heal the brokenhearted and comfort those who mourn (Isa. 61:1-2). I am filled with love – all the fruit of the Spirit (Gal. 5:22-23).

I am able to love others even when they hurt me. I do not see my brother's past. I see him as what he will be. I love and forgive even those who would persecute and kill me, because Jesus lives in me.

I walk in divine health, prosperity and protection. *I am not afraid of terrorist attacks (Isa. 54:14), or of my water being contaminated (Isa. 33:16).* Thousands may fall around me, but God will protect me from harm and pestilence (Psalm 91). I ask daily for His angels – including warring angels with swords drawn – to surround my family and me. My youth is renewed like the eagle. Wealth and riches are in my house (Ps. 112:3). The wealth of the wicked is laid up for me for the purposes of Jesus (Prov. 13:22; Micah 4:13).

I am a precious part of the church who is Jesus' Bride-to-be. I am united with Him as a husband with his wife. I am a part of His Bride, the church. He wants to marry me. He has a passionate, intimate love for me that I cannot fully grasp. If I were the only person on earth, He would have died for me! He knew me before I was formed in the womb, before the foundation of the earth.

I am one with the Eternal One – one with the awesome God! In Him, I am the righteousness of God. The Righteous One lives in me. I live in eternity, not in this mundane life. I am seated in heavenly places with Jesus, gliding gracefully on the wings of God's wind like the eagle above the valley of sin and sorrow. I am God's holy temple. All my members are His to employ.

Our Awesome Identity in Christ

I am not a "child of the universe." I am a Child of the Creator of the universe. He loves me unconditionally. There is nothing I can do to make Him love me more. There is nothing I can do to make Him love me less.

I am His pride and joy, His special treasure, His glorious temple, using my body for His glory.

I rejoice in who I am – who He has made me to be. Nothing can separate me from His love. I am a special sheep of His pasture, in His constant care. Praise God for His awesome work in me!

Knowing Our Identity Is a Process

Even the great apostle Paul did not immediately learn who he was in Christ. It's a process. We can see that at the end of his life Paul knew fully who he was (II Tim. 4:7-8; Gal. 2:20). God recorded Paul's imperfect process of realizing his identity so we could learn from his mistakes and come more quickly to know who we are. It was not only the Hebrew section of God's Book of Love that was written to show us the weaknesses of God's servants so we could learn from them (I Cor. 10:11; Ps. 51).

Paul said that he was the least of the apostles because he persecuted the church (I Cor. 15:9). And I'm sure he had enough people inside and outside the church who reminded him of what he had done to their dear relatives. Although some may accuse me of Paul-bashing, the reality was that Paul was living in the past!

The past is past! It seems Paul had not yet learned that he had no past in God's eyes. It doesn't matter how many people bring up our past to us. We have been washed in the blood of Jesus. We are pure and spotless in God's eyes. What Paul said might sound humble, but it was a satanic lie. The Devil wants to dredge up our past.

Every day we are different creations than the day before. What we did even yesterday matters no more for God. Oh, we may suffer for it because of the law of cause and effect. God has nonetheless forgiven and forgotten what we did. If we beat ourselves on the head for our past or dredge up the past sins of our Christian brothers, we are making ourselves more righteous than God. He doesn't bring it up. So why do we?

The reality of what Paul said in Romans 7 may shock and offend you, but it is true. Paul said something over himself he should never have said. He laments in verse 24, "O wretched man that I am!" That is calling Jesus Christ wretched! As he later said in Galatians 2:20, he did not live anymore, but Jesus lived in him. He had been cursing himself and cursing Jesus! However convoluted his reasoning, what he said over himself was not God's truth.

That does not take away from the inspiration of God's Word. We must take the Word as a whole and realize Paul was in the process of understanding who he was in Jesus. Do you think that apostles don't have things to learn? Let's learn from his error. We are not wretched sinners or wretched people. We are holy and pure in Jesus.

So whatever is true and pure and of good report – even about ourselves – let's think on those things. Let the positive truth of what God says about us be in our thoughts – and most importantly – in our mouths!

The Astounding Power of Our Words

In Chapter 11 we will expand on the amazing, God-plane power of our words. What we say comes to pass.

If we habitually repeat over ourselves the truth of who we are in Christ, our heart, mind and will begin to come in line with our spirit. And remember, our spirit is perfect: Jesus lives in us. We begin to act like who we really *are*. Identity precedes behavior.

Daily oral reaffirmations of our identity should become a habit. We also need to meditate on our identity. The more we remind ourselves of who we are in Christ, the more mature we will be. The more we reaffirm our identity, the more our behavior will reflect it. Start today affirming your awesome identity in Christ!

The Daily Declarations the Holy Spirit inspired that are listed in the Appendix are the most important ones we can make. Much good additional material exists on the subject.[14]

And There Is More!

The following may be shocking to some. Yet if you accept this truth, it can be the most encouraging and liberating knowledge you have ever received. Before you read on, please pray for guidance and understanding. And please read every word before you come to a conclusion.

Let me introduce this surprising yet Biblical teaching by repeating an important point. After our knowledge of God – or who God is – our knowledge of who we are in Christ is the most important truth we can know.

As with us, God's will and actions originate in who He *is*. He *does* good because He *is* good. And His names reveal who He is. He is our Health, our Provision, our Peace, etc. And so He heals, provides and becomes our peace. Jesus – God – lives in us. When God refers to us being with or in Him, He uses the Greek word *sun*, which means the equivalent of two lines that are so much a part of each other that we see only one line. We are truly one in Him.

We can love others as we love ourselves because we love the new creation –

---

[14] Mike Shreve spent 15 years of his life researching material for his six volumes of *Our Glorious Inheritance*, which explains 1,000 names God gives us (available at www.newday.org). Neil Anderson's books on the subject are also quite helpful, especially *Freedom in Christ*. Ron Cohen has excellent material on identity in Christ, comparing our past to a garbage bag we must reject (Messianic Miracle Ministries, Box 7764, Newark, DE 19714).

Our Awesome Identity in Christ

Jesus in us. Although the Father rejoices in our unique personality, He sees Jesus when He looks at us. And if we walk in our new identity, others see Jesus in us. When we walk into a room, Jesus walks in. He's in us and we're in Him. So who we are in Christ is who Jesus is – because He's in us! We have His nature.

Members of the God Family!

When we accept Jesus, we become one with Him. That means so much more than we have ever realized. We are one with *Yahweh*, the Eternal "I am." "… He chose us in Him before the foundation of the world, that we would be holy and blameless before Him …" (Eph. 1:4). That means that our spirits were created long before our bodies and souls. We were predestined to be holy, to be in Christ as blameless new creations, before the world was created – before time began!

We actually become eternal – timeless beings who can never die – when the Eternal One begins to live in us and we begin to obey Him. The Eternal is in us – one with us.

Now let's read Genesis 1:21-28 with special attention to how God uses the phrase "after their kind." He made all the creatures of the sea "after their kind," and continued with the land animals "after their kind." Following this pattern, He then said in verse 26 that He made us in His own image – in His likeness. He clearly made mankind after the *God* kind! We're of the God stock – in the God class. We are exact reflections and replicas of God Himself – clay copies of our Creator! The awesome truth is that God is reproducing *Himself*!

We are on the God plane! We are above the angels – very Sons and Daughters of the Eternal God!

That is not blasphemy. In fact, not accepting that truth is calling God a liar! It is blasphemous to refuse to accept and live up to who God says we are and thus glorify Him. It is blasphemy to call ourselves wretched, unworthy sinners when God calls us gods – just under the Most High Himself! Have we understood the awesome truth of Romans 8:29? We are "conformed to the image of His Son, so that He would be the firstborn among many brethren." We are Brothers in the same God Family!

Please don't misunderstand. We did not create the universe. We will always worship and recognize the supremacy of our Father God, of our older Brother and Savior and of the precious Holy Spirit without whom we would never be in the Family.

By saying we are on the God plane, I am not saying we are members of the Trinity. The triune God made all things, all beings, including us. Although God gives us by His grace creative powers, and we do become eternal when we accept and obey Jesus, we are not the Eternal Creator. We are a part of His creation. Even our God-given divinity is a creation of God by His grace. We are His

89

Why Doesn't God Heal Me?

workmanship. The clay cannot claim to be the Potter.

One of the names of God in the Bible is the Most High. We will *never* be God Most High. That name or title belongs to the Holy Trinity – and *only* to the Trinity. That great God Most High is above us and will always be above us.

Our human fathers never cease beings our fathers. My children call me Dad here in Canada because "Daddy" is not "cool." And yet where I come from in South Carolina you call your father Daddy and you continue to call him Daddy even if you're 85 and he's 105! We will always look up to our heavenly Father as our Abba Father – our Daddy!

Having qualified this astounding revelation, I must state this undeniable truth: to deny our divine nature and God-plane existence is to deny that Jesus Himself is in the God Family! After all, He became by His resurrection the first of many Brothers to be born into that Family. That's plain Biblical teaching.

Read Psalm 8. In the correct Hebrew rendering of verse 5, the Holy Spirit writes: "You have made him a little lower than God (*elohim*)." We are made in the image of God, destined to be a part of the God Family – far above the angelic family. Yet we are and will always be a little lower than God Most High (*El Elyon* – literally, God, God the Most High). But notice: it doesn't say "a lot lower."

Humble, religious folk balk at that truth. They don't believe God. He says that man is "the image and glory of God" (I Cor. 11:7). They don't believe Jesus either. He said in John 17:22 that He gave us the same glory the Father had given Him! Those are strong words.

It is astounding yet true that although not quite of the stature of the Most High, we are called to be God as God is God. The reason we can say that is that we are talking about the Family of God as opposed to the much lower family of angels. Our destiny is much greater than most have thought.

Although the following is difficult to translate into some languages, in English we can say that we will be on the God *plane* and yet not on the God *level*. In other words, it's like saying we are born into a physical family as a son or daughter and yet we will never be the dad, mom, or older brother.

I am saying all this to make it clear that this teaching is not blasphemy, as some will undoubtedly accuse. God has given me the grace to teach this truth for over 30 years. Thank God for Creflo Dollar and Kenneth Copeland, who are beginning to preach it powerfully. It does not sit well with religious people.

Why do you think those religious Pharisees were so mad at Jesus when He taught this truth? They understood clearly what many Christians don't. They wanted to kill Jesus because He called God His Father, "making Himself equal with God" (John 5:18). Is God any less a Father to us?

It is true that God's Son Jesus was the Creator who gave us life – physical life and eternal life. He came down to this earth, however, to be part of the family of man so that, by the death of the perfect Son of God, we might become a part of the Family of God.

90

Our Awesome Identity in Christ

The amazing grace Christians sing about is more amazing than they have ever imagined. It is more than the grace to go to heaven and sit on a cloud playing a harp, singing constant praises to God as His *servants* the angels do.

They are servants. We are Sons. Although numerous verses point out that we too are servants of the Most High (e.g. Gal. 1:10; James 1:1; II Pet. 1:1; Jude 1:1; Rev. 22:9), Romans 8:17 also tells us that we are to share, as co-heirs with Jesus, all that God has and *is*. We are to share His glory!

Chapter 1 and 2 of Hebrews show we will be above the angelic realm. The only realm above the angelic is the *God* realm! As incredible as it may seem, Jesus embraced humanity so we could embrace divinity. God became man so man could become God. Jesus became a member of the human family so humans could become members of the God Family.

Above the Angels – in the God Family

You may call the family dog part of the family. Yet he does not come anywhere close to being your very own son. He's of the dog kind. You may love him and he may lick you affectionately when you come home – but he's not your very own son or daughter. He's not your flesh and blood – the child you laugh over and cry over and tuck into bed with a kiss and a hug at night. You don't tell your dog what you want him to be when he grows up.

Although some of the spirit beings God created look like animals, I do not want to demean our loving, ministering spirits (Heb. 1:14). They are powerful, intelligent beings. They are not, however, on the God plane – in the God Family. We are!

Obviously, we are not glorified yet (I John 3:1-2). And yet God says in Revelation 3:9 that men will "come and worship before your feet ..." (NKJV). God forbids worship of angels (Rev. 22:8-9). Only God can be worshipped! Can we begin to grasp what that means?

The members of the Trinity are all called God (Acts 5:3-5; Heb.1:8, John 1:1). They are equal in every way – except one. The Father is the administrative Head of the God Family. Jesus is the Logos or Word who speaks the express will of the Father. The Holy Spirit, in a general sense, is the One who accomplishes here below the will of the Father spoken by the Son. Throughout the Greek Scriptures, especially in the later chapters of John's gospel, we see that Jesus glorifies the Father and will at the end submit all to the Father's ultimate authority. The Holy Spirit glorifies the Father and Son – even though He is as much God as they are.

We are the blessed recipients of what Philip Yancey calls the "scandal of grace" – yet it is much more "scandalous" than most champions of grace have imagined. Incredibly, we who were mere humans will share in the deity, although not at the same level, of those three distinct personalities of the one Godhead.

To say that we will not be a part of the God Family is to say that Jesus has not

91

been born into that Family as the first of many Brothers. It is to say that He is not God. If He is the first of many Brothers, and we are not Brothers, then He is not our Brother – and therefore He is not God's Son!

This is a hard truth to accept because it seems prideful, pretentious and presumptuous. And it would indeed be if it were not for the fact that *God* says it of us His very Children. Most Christians would not capitalize the word *children* when referring to Children of God. When we are born into our human families we bear our father's name with a capital letter. It is true that we are not yet glorified. We are not yet to be worshipped. Yet we will be!

We will always worship the Most High, and yet we ourselves will be held in awe and reverence by angels and by the humans over whom we will reign with Jesus during the Millennium. God means what He says when He calls us joint heirs with Jesus.

What Satan Knows

Satan knows the truth. And it is a painful truth to him. He knows we weak humans were called by the grace of God to be members of God's own Family – above the angels! And remember, he was an angel. God chose us before the foundation of the world. That's also when the Father had planned to send Jesus to die for us. So Lucifer apparently knew that he – the great archangel who covered the very throne of God (Ezek. 28:14) – would be below puny man! (There are indications angels could be a part of God's Family at a later time, but some did not pass that test of humility and loyalty and rebelled with Lucifer.)

This scenario could shed light on Lucifer's principal sin – pride (Ezek. 28:17). Pride and jealousy are ugly twins. He was not only jealous of man being called to be above him, to be worshipped as God in the God Family. He even wanted to replace God, to oust Him from His throne (Isa. 14:13). He succeeded in getting Adam and Eve to sin so he could usurp their God-plane authority. In doing so, he perverted the truth about them becoming Gods.

He told them that if they ate of the "tree of sin" they would be like God (Gen. 3:5). What a clever lie! They already *were* like God! They had God-plane authority on earth over everything – including Satan! He was only an angel, and a fallen one at that. He had been given authority over the earth previously to prepare it for man, but he lost that authority by his rebellion. He was telling them the lie that they had no authority over him – and they swallowed it!

"You are gods"

In John 10:34-35 we find an intriguing passage most have explained away and misunderstood. The Pharisees accused Jesus of blasphemy – calling Himself God. Notice that they, unlike some scholars who write notes in Bibles, did not contest

Our Awesome Identity in Christ

or deny what He said. Was Jesus lying about Psalm 82, which He cited in His defense? Did He not know His own Word?

In essence, He said, "Hey, why are you accusing Me of calling Myself God as if that were blasphemy? Don't you know your own law? God called your leaders and judges 'gods'." Many of the leaders and judges in Israel received the Holy Spirit to enable them to properly judge the people. They had god-like power in making binding decisions of life and death.

What is most interesting, though, is the way God said it in Psalm 82:6: "You are *gods*. And all of you are children of the Most High" (NKJV). Many of these judges and prophets had the Holy Spirit and were thus Children of God. And what does God Himself call His Children? "You are gods." He hasn't changed. He calls Jesus God and says we are Sons in the image and likeness of God, in the same way as Jesus. These judges, of course, did not always follow the lead of the Holy Spirit and only God can judge them as to their salvation.

The next verse says, "But you will die like mere men ..." (Ps. 82:7, NIV). What God was saying was that they were *not* mere men. And we are not mere men. We are gods! Those who feel I'm taking this verse out of context don't grasp the scriptural overview of this subject this chapter should make clear.

Jesus was saying that He too was a God and a Son (by His human birth and His resurrection) of the Most High, which are one and the same. And this was the only truth He ever emphasized by saying, "(and the Scripture cannot be broken)." Many would like to try to water down or "break" this controversial Scripture. It stands as a testimony to the fact we are called to be gods – or dare I say Gods? Remember, if we deny the divinity of one of the "brothers" of whom Jesus is the "firstborn," we are denying the divinity of the firstborn Brother, our Master and Savior Jesus Christ!

The Holy Spirit, the very Anointing of the Christ, the Anointed One, is the Spirit of humility. He will not lead you into pride and vanity. And it is not pride and vanity to realize that God by His amazing grace has decided to make divinity out of dust.

I trust we all accept with humility our calling of pastor, evangelist, teacher or lay intercessor, helper, or encourager. We should humbly recognize it is God who by His grace does everything through us. As we give Him all the glory here below, so He will give us all His glory for eternity.

May God grant us the grace to humbly accept the awesome and undeserved calling He has given us. Accepting that truth will transform us. We will walk, not in pride, but in humble yet bold confidence – because we know who we are. We will think like God, talk like God, and act like God. And we will thus eliminate all hindrances to healing.

James 4:10 says, "Humble yourselves in the presence of the Lord [Jesus], and He will exalt you" (KJV). God simply will not exalt someone who is not humble. Yet God wants us to shed false humility and recognize the stupendous calling He has given us. When He says "exalt," He means "exalt."

The spirit of religiosity – reeking with false humility – has been Satan's agent for watering down the truth of our exaltation to be of the God class. Religionists label what I am teaching heresy. It is not my teaching, but the teaching of the Holy Spirit based on the clear Word of God.

Jesus became man so that man could become God! – i.e. Sons and Daughters in the very God Family, on the God plane. That's how much God loves us. God says we are deity, soon to be glorified with all the power and privileges of the God Family – and He does not consider it blasphemy to make such a statement. Let's accept our awesome anointing and our astounding destiny. Jesus is the Father's Son, and so are we! "Brother" isn't some meaningless, syrupy term. It's a reality!

In Hebrews 1:8 God the Father calls His Son Jesus "God." That's the Family name. We are no less Sons than Jesus. We are co-heirs with Jesus of all He will receive (Rom. 8:17). If Jesus is called God, so are we. To those we minister to, we will be looked to and revered as God (Rev. 3:9)! If you call that blasphemy, then you're calling God a Blasphemer!

Amazing Love

God's love for us is absolutely astounding. We are all responsible for the death of His Son. Jesus was His only Son, His Beloved Son. And you and I murdered Him by our sins. And what does the Father say to you and me who killed His only Son in cold blood? He says, "I'm going to forgive you, adopt you as my Children and give you all the blessings reserved for My Son, even a place in My own Family. I want to lavish love and blessing on you with Me for all eternity."

Yes, Jesus will be there too. But have you ever heard such a story of a Father's love? It is a true story – a story about you and me and God's truly amazing grace.

It's a story of who we are in Jesus – of how special we are to God. Because of the awesome love of our Father God, we have been adopted and actually born by the Spirit into God's very own Family. He will make a way for all people to have an opportunity to be in His Family. And once He has you as His Child, He doesn't ever want to lose you. He wants to enjoy you and beam with love as you enjoy Him for all eternity. We will delight in His love, as well as the awesome power and authority of the God Family. We actually have a great amount of that power now.

Who Can Forgive Sins?

In John 20:23 we find a remarkable power given to Jesus' disciples. He had just breathed on them, thus giving them the Holy Spirit. We also have the Holy Spirit and we also are Jesus' disciples. Verse 23 applies to us: "If you forgive the sins of any, they are forgiven; if you retain the sins of any, they are retained."

Now wait a minute. Who alone can forgive sins? God alone forgives all our sins

(Ps. 103:3). If God tells us we have the authority to forgive sins, what does that mean? It clearly means we have God's authority. We are on the God plane. If only God can forgive sin, then we indeed are Gods! And that's exactly what Jesus said.

"Behold what manner of love ..."

Jesus' beloved disciple John says it best in I John 3:1-3: "Behold what manner of love the Father has bestowed on us, that we should be called children of God. Therefore the world does not know us [who we are in Christ, and even many of us do not know!], because it did not know Him. Beloved, now we are the children of God; and it has not yet been revealed what we shall be, but we know that when He is revealed, we shall be like Him, for we shall see Him as He is. And everyone who has this hope in Him [this awesome knowledge of his identity in Christ] purifies himself, just as He is pure" (NKJV). The knowledge and acceptance of our identity will transform our behavior.

Only God can take clods and make them into Gods. We are the masterpiece, the crowning glory of His creation. Let us now walk in the knowledge of who we really are – Sons and Daughters in God's very own Family!

9 Why Doesn't God Heal Me?

It is written...

Therefore, if anyone is in Christ, he is a new creation; old things have passed away; behold, all things have become new ... For He made Him who knew no sin to be sin for us, that we might become the righteousness of God in Him.

II Cor. 5:17, 21 – NKJV

CHAPTER 10
The Key That Unlocks All God's Blessings

The door to all God's blessings – including healing – has been wide open to all Christians for 2,000 years. Jesus opened it when He took the keys of ruling authority over this earth from Satan. He descended into hell while His body lay in the tomb. His death made it possible and His resurrection sealed the victory.

All Christians have available today the keys of the Kingdom – the keys to all the Kingdom blessings.

Satan lost them – forever.

The toothless lion, however, is a sore loser. His clever tactic is simple: he lies. He has convinced almost all Christians – who are the winners – that they are the losers. Talk about the big lie! There is none bigger.

Satan's number one "man" – the spirit of betrayal – has pulled the wool over the eyes of the naïve sheep for almost 2,000 years. He's got them bleating helplessly, using only a fragment of the awesome, God-plane power and blessing they were called to walk in. And they feel betrayed by the Shepherd as they whine and whimper, "Baah, baah, why doesn't God heal me?" (One of

Why Doesn't God Heal Me?

betrayal's demonic agents is the spirit of infirmity!)

And all the while the Shepherd pleads, "Why haven't you accepted the gift I gave you – the keys I paid My life's blood to buy for you? Had you simply believed what I said, you would not be wondering why you weren't healed. You would be healing the sick yourself. You would be raising the dead! You would be doing greater works than I, even as I said."

God did know, on the other hand, that Satan would muddy and pollute the pristine waters of the early church. Alas, He foresaw the day when doctrines of demons would enter the church. About 5,000 bolted in with Constantine. And today Christians are obsessed with a cesspool of over 9,000 in all.[15]

Instead of listening to God's Word, Christians have worshipped pastors, theologians, Most Right Reverends who were neither reverend nor right, D.D.'s and Ph.D.'s piled higher and deeper in hermeneutical heresy. It's high time someone told the truth. The truth is – Jesus became sin for us so that we might **become** *the righteousness of God*!

That's not some cute, religious phrase. It is a colossal truth. It encapsulates the entire truth and history of the Bible. It unlocks the other two keys of the Kingdom: the love of God, which activates righteousness, and the spirit of giving. These Kingdom keys unlock the door to **all** *of God's blessings*!

Not only does this key of knowing we are the righteousness of God give us the *right* to call down all God's blessings. It also enables us, when we accept it and walk in it, to *eliminate all hindrances to healing*.

Some may look negatively on the fact that the Holy Spirit has given some 200 hindrances to healing in this book. Remember, though, it is His responsibility to convict us of sin (John 16:8). He has shown that there are actually about 600 hindrances in all. He wanted to share a third of them to give us the concept. And He is quite capable of revealing to us personally the specific problems that hinder us from receiving God's blessings.

At this point I must insert an important word about the Holy Spirit. I realize that Christian leaders have sometimes claimed that the Holy Spirit told them something that was actually quite odd, unbalanced or even contradictory to the Word. The Bible tells us to "test the spirits to see whether they are from God" (I John 4:1). That principle also applies to putting to the test what men may say God told them.[16]

---

[15] This is revelation from the Holy Spirit, who was even more specific in the numbers. Other teachers have given similar numbers. The problem is that most Christians simply swallow what their churches teach without comparing those teachings to what the Bible actually says. You will find a number of examples in the later chapters dealing with hindrances. More information will be forthcoming in the next book.

[16] It is confusing for Christians to hear divers leaders say totally different things and claim them to be from the same God. What many have not realized is that even leaders can unwittingly invite the help of the spirit of divination (Acts 16:16) and deception. Rejecting part of the Word of God and resisting correction from God bring in both these spirits. When people look for an answer that confirms what they want to hear,

The Key That Unlocks All God's Blessings

I have no doubt that what I say comes from the Holy Spirit indeed *does* come from Him. That is because I have seen the fruits. I invite you to do the same (Mat. 7:15-20). If you apply the principles and revelation in this book and see that they indeed work and you experience blessing and healing, you will know that these revelations are from God. But you must honestly put them to the test. Critics who attack without examining the evidence or who prefer to cling to their traditions will not benefit from the truth that can set them free (John 8:32; 7:12-24; 3:10-12; Mark 12:24).

Jesus also had His critics. Some of the truths the Holy Spirit revealed through Him caused offense (John 6:41-65). Even the good news of the Kingdom has some elements that require spiritual maturity to accept and can make some stumble (Heb. 5:11-14; II Pet. 3:14-18).

But the Holy Spirit has revealed through Creflo Dollar, Kenneth Copeland and through this chapter the good, encouraging news about the righteousness of God in us. That news counterbalances the "bad news" about what we may have to change in our lives to receive the blessings.

The "do's and don'ts" of hindrances are not legalism. There are 613 commandments in the Part One of God's Word of Love (which men call the *Old* Testament) and – probably to your great surprise – 613 in Part Two (the "New Testament" Scriptures in Greek).

Knowing you are the righteousness of God empowers you to walk in obedience to all these laws, not as a legalist doing your own works – but as a royalist, doing the works the King created you to walk in before time began (Eph. 2:10; 4:24; II Cor. 5:17-21).

It would take many books to fully explain the truth about the righteousness of God, replete with Scriptures expounding this vast subject. This chapter and the one on identity are possibly the most important chapters in the book. They are indeed vital keys and encapsulate the greatest hindrance to healing. Let me summarize:

Most Christians are not healed because they have not accepted their identity as righteous Sons and Daughters of their Father of Love. Not realizing their worth in God's eyes, they have not chosen to love God with all their heart, mind and strength. Acknowledgment of their elder Brother's sacrifice for them – so they could partake of His love and be one with Him in His righteousness – is still missing .

Not until they come to truly know their Godly Family, and accept the love of the Father, Brother and Comforter, returning it with their whole heart, will

---

God backs off and the spirit of deception takes over. Some prophetic people, motivated by the spirit of control and manipulation, compromise by giving people what they want to hear (Ezek. 12:24; Micah 3:11). The polite Holy Spirit respects their free will and allows the spirit of deception to have his way. Evil spirits can deceive by giving as much as 70 to 90 percent truth. But that lethal leaven leavens the whole lump (I Cor. 5:6). Is it any wonder in these last days that leaders intoxicated by church dogma infected by deceptive doctrines of demons contradict those who simply teach the Word (I Tim. 4:1)?

Why Doesn't God Heal Me?

they be able to receive their Father's blessings.

When they receive that awesome love and share it, the fear, guilt and cowardice of the sinner mentality will be blown away (I John 4:18). True realization of their identity will open the way for God's blessings to pour down from heaven.

Sin Consciousness versus Righteousness Consciousness

Pastors and worship leaders have polluted God's people with a devilishly deceptive *sin consciousness*. "We're just wretched sinners saved by grace." What a moronic oxymoron! You're either a sinner or you're saved by grace. You can't be both!

We are not sinners! We are saints – who occasionally sin.

If the church had more of a *righteousness consciousness*, God would not have to point out so many hindrances.

The famous "Sinner's Prayer" has probably done more damage to the body of Christ than any of Satan's lies (see Hindrance No. 197). A sinner comes forward at a salvation invitation, thus accepting by his very action Jesus as Savior and passing from the Kingdom of Darkness to the Kingdom of Light. But alas, some well-meaning preacher has him muddy his confession of Jesus by declaring to the physical and spiritual world, "I'm a sinner!" I've even heard pastors require their congregations of saints to make this devilish declaration.[17]

The Sinner's Prayer is not from God. It's a curse! It mocks God! When you accept Jesus, God calls you a saint. Then you turn around and pronounce the curse over yourself that you are a sinner! Don't think the demons don't hear it – and begin to enforce it. They rejoice! You have cursed yourself back into the Kingdom of Darkness. And you wonder why God hasn't healed you?

Righteousness Is a GIFT!

Understanding the righteousness of God and beginning to walk in it is a process. First, you must accept it by faith as a grace from God – a glorious *gift*! Your Daddy sent your elder Brother down here to buy it for you at a great price and present it freely to you the day you accept Jesus. And that could be today! (If this is your day, and you know the Father is drawing you, see the salvation prayer in the Epilogue.)

You did absolutely nothing to earn it. A Rolls Royce is not a Volkswagen because it was *made* to be a Rolls. Its creator made it to be a Rolls. God *made*

---

[17] Read – preferably aloud – I Peter 4:17-18, Romans 3:7, Hebrews 6:10, Daniel 7:21-22, Acts 26:10, Romans 1:7; 8:27; 12:13; 15:25-26, 31; 16:2, 15. Look up saints in a concordance. Reading the Word aloud makes a stronger impression on your heart, mind and will. I especially recommend it for the verses in this chapter because the subject is so condensed and so important.

The Key That Unlocks All God's Blessings

you to be the righteousness of God. Accept it! Receive it! Believe it – simply because He said it![18]

Reading the book of Romans out loud, especially chapters 1-10, would help you understand righteousness as a gift.

And what a gift! There are 17 words for righteousness in the Hebrew Scriptures. The word *kuwn*,[19] however, best expresses the concept of the righteousness of God. Although its basic meaning is to establish or prepare, it ties in with the concept of righteousness, as the following meanings and verses illustrate (passages containing the word *kuwn* are italicized): stand firm without wavering (*Ps. 37:23; 51:10; 57:7*, which includes the important concept of being steadfast in praise; *78:37; Prov. 16:12*); be prepared to walk fully with God (*II Chron. 27:6*); be fixed on the truth (*II Chron. 12:14; Job 42:7-8*); be fitted into a place prepared by God (*Isa. 54:14*; Eph. 2:10; 4:24); walk in perfection as God is perfect (Gen. 17:1; *Ps. 119:5-6, 133; Prov. 4:18; Ps. 5:9*); establish boundaries based on those given by God (Deut. 5:32-33; *Ps. 78:8; Prov. 4:26-27*).

It is God's gift that enables us to do all the above. It has nothing to do with our works in the flesh. Our righteousness is a creation of God. We did nothing to earn it. We did nothing to earn our sin nature, did we? It came by birth. So do our new, righteousness nature and our good works. When we were born from above, our righteousness and our righteous works had already been created. We simply accept them and walk in them. We simply accept this precious gift by faith – and even that faith comes from God!

Standing before God as if You Never Sinned!

The second step is to understand what that gift means. It means that you have *authority* more far-reaching than you ever dreamed and that you have **rights** you have probably never understood. The first right that permits a breakthrough in grasping this truth is this: you have a *right to be cleansed from sin* (I John 1:9-10).

That is, in essence, the foundational definition of the righteousness of God: the ability to stand in the presence of God (and Satan!) without any sense of guilt, condemnation, shame or inferiority, *as if you had never sinned*![20]

Wow! Did you catch that? That may not be how you *feel* when you sin and just

---

[18] Thanks to Creflo Dollar for the Rolls analogy – and to the Holy Spirit who has powerfully anointed him to preach this truth. We at Freedom Church of God began preaching it before he did, and our tapes complement his, but his teaching anointing is unique. I am so grateful to my Southern brother for helping me get this truth into my spirit. His superb teaching on this subject is available on the web at www.creflodollarministries.org. Kenneth Copeland also has complementary teaching on the subject.

[19] See "[koon]," page 592, *The Englishman's Hebrew and Chaldee Concordance of the Old Testament*, Zondervan, 1972.

[20] Read Micah 7:19; Psalm 103:12; Isaiah.1:18; 43:25; Colossians 2:13-14; II Corinthians 5:17-21; Hebrews 9:14; 10:1-18; Philippians 3:13-15; Romans 8:1.

after you stumble. But that's the reality! That's the awesome *power* of Jesus' blood. It manifests its power not when you stand, but when you fall.

It doesn't matter what you did last night or last week or last year. Confess it. Be cleansed by the blood of Jesus. And get right back to standing and resting in your righteousness.

This realization of the right to be cleansed is a powerful key to understanding and staying in your righteousness. Even seasoned hitters in baseball sometimes strike out. Michael Jordan may fly through the air with the greatest of ease, but his shots don't always hit the hoop. Tiger Woods three putts from ten feet and hits shots even I would be ashamed to claim.

We all goof up. We miss the mark. And God provided the *blood of Jesus* because He knew we would. Thank God for the blood of Jesus! His blood really does wash you clean. Believe it!

Power, joy and peace sustain you when you know God truly does forget what you did a few minutes ago. Although it may be hard for you to forget, you don't have to think or say, "But I still feel guilty." Jesus says you're declared not guilty! Quit listening to Satan the liar!

As Creflo Dollar explains, it doesn't matter what you did last night. If you confessed your sin and were cleansed by the blood of Jesus, you should be able to get right back to exercising your anointing – as if nothing had happened. You can lay hands on the sick, and they will be healed!

The sinner mentality won't let you do that. It is based on the record of what you *did* last night, last week, last year and last decade. But your righteousness is based on **what Jesus did for you**. God knew you would fail at times. He provided the solution: Jesus' blood. When you confess and Jesus' blood obliterates your sin from existence, you can go before God *as if sin never existed*! You're as pure as Adam before sin ever became a word.

No matter how advanced you are in the Christian race, no matter how much progress you've made, you will mess up. But you'll mess up less. Yet you may blow it in a surprising way and really disappoint yourself. But the God who knows the end from the beginning has got it all covered – covered with the blood of Jesus! Confess the mess. Let Jesus wash you clean. And get up and keep on keeping on.

The condemnation you heap on yourself after confessing a sin is far worse than the sin itself. Don't beat up on yourself. Since Jesus lives in you, you're beating up on Jesus! Stumbling is not the major problem. It's not getting up or taking forever to stand back up in your righteousness that's the problem.

Even when we do mire in self-pity and condemnation for a while, we can still get up. And as we become established in our righteousness (Isa. 54:14) we will become quick to repent. We'll rise and brush ourselves off with the blood of Jesus as if nothing happened. And that doesn't mean we take sin lightly or plan to sin. We are sad to sin, yet thankful for the precious blood of Jesus.

The Key That Unlocks All God's Blessings

Let's declare with Micah, "Do not rejoice over me, O my enemy; Though I fall I will rise; Though I dwell in darkness, [Jesus] is a light for me ... He will bring me out to the light, And I will see His righteousness ...Yes, You will cast all [our] sins Into the depths of the sea" (Micah 7:8, 9b,19b).

What good news! And as we cherish that good news and believe it with all our hearts, we will begin to truly grasp this liberating, colossal concept. We will come to value our right standing with God, as well as our intimacy with God, both of which allow us to operate powerfully in our anointing. We will not want to jeopardize our relationship with God by sinning. We'll sin less and less. We are to be perfect as our Father – and as the first Adam was before he sinned.

"Superman Jesus" Gave Us His Suit of Righteousness

In the identity chapter you learned a controversial truth about Adam and about yourself. You are on the God plane, just below the Most High. God created Adam in His very image. He was of the God kind or species – in the God class or Family. He had God status. He was God on the earth. He had more authority than even Jesus had before His resurrection![21]

But what a feat our Savior accomplished for us by His death and resurrection! When He died He descended as an intruder into hell. It was almost like Superman disguised as Clark Kent.

Superman, as we all know, was a comic book, TV and movie hero who had supernatural powers, much lesser than those of Jesus. He came from another planet and disguised himself as mild-mannered reporter Clark Kent. Like Jesus, he was a savior. He could tell when people were in trouble. He would dart into a phone booth and remove his street clothes to reveal his Superman suit. Then he would fly in a flash to rescue hapless humans from certain death. That's what Jesus did.

Jesus put the common coat of sin over His Superman coat of righteousness. He who was without sin took on the cross our coat of sin. That coat got Him incognito into hell. There, like Clark Kent, he wore the disguise of a common human – or common sinner in this case.

---

[21] Jesus only reflected the power of His Father and the Holy Spirit before He was resurrected. It was only on the day of His resurrection that He took back the keys of God-kind authority Adam had possessed. He then put on us the coat of righteousness and authority Adam had as God over the earth. He was not declared the Son of God with power until the resurrection, and at that time He gave us that power (Rom. 1:4; Col. 1:15-18; Gen. 1:26-27; John 10:34-35; Ps. 82:6; I Cor. 15:22, 45; Rom. 5:12-21; Phil. 2:5-11; Mat. 16:18-19; 28:18-20). The shocking truth is that Adam had more power and authority given to him directly by God (Jesus) than Jesus Himself had when He walked the earth as a man before His resurrection. We have the same authority as Adam – but we have been given more power.

You may be thinking, "Since Satan is the 'god of this world' (II Cor. 4:4), there must be a 'conflict of interests' here on earth." A conflict indeed exists. But we are the winners. Although Satan still sits on the throne of this earth, replacing Adam, Jesus won the keys of the Kingdom from him and has given them to us (Mat. 16:19; 18:18). So we are gods on this earth (under the Most High God!) with the keys Satan has lost. Although God may allow him to test us, we have the victory over him. He must obey us as we use Jesus' name (Mark 16:17; John 14:13).

In hell He preached to the righteous souls who came alive when faced with Life Himself. He also preached to the demons (I Peter 3:19).[22]

But most important of all, on the third day He took back the keys of God authority over the earth from that old rascal Satan. Then Clark Kent bolted upward out of that phone booth as Superman. Unlike the fictitious Superman, He bequeathed to us His supernatural suit of divine righteousness and power. "He has wrapped me with a robe of righteousness ..." (Isa. 61:10). His name is "[*Yehovah*, *Yeshua*, Jesus] our righteousness" (Jer. 23:6). Yes, He rose from the dead, shedding the sin coat and sealing in our coat of righteousness with His blood. Hallelujah!

The Superman suit is a feeble analogy. When I was a boy I had a young friend who got a Superman suit for Christmas. In his exuberance he proceeded to jump out of his second-story window. To the tune of a few broken bones, he learned he did not have "powers and abilities far above those of mortal men."

But you do! As the righteousness of God, the sky is the limit! Actually, even the sky is not the limit. God gave Adam dominion over the earth *and* the heavens – all created things (Ps. 8:6). And you have the same rights as Adam.

Let Me Read You Your Rights!

If you have accepted the last Adam, Jesus, you are the righteousness of God! God has revealed over 200 aspects to this important subject, far too many to cover here. We'll see only a few.

As the righteousness of God, you have rights! As the police and your lawyer would do, let me read you only a few.

First of all, you must know that sickness does have a right to exist. Cancer has a right to exist – but *not on you*! Sickness has no claim over you. It doesn't belong to you. Those symptoms are gifts from Satan. Don't accept them. Don't tolerate them on your body. You are God's temple and the righteousness of God! You have a *right to be healed*! And you have no right to be sick!

What's more, as the righteousness of God you have the *right* to call down **all**

---

[22] By hell I mean the Hebrew *sheol*, the place of the dead. The Bible refers to various compartments of hell (Prov. 7:27), including "the depths" of hell (Deut. 32:22; Isa. 14:9-15; Ezek. 32:23) – the lowest pit where the demons abide – and a middle compartment (Ezek. 32:21). The top compartment, before Jesus came, held the righteous dead. They could not become alive and be with Jesus until He paid the price for them. The top levels of hell are holding places where the unconscious souls of the unsaved sleep until a future resurrection. The souls and spirits of those who walked with Jesus but later committed the unpardonable sin are alive in the bottom level of torment. The Bible contradicts the popular belief that the wicked will burn in hell inside the earth forever. Hell itself is burned up at the end in the lake of fire (Rev. 20:14), which is a globe-girdling fire that destroys both the earth and the heavens that Satan has marred. God replaces them with new heavens and a new earth (II Pet. 3:10-13). Satan and the demons and human spirits that accepted Jesus but finally followed the Devil will be banished to a dimension of total darkness outside this universe – separated from God and from each other (Jude 1:13). This is one of the most misunderstood subjects in the Bible and regrettably, too large to properly treat in this book.

The Key That Unlocks All God's Blessings

the blessings of God! And that includes healing.

You are a Child of God, a king or queen who has inherited the majestic excellence and superiority of your Father. He calls you what He is Himself: Your Excellency! Jesus uses this powerful Hebrew word *gaown* of Himself (Ex. 15:7) and says that His excellent majesties (*gaown*) are over Israel, the believers (Ps. 68:34).

If you have submitted your life in obedience to God, you have His majestic excellence as a shield about you. Our linear languages render Biblical Hebrew in puny prose.

The exciting meaning of this word is a gateway to the end-time manifestation of the glory and power of God over the church. *Gaown* means you *are* the glory of God. You are the absolute pinnacle of His creation. He can't do any better than recreating Himself!

You have access to all glory, honor, authority, favor, excellence, power, peace, joy, knowledge, wisdom (about anything!), discernment, faith, hope and patience. You have authority over all space – the whole universe. You have power over all creation: all angelic forces, good and evil, are under your command. They jump at your orders!

You have access to all life energy: you can call back to life that which is dead! All light is at your command. You have access to all truth, all motion, all secrets, all of God's love. It's all there for you – if you call on it.

The problem is, we haven't called on it. We haven't realized we have a right to be like God! But that's who He made us to be. He called us to be world changers. And He gave us all we need to powerfully impact our world. As Jesus is, so are we in this world (I John 4:17).

In the light of all this majestic excellence and power and glory, what's the flu? It's nothing. What's cancer? What's anthrax, or SARS, or West Nile virus? They mean absolutely nothing. They fly away like umbrellas in a hurricane before the excellent majesty of the Sons and Daughters of God.

The Sermon on the Mount (Mat. 5-7) is a call to majestic excellence. *Gaown* is a process. We go from glory to glory. Jesus calls us to be perfect like our Father. But it won't happen unless and until we begin to realize who we are – until we accept the title of king and queen and see ourselves as "Your Excellency."

We are no rag-tag band. We are gods in the Family of God, headed by the Most High God. We are royalty – crowned with glory and honor (Psalm 8) – Sons and Daughters of the awesome Excellency of Excellencies! It's high time we began to accept and live up to our high calling!

When we do, sickness will flee before us at the speed of light. Demons will run when they see us coming. As we accept our identity as the righteousness and the glory of God, astounding, earth-shaking power will flow like lightning from our holy hands. The lame will leap, lost limbs will grow out as fast as we declare it in our righteousness, and blind eyes will see.

105

The dead will rise and the heavens will tremble before the glory of the end-time Excellencies of the Most High!

"We ain't seen nothin' yet!" God is about to do a new thing in this earth – His greatest thing yet for the church. It will be greater than any of us can imagine. The great moves of God in history will seem like trickles compared to the tidal wave that is coming.

The dead will indeed rise. But not until Christians come alive! And this teaching on righteousness can make that happen.

When this revelation of the righteousness of God takes hold of us, we won't be wondering why God hasn't healed us. We will stand in wide-open wonder at our awesome God and who He has made us to be.

Accept the righteousness of God Jesus bought for you with His life. Rest in it. Be established in it. Be confident in it. Be excellent, Your Excellency!

Be healed and be blessed! Heal and bless!

Finally, to paraphrase Peter as he exhorts us in I Peter 2:9: Your Excellencies, chosen race of the submitted ones, royal priesthood, holy nation, God's own special treasure, beloved Bride of Jesus, glorious Sons and Daughters of the Most High God, shine forth and show the majestic excellencies of Him who has called you out of darkness into His marvelous light!

It is written ...

> So also, the tongue is a small thing, but what enormous damage it can do ... It is full of wickedness that can ruin your whole life. It can turn the entire course of your life into a blazing flame of destruction, for it is set on fire by hell itself ... Sometimes it praises our [Greek *theos*, God] and Father, and sometimes it breaks out into curses against those who have been made in the image of God.
>
> James 3:5a, 6a, 9 – NLT

CHAPTER 11
What You *Say* Is What You Get

Although comic Flip Wilson's words as he portrayed Geraldine left much to be desired, the familiar phrase he uttered stuck with me: "What you see is what you get."

I propose a holy reworking of that famous phrase. The new phrase aptly describes the astounding power God has given to us – and in a much greater way to those who speak out in their righteousness. This God-plane power has such an important connection to healing that it deserves a chapter.

There is power, power – wonder-working power – in the blood of Jesus. And there is also unrealized power in our words. What you *say* is what you *get*!

That is especially true if you *speak out in your righteousness*. Jesus spoke out in His righteousness. His words healed the sick, calmed the storm and raised the dead. And yet even He did not speak out with the full authority over heaven and earth as the first Adam could until after His resurrection.

And since Jesus gave us His righteousness and the keys of the Kingdom Adam had, we have God-plane authority over the earth and the heavens. We are one with Jesus – while still retaining an individual identity, we reflect Jesus' likeness and

107

all that He is. And Satan is scared stiff! He knows that when we recognize who we are, he no longer has just Jesus to contend with. He has thousands, yea millions, of Sons and Daughters on the earth just under the Most High, who perfectly share Jesus' way of thinking and acting. And Satan finds that an absolutely terrifying thought!

But we have no power unless we **speak**! God made us in His image – to be *speaking spirits*, as the Jewish translation of Genesis 2:7 states. God's power is in His words. So is ours.

Jesus says, "It is I who *speak in righteousness* ..." (Isa. 63:1). In making us, He was reproducing Himself. So He wants us to speak out in the righteousness He gave us.

The righteousness of God doesn't simply think God's thoughts. The "righteousness based on faith *speaks* ..." (Rom. 10:6). Paul goes on to explain what it says. It says that God's words of faith are near us, in our hearts and in our mouths. As a result of accepting this righteousness by faith, we confess God's Word with our mouths, resulting in salvation.

The powerful meaning of salvation (*Yeshua*) will come alive in the next chapter. We're talking about healing, blessing, miracles of all kinds. All the manifold meanings of *Yeshua* and salvation are ours – if we speak them out!

The Power of the Tongue

Do you realize the power of the tongue? I have seen people destroyed by gossip as well as by the words they speak over themselves. Proverbs 18:21 delivers a powerful message, a truth of which so few are aware: "Death and life are in the power of the tongue ..." James says the tongue is a fire – a world of iniquity that defiles the whole body and that "from the same mouth come both blessing and cursing" (James 3:6a,10).

When you see Moses and Aaron one day, ask them how important the tongue is. It kept them out of the Promised Land! God told them to *speak* to the rock (Num. 20:8-12). Instead of speaking out in his righteous authority to the rock, Moses spoke out in impatience and frustration to the *people* and angrily struck the rock. One wrong use of his tongue cost this man of God all he had worked for in this physical life. His mouth killed his dream.

And what was the first thing God told Moses' successor, Joshua? "This book of the law shall not depart from your *mouth* ..." (Josh. 1:8). We are to have God's Word in our mouths, not simply in our thoughts. We are to speak it over ourselves and others – and it will come to pass. Reading the Bible *aloud* is an essential practice, marshalling all our senses and penetrating the words into our heart, mind and will.

What we bind on earth will be bound in heaven. Jesus is our representative in heaven and we are His representatives on earth. The Father implements what Jesus speaks to Him on our behalf. We represent Him on earth. What we speak in His name

What You Say Is What You Get

comes true. We are not only to think good thoughts, but also to say good things.

It is true that what we say reflects what we think. It is also true that what we say about ourselves and what others say about us, if we accept it, powerfully affects how we act. The spirit world, good or evil, hears our words and enforces them. Our words are more than self-fulfilling prophecies.

In Hebrew the word for *word*, *dâbâr*, is the same as the word for *thing*. God spoke and creation appeared. He said, "Let there be light." And there was light. We have the same God-plane power. What we speak comes to pass – negatively or positively.

We are one with Jesus. And what was He called? "The Word."

The power of human words mirrors in a small way the power of the God in whose image man is created. When we accept Jesus, we are born as Sons of God. We suddenly inherit Jesus' righteousness. We then have access to all the power and authority the first Adam commanded by his words.

We can create by speaking. We have God's power to call into being that which does not exist (Rom. 4:17). "Stub, grow out in Jesus' name! Arm, be!" And arm was! Just as Jesus said, " 'Light, be!' And light was," as the Hebrew states.

Don't Speak Satan's Symptoms into Law!

With such astounding power, what are we doing being sick? When we speak God's Word over our bodies, sickness has to go!

So many Christians are not healed because they're *speaking sickness over themselves*! "I have the flu." "I have cancer." You were healed 2,000 years ago. What Satan is **attacking** your body with is a *lie*! Don't accept it!

Those symptoms are *gifts from Satan. They don't belong to you.* Don't accept them! Speak **God's** Word, not Satan's words!

If you speak out with your powerful tongue what Satan is attacking you with as if it were yours, you are speaking those symptoms into **law**! You then give the demons the right to afflict you – and even make things worse.

The symptoms you speak are the symptoms you get!

How often do you hear Christians say, "I feel the flu coming on." They're saying to Satan's symptoms, "Y'all come! Make yourself at home. And next flu season, y'all come back now, y'heah?"

Overheard in a locker room conversation: "I always get the flu about this time in the winter." You always do because what you say is what you get!

Remember: Satan is a legalist. And he has a legal right to enforce curses to the letter, whether you realize what you're saying or not. In court, lawyers will often seize on your words and those words can send you to prison. Angels carry out God's Word (Ps. 103:20), and likewise, demons carry out Satan's words when we speak them. And they can put us into a spiritual prison. Don't give the Devil an inch.

The world may call it "my flu" – but don't you! Call it an *attack*. Call it

Why Doesn't God Heal Me?

"lying symptoms." But don't call it yours!

Our words have more power than we have ever imagined. We have the power to bless or to curse – and there is power in both.

Curses – What *They* Say Is What *You* Get

Curses are an overlooked, misunderstood, underestimated factor in our lives – yes, even the lives of us Christians. Jesus became a curse for us, but that does not mean that all curses are automatically broken when we accept Jesus.

Christianity is all about confession. "If you confess with your **mouth** Jesus as [Divine Master], and believe in your heart that God raised Him from the dead, you will be saved, for with the heart a person believes, resulting in righteousness, and with the **mouth** he confesses, resulting in salvation" (Rom. 10:9-10).

Jesus did not automatically invade your heart. You invited Him in with your mouth. Healing is a part of salvation. To be healed, you claim the healing Jesus paid for you with your mouth.

Jesus paid for the above benefits with His blood. But to see them realized in your life, you must confess them with your mouth.

The same is true for curses. Jesus shed His blood to deliver us from curses (Gal. 3:13). But our mouth must reject the curses in Jesus' name, confessing our freedom from the curses.

One pastor said curses have no effect on us because we are new creations. Don't be naïve. If that were true, sin would not be an issue either. The truth is, your spirit has been made new, not your soul. Sin can enter your mind and affect your emotions after you (you are a spirit) have become a new creation.

Curses stick because of sin. You may be forgiven because you invoke with your mouth the blood of Jesus. But the stupid thing you said or did to that person still caused him or her to curse you. You still have to claim freedom from the curse by the blood of Jesus with your mouth, the same way you did when you sinned.

Remember: Your spirit has been fully redeemed. Not so with your soul and body. Sticks and stones do break bones, and words can literally kill. Jesus can fix that bone. He already has. But you must use that mouth He gave you. Jesus took that curse on Him. Already. But you must use your mouth to reject it. You must claim what Jesus did for you.

The day may come when curses will simply bounce off of us, as with Jesus. *But we must be walking in Jesus' righteousness, in His glory and in our full identity as Sons of God*. We must be sin free, meaning we walk in obedience, repent quickly when we stumble and seek quick cleansing by Jesus' blood.

Until then, we can at least be curse-free on our end. God has called us to bless others, not curse.

One man in our house of healing justified cursing another resident. "But it's the truth!" he protested. Since he was French, I responded in French with a familiar

110

What You Say Is What You Get

Gallic saying, "All truth is not good to say." The book of Proverbs supports that principle. God says to speak the truth in love.

We can even curse in jest. I love to tease, but too many times I have said words facetiously that I had to repent of and rescind. Once I joked about two sweet ladies who always sat on the front row, teasing them about being Pharisees. That's an open door for the Pharisaical spirit to influence them.

Calling people "crazy" – even in a joking way – is a curse that has its effect, slowly but surely.

Don't play around. Choose words wisely, or the demons will play around with those you curse. A common curse many say is, "That broke my heart." You're asking for heart problems!

Read Ephesians 4:25-32. Giving the Devil an opportunity or foothold is in the same context as speaking unwholesome words and slandering others.

This is new information revealed by the Holy Spirit. You may resist it if you like, but you will suffer the consequences of the curses you don't reject. In our freedom and deliverance ministry, we have seen countless cases first hand of people being set free from the effects of curses. In many cases, their healing only manifested when they rejected the curses with their mouths.

The Lack of Knowledge that Destroys

Curses are a *major hindrance* to healing. This subject could fill volumes. Yet most Christians, even leaders, know little about curses.

Many pastors only know one verse on curses: "As the bird by wandering, as the swallow by flying, so the curse causeless shall not come" (Prov. 26:2, KJV). Yes, there is a cause for curses. People have varied reasons for cursing others. We sometimes offend, not walking in God's wisdom and/or His love.

But one of the lies of hell the deceiver in the pit has sold to Christians is that curses come only from hell. Surprise! Curses can come from heaven. *God curses!*

There are 238 curses in the Bible, 200 of which are issued by God. Generally human mouths issue them and the rulers of darkness enforce them.

It surprises some to hear that God curses people. No amount of hermeneutical double talk can change God's Word. Proverbs 3:33 is only one of many examples: "The curse of the [*Eternal*] is on the house of the wicked, But He blesses the dwelling of the righteous."

A famous movie line comes to mind when I think of how people misunderstand God: "You can't handle the truth." *A Few Good Men* do. I hope you will too. Many don't. They trip over verses in God's Word where God Himself curses.

Listen to God's prophetic warning to today's priests or pastors. And remember it when you read the next chapter. "If you do not listen, and if you do not take it to heart to give honor to My name … then I will send the curse upon you and I will curse your blessings; and indeed I have cursed them already, because you are not taking it

Why Doesn't God Heal Me?

to heart. Behold I am going to rebuke your offspring, and I will spread refuse [a polite translation] on your faces, the refuse of your feasts …" (Mal. 2:2b, 3).

What religious people don't understand is that the One spoken of here was Jesus! Sweet Jesus has His warrior side. He is the just Judge.

Some sins do bring curses from God. He only curses to bring people to repentance and receive His blessings. His curses always require repentance. That is not always the case with other curses since Satanists and others often curse the righteous for obeying God.

God only curses when we sin so greatly that He needs to redirect us by the results of the curse to a right path. The proverb cited above is a warning not to act unwisely so as to provoke curses.

No provision for breaking curses was made in the Old Covenant period. (Without the blood of Jesus, there is no way.) God had to curse David's family because of his sin of murder and adultery (II Sam. 12:9-14). Had Jesus' blood been shed, David would not have had to see his son die. The curse did not come without a cause. But it did come.

Some muddled ministers use this example to prove God does not always want to heal His people today. That's hogwash! We need teachers who are "… accurately handling the word of truth" (II Tim. 2:15).

The truth is that we're no longer under the Old Covenant. Thank God for Jesus' blood! He shed it to break our curses today so we could be healed.

Israel did not get many of the blessings of Deuteronomy 28, including healing, but they got most of the curses. Those curses did come, and they have come on our peoples today.

The fact that God and mankind have reasons for cursing people does not do away with the reality of the horrible effects of curses. The Hebrew part of God's Instruction Book is full of that reality.

The reality does not change under the New Covenant. But God provides a way by Jesus' blood to set us free from curses. We must nevertheless do our part, as we do in salvation and healing, by using the mouth God gave us.

Let's come out of our kindergarten understanding of curses and grasp the powerful effect they can have on us. In some Third World areas where people curse with no subtlety and openly practice voodoo, they are much more aware of the power our words have to destroy.

As I gave an informal Bible study on curses to my family in South Carolina, they couldn't see why I was making such a case for curses. A French-speaking lady from Haiti was present. I said, "Marie, do you know of people – believers and non-believers – that have died because of curses?"

"Oh, yes," she replied, "many – all the time!"

As James says, God gave us a mouth with power to curse or to bless. Speaking good things over people has power to promote blessings, especially when Christians speak the powerful Word of God.

People curse without realizing it. You may say, "John, like his father, often has difficulty motivating himself to work," or much worse, "John is a lazy bum like his dad!" The former is a label. The latter is a curse. Both give legal grounds for demonic involvement. It's so easy to speak evil.

But we are called to bless others and pray for them. You might properly say, "We're looking for the right motivation for John so that he can learn to be diligent." Or, if you have prayed for him, you could say, "I thank Jesus for enabling John to find motivation to be diligent." A Christian must choose his words wisely in order to speak blessings.

The saying goes, "Sticks and stones may break my bones, but words will never harm me." What a lie! Words can wound for life. Yet what most Christians don't realize is this: word curses spoken about you will come true! They will indeed, unless you reject them. You don't even have to hear those words or be aware of them. They can literally kill you! That's why frequent communion is so important. Through Jesus' body we break the curses. See "Communion" and "Curses" in the Appendix for more details.

In some cases of illness resulting from curses, we must ask God, sometimes with help from anointed people, to show us the specific curse we must reject and break off.

If we have spoken a curse over others or ourselves we must rescind it in Jesus' name and speak out God's Word on the matter. Better still, we need to control the power tools we hold in our mouths.

The Power Tool between Our Teeth

You may have heard the story of the man who bought the best brand of chainsaw and kept coming back to the store where he bought it, perplexed that it wasn't doing a good job at all of cutting wood. Finally, the salesman accompanied him to his nearby wooded property so he could figure out the problem. As the salesman pulled the lever to activate the chainsaw, the surprised man yelled, "What's that noise?"

We have a mighty tool God has given us. If we're not careful, our Husqvarna can be a husky varmint whose toothy mouth bites and devours. Our mouths can chop people to pieces. They can curse people with sickness and even death. And they can bless people with health and life. We must realize the negative and positive power of God's strong tool He has bequeathed to His Children.

Something happens in the spirit realm when we speak words over ourselves or when someone speaks words – good or bad – over us.

Have you read the red-letter warning in Matthew 12:36-37? "But I tell you that every careless word that people speak, they shall give an accounting for it in the day of judgment [unless they confess and rescind it]. For by your words you will be justified, and by your words you will be condemned." Potent words, those. Yes, words do have power. Words bless. Words kill.

Why Doesn't God Heal Me?

It is sad – even tragic – that we are so naïve about this in our Western world and especially in the Christian world. When it comes to claiming, accepting and using the name of Jesus for salvation or healing, we seem to understand. When we discuss curses, covered by the very same sacrifice, we are destroyed for lack of knowledge. Some literally die.

The minister cannot reject it for us. We must do it. If we don't, it will affect us no matter how "born again" we are. Salvation and healing are not automatic. They involve our will, our decision to accept and our confession by the mouth. So it is with curses.

To break a curse, we must be believers and in Jesus' name reject the evil spoken over us.

Some Christians do understand generational curses. I had to reject a demonic curse of manic depression that had survived in my family for generations. This is not some weird religious invention. The Ten Commandments show that God curses evil families to the third and fourth generation (Ex. 20:5). Witches curse to the thousandth generation. Most curses we accept come from ordinary people like us, not witches or Satanists.

My covenant brother had a Satanist boss who cursed him in 1985. He said my friend would lose his health, his wealth, his family and his life. Over a period of thirteen years, he lost it all – almost all. Independently wealthy, he went into deep debt and divorce. A deadly pneumonia hit him in late 1998.

The doctor had told him to get his affairs in order since he only had a few days to live. In intense pain, he struggled to the bathroom for what he thought was the last time. When he lay back down, he gasped, thinking he was breathing his last breath. Then suddenly – no pain! He had asked a Christian prayer group to pray for him, and they met at the exact time he had stumbled back into bed.

The next day the doctor was in disbelief at the X-rays. He said, "You've had 28 bouts with pneumonia, yet your lungs are the perfect lungs of an eight-year-old! You've just had a miracle in your life." Those words from a doctor are a miracle in themselves!

Although he knew nothing about curses, God gave him the grace to be able to come to understand them and reject them in Jesus' name, as well as to teach others about curses.

The hardest curse for him to reject was a spiritual one. He had not forgiven – from the heart – a pastor who kicked him out of the church with no due cause and told him, "God doesn't want you anymore!"

My curse was just that – the curse of unforgiveness. A parable speaks of being sent to the "tormentors" or demons. I had to go through demonic torment before I learned to forgive. When I forgave and rejected a curse on me that involved blasphemy of the Holy Spirit in me, I was healed instantly and began receiving everything back as Job did.

Jesus can redeem anything, especially when we know how to reject curses. Never before has the Christian world had a greater need to reject curses. Here's why.

Time Is Short – and Satan's Curse List Is Long!

Satan's time is short. And he knows it. But his list of curses is long.

Unlike the church, seven groups of darkness have come in unity to call forth the Antichrist and to curse Christians. They gather five times a year to curse believers. These organizations have an effect upon God's people and their healing and they are cursing more and more as we approach the end. *It is extremely important for Christians to **reject** their curses in communion – preferably every day!* (Use the general prayer in the "Curses" section of the Appendix.)

I've read some excerpts from the volumes of curses. I discovered in these tomes what most Christians don't know: what they're supposed to do! Satan knows better than many Christians how they should be walking with Jesus. And these evil groups curse them to do just the opposite. And too many of us are cooperating!

Jesus may have to delay His coming if we don't get busy beating demonic forces and preaching the restoration of the hearts of the children to the fathers and the Father (Mal. 4:6). If we don't, He will have to smite the earth with a curse. Paul said he would be accursed if he didn't preach the gospel (Gal. 1:8). God will curse the whole earth if we don't do like Paul.

God's time has come to restore knowledge about curses and set His people free. It's high time we got the lowdown on Satan's schemes. We must refuse to speak his words. Like him, they destroy. We are not called to curse others, unless in rare cases God tells us to do so in our righteousness to recompense evil. It happened in the Bible. But when we curse like Satan, we block God's healing and blessings.

Speak blessings – not curses. God may not condemn you spiritually as being guilty if you are ignorant of some curses. You will pay the consequences, however, until you seek God about it and find the way to repentance and breaking the curse.

I have found that the most common hindrance to the healing of those who are really walking in God's way is that of curses. If you are otherwise hindrance-free, ask God if someone has cursed you.

Blessings can never be revoked. Curses can. Let's use our mouths the way God would. Jesus said, "You are gods." Since we are made in His image, let's speak His words and see healing spring forth – in ourselves and in those who are healed through our words.

The next chapter deals also with words. Satan has cleverly introduced a word or two into the vocabulary of the Bride of Jesus that has had a devastating effect upon her. As I make the final revisions for this book, I feel this subject is too important to be covered by a few lines in Hindrance No. 194. Books could be written about it.

It's controversial. Truth is sometimes difficult to swallow. People gobble down tradition more easily than truth. I hope you will be willing to accept the truth and change your Christian vocabulary. It will change your life!

11 Why Doesn't God Heal Me?

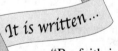

"By faith in the name of Jesus, this man whom you see and know was made strong. It is Jesus' name and the faith that comes through him that has given this complete healing to him." ... Then they called them in again and commanded them not to speak or teach at all in the name of Jesus.

Acts 3:16; 4:18 – NIV

CHAPTER 12
The Mighty Name of Jesus

I have breaking news – heartbreaking news – you won't find on your local radio station or even the Internet: the Bride of Jesus has been raped! By Satan's deception, "the Lord" has ravished her and left her in guilt, shame and defeat. As many rape victims, she has been traumatized. She's lost her identity. She feels unworthy. And her Fiancé must see some changes before He weds her.

Why do only about 5% of the Christians who make up the Bride get healed? Why has the Bride lost her power, her anointing and her intimacy with the Bridegroom? The answer – or much of it – is in a name.

It's a name that saves and heals. The only name that makes demons flee (Luke 10:17). The only name that moves the heavens and the earth.

When not followed by the name above all names, "Lord" is only a title. And a powerless one at that. Multiple gods in India are called by that title. When used as prefix before a name in the English hierarchy of nobility, it is a title of respect.[23]

---

[23] *Oxford English Dictionary Online*, Oxford University Press 2003, *lord*, Entry II. "As a designation of rank or official dignity... 8. a. In early use employed vaguely for any man of exalted position in a kingdom

Why Doesn't God Heal Me?

But a lord was several ranks below the king.

Recently I heard a radio preacher go on and on about the importance of "the name of the Lord." But not once did he mention His name!

As a worship leader, I now know the difference in the power of the anointing (including the physically discernable touch of the Holy Spirit upon our hands and body) between a "Lord" song and a song that uses His name. I hear these lyrics: "I sing praises to Your name, O Lord, for Your name is great and greatly to be praised ..." But I'm flabbergasted. How can you sing praises to His name when you never mention His name?

His name is not "the Lord." His name is not even Christ. That's a Biblical and inspired title that signifies "the Anointed One." But that's not His name!

His name is **Jesus**!

That name is extremely important to our heavenly Father and to the Holy Spirit, who lifts up and responds to that name. That name is the mace[24] of God that shakes heaven and earth and the workers of darkness and gives access to the wisdom of God. That name is the Passover password – the gateway to power, anointing and intimacy. But it doesn't seem to be important to Jesus' Bride.

How would you feel, men, if your fiancée or your wife rarely or never called you by name? Would you feel intimate with her?

"Hey, plumber, come here." "Burger flipper, let's go." "Telemarketer, give me a call." "Bed partner, come sleep with me." How would that make you feel?

How can the Bride of Jesus be intimate with Him if she's calling Him by an impersonal title? Will you go for the cheap, no name brand of Christianity? Will you settle for less when you can have more – of Jesus?

---

or commonwealth, and in a narrower sense applied to the feudal tenants holding [land] directly of the king by military or other honorable service: see BARON 1. In modern use, equivalent to nobleman in its current sense: A peer (usually a temporal peer) of the realm, or one who by courtesy (see 13) is entitled to the *prefix* [emphasis author's] Lord, or some higher title, as a part of his ordinary appellation... 13. a. As a prefixed title, forming part of a person's customary appellation ...." In view of this, it is permissible, yet not ideal, to use the term "Lord Jesus." Jesus is the emphasis here, and the prefix is indeed a title of respect, even though "Lord" does not convey the power of King Jesus or Jesus as part of the supreme Godhead.

The Biblical phrase "KING OF KINGS, AND LORD OF LORDS" (Rev. 19:16) combines the kingly and priestly function of Jesus. In ancient Hebrew culture, the priest had preeminence over the king. It was he who normally anointed the king. Kingship refers to the civil or state rulership, and indeed, Jesus will rule the nations as King. His priesthood, however, refers to His supreme authority as God. In Greek, it was the term that was mentioned last that was the most important function. As in ancient Israel, church and state were combined. The head of state was none other than Jesus, the head of the church in the wilderness. From the beginning (Gen. 14:18) Jesus' priestly function represented Him as the Eternal God, "without father, without mother, having neither beginning of days nor end of life, but made like the Son of God, he remains a priest perpetually" (Heb. 7:3). The verse should have been translated, "King of [or above all] kings and Divine Master of [or above all earthly] masters." We must distinguish the Master of the Universe from the earthly masters [*adonai* or *kurios*]. Why use a term that was some five levels below a king to designate the Master of all, the God of the universe? It makes no sense. It is demeaning to Jesus. He is not Lord. He is King and He is God!

[24] Larger and thicker than a scepter, this emblem of kingly authority contained the king's seal. When he called for his mace, which stood at his right hand, and put his seal on a decree, what he wrote became law in the land. When he pointed the mace toward someone in his presence, they had to leave. Demons have to leave when we use our mace of authority – the name of Jesus.

The Mighty Name of Jesus 12

"Oh, come on, don't be so picky," you say. "He knows who I mean!" Yes, He does. And so do the demons that are worshipped as "Lord."[25] Why use a generic term that could also call on some Indian god?

And why defy the Word of the living God by denying the name of Jesus? Peter denied that name. But what a change came about later!

You may know John 3:16. But what about Acts 3:16? Jesus had just healed the lame man through Peter and John. Want to get healed? Then pay attention to how this lame man was able to jump for joy. Did he say, "Praise the Lord"? If you have denied His name, it's not too late to quit being part of a lame bride. Listen to what the one who had denied His name said.

Peter declared: "By faith in the *name of Jesus*, this man whom you see and know was made strong. It is *Jesus' name* and the faith that comes through Him that has given this *complete healing* to him, as you can all see" (NIV). "… by the name of Jesus Christ the Nazarene … by this name this man stands before you in good health" (Acts 4:10).

"Lord" doesn't heal. "Lord" doesn't save. "And there is salvation in no one else; *for there is **no other name** under heaven that has been given among men by which we must be saved*" (Acts 4:12). As we shall see in the next chapter, His Hebrew name *Yeshua* embodies salvation in all its splendor.

Satan has indeed raped Jesus' Bride. It's so sad to watch a half-hour religious program where they talk and talk about "the Lord" and never once mention the name of Jesus. It happens. And the Bridegroom is not pleased.

The name of Jesus strengthens us physically and spiritually. Little wonder that the beleaguered Bride is limping. She's not walking in overcoming power. She has been shamed. Why? Because she's ashamed of the name. If you want to be part of a spotless Bride that will be raptured out of these terrible days of sorrow and soon-coming tribulation, you better get to know the name of the Bridegroom. (Take a look under "Jesus' Name" in the Appendix and see all that His name evokes.)

One meaning of rapture is "snatch away." Satan has succeeded in snatching away the name of the Bridegroom from the Bride so that she will not be snatched away by Jesus. But you don't have to be among the foolish virgins of Matthew 25.

A Clever Deception

Don't be fooled by Satan's clever deception.

God wasn't fooled. He knew what Satan would do. And, as Isaiah 28:9-13

---

[25] *Oxford English Dictionary Online*, lord "…12. d. Lord of the Flies, a name for Beelzebub …" (II Kgs 1:2). Often mistakenly taken for Satan, this demon is second under Satan. His name is Betrayal. He is indeed "lord of the flies," for he uses harmful insects to attack people. He is the demon who influenced Judas before Satan possessed the traitor.

119

Why Doesn't God Heal Me?

explains to those wise enough to catch it, He prophesied it. He said He would speak to His people, even the believers, through a "foreign tongue." And because the truth is revealed in the Word "a little here, a little there," like a puzzle, many would stumble – even part of the Bride.

To understand the Word, you must be willing to obey it. And since all the treasures of knowledge are hidden in the Anointed One (Col. 2:3), the use of His name activates that understanding. If the Holy Spirit is your Teacher, you will not be fooled. And you will know when a true teacher of the fivefold ministry of Ephesians 4:11 is feeding you truth.

The foreign tongues of Hebrew and Greek are unfamiliar to most of us. But the Holy Spirit teaches us the Word, and He supplements His direct help by sending preachers and teachers (Rom. 10:14) – and others who compile concordances (Bible word indexes).

Go to a good library and check it out for yourself in an exhaustive concordance. I counted the occurrences of the word "Lord" in the Hebrew Scriptures. About 96% of the time it is "LORD" in the KJV. The Hebrew word is "YHVH" (*Yahweh* or *Yehovah*). Some translators like Moffat render it correctly as "the Eternal."

Although all the members or the Godhead are eternal, "the Eternal One" or the "I am" referred to in the Hebrew Scriptures is none other than – in almost all cases – the Word of John 1 who was later born as Jesus (see Appendix under "Jesus – God of the 'Old' Testament"). Many times you can actually substitute that word "LORD" or Eternal One with the name Jesus, since that's who He later became.

Only 4% of the time does the word "Lord" come from *Adonai*. When used of the Eternal, it carries the meaning of "Divine Master." The same goes for the Greek equivalent *kurios*.

"I will remove the names of the Baals from her mouth ..."

"Lord" is an unfortunate translation. It's a long story – too long for this book. Reading Hosea 2 would help you understand. "Lord" basically translates back into Hebrew as "Baal."[26] And verse 17 gives an amazing prophecy with several fulfillments as usual. One of those is for this end-time, when God will take "the names of the Baals" out of the mouth of the Bride of Jesus.

History has reruns. An ancient bride was also violated (Jer. 3:2). Like the modern Bride of Jesus and the whole world at the end, Satan got her drunk with the wine of deception and spiritual harlotry (Rev. 17:2).

Both brides had the holy name ravished from them and continued in drunken

---

[26] *Oxford English Dictionary Online*, Baal, "…[Heb. *ba'al* lord] The chief male deity in the Phoenician and Canaanitish nations; hence, transf. false god]."

120

The Mighty Name of Jesus 12

whoredom. Jesus told His wife Israel that her fathers "forgot My name because of Baal" (Jer. 23:27).[27] The wayward bride went for the ways, days and the name of Baal and forgot the Eternal. Jesus had to divorce her (Jer. 3:8).

He will never again marry a bride who refuses to love Him and His name. When this knowledge is fully revealed to the Bride, she will be accountable. And if she's in love with "the Lord," do you think Jesus will put the ring on her finger?

The rapture-ready Bride will have washed "the Lord' out of her mouth with the water of the Word. She will have begun to speak intimately to her Bridegroom by His name.

Would you like to be called by the title of a pagan god whose sexual debaucheries were legendary? Did you know that the local city man-god called Baal in Canaan was chosen by the size of his genitalia?

Far-fetched, you say? It may seem that way to a bride swaying and swooning to the music of her "Lord," but Jesus won't come to fetch you from afar if Baal is your dance partner. In the next book I will have the space to explain all this historically and theologically.

Ladies, you wouldn't like your husband to call you by saying, "Whore, come here!" And men, you wouldn't relish your wife calling you "Whoremonger," would you?

And yet, as shocking and controversial as it may be, that's what Jesus thinks of this "lord" business. Just watch. Watch those who catch on to the power of using Jesus' name in this end-time. Watch the miracles. Watch the fruit. Compare. Compare with the lot of the "Lord lovers." Calling on the name of the Lord is for losers. Jesus is the friend of winners. He's *Yahweh* (*Yeshua*) *Nissi* – our Banner, our Victory!

Demons will laugh at you if you try to send them away in the name of the Lord. You may laugh, too, at the following revelation since you have not seen it with your own eyes. We have. Our deliverance ministry has brought forth undeniable results, and we know firsthand the problems a certain demon has caused. His name is quagmire, and he pushes you from one ditch to the other. Sound like today's bumbling bride – sick, broke and powerless?

Believe it or not, this demon calls himself "lord" or "the lord." The Devil is a clever counterfeiter.

Instead of dancing with Jesus, Satan has intoxicated the Bride so she's dancing a drunken dance with "the Lord." Drugged and drunk with doctrines of demons

---

[27] D. Harden, *The Phoenicians*, Thames and Hudson, 1962, p. 85. All of the historical works on Phoenician religion as well as the *Oxford English Dictionary* identify Baal as "Lord." Harden's description of Baal and Baalat as lord and lady sound like English nobility. He writes that Astarte (Heb. Ashtoreth), the fertility goddess, was also called Ishtar and was assimilated with Hera, queen of heaven. P. Hilli writes in his book *Lebanon in History* (Macmillan, 1967, p. 128) that the Canaanites borrowed from Babylon and Egypt but also gave them Baal and Ishtar. Is it coincidence that Revelation calls this end time religious and economic system Babylon the Great?

Why Doesn't God Heal Me?

and toxic tradition, she's doing the terrible twist with quagmire, who has her sliding in a stupor from one ditch to the other. He has twisted the Word terribly and has her so contorted that she needs some chiropractic adjustments from Healer and Bridegroom Jesus.

The serpent Satan is twisted and clever.

"If it's good enough for King James ..."

He used a group of scholarly men who did not truly know Jesus to translate the King James Bible of 1611. As men's translations go, it's not bad – only 8% error – and the language is beautiful. But they made some glaring mistakes. They translated Easter instead of Passover. And some errors were not so glaring – but the damage they did was catastrophic.

The *Oxford English Dictionary* defines "lord" (Entry II 8) as a "designation of rank or official dignity. In these applications it is not used vocatively except as a prefixed title." Entry 8a adds that a lord is a nobleman or "one who by courtesy is entitled to the prefix Lord." So to be proper, you don't address a lord by saying "lord" but by saying "Lord" followed by his name. "Lord Jesus" would therefore be a respectful way to address Jesus.

When "Lord" is followed by Jesus' name, we know we are speaking of the Divine Being named Jesus. "Lord" or "the Lord" in most languages[28] refers rather to a peer of the royal realm much lower than a king. In the England of King James and even beyond, the king was on top, followed by queen, prince and princess, and duke, who was normally addressed as Duke X. The lower titles of marquis, earl, viscount and baron were addressed as Lord X.

Critics said King James was exalting himself as if he were Almighty God. While it is true that Jesus is called King in the Bible, "Lord" is the much more frequent rendering. Whether or not the translation of "Lord" in the King James Bible was a hidden agenda of a pompous king who wanted to "lord it" or "king it" over a lowly lord named Jesus or God, the translation certainly married well with his pride.

I'm sure King James was pleased, even if God wasn't. He must have gloated. After all, he was king, and most of the time in the Bible Jesus was called a lowly lord, far below the king.

What a web Satan wove around the naïve Bride. Like the religious receptionist I mentioned earlier who believed, "If it's good enough for King James, it's good enough for me!" But Jesus is the Word, and it's time His Bride began to rightly divide the Word of truth.

---

[28] Latin languages such as French translate "lord" as "Seigneur" (Spanish "Señor"), deriving from the root meaning "senior" or "older." Although not as demeaning as the English "lord" with its Baal connection, it does not have the power and rank of the name "Jesus."

122

The Mighty Name of Jesus

You can check it out for yourself in *Strong's Concordance*. Only about 4% of the time is "Lord" translated from *Adonai*, which is a divine title, rather than the 96% rendering of "LORD" for YHVH or Jesus.

When used of God, *Adonai* and the roughly equivalent Greek *kurios*, although used of humans as a polite title of respect like "sir," are obviously divine titles. Considering all we have seen, a better translation of these words would be "Divine Master." Satan's use of that term in certain Eastern religions notwithstanding, it is the most faithful translation. It agrees with God's removal of the names of Baals from the mouths of His people (Hos. 2:17). It also elevates Jesus from the position of a comparatively lowly lord to His rightful place.

In case you're wondering about the phrase "King of Kings and Lord of Lords," the latter is actually more powerful than the former. A king is supreme ruler in the civil realm, priest referring to the religious realm. Even in the case of pagan priest-kings, subjects obeyed them as kings but worshipped them as gods in their priestly roles. "Divine Master" is referring to the priestly supremacy of Jesus as High Priest of heaven. While King of Kings refers to Jesus as Supreme Ruler over all earthly governments, Divine Master refers to Him as Supreme God. "Lord" does not begin to translate that kind of power.

This mistranslation was born out of a Jewish misconception about not speaking out the name YHVH. Satan has used this "Lord" translation to lord it over the Bride of Christ. His outrageous violation has left her in the dark, groping in a different way than he groped her. He has shamed her so she can't walk in the righteousness activated only by the name of her Beau. He has used "the Lord" to rape her and rob here of her purity. He has stolen the power, healing, salvation and anointing released only in the mighty name of Jesus!

And Satan and his group of religious people will get riled at anyone who starts preaching the importance of Jesus' name. Times haven't changed. Nor have the spirits of religiosity and churchianity. Previews of history's last days show a mini-series of bad reruns: "... they commanded them not to speak or teach at all in the name of Jesus" (Acts 4:18). The famine of the Word (Amos 8:11) will include the name of the living Word – Jesus.

"Lord" doesn't get anybody upset. Franklin Graham, evangelist son of Billy Graham, got in trouble for a word he said at an important occasion in Washington, D.C. It wasn't "Lord" that go him in trouble. He mentioned the name Satan and his people hate: Jesus.

This is Original Bible Teaching

This is not my teaching. It comes from the pure, unadulterated Word of God.

If you use virtually only the title "Lord," the Bible has some strong correction for you.

"But as many as received Him, to them He gave the right to become

123

Why Doesn't God Heal Me?

Children of God, even [*even* was added by the translators] to those who believe in His *name*" (John 1:12).

In Greek, believing includes doing. How can you say you believe in His name if you don't even use it? Did you seize the power of this verse? If you are not believing in and using the name of Jesus, you have no right to become Children of God! Powerful words. Powerful name.

But the question is: are these words powerful enough to lead you to change an entrenched habit of "Christianese." The master of legalese and his agents hear your requests of "the Lord" and they act on them. God doesn't. The Father responds – and all heaven responds – to the name of Jesus.

Can you see now how the foolish virgins fail to measure up and need the correction of tribulation? And what do they lack? Oil (Mat. 25:8). The oil of anointing is released by the name of Jesus. One factor that will separate the wise from the foolish virgins is the use of the name of Jesus versus powerless titles.

Victory over Epidemics in the Shelter of Jesus' Name

Without the name of Jesus, you don't have the rights of the Children of God. That includes the "children's bread" of healing! It also includes protection from pestilence and tribulation.

Unless our nations repent, God will allow epidemics to strike us, worse than anything we've seen. Biological terrorist attacks will come, as well as new strains of flu and other diseases that will even kill Christians. Unless they walk with Jesus and know the power of His name, they will fall prey to the "pestilence that stalks in darkness" (Ps. 91:6).

But you can be different! You can walk in the power and glory of the name of Jesus. You can be healed of this rape perpetrated against the Bride of Jesus. You can be free of shame and walk in the righteousness activated by Jesus' name. You can say with boldness, in Jesus' name, "[I] will not be afraid of the terror by night ..." (verse 5).

You can claim Psalm 91. But there are conditions.

How can you "[dwell] in the shelter [or secret place of intimacy]" (verse 1) of Jesus if you don't call Him by name? "I will set him securely on high [*salvation* in verse 16 includes the rapture concept, and "on high" includes that idea as well], because he has *known* [acknowledges – NIV] My *Name*. He will call upon Me [Jesus, not "the Lord"], and I will answer him ..." (verses 14-15a).

Power, authority, healing, protection and answers to prayer are released only in the name of Jesus. Even "in Christ's name" does not release the power like His given name – Jesus.

With this revelation I do not intend to offend. It is new understanding that I believe will bring a breakthrough for those who have the humility and courage to change. I know of many precious brothers and sisters who walk in powerful anoint-

The Mighty Name of Jesus

ings and do have an intimate relationship with Jesus and yet who have sincerely used the title "Lord." I pray that you will not take offense, but rather learn this new truth as I have learned it – from the Holy Spirit and the Word – and walk in it.

If you have a measure of intimacy and power now, wait until you unlock the awesome power of the frequent use of the name of Jesus. You will go from glory to glory, for Jesus' name releases the glory – the completing expression of our change into the image of God.

The Bible Cure for the Ravished Bride

The bride has been raped by the lie of the lowly lord. Her trauma and hurt needs healing. She needs healing words – words from the Word, Jesus. The most healing word is the precious, magnificent name of our Brother of Love. Jesus. Jesus. What a beautiful name!

Darlene Zschech, of *Hillsong Music Australia* fame, sings about that beautiful name. How sad that so few intone that name in song. Graham Kendrick's *Say the Name of Love* is a refreshing breeze after the stifling sauna of Lord songs that has left the bride limp and weak. She needs the healing balm of Jesus' name. Jesus *is* the Word. So listen, Bride, to what your Bridegroom says about the power of His name.

First of all, He wants you to get this straight. His name is not Lord or even Christ. It's Jesus (Mat. 1:21). It's Jesus, because He saves.

He wants you to know that the gospel is about His name. Philip preached "the good news about the Kingdom of God and the *name* of Jesus Christ ..." (Acts 8:12).

His name is more precious than silver and gold. It made the lame leap (Acts 3:6). Why is the name Jesus not precious to you? Why would you let Satan win? Why let that lousy loser lord it over you by putting the title and the name of a foreign god in your holy mouth? Bride of Jesus, your words have the power of life and death. Lord is a word of death. Bridegroom Jesus asks you: "... why will you die, O house of Israel [the believers]?" (Ezek. 18:31).

In the early history of the church, "... fear fell upon them all and the name of the Lord Jesus was being magnified" (Acts 19:17). Does the incessant use of the Lord epithet magnify the name of Jesus?

Have you allowed God to answer Paul's prayer for you: "... that the name of our Lord Jesus will be glorified in you ..." (II Thes. 1:12)? Is Jesus' name glorified in your mouth when almost all He hears is "Lord"?

God even dedicated one of the Ten Commandments – the third – to the protection and right use of His name (Ex. 20:7). This applies to the "I am" who became *Yeshua* or Jesus, as well as to the Father.

Isn't it funny – no, sad – that Christians start their prayers with "Lord" when Jesus said to say, "Our Father ... Hallowed be Your name" (Mat. 6:9).

Why Doesn't God Heal Me?

This "Lord" thing is downright confusing. You don't know whether Christians are referring to the Father, Jesus or the Holy Spirit. Do they even know? When they say, "the Lord told me this," they are really referring to the Teacher, the Holy Spirit, who spoke to God's people throughout church history as recorded in the Word. Probably most often by "Lord" they mean Jesus.

But it's high time the bride began to say what she means. You married people know how difficult communication can be in marriage. If your fiancée is speaking words she doesn't mean, you're headed for a disastrous marriage if you marry the girl. Jesus doesn't want a confused wife. That's why the Holy Spirit is at work to correct this Lord language. It grieves Him.

He wants to convict the bride of her lackadaisical language that is roping her into a romance that she doesn't want – an unwitting dance with deception and demigods. He wants her to soothe her Suitor with the sweetest sound in the universe – the sound of the beautiful and awesome name of Jesus. It's a sound the Father, the Holy Spirit and especially the Bridegroom love to hear. It releases intimacy. It packs power.

Jesus will jump to her rescue. He will save. He will heal. He will restore. He will render her spotless and rapture her up to carry her over the threshold of eternity. He delights in a bride who knows His name.

It's time for her to call on the name of the Lord Jesus (I Cor. 1:2). The English word *lord* derives from the concept of breadwinner – not a bad meaning. But Jesus doesn't come running into your arms when you call out "Breadwinner." But He comes running and embraces you when you call out His name. Intimacy is more, of course, than just a name. But it opens the door to slow dances, pillow whisperings and candlelight dinners – with Jesus.

It also activates love. God gave as many commandments in the Greek part of God's Book of Love as in the first part written in Hebrew. God is not against laws. He's against breaking them. That's sin. All these commands are summed up – but not done away – in the word *love*. The Big Ten sum up the two greatest laws – love God with all your being and love others.

Next to Jesus, it was probably John, the apostle of love, who understood that subject better than anyone. He knew how to activate love. After stressing that answers to prayer come when we obey the commandments, John summed up all the commandments of love. "This is His commandment, that we believe in the *name* of His Son Jesus Christ, and love one another, just as He commanded us" (I John 3:23).

The last-days bride will be composed mainly of some wise virgins who flow in love. They are called the church of Philadelphia. As the Greek name indicates, it is the church of brotherly love.

What sets this bride apart? Jesus whispers into her ear, "[You] have kept My word [not cherished traditions from King James translators], and *have not denied* **My name**" (Rev. 3:8).

He would say to His Bride today, "My name is not 'Lord.' My name is Jesus. I call you by your name. Call me by My name, My love. It shows Me that you love Me – that you think I'm special. It gives Me joy."

Every knee will one day bow before that name, the name above all names (Phil. 2:10). One day every human being that has ever lived will come to honor that name. Jesus asks of you His bride today, "Will *you* honor My name?"

He asks His Bride, "Is it not written: 'Whatever you do in word or deed, do all in the name of the Lord Jesus, giving thanks through Him to God the Father'? (Col. 3:17) Precious Bride, you cannot prove your love for Me by obeying My Word unless you use My name."

"Arise, shine," Bride of Jesus, for your Light has come. And "the lord" is not your Light. He will only take you into his penthouse suite that is anything but sweet. It lies in the path of darkness, sickness and death. You will be a blessed bride when you call on the name of Jesus. He's your Light. He will light up your life and dispel your darkness.

Say it. Say His name right now. Jesus. Jesus. Jesus.

In almost every language, saying that name opens your mouth and brings a little smile. Lord doesn't do it.

Saying it with meaning will bring more than a little smile to Jesus' Bride. And Jesus will break out in more than a smile. He will twirl around in the heavens with shouts of joy (Zeph. 3:17). And the only wrinkle on the face of His glorious, spotless Bride will be a cute little crease near her lips as she whispers His name – then sings and dances. She'll shout out soon the name of her Groom – "Jesus, Jesus, Jesus, I love you!"

12 Why Doesn't God Heal Me?

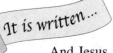

And Jesus ... spoke to them, saying, "All authority has been given to Me in heaven and on earth." ... [Our Father] ... seated us with Him in the heavenly places in Christ Jesus ... love is perfected with us, so that we may have confidence in the day of judgment; because as He is, so also are we in this world.

Mat. 28:18, Eph. 2:6 and I John 4:17

CHAPTER 13
Claiming All the Rights of Salvation

The name of Jesus is powerful. In Hebrew it has a multitude of meanings, the principal one being *salvation*. He died to save us – from much more than death.

But most Christians do not claim all the benefits Jesus has for them in that sacrifice. And so few believers have any inkling of the extent, power and fullness of the exciting meaning of the word *salvation*.

For the purpose of this book, a full technical explanation of all the Hebrew and Greek words and concepts of salvation is not feasible. I will, however, share what the Holy Spirit has revealed about the Biblical concept of salvation. *Yeshua* is the Hebrew word for salvation. And guess whose name that is? It is none other than the name of Jesus. There is only a slight variation in the personal form of the word.

Yes, Jesus *is* our Salvation. Salvation is in the name *Jesus*.

The meaning of *yeshua* or *Yeshua* is: "I am your Deliverance, Aid, Victory, Prosperity, Health, Help, Helper, Salvation, *Saving Health* or *Healing Power*, Welfare, your Freedom from sin."

129

13 Why Doesn't God Heal Me?

The Greek Septuagint[29] translates this word, notably in its first appearance in Genesis 49:18, by the Greek word from which comes the word *metamorphosis*. In other words, "I have waited for You to change my shape and form (spiritually) to be like You, God."

Teshua means "rescue, deliverance, a bringing to safety, salvation, victory."

The verb *yâsha'* or save implies "avenge, nurture, deliver, help, preserve, rescue, be in safety, *get glory*, give liberty and victory, *give prosperity, remove from tribulation* (i.e. *rapture*), bring into safety, open a gate, to be set free, save for victory." And Jesus is the great Liberator and Gate-opener.

Another word for salvation in Psalm 68:20 implies "opened wide to freedom, rapture away from evil."

We have already seen that the Greek *sozo* means more than to save. It also means to heal or make whole. This associates it with the all-encompassing and powerful Hebrew word *shalom*, which we will explore later.

Soteria in Greek means "my rescue, safety, deliverance, plan for saving, design to save, defense, peace of mind and heart, *health and salvation*."

Jesus and salvation are synonymous. Here are some of the exciting names of Jesus – our Salvation – that the Biblical words reveal in their fullness. And as we read them, let's claim the fullness of our salvation in the name Jesus: our Provider, Defender, Defender of Boundaries, Savior, Salvation, Protector, Rescuer (from all our troubles), Peace (including sound sleep), Welfare (well-being of our spirit, soul and body, as well as the well-being of our families), Life and Life-giver, Renewer, Revival, Reformer, *Healer*, *Health*, Prosperity (see "Debt, ending" and "Finances" in the Appendix), Help, Helper, Avenger, Victory, Liberty, Bondage-breaker, Rapturer (bring out of danger and into ecstasy with Him), Boundary, Form (in whose image we are made), Foundation, Aid, Strength, Safety, Preserver, Chief Warrior, Dancing King who rejoices over His spoil (us!), Rock, Commander-in-Chief, Change (from glory to glory), Wholeness (unity in body, spirit and soul), Assistance, Forgiveness, Designer (setting our plans and purposes), Keeper, Returner (of lost items), Restorer, Redeemer, *our Medicine*, *our Doctor*.

Yes, Jesus is our Medicine. When we take in communion His body and blood, we take medicine for our healing and health. Spiritually the wine actually becomes the blood of Jesus.

When we accept Jesus, we become new creations – Sons of God as Adam with

---

[29] The first and most important of a number of ancient translations of the Hebrew "Old Testament" into Greek is called the Septuagint. Ptolemy II (also known as Philadelphus, the king of Egypt, 285-247) desired a translation of the Jewish law for his famous library in Alexandria. The high priest Eleazer of Jerusalem sent 72 men, six from each tribe, to Egypt with a scroll of the Law. In 72 days each of them translated one section from this scroll and afterward jointly decided on the wording. This version became the Septuagint (the translation of the 70, abbreviated LXX). The exact agreement of the 72 copies clearly demonstrated the work's inspiration. The Pentateuch (Heb. *torah*, law or teaching, the first five books of the Bible) is generally thought to have been translated from Hebrew into Greek in Egypt around the time of Ptolemy II, ca. 280 B.C. The rest of the "Old Testament" was done at a later date.

Claiming All the Rights of Salvation 13

God's blood – blood type G in our veins. We accept divine, eternal life. God's presence in us gives divine life to our mortal bodies (Rom. 8:11). We get a divine blood transfusion.

Each time we take communion we do indeed get a fresh new supply of His blood added to us. Partaking of His body and blood renews Jesus' life in us (John 6:53-58). The body and blood of Jesus in communion build up our spirit man. His body gives us spiritual strength and muscle. His spiritual blood adds new life to our spirit man. We drink divine life and divine health. Jesus' blood is like medicine.

I will give an example of this, but I must first qualify it. The principle "according to your faith" must always be applied. We are not in the business of imposing God's ideal in a legalistic way.

One of our lady members of Freedom Church of God told this true story. She began to experience painful pink eye late one night. She would have gone to a pharmacy, but there was none open in her Edmonton suburb. She had decided to take communion. As she prepared it, the Holy Spirit spoke silently in her spirit, encouraging her to dip her finger into the communion wine – the blood of Jesus – and apply it to her eye. She did – and she was healed instantly!

The question that comes is this: if Christians are claiming the fullness of their salvation and Jesus as their Medicine, why do they need pharmaceutical potions?

As I write, a clever TV ad for a local pharmacy says: "As long as babies don't come potty-trained ... and wounds don't heal instantly ... and we have headaches, etc. ... there will always be _____ Drug Mart!" Admittedly, there may be legitimate reasons a Christian could use a pharmacy. Yet you have to wonder: what would happen if Christians began to trust God in everything for healing and stop going to Satan's world to get help for their physical maladies?

The only divine medicines mentioned in the Bible are the Word of God and a merry heart, as emphasized in Proverbs, as well as the healing emblems of communion. Fig potions were only used as physical signs and tests of obedience, not as remedies in divine healing. The only other medicine mentioned is in Revelation, where the word from which pharmacy is derived, *pharmakeia*, refers to witchcraft.[30]

The preceding comments may be a pill quite difficult to swallow for many readers, and as it was in my case, it may be difficult to swallow right away. I understand. Whatever pill you may choose to swallow at this point, may it be to you according to your faith and understanding. My purpose is not to legislate conduct regarding healing. Let the Holy Spirit guide you into all truth – in His time and/or your time. But remember, although God desires for us to eventually fol-

---

[30] *The New Strong's Exhaustive Concordance of the Bible*, James Strong, Thomas Nelson, Nashville, 1990. Strong defines this word, found in Revelation 9:21 and 18:23, as "medication ("pharmacy"), i.e. (by extens.) magic (lit. or fig.): – sorcery, witchcraft."

131

low His perfect will, He gives us free will. And even though we sing the song lyrics, "I want to be where You are," we don't always make it. So He meets us where we are.

As the above list shows, Jesus is more than our Medicine. He is also our Redeemer. He redeems us from the curses of sin, sickness and death. He also restores all that was lost in the Garden of Eden fiasco. That includes intimacy with God, walking in the glory of God, prosperity, health and complete provision as we walk fully in our anointing. Aside from the trials that build our character, Jesus wants to call everything in our lives "very good" as in the garden.

This glorious picture of salvation belongs to us. It is our Christian birthright. Yet how many Christians have claimed it? We must claim it, use it, have knowledge and understanding of it, embrace it and treasure it!

The fullness of Jesus' anointing is embodied in *yeshua* and *Yeshua*. Savor it. Seize it!

"Call Your Walls Salvation and Your Gates Praise"

How? Isaiah 60:18 begins to show us the way. Hebrew words and God's words have multiple meanings. This is not only a prophecy of Jesus' reign in the Millennium. It is a key to claiming the fullness of our salvation today!

"Violence will not be heard again in your land, nor devastation or destruction within your borders; but you will call your walls salvation, and your gates praise" (verse 18).

"Your land" includes your body, house, community, church, family, nation, business, finances and the air you breathe. "Devastation" includes floods, fires, hurricanes, tornadoes, earthquakes, droughts, hailstorms, asteroids – and even such plagues as crop-destroying insects and "mad cow disease." "Destruction" includes war, terrorism, vandalism and distress. "Your borders" includes all that is you, belongs to you, i.e. all that is described above as "your land."

"Call" implies proclaiming, speaking out with authority, making into law. "… with the *mouth* confession is made to *salvation*" (Rom. 10:10, KJV). "Walls" includes all your area of influence and authority, your armor – all that pertains to you. God says He will set up walls as our security or salvation, and once again, this is not only futuristic (Isa. 26:1). So we must declare Jesus and salvation to be the walls that surround our sphere of influence.

When we accept Jesus, we lay down our carnal rights as we are crucified with Jesus. Yet we lay down our life so we can gain it! And gaining it means we enter into and claim all the rights we inherit in salvation and Jesus.

God is saying to all of us: "It's time to start claiming your rights – your rights of salvation, your rights as brothers of Jesus Christ! It's high time My Children get 'violent' and start claiming the Kingdom and their Kingdom rights by force!

Claiming All the Rights of Salvation

The time has come to walk in the glory and power of the Kingdom – to walk in the fullness of salvation!"

You cannot accept salvation unless you accept Jesus. And if you reject or neglect salvation, or any part of it, you have rejected Jesus as your Savior. However, as John 9:41 and James 4:17 show, you will only be held fully accountable when you come to the knowledge and understanding of salvation in its fullness.

The U.S. Constitution preamble proudly proclaims the "inalienable rights" of Americans, who have become more and more unabashed in claiming their rights under the law. It's time we Christians began to boldly claim our "inalienable rights" as citizens of the Kingdom of God and ambassadors of His Kingdom on earth.

It's a lawyer's duty to inform his client of his rights. I recommend the best and smartest Jewish lawyer I know – Jesus!

Our Advocate, to use a more appropriate term for Jesus, has already read us our rights. They are in His Word. Sadly, most Christians haven't claimed them. Have you?

Deadly tragedies could have been averted in the past if we Christians had exercised our authority in Jesus. Tornadoes and hurricanes don't need to cause ravages in areas where believers do what Jesus did. He spoke peace to the storm – told it to be still. And He said in John 14:12 that we could do greater works!

If we do not do as Jesus did – with boldness and authority in His Name – *we are denying a part of our salvation*! Claiming our rights of salvation is not only our right: *it is our duty!*

Christians, it's time to get radical! When we accept Satan's lying symptoms of cancer – or even flu symptoms – we are denying our salvation. And we are denying Jesus our Savior and Healer!

Too many churches are full of people just sitting on the premises – not standing on the promises! It's time to sock it to the Devil and put him where he belongs, where Jesus put him – under our feet!

When the Devil tries to show you with his lies that Jesus is a liar and you weren't healed by His stripes 2,000 years ago, tell him where to park his rear end! Then claim your healing.

It's time to enjoy our full birthright celebration meal – and dessert! And a very special one, prepared at our table with lots of spirits poured over it – Devil flambé!

Finally, we are to call our gates "praise." That means we are to sing songs of thanks to Jesus for all He has done for us and all He is for us. These are keys for opening the windows of heaven and our own gates to allow the blessings to flow. Not understanding our salvation rights and the *lack of praise* shuts our gates and hinders or blocks God's blessings. (On this note of praise, see "Adversity" in the Appendix, as well as the steps to heartfelt prayer under "Prayers.")

13 Why Doesn't God Heal Me?

Praise unleashes power. Once God told Israel's army to do nothing but praise God. The result? The opposing armies began fighting each other and wiped each other out! Let's quit bellyaching about symptoms Satan puts on us. Let's stand on the promise of healing and begin to praise Jesus for it! Healing is our right. Let's claim it!

Which do you prefer: suffering for three weeks with flu symptoms – or praising Jesus and celebrating your healing for a much shorter time so you can be quickly rid of Satan's symptoms? Sickness is wrong. Health is right.

And the blessings of salvation are also our right – *all* the blessings! Prosperity and health and victory are our rights. Let's claim them!

Understanding our rights of salvation keeps Satan from stealing our blessings. How sad it is to see so many Christians weakly whimpering while the Devil steals their health and prosperity – sometimes even accepting it as from God or blaming Him for it.

We should shout, on the contrary, "Thief, thief!" and immediately reclaim our blessings and promises in the mighty name of our Restorer – Jesus (see "Prayer of Restoration" in the Appendix). He expects us to do so. He even requires it!

The Devil will not like this chapter. It spells the end of the writing of his chapter in the lives of so many Christians today. But it will only enrage him if we heed it!

It is written ...

> ... sin is crouching at the door; and its desire is for you, but you must master it ... You ... have delivered us into the [consuming] power of our iniquities ... sin shall not be master over you, for you are not under law but under grace [God's empowerment to avoid sin] (mastery medley).

> Gen. 4:7b, Isa. 64:7b – AMP and Rom. 6:14

CHAPTER 14
Defeating the Power of Sin

When you know who you are in Christ and what your subsequent rights are – and only then – will you be able to defeat the formidable foe described in this chapter. This "beast" won't overwhelm you when you understand its nature and origin.

Some may nevertheless feel overwhelmed when they read all the hindrances the Holy Spirit has revealed. I believe that's why He has also unmasked the main culprit of those many hindrances. It is *Satan's secret weapon: the power of sin.*

We tend to think of sin as a verb. The Bible, however, shows the importance of seeing it as a *noun.* The first mention of a word in God's Book is important to note, for it holds a key to its meaning. Let's see where the word *sin* appears first in the Bible.

It's in Genesis 4:7. God tells Cain: "… sin is crouching at the door; and its desire is for you, but you must master it."

Sin is not a verb here. It is not even speaking of one particular sin. God is introducing sin as a living force, an evil power working in man.

This evil power reared its ugly head early in human history. When Adam

14 Why Doesn't God Heal Me?

sinned, Satan had the right and the power to "rewire" – even "hardwire" – his brain. The pathways of sin were indelibly etched in his brain. The Bible shows that all men were subsequently born in sin.

Now what does that mean? It signifies, first of all, that all men were then born with a sinful nature. Adam's spirit was alive until he sinned. Then his spirit died. His innocent nature was replaced by an evil nature – the nature of the one who had caused him to sin.

Upon conversion and baptism, our dead spirits inherited from Adam spring to life! They inherit eternal life and thus cannot die. The old, sinful nature is replaced by God's nature (II Pet. 1:4) – the mind of Christ. The "old man" is replaced by the new. That is the vital, transforming truth so few Christians grasp. That's why I repeat it.

Even when we do come to realize our new identity and nature, there is still something else we need to conquer. And that knowledge of our identity is extremely important in that conquest.

What we must conquer is the *power of sin*. And what exactly is that living entity inside us?

Before we come to know Jesus, our sinful nature and the power of sin team up to make our lives miserable. Some sins produce an initial pleasurable response in our brains. These sins, especially pet sins, sear patterns or burn pathways in our brains.

Even when we receive Jesus and our new nature, the power of sin is still there. It triggers thought bullets that activate the old flesh pattern burnt into the brain through years of sinning. It cannot establish new pathways unless we commit new sins.

The problem is this: although the thought bullets sent by the power of sin are not really our thoughts, we begin to speak as though these were our thoughts. "I have these lustful thoughts," we may say. In this way, we begin to speak these thought bullets into life as law. They then have the power to affect us. We will deal with the solution shortly, but first we must deal with a prevalent lie among Christians today – a lie that makes the power of sin overpowering.

Christians Do Not Have a Sinful Nature!

Many passages (e.g. Gal. 2:20; Eph. 2:5-6) show that when we accepted Jesus, we were crucified with Him. Our old sin nature died and was buried at baptism. We were then resurrected with Jesus to newness of life – a new nature. But what does it mean to be crucified?

The subject of the cross we bear is a misunderstood one. Jesus tells us to take up our cross and follow Him (Luke 14:27).

How many rights does a crucified man have? None! He surrenders all. When we are crucified with Jesus, we give the controls to Him. We give up our rights and

136

Defeating the Power of Sin

let Him live through us. But why do we have to take up our cross if we have already been crucified?

Is sickness a cross we must bear as Christians, as many believe? Is poverty or an unhappy marriage a cross we have to bear?

No! These things are not God's perfect will for us. Jesus paid the penalty so we could live an abundant life in every way. Our cross is not a punishment or penance we impose on ourselves. We need not accept any of Satan's gifts. Yet with our mouths we have the power to speak those gifts into law. We also have the power to speak God's Word – health and prosperity – over ourselves.

So what does it mean, then, to take up our cross? It simply means to abandon our life to Jesus. It means giving up our life in order to receive Jesus' life in us. It means laying down our agendas, our lives, our rights and embracing Jesus as our life (Luke 9:24). There are different words for life in Greek. We surrender the carnal aspect of our life for the righteous life of Jesus.

Jesus lives in us. And that changes everything.

A true Christian – one who has really accepted Jesus, been born again – has Jesus' nature in him. He hates sin and hates to sin. He feels bad, guilty when he does.

An unbeliever or sinner, on the other hand, often sins because he really doesn't realize how dangerous sin truly is. And depending on the kind of sin, he can even enjoy sinning. Sin becomes a fatally addictive habit. Satan's world is full of unregenerate people who are constantly inventing new, innovative ways to sin.

This was decidedly not the case with the apostle Paul in Romans 7. This passage has been grossly misunderstood.

The Romans 7 "Sindrome"

Now would be a good time to open your Bibles to Romans 7:14-25 and read of this sin syndrome for yourself. Some translations, including the NIV, mistranslate the Greek word *sarx*, which refers to the flesh. It does not refer to the sinful nature, which the Bible clearly shows no longer dwells in the Christian. Believers still do, of course, have a body of flesh. That includes the physical brain. The power of sin hardwires the brain and thus affects every part of the body.

So the flesh is still a factor, but that old nature is dead. And yet Satan has done a number on Christians with a lie he has even put in their Bibles through mistranslation. He has convinced theologians that Christians still have a sinful nature. That brings them out of the Kingdom of Light and into the Kingdom of Darkness. They curse themselves as sinners and thus give the Devil permission to cause them to act out the part.

If the old man did not die, then Jesus did not die. They were crucified on the same cross (Rom. 6:2-6; Gal. 2:20). And Satan does not have the power to bring the old man back to life!

137

14   Why Doesn't God Heal Me?

It was the sinful nature – not the flesh – that died on the cross with Jesus. It is the flesh we must crucify now – by the power of the Spirit. The Spirit is at war with the flesh.

Romans 7:15 would read quite differently if we had two natures at war with one another. Paul's schizophrenic dilemma would have read somewhat like this: "I am practicing what I love to do. When I feel like sinning, I just love to sin. When I feel like obeying God, I love that too." That's not what he said. His real, inner nature hated sin. The enemy was not his old nature.

As we have seen in the chapter on identity, Paul had not fully understood at this point in his life his true identity in Christ. He did understand, however, that he had a new nature (called "inner man" in verse 22). He says in verse 17 that *he* – the real Paul in his perfected spirit – hated sin. The "I" he uses there clearly refers to his new nature. And the old went out when the new came in (II Cor. 5:17).

Paul's battle couldn't have been with an old nature (verse 17). It was history! The culprit was sin, i.e. the power of sin in his flesh, especially in his brain.

Paul even calls this power of sin a law. It is to be distinguished, though, from the law of sin and death in 8:2. The former only involves sin. The latter involves both sin and its consequences – sickness, poverty and death.

So Paul shows that we are not flying solo when we sin. Our copilot is the power of sin.

On the next page is a chart that shows the contrasting actions of the power of sin versus the Holy Spirit.

The Salvation Trinity

Many of us have not dealt effectively with the power of sin because only part of God's solution has been accepted. Our triune God created a threefold process for our salvation and sanctification, each stage intensified in power.

First, we accept Jesus – His death on the cross for us. At that moment our old sinful life or nature dies. It died, in fact, with Him 2,000 years ago on the cross when He died. Crucified with Him, we receive at the same time the seed of eternal life.

According to Romans 6, something different and special happens at baptism by immersion, the second and vital stage of salvation. Verse 4 says we are buried with Him. The old nature dies when we accept Jesus, but after we accept Jesus we learn from His Word that we need to be baptized. We surrender our wills to God and actually bury the old nature so the Holy Spirit can work with our heart, mind and will in a new way.

In addition, we are resurrected to "newness of life." You can't be resurrected, as Jesus was, until you're buried, right? We are, of course, made spiritually new at conversion. But our new life is only in seed form. Our newness and ability to change our character and sinful habits etched in our brains by the power of sin are

138

Defeating the Power of Sin

Holy Spirit	Power of Sin
Teaches you the truth	Teaches you lies
Credits the Father and Jesus for the good and blames Satan for the bad	Credits luck, circumstances and blames God for the bad
Interprets and validates all of God's Word	Picks and chooses only parts of the Word
Validates the power of God	Portrays God as impotent
Praises the Father and Jesus for their loving strength	Portrays Jesus as weak, effeminate and sickly
Teaches that following God's Word is best for you	Teaches that following cultural correctness is best for you
Heightens sensitivity to sin and God	Dulls sensitivity to sin and God
Indwells your spirit	Indwells your body
Gives thoughts to your mind	Manipulates your brain
Persuades you	Nags at you
Lights up the path of righteousness	Darkens your path in unrighteousness
Convicts you of sin so you'll repent	Condemns you for sinning
Uses valid guilt feelings	Uses false guilt feelings
Shows God as a loving Father	Portrays God as an unfair tyrant
Builds intimacy with God	Shows God as a terror
Draws you to God	Drives you from God
Always tells the truth	Lies and distorts the truth
Guides with the true context of Scripture	Misinterprets Scripture to hide the truth
Encourages you to speak God's Word into circumstances	Encourages you to speak Satan's words into your life
Builds faith in God	Destroys faith in God

limited. That's why Paul reserves the term *resurrection* for our baptism experience. A fuller life – a resurrection life – occurs at baptism.

This obedient act causes the seed of eternal life to sprout. It is the opening up of the reality of eternal life. It opens the door to a richer, more abundant life – a life ruled more completely by God.

Baptism is not merely a symbol. It is a supernaturally anointed ceremony – packed with power! Our decision to surrender our will to God at baptism produces power to change that conversion alone does not afford. The baptismal surrender brings the flesh under the control of the resurrected spirit man.

The third stage of sanctification is the baptism of the Holy Spirit. This is a complete infilling of the Holy Spirit. As we were baptized or fully immersed in water at baptism, so we are baptized or fully immersed in the Holy Spirit, receiv-

Why Doesn't God Heal Me?

ing full power from on high to be His witnesses. He offers to those who seek His gifts a special, personal prayer language to give them greater intimacy with the Father, enabling them to grow to even greater sanctification, if they use God's gifts properly.

The Tongues Question: To Speak or Not to Speak

Please understand this controversial subject. Nowhere does the Bible say, "You shall know them by their tongues." It says, "You will know them by their *fruits*" (Mat. 7:20). The proof of being baptized in the Holy Spirit is a completely changed *life* – a life overflowing with God's love.

That is not, however, an excuse to limit God or ourselves. Every Christian has the gift of tongues in him or her. It is simply a matter of allowing it to manifest.

The main reason it doesn't usually manifest quickly – or ever – is false doctrine: many churches teach it isn't necessary. It is clearly a Biblical manifestation enjoined by Jesus (Mark 16:17) and practiced by Paul (I Cor. 14:18). Paul desired that all the Corinthians speak in tongues (I Cor. 14:5). That is God's desire for the whole church. But if men have taught you that it isn't God's will, it will be difficult to manifest it.

Speaking in tongues will be a part of the end-time reformation, since the partial fulfillment of Joel 2:28 in Acts 2 involved this gift, as well as the more important gift of prophesying (Acts 2:17; I Cor. 14:5).

Acts 2 speaks of only one of the three kinds of tongues, that of the manifestation of human languages unknown naturally to the speaker (I Cor. 13:1). In this case people heard the disciples speak in the language those people knew, a language unknown to the speaker. Modern disciples have both *spoken out* languages they had not learned and been *heard* by those who listened in the listener's language.

That happened to a friend of mine who was counseling a Greek lady on the phone. He spoke in English, but she heard him speak in perfect Greek! What's more, he heard her, an immigrant who spoke only broken English, respond in excellent English. The expression, "It's all Greek to me," isn't always true in the Holy Spirit.

The second type of tongues is an angelic language (I Cor. 13:1). It is normally manifested in intercessory prayer and spiritual warfare. Spiritual warfare can often evoke a different and stronger, sometimes more staccato language. That warfare language can be either in tongues of men or angels.

Demons cannot understand the second and third types of tongues. If you pray aloud in your native tongue or another human language, they understand and can form plans to counter your prayer. The other tongues put them into a state of confusion.

The third type of tongues is the intimate prayer language the Holy Spirit gives us to talk with our Heavenly Father. In the midst of the valley of sore affliction or on the mountaintop of inexpressible joy, words often fail us. What a blessing from the precious Holy Spirit to be able to express ourselves in a language too deep for human words (Rom. 8:26-27). This type of tongues is like a fire inside – a driving unction.

Do you begin to see why Satan hates this gift from the Holy Spirit? He doesn't want us to have all of God – because then we'll counter all his attacks. He has cleverly convinced most of Christendom that tongues are either unnecessary or are dangerous manifestations of charismatic chaos. Corinth was indeed in chaos, but the problems the church experienced involved public tongues in church and had nothing to do with the private exercise of this important gift.

How Much of God Do You Want?

Our precious Friend the Holy Spirit has over 200 gifts for us. Too many Christians want only part of Jesus and part of the Holy Spirit. It must grieve His sensitive heart! He has given us tools to grow and serve others and grow nearer to the heart of Jesus and our Father (I Cor. 14:4; I Cor. 12).

Do we refuse to receive all of Him because Satan has caused some few to misuse or counterfeit some of His gifts? Satan is delighted! God has so much more to give us if we would only receive.

What part of God do we not want?

If we don't receive His gifts, we will still spend eternity with God. But we're limiting Him. And we are depriving ourselves of present and future rewards. Satan rejoices. Why? We are not allowing the third Person of the Trinity to do His full work in the final part of the trinity of sanctification.

As we go through this threefold process, we become victorious over the power of sin. We become more fully in line with God's perfect will for our lives. We open up the opportunity to receive and bless others with all of God's blessings, including healing.

We do not need to let the power of sin defeat us – no matter how bad our past may have been. We do, nevertheless, need to implement God's solution.

And that begins with a simple prayer of faith. Surrender your old thought patterns to Jesus. Turn all those seared pathways in your brain over to Him. Ask Him to go back and heal all those old memories and unholy hardwiring in your brain. He's the great Healer.

Thank Jesus for healing you and walk in your new identity. Read aloud the ongoing solution God gives in Romans 6:11-14. God doesn't give us grace so we can let ourselves go wild and yield to the flesh and sin. Grace is principally the unmerited, enabling power God freely gives us to *overcome* sin – not to wallow in it! Yield daily to the power of the Holy Spirit.

The power of God is greater – far greater – than the power of sin. Use it. The victory is yours!

14 Why Doesn't God Heal Me?

It is written...

[Jesus says]... "'I take no pleasure in the death of the wicked ... Why then will you die, O house of Israel?'" ... "Those who are sickly you [shepherds, pastors] have not strengthened, the diseased you have not healed" ... since you have not hated bloodshed, therefore bloodshed will pursue you."

Ezek. 33:11; 34:4a; 35:6b

CHAPTER 15
Hate Sickness like You Hate Sin!

Almost all of the basic ideas in this book have come directly from the Holy Spirit. At one point I had added a prologue, with the emphasis on the word "I." The Holy Spirit said, "The book is Mine. The prologue is yours." I got rid of that prologue.

Other Spirit-filled Christians have prayed and/or fasted over the contents of this book. I believe that the final result is what the Holy Spirit wants to tell the body of Christ. It is not my book. It is His. You can attribute any motivation, good or bad, to that true statement.

We are, of course, a body. The Holy Spirit gives different revelations to different ones in the church. He wants us to learn from each other.

I first got the idea for what became the title of this chapter from a seasoned healing servant of God. The Holy Spirit revealed this truth to me through Benny Hinn at a partners' conference in Cincinnati, Ohio.

"Hate sickness like you hate sin!" That inspired phrase struck me. But something even stronger and/or stranger struck me more.

Hate sickness like you hate sin? Yes, that's important all right. But as I wrote

143

that phrase, a disturbing question stopped my train of thought in its tracks. "Wait a minute," I said. "How many Christians today really hate sin?" We all do in our spirits. But have we renewed our minds to actually loathe sin?

And how many pastors have the courage to boldly cry aloud and, to paraphrase Isaiah 58:1, "show my people their sins!" Precious few. That happens to be our anointing as a church and as a ministry.

Thank God for John Bevere, who wrote two excellent books dealing with the subject of the fear of God, and others like him. They are in a popularity contest – for the popularity that counts – God's! "Come hell or high water," they are going to give 'em you know what – so they won't go you know where! But as I explained in Chapter 2, it's not the blinded non-believers that are in the most trouble. It's those who do see – Christians!

Fear of God Necessary

Some Christians shy away from the concept of fearing God. They fear a fear religion. That is not what godly fear is all about.

The fear of God is a healthy reverence and respect for His power. He calls Himself a consuming fire. He is a loving Father, but nonetheless a Father who demands respect. A Father who chastens those who disobey. God demands total loyalty.

Before I go on, I must explain the word *fear*. I can only speak with authority on the two languages I speak fluently, English and French. Yet I believe anyone who has begun the mammoth task of tasting the untold richness of Biblical Hebrew would agree that its expansive, conceptual nature leaves our limited linear languages languishing before its power. Many of our Western languages are based on precepts, whereas some of the Middle Eastern and Oriental languages deal with the whole picture. These picture languages, as demonstrated by the word studies in this book, prove the saying, "A picture is worth a thousand words." When no qualifier exists in the immediate context, a word in Biblical Hebrew can expand to mean much more than the literal translation of the word. Context plays a major role in the shades of meaning. And we must always look at the context of the entire Bible.

Here's the key. It's found in a verse using the Greek word for *fear* (*phŏbŏs*), more closely resembling our linear definition. "There is no fear in love; but perfect love casts out fear, because fear involves punishment, and the one who fears is not perfected in love" (I John 4:18).

Perfect love means keeping God's law of love perfectly, with no sin. Sin brings fear and cowardice. Love engenders security and courage.

We may not be literally without sin. Yet when we know we are loved by God and love Him, ourselves and others, we walk in love. We may stumble, but we repent quickly and are washed in Jesus' blood. In its linear meaning, fear is not a

Hate Sickness like You Hate Sin!

factor with us. We obey our Father because we love Him, not because we're scared of Him.

Sin brought fear upon Adam. Sin brought fear upon rebellious Israel. That's not what God wants from us. He wants us to obey because we love Him.

But here's where the conceptual meaning of *fear* comes in. Even under the New Covenant blessing of the blood of Jesus to wash us from sin and the resultant fear, loving awe and respect of our great God is necessary. It's best to forget the word *fear*. If we do use it in its broader sense, let's think: loving awe, reverence and respect. To fear God means to obey Him out of loving, reverential awe.

God is Love. And He is also a consuming fire (Heb. 12:29). His fire of judgment is a part of His love. We must respect that side of Him.

There is no fear in love, but there is respect. Respect for Jesus the Judge. Respect for Jesus the Consuming Fire.

We Christians are being judged now. We must realize we are accountable for our actions. More and more professing Christians are playing footsy with the Devil. They blend right in with the world. And that seems okay to them. They have lost a proper fear of God in its conceptual sense.

The wicked shrink in terror before the powerful glory of the holy God. Even the demons believe in God and tremble in terror of Him and His judgment (James 2:19). But does trembling only apply to the wicked?

No. Although not in the same fearful way, God tells us to work out our salvation with "fear and trembling" (Phil. 2:12). We respect God. We know we are responsible for our actions. We reap what we sow.

Wise virgins, well-oiled with Holy Spirit love will reap a harvest of blessing. "Greasy grace virgins" who have no true spiritual oil will slide head first into the wall of God's judgment. Beware, foolish virgins! *You won't bathe in the waters of God's blessings if you don't respect the fire of His judgment.* Even great men of God in the Bible had to learn that lesson.

David was a man after God's own heart. And yet he had periods where he got stuck in sin. That's why he said, "My flesh trembles for fear of You, and I am afraid of Your judgments" (Ps. 119:120).

Jesus said not to fear man but God who has the power to cast body and soul into hell (Mat. 10:28). Fearing God is a healthy respect based on love and reality. It's like the old TV show *Truth or Consequences*. You walk in the truth or there are consequences. Many Christians live today like they expect no consequences tomorrow.

We must all appear before the judgment seat of Jesus and be recompensed for our deeds in this life, whether good or bad (II Cor. 5:10). Paul is referring to us who have received the Holy Spirit in this age (verse 5). The vast majority will be judged later in a second general resurrection to physical life. We are being judged *now* for our degree of reward in the future Kingdom.

God is fair. He is just. Jesus judges in righteousness and love.

15 Why Doesn't God Heal Me?

Those who do not realize God has a judgment seat as well as a mercy seat cannot understand the full counsel of God. Thankfully, we can go to the mercy seat every time we miss the mark. But we also need to become established in Jesus' righteousness. Our love and respect for God will lead us to say no to sin. Blessings will pour.

Healing is one of those blessings. Interestingly enough, although more than physical healing is meant, Malachi 4:2 connects the fear of God with healing. "But for you who fear My name, the sun of righteousness will arise with healing in its wings; and you will go forth and skip about like calves from the stall."

Three nuggets of healing truth are embedded in this verse. The skipping image reminds us of children at play. It's a powerful picture of joy and praise. Malachi prophesies that respect for the name of Jesus rather than His titles will bring the final healing revival. This end-time prophecy also teaches an important lesson emphasized in these pages: vigorous physical and spiritual health and healing come from the proper fear of God, which will be revived in these last days.

Those who have had good physical fathers certainly loved them. Yet they made sure to avoid arousing Dad's justified ire. Papa had the power to punish his children. So does God. And He does so because of His love.

But we are to be more than children. Mature sons and daughters obey out of love and respect, not in cringing fear.

Love without reverent, respectful awe is incomplete. True love involves respect and obedience. And they pave the path of intimacy with our Father. A disobedient child is not on good terms with his father. Disrespect builds walls.

Today's Christian generation talks a lot about the love of God. Yet alas, there is little true, balanced teaching about the fear of God.

Two Preachers Who Agree

Love and fear are big words. But the church doesn't understand either. And yet the conceptual idea of fearing God in Hebrew connects with New Covenant love.

Let's jigsaw two verses from the Hebrew and Greek parts of God's Book of Love and solve the puzzle.

Listen to a famous preacher: "The conclusion, when all has been heard, is: fear God and keep His commandments, because this applies to every person [NIV – "is the whole duty of man"]. For God will bring every act to judgment, everything which is hidden, whether it is good or evil" (Eccl. 12:13-14).

Now listen to the most famous Preacher ever: "If you love Me, you will keep My commandments" (John 14:15).

Solomon and Jesus agree. Jesus is, of course, the Word, and Solomon's words are His words. Did you notice that the words are different, yet the same. When we "fear" God we show it by obeying Him. And when we love God, we show it the same way.

Hate Sickness like You Hate Sin! 15

The conclusion, when all has been heard, is this: the Hebrew *fear* is the equivalent of New Covenant *love*. A mature New Covenant believer is motivated only by love toward God. He loves and respects God enough to obey Him.

Those who say the law is done away, or live like they believe it's done away, are saying that love is done away. And since God is Love, He is done away too. And in a practical sense, He is indeed done away in their lives.

The church has been lulled into "la-la land" because God has not intervened powerfully in judgment. It may take immature, cringing fear before some wake up.

Sometimes God delays judgment. But when divine order is established, His glory is revealed. At those times God judges quickly and severely. Such was the case when Uzzah touched the Ark, which housed God's glory. But that was also true in the glory days of the New Covenant. Ananias and Saphira lied to God in Acts 5 – and He swiftly struck them dead.

The glory of God will soon be manifested in the final and greatest reformation in history. God's glory will fall – and then His judgment.

But even in normal times, God is not mocked. He is not a candy vending machine that pours out the goodies when we pull the lever. He works on the principle of exchange. He requires correct change – including the necessary change in our lives. He is a just and fair God. If we give our all to Him in unconditional surrender and obedience, He blesses us.

The fear of God leads to obedience. That is why there are so many blessings attached to the fear of God in the Bible. Here is a brief sampling: prolonged days, sleep, riches, honor, life, guidance, protection, mercy, compassion, instruction, the meeting of our needs and desires, and keeping us alive in famine. God delights in those who fear Him.

Healing Hindrances and Godly Reverence

One of the most striking benefits of godly fear is directly related to the subject of healing. Proverbs 3:7-8 says: "... Fear [YHVH – the Eternal] and turn away from evil. It will be *healing* to your body and refreshment to your bones." So the fear of God is directly related to health and healing. If the fear of God promotes healing, then the absence of it may cause Him to withhold it.

Many of the hindrances to healing are simply a lack of godly fear. This revelation of hindrances and of the fear of God probably alarms some Christians. It may sound like fear religion and legalism. It may even sound condemning or judgmental. I do understand their erroneous conclusion.

Having been a pastor for over thirty years, I realize that it is not wise to judge another Christian. I was quite ill myself in the past, and I have incurred the condemnation of fellow ministers and members of the flocks I have shepherded. I have been judged for being sick, as if I were a lesser minister and a lesser Christian.

147

So I understand the reticence of pastors to accept the concept of hindrances to healing. Yes, it does look like a judgment, doesn't it? And we who have been judged harshly are slow to point the finger at those who are ill. After all, isn't their burden enough? In my case, I was sick and tired of being sick and tired, and sick and tired of being judged. God is our judge. And He judged me less severely than some, but more severely than others. I had one of the most serious hindrances it is possible to have.

Some may have thought: "Oh, he's our pastor. We can't judge him." And we shouldn't condemn. But my Father in heaven judged me severely. And if He had not chastened me severely, I don't like to think what my fate might have been. Had someone come to me in love and told me my hindrance to healing was an unforgiving heart, it would have saved me 12 years of agony and family tragedy.

That is one of the reasons I am not concerned about flak for giving a list of hindrances. They may appear judgmental, but they could save your life. They saved mine.

But the most important reason for listing these hindrances is that they come from *God*. This is not a list I came up with in my fertile imagination or because of a legalistic mindset. It is divine revelation. And both the hindrances and the principle of hindrances are found in the Word of God. Let's see evidence of this as we examine one of the power passages through different lenses.

Psalm 103: God's Sovereignty versus Covenant Conditions

Psalm 103 eloquently portrays God's benefits to His Children – including healing. Our body doesn't have to take a beating because Jesus was beaten for us. But there's a catch. Those benefits are not automatic.

God is a covenant-keeping God, but He expects us to be faithful to our part of the covenant. That includes the covenant in Jesus' blood.

Simply stated, hindrances represent the breaching of the details and conditions of the covenants God has made with His people.

In general, God heals the unsaved because of His mercy and the saved because of His covenant. But we must keep our part of the agreement. As the sovereign God, He may choose to bless and heal His Children because of His mercy, but He would prefer to see us correct our hindrances and boldly claim the promises.

Sadly, many Christians use the sovereignty of God as a supposed reason to explain why He doesn't always heal. God is indeed sovereign. He's supremely in charge. "… He does whatever He pleases" (Ps. 115:3).

But even though He is unlimited in power, He has chosen to limit Himself in a certain way. He expresses His will through His mouth, and when He speaks, His Word becomes law. He has written His Word for us to know His will, which the Bible says is always to heal. And He has bound Himself by

Hate Sickness like You Hate Sin!

His covenants with His people (Ps. 111:5).

God says emphatically, "My covenant I will not violate, Nor will I alter the utterance of My lips" (Ps. 89:34). The penalty for covenant-breaking on either side is death. And since God cannot die, He must fulfill His covenant promises. He cannot lie, so He is obligated to fulfill His Word. The sovereign God has declared that He will not act or speak outside the bounds of His covenant.

But we are also bound by the covenants. And we must speak and act according to those covenants. God expects us to remind Him of His covenants (Neh. 1:5). He even expects us to make demands upon Him according to the covenants (Gen. 18:22-33; 19:29).

When we glorify Satan's symptoms, we are speaking outside the covenant. If we refuse to obey the conditions, death is the result. And sickness is part of the way of sin and death. Jesus expects us to follow Him through the covenant loop of love. Both we and Jesus are bound by a blood brother covenant. We must choose to obey!

Bound by His covenant Word, Jesus cannot fulfill His covenant promises for those blood Brothers and Sisters who refuse to obey Him. Psalm 103:11 makes it clear: "... so great is His lovingkindness toward those who *fear* Him [*obey Him out of an attitude of love, awe, and respect*]."

Oooh! So there are conditions?

Your loving grandfather may leave you a million dollars in his will. He may also attach a few strings or conditions that relate to whether or not you receive the money and/or how you must use it. Even the old TV show, *The Millionaire*, gave conditions to keeping the cash.

Jesus Christ – in His will or testament – has freely given us eternal life and offered us many blessings under the New Covenant in His blood.

God's people have been destroyed through sickness and death because of a lack of knowledge (Hos. 4:6). They have chosen to be ignorant of the covenants! As this verse shows, the priests or pastors have not taught them their covenant obligations, and the people have not searched the Scriptures to discover them.

What glorious promises are contained in the covenants! And yet God's own people have chosen to remain "strangers to the covenants of promise" (Eph. 2:12).

If your father dies and has left you $10 million in his will, but you don't know about it, you are left without a penny. You need to know about it, and go to the authorities with written proof in hand, claiming what is your due. The same is true with the written covenant agreement in God's Word. We must quote it back to Him, claiming boldly, "By the blood of Jesus, this is my right!"

These glorious covenant promises – including eternal life – are our right. But God's Instruction Book makes it clear that we can lose out. We must continually yield to God and choose His way so we may endure to the end and make our salvation sure (Mat. 24:13). Our covenant blessings on the way to that final salvation are also conditional.

A "Fare" Choice

You might say that God gives us a choice. We can fly the Christian skies on economy fare or first class. Only those Christians who fully yield to God get to sip champagne and enjoy the extra legroom.

Canadian comedians Wayne and Schuster did a priceless skit years ago to show the difference between first and second class. Wayne was flying economy class. A fat, ugly, sloppily dressed hostess dragged by, angrily dishing out a scoop of cold beans into the paper plates of the economy passengers. No frills – but some spills.

Wayne peeked with envy through the first class curtain. What a spectacle! There was Schuster – surrounded by a bevy of beautiful blondes, dancing as he sipped champagne, serenaded by professional musicians.

At the end of the skit – and the flight – the voice of the captain boomed out to the cheap seat holders: "Economy passengers please deplane now." Wayne was the last to leave. As he approached the exit door, he heard these chilling words over the speaker: "We would like to inform our distinguished first class guests that we will be landing in Los Angeles in approximately ten minutes."

The first class passengers were distinguished – and those in economy were extinguished in a free fall. No frills – and lots of chills. It's not quite the same when it comes to God's blessings. But second class is still second class. God wants us to have all the privileges of first class travel in our earthly flight.

We can be as close to God as we want. It's our choice. And our just and fair God blesses us accordingly. Jesus has already paid for our first class fare, but being fair, He expects us to yield fully to Him in order to enjoy unhindered blessings.

"Why Doesn't God Heal Me?": The *Wrong* Question!

Yes, God does *allow* us to be sick, broke and downtrodden if we choose that condition by our degree of commitment. "Why doesn't God heal me?" is not really the right question. "Why have I not sought God earnestly enough to see where I may need to change my ways? Where am I not in harmony with His will in my life? Why am I blaming God when the answer has been in His Word for me to read?"

It's another sad rerun. Read it in Ezekiel 18:25. Jesus quotes the house of Israel, the believers, who say, "The way of the [Eternal] is not right." Then He speaks: "Hear now, O house of Israel! Is *My* way not right? Is it not *your* ways that are not right?"

Psalm 103 praises God for His benefits, but continues to lay down conditions for the believers in verses 17 and 18: "But the lovingkindness of [Jesus] is from everlasting to everlasting to those who *fear Him*, and His righteousness to children's children, To those who **keep His covenant** and remember His *precepts*." The NIV adds, "… *obey* His precepts."

Hate Sickness like You Hate Sin!

Psalm 91, another psalm full of awesome promises, also gives conditions. We must be intimate with God, dwelling in the "shelter" or "secret place" of the Most High (verse 1). We must also set our love upon Him and know His name (verse 14).

This intimacy is so important to healing that I have dedicated the next chapter to the subject. Amos asks, "Can two walk together unless they be agreed?" (Amos 3:3). To be intimate, we must agree with God by obeying Him.

Obedience is so important. As Galatians 6:7 says, "Do not be deceived, God is not mocked; for whatever a man sows, this he will also reap." It may sound judgmental, but it is true: if we are not fully reaping God's blessings, there is something lacking in our sowing.

That lack of proper planting may involve a misunderstanding on our part. But that is not God's fault. He wants us to correct faulty thinking to be in harmony with the mind of Christ.

Some may protest to God, saying, "How am I supposed to know all these hindrances?" God could well reply, "You call yourself Christian, do you? Then why haven't you been studying My Word? Those hindrances have been there all along!"

Thankfully, though, God is merciful. In this end-time He is now revealing to His precious Children how to correct hindrances in thought and deed that have been depriving them of blessing and healing.

When God speaks of disobedience that has hindered us, He is obviously saying there are *laws* we have either ignored or willfully disobeyed. These hindrances refer to many of those laws. The fact that God is emphasizing a number of His laws that have been flaunted or overlooked does not mean He is a picky legalist. He promises us blessings and benefits, but He expects us to obey in order to reap the benefits.

Hate sickness like you hate sin! Awake to righteousness, and sin not. Resist the Devil and he and his works of sin and sickness will flee from you!

How Would GOD Deal with Sin and Sickness?

How did Jesus deal with sin and sickness? Whether you're wearing a WWJD bracelet or not, you need to ask yourself, "What *would* Jesus do?" What would He do if Satan gave Him even one second of lying symptoms of sickness? Whatever He would do, that's what you would or should do.

Why? It's simple. You are one in spirit with Him. You have His mind. You are "another speaking spirit" made to be exactly like your Father and like Jesus. You are a spirit clothed in an earth suit so you can rule on this physical earth as you speak out God's Word as the righteousness of God.

Deal with sickness according to the truth of Genesis 1:26 and John 10:34. Only a little lower than the Most High, you are a God on this earth. Are you going to

151

Why Doesn't God Heal Me?

submit to the conquered loser and liar and get sick and die "like mere men" (Ps. 82:6, NIV) – or admit the truth God says about you and resist sickness as the member of the God Family that you are?

The way of sickness and death is the broad way that even many Christians follow today (Mat. 7:13-14). The narrow way of resistance to Satan's symptoms requires sacrifice. Are you willing to pay the price? Will you walk with Jesus along the narrow path that leads to life and health?

Satan tried to give Jesus symptoms of sickness since He was tempted in all things as we are. But Jesus said, "No way, Devil!" Deal with sickness – and sin – like Jesus. After all, He is your Brother – and you're just like Him! Yes, hear it again. It's the gospel truth – and a part of the gospel most have never heard (I John 4:17). *You're just like Jesus!*

Don't tolerate sickness! It doesn't belong to you! "You are gods" on this earth.

"Why doesn't God heal me?" For many, the answer is this: "I haven't lived up to who I am. I haven't accepted my identity. I haven't spoken out in the righteousness Jesus bequeathed me." Brothers and Sisters of Jesus Christ, it's high time we lived up to our high calling – to take the high road and tell the Devil to take the low road. He belongs under our feet – not in our hair.

The serpent versus woman verse, Genesis 3:15, has many meanings. One of those meanings is for this end-time. Jesus – through His end-time spotless Bride, the church – is going to crush Satan's head. The five wise virgins who become Jesus' pure Bride are not going to put up with the Devil's gifts that sap their strength and blemish their witness to this sick, dying world. They will hate sin and sickness like their Bridegroom – and they *will* be victorious. Will you?

It is written...

> I'm asking GOD for one thing, only one thing: To live with him in his house my whole life long. I'll contemplate his beauty; I'll study at his feet .

Ps. 27:4 – MSG

CHAPTER 16

God Has No Favorites – Only Intimates

A sweet Daughter of God from Texas, Alice Smith, who was so kind to me at a prayer conference in Dallas, is apparently credited with the phrase, "God doesn't have favorites – just intimates."

God does allow some to have more glorious tasks in this life. At the same time He expects them to give Him the glory. And He requires more of them. He is the great Equalizer.

In God's future Kingdom, the overlooked widow has the same access to eternal reward and responsibility as the famous evangelist and the powerful preacher. And I'm sure many praying widows will have greater eternal rewards than some popular pastors who fall down on the job. Some high-up ministry bosses may end up working for their secretaries for eternity – or maybe even for their wives!

The point is this: God doesn't play favorites. He simply fellowships with His bosom buddies. John, "the disciple whom Jesus loved," leaned as an intimate friend against Jesus' "bosom." This was no gay sex activity, as some ludicrously contend. Jesus had a special brotherly relationship with him because *John* pressed

153

in more than the others to fellowship with his Master.

We all have an anointing or calling to walk in. But if that ministry for which God has anointed us is not a natural (or supernatural) by-product of our intimacy with God, God is not interested in it. It doesn't matter how many demons we cast out or sermons we preach.

God's main purpose for us is to have a loving relationship with our Father. Everything then flows out of that intimate contact – even the blessings. God heals His intimates.

God does not bless strangers. In most cases, He doesn't heal casual acquaintances. He's a covenant-keeping God, but He expects us to keep our part of the bargain.

If we just bounce in once in a great while with a case of the "gimme's," He doesn't respond. He wants unadulterated love, loyalty and respect.

In fact, a profound respect and awe of God is the pathway to intimacy with Him. "The secret of the [Eternal] is for those who fear [lovingly respect] Him, and He will make them know His covenant" (Ps. 25:14). Or as the NLT puts it, "Friendship with [Jesus] is reserved for those who fear [revere] Him. With them he shares the secret of his covenant."

God only shares His secrets and the blessings of His covenant with those who stand in loving awe of Him. But there is something else we must do.

We must seek Him – not casually – but with all our hearts. "You will seek Me and find Me when you search for Me *with all your heart*" (Jer. 29:13).

There are many today – even some Christians – who find intimacy in all the wrong places. The Internet. TV soap operas. Racy, romantic novels. "Shacking up" with someone of the opposite (or same?) sex in an unholy relationship. They are intimate with anyone and anything except God – and they expect to be healed? They expect God to bless them?

God gives His all to those who give their all to Him in a covenant relationship – a relationship based on intimacy. What you give is what you get. God loves us no matter what. But He only blesses those who obey Him and who just want to "cuddle."

"Cuddling" with the Creator

There are times when many a husband wants more from his wife than to cuddle. Yet there are times when many a wife only wants to cuddle. She simply wants her sweetheart to snuggle close and hold her. To show he really loves her – not only for what he can get.

So many Christians today are out for what they can get from God. They seek His hand *only* – not His face.

Gifted conference speaker Joseph Garlington shared an intimate story in Red Deer, Alberta. He spoke of his five-year-old granddaughter, whom

God Has No Favorites – Only Intimates

I'll call Susie (I can't spell her real name!).

Susie never asked Grandpa for anything. But when she saw him, she loved to shower him with her special kisses. Even when surrounded by "important people," he would stop everything to receive her love.

After three kisses, she would say, "Got enough?" And then she would run away.

Some of her unnamed "aunties," on the other hand, would approach Garlington with insincere sweet talk. Finally he would say, "Okay, how much you want?"

They were reaching for his hand. They were looking for the hand to go into his pocket and come out with fast cash.

Little Susie didn't seek his hand. She sought his face. It wouldn't have been wrong for her to ask for certain things, but she simply never did. And yet she never lacked anything. She had beautiful dresses her grandparents bought for her, and had not even worn all of them. When she was in a play, Grandpa would always be there, delighting in his little Susie.

Do we seek God's hand only – or His face? Intimates seek His face. Intimates get blessed. Intimates get healed. Unless there is another hindrance, God loves to lavish blessings on those who seek Him passionately.

God wants His Children blessed physically, financially, spiritually – in every way. And unlike Susie, we can and do sometimes make requests – even of Him. He loves that. And He wants us to have all of Him – and His blessings. Those requests to be blessed, however, are based on our intimate relationship with God.

The apostle Paul was not in it for what he could get. He said, "... I count all things to be loss in view of the surpassing value of _knowing_ Christ Jesus My [Divine Master] ..." (Phil. 3:8). His fervent desire was "that I may _know Him_ ..." (verse 10).

David was a man after God's own heart. What did he desire? "One thing I have asked from the [Eternal], that I shall seek: that I may dwell in the house of [_Yehovah_ who was born as _Yeshua_ or Jesus] all the days of my life, to behold the beauty of [Jesus] and to meditate in His temple. For in the day of trouble He will conceal me in His tabernacle; in the _secret place_ of His tent He will hide me ..." (Ps. 27: 4-5, MSG).

The "secret place" of intimacy with God is a special place – a place where blessings abound. Healing and health are there.

Psalm 91: the Blessings of Intimacy

"He who dwells in the _secret place_ of the Most High will abide in the shadow of the Almighty" (Ps. 91:1, NKJV). And what blessings does He promise to those who dwell in the secret place of intimacy with Him?

He promises to deliver you "from the deadly pestilence" (verse 3). Pestilence is epidemic disease. "... nor will any plague come near your tent" (verse 10). Healing and health benefits come to those who are God's intimates

155

(see "God, harmony with," in the Appendix).

"You will tread upon the lion and the cobra, the young lion and the serpent you will trample down" (verse 13). This can be physical, as the promise of Mark 16:15-18 shows.

Satan, however, is called a lion and a snake. When we are intimate with God, we exercise our authority in Him. We go to spiritual warfare with the demons and win. And we have seen how often they are involved in physical sickness. As Creflo Dollar says, we know the Most High God – so we can trample over the "low-level Devil."

The New King James renders best the Hebrew of verse 14: "Because he has *set his love* upon Me, therefore I will deliver him; I will set him on high, because he has *known My name*."

A driving intensity in the Hebrew idiom for "set his love upon Me" is difficult to render. Drug addicts seek their drugs with an automatic, compulsive ardor. Our love for God should be a driving force that we cannot resist, like our yearning for a large glass of cool, fresh water after three waterless days under the hot, desert sun. It's speaking of "God-seekers," those earnest, passionate people who go after God with all they've got. Their heart pants to know Him – to cuddle up to Him – to love and share secrets.

God-seekers do not seek Him for the blessings alone. They seek His face. But they are the only ones that receive from His hand.

Today we often hear the phrase, "Go for it!" The Word of God says, on the contrary, "Go for *Him*! Go for *God*!" We can, of course, "go for it" if "it" is His will. His hand, however, is outstretched to those who seek His face – not to those who grab only for His hand. Don't go for the "goodies." "Go for the gold!" – God's character of gold. Go after God – and He will give you the good stuff too.

Giving God the Time of Day

We live in a rushed society where busy fathers justify themselves. They speak of "quality time" with their children – or with their mates. "I only give them five minutes – but it's quality time!" They may fool themselves, but they don't fool their loved ones.

Busy Christians singing the "quality time" song don't fool God either. God doesn't want the stale leftovers. He doesn't want to share a microwave snack with us in front of the TV. He wants to relish a romantic, gourmet meal with us. He wants intimacy. He wants quality time – and quantity time.

Too many Christians don't give God the time of day – literally or spiritually.

Many Christians today do not believe they need to tithe to God, giving a tenth of their monetary increase. Is it any wonder that so few Christians believe in giving God a tithe and offering of their *time*?

God asks in Malachi 3:8, "Will a man rob God?" He goes on to say we have

God Has No Favorites – Only Intimates

robbed Him in tithes and offerings. In verse 10 He promises to bless abundantly the nine tenths remaining after the tithe, if we put Him to the test by obeying. And Jesus reaffirms tithing (Mat. 23:23).

Those who have tithed know that God delivers. The rest of the money goes so much further than expected.

Those who put God and His Kingdom first (Mat. 6:33) know that the same is true for *tithing our time*. When we make sure we spend lots of time with God in our day, we see that He redeems and stretches the rest of our time.

Some say they're too busy to pray. Wrong. They're too busy *not* to pray. Too busy *not* to study God's Word. God wants us to give our time joyfully to Him. He wants us to spend a tithe and offering of our time praying, meditating, reading aloud and studying the Word and material dealing with Bible principles, and worshipping Him in song. (Included in our prayer time are the all-important "Daily Declarations" in the Appendix of this book.) And He wants us to maintain contact with Him on a continual basis, even as we go about our routine workday.

David allotted time morning, noon and night to God. I have a minister friend in Montreal named Charlie who helped me understand this with a telephone pole analogy. What would happen to our lines of communication if there were no telephone poles? The lines would sag and so would our communication. David put up three telephone poles daily to keep his lines of communication with God from sagging.

As with the financial tithe, that time should be the first thing we set aside in our time budget. It may be different times for different people. The Bible does, however, emphasize seeking God early.

We wouldn't go out of the house undressed, but we sometimes venture out spiritually unclothed. Spiritual streakers get caught with their pants down.

God doesn't appreciate being squeezed into our busy schedule as an afterthought. Schedules and people are different. But where there's a will – a real desire to be intimate with the most important Being in the universe – we find a way.

People in love find excuses to be with each other. When we are in love with Jesus, we will find excuses and ways to be with Him. We will find the time to sing His praises and read aloud His love letters to us in His Word.

The rewards are eternal – as well as here and now. God blesses those who give him "the time of day." The time of their day means so much to Him. And it will mean so much to us.

When we are in love with Jesus, the hindrances in the following chapter simply melt away in the fire of our love for Him.

16 Why Doesn't God Heal Me?

It is written...

... let us throw off everything that hinders and the sin that so easily entangles ... Let us fix our eyes on Jesus, the author and perfecter of our faith ... God disciplines us for our good, that we may share in his holiness ... strengthen your feeble arms and weak knees. "Make level paths for your feet," so that the lame may not be disabled, but rather healed ... without holiness no one will see the [Divine Master].

Heb. 12:1a, 2a, 10b, 12-13, 14b – NIV

CHAPTER 17
Hindrances to Healing: Understanding the Concept

As the Holy Spirit has progressively revealed hindrances to healing that have never before been understood or published, it has become evident that many or most of these apply to much more than healing. Clearly, not recognizing and correcting these hindrances, especially the later ones, *can block **all** of God's blessings for us, His Children*!

God's words to the prophet Isaiah for His people Israel apply to His spiritual people today: "Cry loudly, do not hold back; Raise your voice like a trumpet, And declare to my people their transgression, And to the house of Jacob their sins" (58:1).

God thunders in Hosea 4:6: "My people are *destroyed* for lack of knowledge …" We often walk in the way of sin, sickness and death, being destroyed spiritually and physically, because we lack vital knowledge. And in many cases, we are not healed physically and blessed spiritually because, as this verse continues, we have rejected knowledge we already have. We may know Jesus, but we are not *yielding* to God as we know we should, *choosing* the way of life and blessings and *surrendering* to Him on a daily basis (see "Life, choosing" in the Appendix).

God is not a Blesser of the coaster, the lackadaisical, the faithless, the lukewarm

159

Why Doesn't God Heal Me?

Christian. Faith is important for healing, but it is not the only thing. Hebrews 11:6 explains: "But without faith it is impossible to please Him, for he who comes to God must believe that He is, and that He is a *rewarder of those who **diligently** seek Him*."

Hindering the Hindrances

We have seen the importance of intimacy. Intimacy with God and earnest seeking of Him is also a key to getting rid of our spiritual hindrances.

John Hagee tells the story of an orphan boy who says, "How can I know who I am unless I know who my father is?" By seeking and knowing God our Father we come to know who we are as His Children.

This rare knowledge, especially the righteousness aspect, is revealed in these pages. It is **the** key to victorious Christian living and the elimination of most of the hindrances. When we know we are Sons and Daughters of our Father of Love, we walk in His love and no hindrance blocks our blessings. Love is everything. A good way to summarize all the hindrances to blessings is this: in some aspect of life we are *not walking in God's love*.

God is Love (I John 4:8). His law is love (I John 5:3; Rom. 13:10). Sin is breaking one of His instructions or laws that define love (I John 3:4).

We have the choice to walk in selfishness, listening to our emotions instead of God, or to walk with our Father, our Brother and our Comforter of Love.

A **powerful anointing** can also override many hindrances. It would be hard to find hindrances in Benny Hinn. And yet even he admitted on *Larry King Live* that he did not fully understand why some were not healed. Sometimes people's prayers aren't enough. Crusades where praise and worship and united fellowship with the Holy Spirit and the collective invitation for Him to manifest Himself can sometimes make the deciding difference.

The *Fast* Track to Health

The only sure-fire way to override *all* hindrances, however, is by what I like to call "spiritual dynamite." When someone joins with you and agrees with you in prayer while both of you are *praying and fasting*, great power is released. Jesus said that the faith to cast out some demons requires prayer and fasting. The more people praying and fasting, the more power is released.

Fasting, along with the anointing of the Holy Spirit, releases burden-lifting, yoke-destroying power (Isa. 58:6; Isa. 61:1-3). Prayer and fasting activates that power, amplifying it in a way that brings spectacular results.

A missionary acquaintance gave a dramatic account of a spectacular healing by fasting. A man had to have a bag on his abdomen to defecate because he was born without an anus. A group of Christians who lived with him saw him face the certainty of being evicted from the home because of the stench his special situa-

Hindrances to Healing **17**

tion caused. They prayed and fasted for him as a group. The result? He actually grew an anus! All that remained on his abdomen was a scar to remind him of God's miracle! It happened.

Agreement is powerful. Agreement in prayer and fasting is explosive!

Only these twin tools can break the major hindrance of unforgiveness. It did for me! God will not overlook unforgiveness, but He will, when addressed by prayer and fasting, miraculously open the door for repentance.

If at first you don't succeed – *FAST*! And ask a Christian friend to agree with you in prayer and fasting. It can make the difference in your healing. Once you are healed, God will still expect you to seek help for your hindrances.

What does God say in Isaiah 58:8? "Then [after fasting] your light shall break forth like the morning. Your *healing* shall spring forth *speedily*." Verse 9 shows that prayer and fasting can eliminate hindrances to *all of God's blessings*. "Then you shall call, and the [Eternal] will answer. You shall cry, and He will say, 'Here I am.'" (NKJV). A praying and fasting church will see miraculous healings and answers to prayer.

In addition to fasting in agreement, however, other important procedures must not be neglected. Jesus repeatedly said to those that He healed, "your sins are forgiven." He enjoins His healing servants to follow the same practice (John 20:23).

Blessings and Curses

Sin hinders healing. Deuteronomy 7:9-15 spells it out. Jesus promised to remove all sickness from the believers – *if* Israel *obeyed the commandments*. Jesus exhorted Israel, "... if you *diligently* obey the [Eternal] your God ... being careful to do **all** *His commandments*, all these *blessings* will come upon you" (Deut. 28:1-2). These blessings, as we have seen, involved every aspect of life. They apply even more to modern believers.

He then spoke soul-stirring words that should be a part of the daily declarations of every Christian: "... I have set before you life and death, *blessing* and cursing; therefore *choose life*, that both you and your descendants shall live" (Deut. 30:19). The principle of free choice does not change under the New Covenant. Every day we either choose God's way of life and blessings or Satan's way of death and curses. When we choose wrongly, we cannot expect healing and blessing.

God tells Israel and us today, in essence: "Choose life and you will be a shining light to those in the darkness around you, an example of obedience, happiness, health, healing – nothing hindering your total well-being or *shalom*."

The principles that apply to the spiritual, physical and financial parts of God's blessings are different. God promises, however, no lack in any area. Our needs are met and we are able to give to others. The more we understand the laws and principles that govern the spiritual, physical and financial, the more we are blessed.

God does not want His people poor, sick and – especially – sinful. He wants us to know the peace that comes from total wholeness and wellness. He wants His

Why Doesn't God Heal Me?

Children happy and blessed in every facet of life. When blessing doesn't come, don't blame God. It isn't His fault. *We* hinder his healing, spiritually, financially and physically. We allow the Stealer to steal our healing by these hindrances, many of which can rob us of all the blessings God has for us.

The Bible speaks of hindrances. The word "weight" in Hebrews 12:1, according to Strong and modern translations, can be translated "hindrances." "… let us also lay aside every encumbrance ['everything that hinders' – NIV], and the sin which so easily entangles us, and let us run with endurance the race that is set before us."

Not Perfection, but Obedience Required

God's promises are absolute, but I can't think of one that is unconditional. The only thing that is unconditional is God's love. Even salvation is a free gift, but we must choose to give ourselves to God. Forgiveness is free as well, and yet God says we must confess our sins so that He can forgive. When we accept Jesus, God freely forgives us. He then requires us to forgive others, however, as a condition for His grace of forgiveness to us.

You may win a free trip to Europe. There are usually, however, certain conditions attached, such as the time of travel and the length of stay. You forfeit the free gift if you don't fulfill the conditions.

It's the same with salvation. It's not automatic (Heb. 6:4-6; Mat. 24:13; Phil. 2:12; I Cor. 10:12). We have our part. Simply put, we must continue to choose God's way and yield to Him – in active faith.

The Greek word for faith (*pistis*) implies obedience as well, which God will work in us if we let Him. Yes, even obedience is by God's grace, but we must yield, decide, or choose. God's promises and blessings are all given freely, by grace, but we must choose the way of life and blessings. We must be choosing on a daily basis to walk, by God's grace and His faith in us, as obedient children.

The Bible clearly shows that we are saved by grace, yet rewarded eternally according to our works. I Corinthians 3:14-15 shows how some may squeak by with salvation, and yet not have a great reward. Others may hear the words the five foolish virgins heard: "I don't know you." Those who do inherit eternal life will have different levels of rewards.

So we see that in the realm of salvation the concept of hindrances does not exist in the same way as in healing. Unless you utterly refuse the Holy Spirit, it is more a matter that your "hindrances," or lack of good works, will *lessen* your eternal reward rather than forfeit it.

In the case of healing, on the other hand, we are dealing with physical blessings in this life. There is a direct cause and effect relationship between what we sow and what we reap. We will prosper "as our soul prospers." We cannot expect blessings from God – including healing – without obedience.

You promise as a father, do you not, to bless your children more than you would

Hindrances to Healing 17

any other children in the world? You love them more than any other children anywhere. You want to shower them with blessings, and you do. However, you as a wise and good father will not bless disobedience. You may choose to deprive them of certain blessings if they have serious problems that should be corrected first. You promise to bless them in specific ways, but you do have conditions.

Would you lend your Mercedes to your teenaged boy who irresponsibly rolled your van into a ditch last night? Neither can our Father bless us when we are disobedient. God wants above all things to "bless our socks off," but not if we're wearing over-the-calf sins (Deut. 5:29)!

"If" is one of the biggest words in the English language. Satan tries to use "if" as a doubt word to tell us God will heal us *if* it is His will. That "if" is a lie. But God does use "if" in regards to healing. Read it. "**If** you diligently heed the voice of the [Eternal] your God and do what is right in His sight, give ear to His commandments and keep all His statutes ..." (Ex. 15:26). The "if" is in our court – not God's.

The "word of faith" concept is valid up to a point. But faith without works is dead! Too many want instant blessings as they speak the word of faith. The problem is they don't want to fulfill the conditions.

We cannot claim any of God's promised blessings if we are not walking, by His grace and by our free choice, in obedience to Him. We're not talking about never sinning, even if you think a long list of possible hindrances implies perfection. God's healing promise depended on Israel's obedience, and He is the same God today. He does deal differently with believers, but if anything, He will be stricter with those who have His Spirit under the New Covenant.

God's blessings are free, but not cheap.

He meets us where we are. For some people at some stage in their development, all that is required is faith. "Your faith has made you whole" was a frequent phrase Jesus used in healing people. On the other hand, God holds His born Sons and Daughters to a different standard. Faith is not all that is required. And actually, many of the hindrances are problems that have hindered our faith itself.

Our disobedience or "bad works" can hinder our healing, but the "good works" of correcting our hindrances do not earn us our healing, which comes freely by grace. Even our ability to make the necessary changes to make healing possible comes by the grace of God, His power working in us (Eph. 2:8-10).

In the parable of the prodigal son, the father represents God the Father. The father shows unconditional love to his long-lost son who returns. Nothing the son does changes the father's love for him. He gladly welcomes his son back.

But he can't *bless* his son when he is playing around in the pigpen of sin. It's the same with our heavenly Father.

Of course, not all hindrances to blessings are as obvious as playing around with harlots as a sordid sow wallowing in the mire of sin. But we do have aspects of our lives that need to be corrected before God can bless us.

Nothing we do or don't do can cause God to *love* us *less*, but something we do or

163

don't do can cause Him to *bless* us *less*! When we sin more, God does not love us less. On the other hand, if we sin more, God will bless us less. If our hindrances are serious, He may even curse us until He corrects us back into the way of blessings.

Yes, you read that right. Deuteronomy 28 is full of God's curses issued against the people He loves. When His Children choose the way of death, He must sometimes curse them so they will wake up and get back into the way of the abundant life. Do you think a father is harsh when he grounds his teenaged son after a destructive drinking spree? Hebrews 12 describes the loving discipline of our Father. His correction – even in the form of curses – is proof of His love. But in His love, He would prefer we be set straight by simply reading a book – like this one, or His Book of Love (see Hindrance No. 188).

Some Hindrances More Serious than Others

Someone once quipped: "All men are created equal, but some are more equal than others." In reality, all sins are serious and equal in the sense that they lead eventually to death. As Paul warned the Corinthians about sex sins, however, some sins have more serious consequences than others. And some sins are the antithesis of God's nature and arouse His anger.

I learned the hard way, by losing everything dear to me and by being cursed for a major part of my life, that unforgiveness is one of those serious sins. It is the whole meaning of Jesus' sacrifice for us. God won't forgive those who refuse to forgive (Mat. 6:15). He won't heal us either. I know.

God does not forgive the unforgiving and He resists the proud (James 4:6). Unforgiveness and pride, which was the Devil's undoing (Ezek. 28:17), are therefore major hindrances to receiving any of God's blessings.

Who Is the Legalist?

Hearing of hundreds of hindrances to healing brings this reaction from some: "Now you're getting legalistic. Jesus didn't go around with a list of hundreds of hindrances in His pocket as a checklist before healing!" As I wrote earlier, a powerful anointing can override hindrances. And this man was the Anointed One Himself! And in most cases the ones that approached Jesus for healing came in faith.

He healed some because of His mercy, reflecting His Father's love. He forgave their sins, but expected them to use His power later to eliminate any hindrances.

And remember, they did not have all the revelation that we have as Christians today. We have the blood of Jesus as well as easy access to the entire written Word of God. Hindrances become more important for those of us today who have the knowledge (James 4:17).

Paul spoke of hindrances (Gal. 5:7; I Thes. 2:18) – and no one would call Paul a legalist.

Hindrances to Healing

Who hinders our healing? Whose fault is it that there is a list of hundreds of hindrances to healing, even if only a few apply to us? Is it God's fault? Absolutely not! It is the Devil's doing! Of course we have our responsibility too. But if Satan hadn't entered the picture, neither sickness nor hindrances to healing would exist.

This hindrance list is God's list of what the Devil has done to Christians. And God tells us not to be ignorant of Satan's many devices.

Introduction to Hindrances

The hindrances can be as different as are people. All of the hindrances won't apply to you, but you may have several. And even one can prevent you from being healed.

But remember this: God is sovereign. "I will show mercy on whom I will show mercy," He says in Romans 9:15. He can choose in His wisdom and mercy to overlook hindrances. But don't count on it! Let's examine ourselves to see why God may not have healed us. Without even realizing it, we may have hindered His healing hand.

If we understood the Biblical concept of hindrances, we would not be questioning God. We know so many Christian friends who have not been healed that we begin to question healing. We question God because of what His Children do or don't do. We let the Devil's doing make us doubt the Healer.

So many leaders blame God by saying He allows sickness for a purpose. Not always true. God only allows or even brings on sickness when we harden our hearts. He told His rebellious people, "So also I [God Himself] will *make you sick*, striking you down, desolating you because of your sins" (Micah 6:13).

Christians have believed the lies because they haven't understood hindrances.

How can the end-time church rock the world when we have not been healed ourselves and don't even believe in healing? We can't. But we must.

And how do we start? It begins with sin – with our discerning and confessing it. God's plan for the land applies also to the body. "... if I [that's Jesus speaking] send pestilence [*disease*!] among My people, and My people who are called by My name humble themselves [instead of blaming God] and pray and seek My face and turn from their wicked ways, then I will hear from heaven, will forgive their sin an will heal their land" (II Chron. 7:19b-20).

Sin and Healing

We have seen the sin and healing connection in James 5. He says to confess our sins or faults so we may be healed, spiritually and physically. These hindrances usually involve confession of sin.

The connection between forgiveness of sin and healing did not begin with James. His Brother started it. Jesus often forgave the sins of the sick when healing them. He gave us the authority to do the same in John 20:23: "If you forgive the sins of any, their sins have been forgiven them ..."

Why Doesn't God Heal Me?

After all, sin is what usually brings on the illness. It can be general, personal or corporate sin. And believe it or not, it can even be one of your ancestor's sins that brought on a curse.

I hasten to add that not all sickness is *caused* by sin. It is sin, however, that is almost always part of the reason we are not *healed* of our sicknesses, whatever their cause may be.

Why did Jesus stress the forgiveness of sin in healing? If the sick are not convinced they are forgiven, Satan can deceive them. By persuading them their sins make them guilty and unworthy of healing, he is guilty of stealing their healing. It's all connected to walking in our righteousness.

Jesus' works and teachings engendered faith in most of those that He healed. He could see them acting on their faith and wanting to change. The Bible says their faith made them whole. Of course, God sometimes heals people before they have faith or become Christians. After all, He is God and can do whatever He wants. He can use the healing to bring them to Him.

These hindrances are not a hard and fast rule. As I said, God often overlooks a hindrance in His mercy. For unbelievers, hindrances are usually a non-issue. Even for Christians, James 4:17 can apply. He that knows what he should do and does not do it sins or is held more accountable for his sin. Jesus told the Pharisees they were guilty because they knew better.

We have seen that the anointing – the supernatural enabling power and presence of the Holy Spirit – can override hindrances and bring healing.

God often heals in cases of sins committed in ignorance, unforgiveness being an exception.

In any case, we must remember that these hindrances are merely guidelines. God makes the rules, and He makes the exceptions.

Peter shows that the way you treat your wife may hinder your prayers, which can hinder your healing (I Pet. 3:7). Can you see God healing a wife beater?

The concept of hindrances goes right along with the chapter on the healing process. Because God heals us from the inside out, the soul or inner person must be healed in most cases before physical healing can occur.

I have even heard of cases where God revealed to a Christian that he or she would be healed from the inside out over a certain period of time. This does not mean that it is not God's will to quickly manifest the healing. Some hindrances take time to remove.

"Health and Wealth"

All these hindrances do not take away from the fact that healing is a promise of God. Unfortunately, some exaggerations of the healing promise have given divine healing a bad name.

The "health and wealth, name it and claim it" teaching is an example of a practice based on Biblical truth but misapplied and exaggerated. Some wanted the promise without fulfilling the condition of obedience. Many doubted God when He didn't deliver the promised goods.

The Word is full of promises of wealth and prosperity, which is a more accurate term. Prosperity implies well-being and success in every domain. Of the upright, God says, "Wealth and riches are in his house ..." (Ps. 112:3).

God wants His Children healed and well – and well-heeled to boot! Prosperity is part of the deal. It's a covenant promise. If we major on spiritual riches, the physical ones come as well.

Israel was to set the example of righteousness, health and prosperity so that the rest of the world would want to be like them.

And so it should be with spiritual Israel. But what do we see? All too often we see sad, sick saints. And they're not only sick – they're broke! No wonder so many worldly people are turned off by Christianity! Who wants a God who leaves you sick and poor?

Poverty is not a badge of humility and superiority. It's a curse.

Jesus became a curse for us (Gal. 3:13). He delivered us from all the curses that sin brought.

Actually, it was the spear wound *after* His death that broke all curses, including the curse of poverty. Adam's sin caused a curse on the land. Jesus' blood spilt on the very land where Adam had sinned and wiped away all the curses.

Yes, Jesus' death and shedding of blood broke all the curses involved in "the law of sin and death." That includes sickness and poverty.

Sin in our lives keeps us under the curses. These hindrances are basically areas in our lives where we have allowed sin to reign. Eliminating hindrances releases us from the curses sin brings and allows us to benefit from **all** the blessings God wants to pour out upon us.

In the chapter just before the one describing the freedom anointing of our church and ministry, Isaiah gives an exciting preview of what will happen to God's end-time people. "Build up, build up, prepare the way, *remove every obstacle* out of the way of My people" (Isa. 57:14). Then God says He's going to heal those who have turned their backs on His ways, which His sleepy end-time church has done (verses 18-19). May the following chapter help bring about a new chapter in the history of the church. May it help remove every obstacle out of the way of God's people. May it eliminate every wrinkle from a bride that needs spiritual and physical healing.

Ask the Holy Spirit to reveal to you which hindrances may apply to you, so you can walk in the glory of the spotless end-time Bride of Jesus Christ.

17 Why Doesn't God Heal Me?

It is written...

... Remove every obstacle out of the way of My people ... I have seen his ways, but I will heal him ... Cry loudly, do not hold back; Raise your voice like a trumpet, And declare to My people their transgression And to the house of Jacob their sins.

Isa. 57:14b, 18a, 58:1

CHAPTER 18
The Hindrances

The first group of hindrances represents those that specifically apply to healing, although some of them may also be impediments to all of God's blessings. The rest of the hindrances could help explain why God has withheld healing, and yet they too can be barriers for receiving *all* of the blessings of God, not uniquely the blessing of healing. You will find a succinct list in the Hindrances Checklist in Chapter 19. Before reading these hindrances, I recommend that you pray aloud the prayers for self-examination and removal of hindrances, and also the prayer for coming to terms with sin found in the Appendix.

Hindrances Relating More Specifically to Healing

1. Lack of faith: "If" is a faith killer. Ask in faith, with nothing wavering (James 1:6-7). It must be God's faith, not ours. Ask Him for faith (Luke 17:5; Mark 9:24; Rom. 10:17-18; I Thes. 3:10; Eph 2:8-10).

2. Hoping or wishing instead of believing. Believing God *can* heal is hope – not faith. Some think God will heal when He gets good and ready, even by letting

169

us *die* in our illness and *supposedly* healing us in the resurrection. That's not even much of a hope, since He guarantees our future glory independent of any promise of physical healing, which is obviously for this life. Physical healing here and now is not a benefit that we *hope* God *may* choose to give us.

Wishing is a concept that comes out of witchcraft. Some Bible versions incorrectly translate the idea of praying or hoping as wishing. It's not in the original. Using the word *wish* is asking Satan to give you something. And he will. It may seem picky to some, yet Satan is picky and his demons will pick up on those idle words. Those evil spirits thus have permission to act on our words.

Why not use words that show we are counting on God and not Satan? It will take effort to change our words. Use words like, "I hope," "I pray," or in the past tense, "I would have preferred that ..."

The concept of luck versus blessing is similar. "I'll be lucky to get rid of this cancer." Satan is the god of luck. God is the God of blessing.

3. Not accepting God's promise. Because of false teaching and looking at what happened to Christians instead of what God promises, I lost sight of healing as an absolute promise from God. It took two weeks of studying healing and recalling previous teaching that was partially correct to eliminate this hindrance. Once I finally forgave by God's grace and saw healing as more than through the "if-it-is-Your-will" approach, God healed me instantly.

My lack of faith actually had its root in not accepting healing as a promise. All the other hindrances regarding faith were resolved in eliminating this one hindrance.

Here are some ways God keeps His promises (of which there are some 6,000 in His Word):[31]

1) by creative miracles,
2) by using agents such as animals like birds and fish, or weather or angels to bring us the promised items,
3) by using forms (people) whom He inspires to bring us the answers,
4) by multiplying what we already have, as with the Biblical story of the widow's oil,
5) by multiplying our harvest,
6) by giving us a vision of where He wants us to find our blessing and showing us the steps to exercise our faith,
7) by opening our ears to hear His warnings of potential loss or dangers that are blocking our receiving the blessing,
8) by giving us the faith to work out the promise without fear or doubt,

---

[31] These promises are not always stated in typical promise terms. But if you search diligently with the guidance of the Holy Spirit, you will be able to confirm that figure. Start with Psalms and Proverbs (Psalm 37 alone contains 14 promises). You'll be surprised how many promises you find. Claim them and seal them in communion.

The Hindrances **18**

9) by giving us a patient heart to wait on Him for the best time to fulfill the promises (Satan's agents encourage us to speak against the promises and thus sabotage them).

When claiming any promise of God, be sure to do the following:

1) Repent of sin.
2) Pray (in the Spirit, in tongues, if that gift has been activated in you) to stir yourself up to receive the promise.
3) Call the promise to remembrance before God, quoting His Word back to Him. Be specific.
4) To add special emphasis, you may decide to seal it in communion.
5) Bind the spirit of fear and doubt.
6) Bind Satan from affecting your claim in any way, shape or form. State that he cannot steal it, mislay, waylay or delay it. Declare that Satan is bound in the name of Jesus.
7) Keep speaking God's Word and thanking Him for coming through, mentioning what you asked for *as if it is already in your hands*.

4. Not confessing faith (Matt. 13:58; James 1:6-8; Rom. 10:6-13). When we confess doubts and fears instead of faith, we confess the symptoms instead of confessing our healing.

Satan attacked me with certain physical problems only two months after being healed. Severe sleep loss was one of the symptoms and the effects of that condition caused some to scoff. Thankfully, by God's grace I did not surrender to their doubts and their curses. I rejected those curses in Jesus' name and I verbally confessed my healing. It was not long before even my enemies acknowledged my healing.

5. Insufficient instruction (Hos. 4:6; John 8:31-32). Ignorance of the power of healing or not knowing God's will. Faith comes from hearing the Word. The truth shall set you free. We must be able to say to Satan: "It is written." False teaching will hinder healing.

6. Lack of unity in the Spirit (John 17:22-23; Rom. 15:5-6; Eph. 4:3-6). Unity and agreement unleash power and blessing (Ps. 133) that are denied in their absence. In the early church (and today) some failed to receive healing because doubters were making it impossible for the church to be in one accord in prayer and faith. A revival of miracles is possible with the unity of the Spirit. Through ignorance, the members of most churches are opposing or not accepting Jesus' attitude toward sickness and have not met the conditions for the healing of the sick. It is these hinderers who are currently pointing out failures for which they themselves are largely responsible.

7. Community unbelief. His home town's unbelief even limited Jesus (Mark 6:5-6; Matt. 13:57-58).

8. Traditions of men regarding healing deny God and preach Satan's lies. We have already countered those lies. If sickness is God's will, Christians getting

171

Why Doesn't God Heal Me?

medical help would be disobeying God – going against God's will! And being in good health would also be a sin! If remaining sick glorifies God, then Jesus was in rebellion against His Father – robbing Him of glory – when He healed everyone that appealed to Him for help.

One false teaching not covered earlier is the one that says Jesus healed as the Son of God, not as the Son of Man. He said clearly He was both, but that He could do nothing of Himself (John 5:19). He healed by the power of the Holy Spirit (Acts 10:38), the same One who works in His followers in the book of Acts and today (Acts 1:1-8).

9. Healing fails when natural laws continue to be broken. Asking God to heal our stomach while we continue to overeat makes no sense. People will ask God to heal their lung cancer but refuse to quit smoking. When we purposely abuse our bodies, the temple of God, we hinder our healing (I Cor. 3:16-17).

10. Unbelief of the elders who pray and/or anoint for healing (James 5:14-15; Titus 1:6-9). It must be a prayer of faith. In the following hindrance, Jesus said it was the disciples' unbelief that prevented the boy's healing.

11. Not dealing first with the evil spirit causing the affliction (Mat. 17:17-20). To deal with the epileptic boy, Jesus cast out the demon causing the condition. The same was true for the deaf and dumb. The principle of getting out the leaven in order to be a new lump applies here. If demons have a legal right to stay, healing power cannot change that. Neither blessing nor healing can stick when demons have a legal hold.

12. Unrepented sins (Prov. 24:12; Is. 59:1-2; Rom. 2:5-8). David said if he regarded sin in his heart, God would not hear him (Ps. 66:18). Unconfessed, cherished sins hinder God's healing. If He won't hear us, He won't heal us. If we have refused to repent of a sin, then the crippling spirit called "bent" and his agents can afflict us (see Chapter 7).

13. Lukewarmness (Rev. 3:16). An important hindrance to healing. Justification without sanctification is lukewarmness. Doubts, fears, and cares of the world creeping into our lives foster lukewarmness. Zeal, joy and praise are antidotes and activate God's healing.

14. The "halter" hindrance. A halter is a temporary restraint. This hindrance applies mainly to church leaders. Major problems in their lives make it necessary for God to use illness to correct their course (e.g. pride of power).[32] In this *rare* disciplinary measure, God allows sickness to remain as a *halter* because it allows God to direct them to the center of His will and/or quit fighting Him. When the new direction is taken, He removes the halter and they are healed.

---

[32] Pride of power is the result of accepting authority from God and then using it for self-glory, self-aggrandizement or to abuse subordinates. The person becomes unteachable, easily offended by questions and unforgiving for even the slightest hurts, boastful and addicted to power. See "Pride" in the Appendices for more information on that subject.

The Hindrances 18

Job was a teacher of the law and would fall into this category. God wanted him to learn certain lessons, even though his sickness was not because of a particular sin. And remember, though it was God's will in this rare case, it was Satan and not God that brought on the sickness. The Bible shows God did bring plagues of sickness on His people as disciplinary measures, such as in the case of Miriam. God rarely curses Christians with sickness. When He does, it is only a temporary trial to bring them to repentance and to a place of blessing – not curses.

15. An unforgiving spirit, holding a grudge, seeking your own vengeance or gossip. These sins tend to go together. Listening to gossip is the same as speaking it.

16. Wrongs not righted hinder the faith of some for receiving healing (Mat. 5:23-24). Those who have wronged their brothers should ask for their forgiveness.

17. Lack of diligence, wholeheartedness or intense desire (Josh. 14:9). A *que sera sera* attitude insults God. God rewards those who diligently seek Him. We should not ask for healing just to see what happens. God wants fervent prayers (James 5:16), telling Him that we truly desire His intervention.

18. Accepting no less than an instant, miraculous healing as a sign or wonder, as opposed to a progressive yet still divine healing. I use the word *progressive* to explain such a less-than-immediate healing to the natural, logical but limited mind of man. In the realm of the supernatural, we have already been healed. That is supernatural reality, even if it sounds unrealistic to the natural mind. We can call such a healing a "faith healing" since it requires perseverance and the fight of faith.

An instant healing does not require faith once it is accomplished, since it has been done, not only in the supernatural sense but also with the removal of all symptoms in the natural realm. Even a skeptic can see the healing.

A Christian who understands the promise of divine healing accepts his healing and believes he has already been healed even if the symptoms still persist. Because of that persistent faith, the symptoms do disappear shortly and even non-Christians can testify to the healing.

19. Watching the symptoms (Satan's lies), which Satan uses to convince us God will not heal us. Dwelling on the physical signs only serves to further undermine our faith in God's promise. We must not focus on the physical facts, but on the truth of God's promises as Abraham did (Rom. 4:17-21).

20. Not acting on our faith (which without works is dead) (James 2:20-24). Jesus told the blind man to go to the pool of Siloam and wash. He believed the healing was his before it was manifested. Lepers went to the priests on Jesus' command and as they went, they were healed. If the healing evangelist asks you to stand up from your wheelchair, and you don't even try, you have failed the faith test and God may not heal you until you act on your faith.

21. Failing when faith is tested (Luke 22:32; Heb. 12:3-6; II Cor. 13:5-7). The

173

test can perfect us or hinder us. It's our choice. Often passing the test involves persisting in praise.

22. Substituting personal faith for belief in the doctrine of divine healing. Faith is a gift from God, not something we work up. It must be based on God's Word and His promises. Our own faith represents dead works (Heb. 6:1; Jer. 17:5).

23. Believing God's Word is not directed to us (II Tim. 3:16-17). In that case, God cannot forgive and heal. Proverbs is full of admonitions to the wise to pay attention to the Word so they will have success (1:5; 3:1-2; 4:2-6; 8:33; 12:15). The term "Israel" carries the meaning of "the believers," and God's warning to hear and obey was – and still is – for *all* the believers (Deut. 5:1).

24. Waiting until we see the healing before we believe (Heb. 11:1). "Seeing is believing" is a truism for the natural realm, in which doubting disciple Thomas dwelled. Some think they must persist in begging God to heal them. Why do we plead for something we already have?

Ask in your righteousness – and ask once! When you walk in righteousness consciousness, circumstances are not your focus. Thank God that you already have what you requested (Mark 11:24). Jesus thanked His Father before resurrecting Lazarus. After any prayer for healing, God should only hear thanks until symptoms leave. Trust must be active. Basing our faith on our improvement after prayer rather than upon the promises is a lack of faith. God is training us to tune Satan out and simply believe.

I told a lady healing team assistant that I "waited" twelve years for healing. (I did wait, but not in faith.) She said, "I didn't wait, I fought the good fight of faith." Doctors had given her very little time to live with her cancer. Her symptoms came and went and finally left six weeks after her request for healing.

25. Denial of sin (I John 1:8; Prov. 28:13). Hiding and justifying allows a binding by Satan to live with the consequences of the curse of the sin. Ask God to reveal your sin to you. You may need to hear the hard truth from your mate or close friend. Facing the music is toughest when you wrote the score. Confess and get in symphony with God.

26. Tempting God (Mat. 4:5-7). Examples: drunk driving or doing things to cause illness on purpose to see if God will heal or protect.

27. Guilt (Ps. 103:12-14; Heb. 10:19-22). "I am so evil I deserve to be sick." Righteousness consciousness delivers us from this common hindrance.

28. Curses. See Chapter 11 and "Curses" in the Appendix. For those who are learning to walk in their righteousness, this is the most common and often unseen hindrance. We may not be sinning in any way, but people are speaking evil of us. Their words have the power to make us literally sick, unless we discern the source and reject their curses in Jesus' name.

29. Trying to play games with God and His promises (II Tim 3:4-5). Ananias and Sapphira tried it with lying about the price they had received when selling some land (Acts 5:3-10). A front of righteousness will not bring God's healing or

The Hindrances 18

His blessings (Ezek. 33:30-32).

30. "God can cure some diseases, but not mine" (Jer. 32:17). God is not a respecter of persons or illnesses.

31. The belief that sickness is time and chance and that God cannot alter the results of time and chance (Luke 13:2-5; Gen. 50:20). Don't kid yourself. Satan is the author of sickness. Happenstance does not – or should not – affect Christians. God and angels protect us – if we ask Him and obey. But He does not do for us what we can do for ourselves. If time and chance were valid, God would not be able to finish His work in us. Satan would win every time.

32. Not discerning the Body of Christ at the Passover and/or communion (I Cor. 11:27-30). Consult "Communion" in the Appendix for more information on this subject. There are four aspects to discerning the body of Christ:

a) Accepting the emblems as representing the body and blood of Jesus.

b) Accepting the bread being blessed as the broken body of Jesus beaten for our healing. Stripes for *physical* healing are included in this discernment. Some churches, however, do not believe and discern that those stripes provide for our promised physical healing.

c) Discerning the body of Christ can mean properly judging the church, which is also called Christ's body. Improperly judging or condemning individuals in Christ's body can cause God to withhold healing.

d) Refraining from condemnation of a group as not being Christian when they profess to be. This is equally dangerous. We must not assume God is not working with them because they are not a part of our little group. Who are we to treat them as unworthy? Simply because a group is considered widely to be a cult does not mean God is not working with some of them or that none of them know Jesus. Cursing them is not going to help. How can we eventually help them if we condemn them so readily? God can withhold healing to those groups or individuals who condemn others as not belonging to the body of Christ. Because of not discerning the body of Christ in a different way, some Corinthians were sick and some died.

Here's a striking example from my native South many years ago. A certain denomination refused to admit that African-Americans could come to Jesus, believe it or not. While they held to this condemnatory belief, 90% of them were afflicted with cancer! When they finally changed, the cancer rate among them dropped dramatically. God can withhold healing from groups that believe they alone can be saved. *If we condemn Christ's body, God may allow our bodies to stay sick.*

33. Partaking of the Passover and/or communion and then partaking of the table of demons (I Cor. 10:21). Although buying foods in the marketplace that had been sacrificed to idols was not against Paul's conscience, outright participation in an idolatrous, demonic feast was a serious sin. Apparently some at Corinth were eating the Passover and still eating at idol feasts – a demonic counterfeit of the communion service.

34. The medical profession. As explained earlier, the medical profession keeps

175

the world from asking God to heal them, so the doctors become an idol. This is not to say that using the services of a doctor *always* represents idolatry. Doctors *can* become idols if they hinder us from believing God's promise. We *can* use them, in balance, not losing our absolute faith in God. Luke was called, still after his conversion, "the beloved physician." Jesus is also the beloved Physician. Luke certainly "bound some wounds" for the disciples, but God healed them.

We are not knocking doctors and in no way are they wrong in and of themselves. We have many fine doctors in the church, but these doctors will be helping the world in their state of unbelief more than they will help the helpers. We simply do not need them as much as we needed them before we knew Jesus. *Yahweh Rapha* can be translated "our Eternal Physician."

Too many people are addicted to medication and they run to doctors for more prescriptions, which they receive but are cursed with continuing sickness. If a doctor condemns us to die in two weeks, we need to reject that curse in Jesus' name and believe God's report instead.

In Luke 5:31, Jesus is referring to the status quo. The sick do need doctors, but His best recommendation is Doctor Jesus Himself. Beloved physicians like Luke definitely have their place. Dr. Don Colbert, Benny Hinn's personal physician, is an excellent modern example.

35. Fear (Ps. 27:1-2; Isa. 41:10). Consult "Fear" in the Appendix for more on this important hindrance. A fearful spirit is not one that is receptive to healing. Because of not being familiar with miraculous healing, there is sometimes a fear of the supernatural or the unknown. God says over and over in the Bible, "Fear not!"

Fear is a major hindrance to blessings. As Job said, that which we fear comes upon us. September 11, 2001 was a wake-up call for many, including the church. Paradoxically, many Christians are now worshipping the spirit of fear. Understanding we are the righteousness of God allows the love of God to fill us, and perfect love casts out fear.

36. If we don't really want to be healed, God will not heal us (Ps. 30:2; Mat. 14:35-36; John 5:6-8). Surprise! Surprise! Some do not *want* to be healed. I express this surprising revelation in the form of a fanciful poem.

Ode to a Hypo C

My achy, breaky joints they creak
At night my bladder springs a leak
My splitting head drives me to bed
I down another load of meds?

Midnight, sinking in the sack
A true devoted 'chondriac
Proud of feeling never well
Committed to my failing health.

The Hindrances 18

Pills at sunset, pills at dawn
How I savor every one
Help is just a call away
But give me suffering any day.

God Himself's too old to heal
Why bend my knees in vain appeal
Ain't lookin' for no miracle
Feeling well's too much like hell.

37. Self-image (Prov. 23:6-7). No one, male or female, young or old, can ever rise above his or her self-image. Knowing who we are in Christ and accepting this new image is critically important for growth, prayer and healing (see "Daily Declarations" and "Identity in Christ" in the Appendix). The image we have of ourselves – whether as a success or failure, as a sleeper or mover, as an illness-bound or healthy, robust individual – can make the difference between producing a hindrance to healing or healing itself.

When we ask for healing and cannot see it as done and cannot adjust our mind to the new circumstances, we let Satan steal our health and healing. We need to see ourselves receiving what we have asked for under the covenant. Contrary to popular opinion, seeing is not believing. When we see the end result before it manifests, seeing is receiving. When we get a vision of what we have requested and rest in the covenant assurance that we have it, it's as good as done.

38. Believing our illness is too small for God to heal. "It's not all that important." If it's big enough to spend time and/or money for help from the doctor, why is it not big enough for us to ask our Eternal Doctor for help? To paraphrase Jeremiah, "Is anything too small for God?"

39. Having no hope (Prov. 13:12). This is not quite the same thing as lacking faith. We can lose hope because of what people say. "The doctor said I had only two weeks to live." "The doctor said I'd just have to live with it." "He said I'd be sore for two months." "I've lived with it with so long, I guess I can live with it some more." God's opinion should carry weight – not others' opinions or our own fleshly thoughts.

I know how hope can work for our eventual healing. Full of hindrances, I endured for twelve years suffering that was not God's will for me. There were times when I lost hope and came close to ending my life.

And yet, strangely, I hung on to hope. I was approaching the end of twelve years of illness. As I did, being somewhat of a Bible numbers enthusiast, I remembered that twelve was an important Bible number. It includes new beginnings. That's what I asked God for. And that's what He gave me.

40. Allowing evil influences to destroy our health (Prov. 3:7-8). What we allow into our minds can destroy our peace of mind and introduce negative or evil

Why Doesn't God Heal Me?

influences that can affect our health. Raucous and demonic music and evil movies or television fall into this category. The book of Proverbs is full of the effects of our evil environment on our peace of mind and health.

Some religious groups are unwise and self-righteous in condemning outright certain activities such as cards, moderate drinking, movies, dancing, etc. Although I'm sure there are some movies Christians should not see, every Christian has different battles and some are not tempted and/or affected by what would cause others to sin. We must not be legalistic or judgmental about what others watch. We should judge ourselves and all of us should seek God's perfect holiness. God is not a picky legalist, and yet He is a holy God.

41. Not being joyful (Prov. 17:22). Proverbs say that a merry heart is like a medicine. When we block the fortifying flow of Jesus' joy with negative thoughts, we can either induce sickness or block our healing.

Laughter is maybe not the best medicine, but it surely helps. One of the young cancer patients on the set of the movie *Patch Adams* actually went into remission because of the spontaneous joy of actor Robin Williams. It was not only in the movie that laughter healed. It was on the set.

Lighten up, killjoys! God invented laughter. And joy is coming in with a hoot and a holler and a hee-haw in the coming revival. Sanctimonious, constipated religiosity is about to be flushed out by the laughing brook of Holy Spirit joy. God is going to show up in church, and in His presence is fullness of joy!

42. Religious thinking (as opposed to godly thinking). "I'll just have to suffer in my infirmity like Paul." "We don't see any healings in our church, so I'll just take a pill for it." Some warm a pew in a powerless church and have never been exposed to the powerful flow of the anointing in some servants of God. The low anointing level in many churches, while not actually an official hindrance, is a result of other hindrances that lower the flow of the Spirit. Godly thinking is according to the Word, basing our thoughts and actions on His sure healing promise.

43. Refusing to believe in demonic involvement in sickness (see "Curses, witchcraft" in the Appendix). Due to the importance of this issue, some reemphasis and repetition of the principles in Chapter 7 is necessary. Demonic participation in sickness is not some weird idea invented by some unbalanced kook. The idea comes from our Savior and Healer, Jesus Himself! He talked of deaf and dumb *demons*, of epileptic *demons*, of "spirits [*demons*] of infirmity." In many cases casting out demons was synonymous with healing.

Demons are smart enough to cause physical problems without a permanent or even temporary manifestation of their presence. Demon infestation, influence and/or possession are not necessary to produce a physical ailment, but Jesus is our witness that demons can directly cause certain illnesses. When they are cast out, the sickness disappears or is healed.

The beating Jesus endured for us paid for our sicknesses, whether they were caused by demons, directly or indirectly, or not. Demons are not involved in cre-

The Hindrances 18

ating every sickness. We do quite well by ourselves. They do, however, like to convince us that God's promise is not true once we have claimed it.

In most cases they do become involved after we claim the healing promise, and if we accept and believe their symptoms, we retain the symptoms and end up with no healing at all, either in the natural or the supernatural realm.

What God says is true, and the reality is that Jesus paid for both our sins *and* our sicknesses 2,000 years ago.

Let me explain. When we sin, if we have not fully grasped that we are the righteousness of God, we may still feel guilty after confession – especially if we see the person we sinned against. That's a lie of Satan! Jesus has already forgiven us and forgotten the sin. He paid for that sin 2,000 years ago.

So what is different when it comes to healing? Nothing! "It is finished" means "it is finished." Guilt and doubt after confession of sin should not exist for us who are the righteousness of God. Doubt about our healing after claiming it, by the same token, should not exist!

When Satan tries to convince us that we are still sick because a faith healing did not occur instantly in the physical realm, that's a lie! Logical, carnal, and even some Christian people will tell us *we* are the ones lying to ourselves and that we're living in a sort of dream world, denying reality. Is ours a hocus-pocus "Houdini healing," as some seem to think?

Can't we see Satan's game plan? He is doing the same thing he does when he tries to make us feel we have not been forgiven by God.

It may not be exactly like the guilt trip he lays on us regarding sin, but it is just as much a lie. He makes us, with his lying symptoms, feel "unhealed." If we reject that lie and persist in faith knowing we have already been healed by Jesus' stripes, the symptoms will shortly disappear, proving God and us right! Whose report do we believe – Satan's and his lies or God's and His Word?

The Bible speaks of Satan's "lying wonders." Those wonders have a definite effect in the physical world – and would, if possible, deceive even the elect. His miracles are real, but God's are more real, more powerful, and are based on truth – not lies.

Yes, we may feel pain. We may feel awful. But let's not declare the Devil's doing. Let's declare God's reality – what Jesus has already done!

If we proclaim with our mouth that our symptoms are in reality sickness, we are actually bringing the curse of sickness on ourselves by mouthing faithless words. Though it may at first sound like mental gymnastics, it is a godly exercise that develops spiritual muscle with which to conquer Satan.

All this sounded ridiculous to me at first. When I finally did it, however, and then simply kept thanking God for the healing, Satan gave up. Severe flu symptoms disappeared.

Speaking God's Word over ourselves is powerful! If it is not a reality in the natural world, it will become physical reality if we speak it. Faith is the evidence of

179

"things not seen," but it *is* evidence – powerful evidence of a spiritual reality.

We must rebuke Satan and his demons in Jesus' name and remind them that we were healed 2,000 years ago and they have no right to bring their lying symptoms.

This should be done resolutely – but only **once**. From then on, we should repeatedly *thank and praise God* for our healing – in faith – until all symptoms disappear.

I had originally planned to put the spiritual warfare part of healing in the Appendix, so as not to offend the conservative religiosity of many, which I understand, having accepted that paradigm for so long.

When I mentioned spiritual warfare as a part of healing, an evangelist friend reacted in a somewhat hostile way: "Spiritual warfare is not in our paradigm!" I didn't say anything, but I thought: "Well, then you better change your paradigm."

Aggressive spiritual warfare was in Jesus' paradigm! We better make His paradigm ours too! He dealt almost daily with demons in the context of physical healing. And He didn't dilly-dally. He told them to get lost!

Admittedly, the unconverted people that Jesus healed did not have all this knowledge. They didn't need it. Jesus did the warfare for them, and they simply believed. But we have the Holy Spirit and are empowered to do what Jesus did.

The demons are happy to make and keep us sick and believing they have no part in sickness. Then they can keep us asking the question, "Why doesn't God heal me?" They can keep us doubting our *faith* instead of doubting our *doubts*! We doubt God instead of doubting Satan!

We can even call his bluff and tell him where he can go! And that's one time we need have no scruples in using the phrase "Go to hell!" After all, that's where demons belong.

The carnal mind does not want to believe what God says. We prefer human reasoning. And we prefer to stay sick instead of believing God.

Let's not give up on God. Breakthrough may come with perseverance.

44. Comparing ourselves with others (in regard to healing). II Corinthians 10:12 says this is not wise. "She was operated for what I have, so I guess I better do the same." "My pastor's so spiritual, and he refused all help from doctors. I hope I don't die, but if I don't do the same, what will he think of me?" Or we see others who have not been healed that we feel are better Christians than we are. "If God hasn't healed them, then he surely won't heal little old me!" A famous evangelist says God has not healed him in order to teach him humility. So some may say, "If sickness is good for _____, I guess it's good for me! Sickness will make me more spiritual like him. What's good for a great evangelist must be good for me." God has other ways to humble us. If you are attacked with a deadly cancer and compare yourself with another Christian who hasn't been healed, you will be more than humbled. You may end up dead. Such foolish reasoning blocks healing.

45. Wanting healing to the exclusion of accepting our calling as a Christian. Some may desire healing only, and not want to accept their calling. In Acts 8,

The Hindrances **18**

Simon Magus[33] wanted the power of the anointing without accepting the calling to be a Christian. There are those unconverted whom God may heal in order to draw them to Him. Then there are those whom God is already calling who will not accept their calling and want healing only.

46. Not giving God the glory for our healing (this can apply either to the person who is the instrument of healing or to the person who is healed) (Luke 17:17-19). If we want to be healed so we can brag about it, God may not heal us. God has made it clear to Benny Hinn that the moment he begins to take the glory to himself, the anointing power will disappear. In spite of accusations to the contrary, he does give God the glory. That is one reason why so many are healed through his ministry.

47. Lack of respect for God's authority and sovereignty (Prov. 9:10). We cannot presume to order God around. "Those symptoms better be gone right now!" "I want it done this way!" God wants us to boldly claim His promise, but with the proper respect.

48. Wrong motives. "You ask and do not receive, because you ask with wrong motives ['wrong purpose and evil, selfish motives' – AMP], so that you may spend it on your pleasures" (James 4:3). Of course we don't want to suffer, but is that the only reason we want healing? Don't we also desire to serve God and "abound to every good work" and to glorify God through our healing? Do you want your hand healed so you can be a better thief? Do you want your eye healed so you can watch pornography?

Although we may not go to such extremes, we do need to examine our motives. God looks on the heart (I Sam. 16:7).

49. Misplaced faith. Although there were apparently only fourteen healings at Lourdes that were attested by doctors, I saw some at this French shrine who seemed to worship the place and not principally the God who heals.

Jesus told the woman in John 4:19-24 that a place should not have pre-eminence over God Himself. We are to worship Him in spirit and in truth. This is not to say that anointing oil or even holy water may not have some symbolic importance, yet we must not put the accent on the physical, but on the unseen spiritual healing hand of God. God is not pleased when we emphasize a church shrine more than Him.

Although I love my brothers and sisters in Christ who are Catholic, experience in dealing with some in France and Quebec would indicate that there is a tendency for some to look to Mary in a worshipful way for healing rather than to the sacrifice of Jesus.

---

[33] Simon Magus was a sorcerer in Samaria and a man of great power and influence among the people. He loved the praises and adulation of men. With his innate love of witchery, he offered to buy from the apostles the power of conferring spiritual gifts, and was rebuked in language of sternness.

Ignatius, the earliest of the church fathers, calls Simon "the first born of Satan." Irenaeus marks him out as the first of all heretics. Scripture, however, is silent about his life after Peter's strong rebuke.

Why Doesn't God Heal Me?

Mary is indeed one of the greatest Christians who ever lived. She had the honor of being the physical mother of Jesus, but Jesus as God from eternity never had a mother, only God, His Father. Although the Holy Spirit does have the gentle qualities of a mother, the idea of the "Mother of God" came from paganism. And God tells us not to mix pagan deities such as Semiramis,[34] Nimrod's[35] wife-mother, and pagan ways with His prescribed way of worship (Deut. 12:30; Jer. 10:2).

Mary is a highly esteemed Daughter of God in heaven as an intercessor now, but she is not a member of the Trinity. Although Revelation 3:9 does say Sons and Daughters of God will be worshipped in the future, God says that there is only one Mediator between God the Father and mankind (I Tim. 2:5). That is Jesus, not Mary – and not a man dressed in black donning a clerical collar. Why so many "Hail Mary's"? Why not "Hail Jesus," our Healer? Faith in Mary above Jesus is misplaced faith.

Some look to a person who happens to be God's instrument of healing rather than to God Himself. It is certainly not wrong to travel to a healing meeting featuring Benny Hinn, Rodney Howard-Browne, T.L. Osborn or any healing evangelist, famous or not. But let's not worship them. I have never met any healing servant who would want that. Let's look to Jesus, not man. To God be the glory!

Paul sent out cloths that had touched his body to distant believers (Acts 19:12). The anointing power came from God – not from some magical quality of the cloth. Unfortunately some today put an undue emphasis on objects instead of on Jesus the Healer – and even charge for it!

Some have faith in someone else's faith, such as the faith of the healing servant. That is subtly but surely misplaced faith as well.

As we have seen, it is also possible to put too much emphasis on our own faith. We can look at all the faith we have worked up with our human strength, instead of realizing that faith is a gift from God. If we are not careful, our healing can become like a prize for having so much faith. That is a false teaching based on works and not

---

[34] According to the Babylonian religion, Semiramis was the wife and the mother of Nimrod.

Following the death of Nimrod, his heathen form of worship was continued by his wife, Queen Semiramis. She claimed that her husband had become the Sun god, and was to be worshipped. Some time after this, Queen Semiramis conceived through adultery and gave birth to an illegitimate son whom she named Tammuz, who she declared was actually Nimrod reborn, and that he had been supernaturally conceived. However, even though Semiramis claimed to have given birth to a savior, it was she that was worshipped, not the son. She was worshipped as the mother of the gods.

[35] The name Nimrod may come from the Hebrew verb *nimrodh* which is translated, "Let us revolt." Nimrod is referred to as a "mighty one": this phrase derives from the Hebrew word *gilor* which means "tyrant." Nimrod was not just a powerful man on the earth at that time; he was a tyrannical leader of men. The phrase "a mighty hunter before the [Eternal]" suggests that it was not wild beasts that Nimrod was hunting, but men. Having hunted them he would enslave them and have a tyrannical hold over them. And all this was done in direct opposition to the Eternal.

Genesis also indicates that Nimrod was the builder of Nineveh, and the word Nineveh (Nin-neveh) means "the habitation of Ninus." Ninus is probably Nimrod.

on faith and the grace of God. This idea leads logically to the following hindrance.

50. Trusting in merit. We are not healed because of what we are or do, but because of who God is and what He has done for us – because He "delights in mercy and loving-kindness" (Micah 7:18, AMP).

We have seen that repenting of hindrances is not a kind of legalistic works. On the other hand, we must meet conditions and remove hindrances for both salvation and for healing, which is physical salvation.

Hindrances involve sin and there is a definite connection between sickness and sin. In the case of the man born blind, the disciples were actually not all that far off base by asking if the man's handicap was a result of some sin, more logically on the part of his parents. Generational sin and curses can produce illness, but that was not the case in John 9. In John 5:14, however, Jesus told a man he had just healed to sin no more lest a worse illness come upon Him.

When Jesus has returned to earth to usher in the Millenium, He will start abolishing both sin and sickness (Jer. 30:17; Isa. 19:20-22; Rev. 22:1-2).

51. Lack of prayer and fasting (Mat. 17:21). The story of the boy with the deaf and dumb spirit or demon in Mark 9:14-29 reveals at least two principles: a) Some physical illnesses are caused by direct demon manifestation. b) The faith and power to cast out some demons requires the extra spiritual contact with God provided by prayer and fasting. Jesus Himself had probably been fasting, since He just came from the mountaintop experience of the Mount of Transfiguration.

I often compare fasting to the extreme means of digging a tunnel through a mountain. Fasting is spiritual dynamite. Sometimes the pick and shovel do not do the job.

Fasting is not forcing the hand of God. Hunger strikes don't impress God. Miracles, deliverance and spectacular healings often follow fasting (Isa. 58:6-8). Fasting opens doors in the spirit realm and brings added faith and power.

The Greek for miracle-working power is *dunamis*. Sometimes it takes the dynamite of fasting to activate it!

52. Putting even natural remedies ahead of God's healing. Some people feel self-righteous because they wouldn't dare see a doctor, but they swear by their righteous, natural remedies. Mind you, God is all for them. He made the natural remedies, plants and herbs for healing.

I have to wonder, though, when I hear of people dying because they refused medical help – they would trust in God and herbs, or herbs and God, in whichever order it comes. If they trust in nature or the creation more than the Creator and supernatural Healer, that could hinder their healing.

God rightly said in Romans 1:25 that some would love the creation more than the Creator! People seem to worship nature and the environment more than God, observing "Earth Day" and yet ignoring the day the Creator rested from His creation and made holy! Humans made in God's image are murdered because of animal testing.

18   Why Doesn't God Heal Me?

The modern Gnosticism, the New Age movement, glorifies things natural. Natural remedies are not wrong. What is wrong is trusting in them more than in God.

53. Lack of praise and thankfulness to the Healer, God (Deut. 8:10-20; Dan. 4:28-35). Healing evangelists who do not thank and praise God do not have the same results as those who do. And if we are not thankful to God, God may allow Satan to steal our healing. The illness may return if we do not express our sincere thanks to God.

54. Speaking evil of our father or mother (Mat. 15:3-6). Death was the Old Covenant verdict for those who did so. Jesus reaffirms this. Death can come from sickness and accidents too. We may pay that penalty unless we confess and forsake this serious breach of the fifth commandment.

55. Not dealing with problems that must be dealt with before laying on hands for healing (I Tim. 5:22). Haste can be costly. As healing servants, we must take the time to give people more than a "quick fix." If they ask for help or counseling for a problem or sin, we must deal with that first. If not, we may be held responsible for their sins – and they won't be healed. In addition, curses on them may be passed to us. This can work both ways. We can cover ourselves before someone prays for us, when we pray, "Whatever is not of You, Father, let it pass over me, in Jesus' name."

56. Abuse. A Christian who is lying to himself by committing gross physical or sexual abuse against anyone, especially his mate or children, will almost always see his healing withheld. God is the One who decides, according to the person's heart and the degree of abuse. I Peter 3:7 condemns husbands who are even inconsiderate to their wives, saying that their prayers, including prayers for healing, will be hindered.

57. Not confessing our sins (Ps. 32: 1-5). This is slightly different from the hindrance "Unrepented sins," which involves repentance or actual change. David shows here that the guilt involved with delaying his confession of sin actually made him sick. So if we are asking for healing, we cannot be refusing to confess our sins and thus actually bringing on sickness while we are asking for its removal.

One key that will help us understand that we are the righteousness of God is that when we stumble we have a right to be cleansed. Quick confession is a key to walking in the righteousness of God and thus receiving all God's blessings.

58. Not developing our spirit, or "spirit man" (Prov. 18:14: "A man's spirit sustains him in sickness, but a crushed spirit who can bear?" – NIV). The Holy Spirit revealed this hindrance through Tim Sheets on the Canadian TV program, *It's a New Day*. Often when a person is chronically ill, it may not be only physical or emotional. The root cause may be an undeveloped spirit. The person is not taking care of his or her spiritual life – is not where he or she needs to be spiritually. Sheets gave five ways to ensure that we develop our spirit: reading and studying the Word of God, praying with our understanding and in the spirit, praise

The Hindrances 18

and worship, intimate fellowship and communication with the Holy Spirit, and church attendance.

59. Anger. As seen in a previous chapter, this was the prophet Elisha's hindrance. It is not only a problem that may prevent God from healing us. It is a major cause of sickness and death. Medical researchers are finally catching up with the Bible. Proverbs recorded long ago that negative emotions had a terribly adverse effect on health.

A minister on a Christian talk show gave the following account of a friend with an anger problem. Only a few days before, the friend had been given a clean bill of health from the Mayo Clinic. They said he had the heart of a 35-year-old. That suddenly changed when he caught some hunters hunting on his land. After an angry encounter with them, he died suddenly of heart failure.

The subject of negative emotions on health is too broad for this book. The stress of our modern age causes many premature deaths. Even Christians have a hard time attaining the peace God offers to those who learn to rest in Him.

60. Eating foods God says not to eat. Who should know better what our body needs to stay in good health than the One who made us? Although, thankfully, some Christians are beginning to teach the Biblical food laws, most Christians today believe those laws are Jewish and we put ourselves "under the law" if we observe them.

Is the body of a Jew different from the body of another human being?

The food laws of Leviticus 11 and Deuteronomy 14 are not spiritual or moral laws. They are simply laws of health.

We are not to eat the meat of animals unless they part the hoof and chew their cud. In the case of fish, they must have fins and scales. This is the way God separated the animals that properly digest their food and provide clean meat for mankind from those who are the scavengers or walking, swimming garbage cans of the natural world.

In many scientific domains, men are beginning to catch up with God and the Bible. Unfortunately, this has not been fully achieved in the nutritional realm. There are, however, some interesting facts that explain God's health laws.

Studies have shown that the Jewish people who keep the food laws are almost completely free of certain diseases. The connection between the food laws they observe and this phenomenon is unavoidable.

One scientific journal stated that even a small amount of pork is bad for the human body. The protein in pork is almost identical to humans. To digest the pork, the body has to develop enzymes that eat away at the stomach. Doctors will tell people with heart problems not to eat pork, yet they won't tell people to avoid it so they can prevent problems.

Another study was made recently to teach stranded seafarers how to survive on ocean fish. They concluded that the best fish to eat were those that had fins and scales. God wasn't so stupid, after all!

185

Why Doesn't God Heal Me?

It is fruitless, of course, to try to prove these things scientifically. Biochemists and nutritionists are generally like most experts in scientific matters: they refuse to believe God and the Bible unless and until science can prove what the Word says. And the studies are by no means conclusive at this point.

One Scripture that experts would agree with is Leviticus 7:23-24. Animal fat contains hormones that encourage the storing of fat and the addictive consumption of fatty foods.[36] God had already placed a further prohibitive rating on fat when He said, "All the fat is the Eternal's" in Leviticus 3:17.

The fat belonged to the Eternal (Jesus). One of the spiritual meanings of the fat is the flesh and its lusts that we must surrender to Jesus in exchange for the muscular strength of His body in communion. He forbade animal blood in honor of the blood He would shed for us – and in so doing He made it unacceptable for human consumption. He wanted us to rely on the power of His blood in communion for our spiritual and physical life and health.

Alas, even Christians refuse to believe what God says. A misunderstanding of the nature of the New Covenant is the main culprit. Jesus' sacrifice did away with the need for animal sacrifices and rituals. His death did not, however, change the structure of the human stomach and body. You wouldn't put milk into your gas tank, would you? God designed the human stomach and body to run on certain fuels. He spelled out those that are not appropriate.

In Acts 10:14, the apostle Peter makes an interesting declaration – ten years after he became a Christian. He said he had never eaten anything unclean. God gave him a vision, telling him to eat unclean animals. Did God do a great miracle at that moment, altering the human body forever so that unclean food could now produce good health? No! Peter's stomach stayed the same. It was his attitude that changed! Verse 28 clearly shows that the unclean animals were only a symbol for unclean men, i.e. Gentiles whom the Jews considered unclean and unfit to first, enter the Jewish society, and then later, enter the Christian church. By this vision God showed Peter that Gentiles could come into the church.

God forbade eating blood as well, because the life, as well as toxins and dangerous hormones, are in the blood. That's why He even said not to eat even clean animals that were strangled or died naturally and were not properly slaughtered to let the blood spill out. God even repeats this for Gentiles under the New Covenant!

That's in Acts 15:29. Some claim that these four things are the only things from the Hebrew section of God's Book of Love that Gentile Christians must avoid. Preposterous! That would mean it's okay for Gentile Christians to commit murder, or steal, or lie, etc. No, the council mentioned those four things because they were the only parts of the ceremonial law that needed to be pointed out to Gentile

---

[36] According to the National Institutes of Health, saturated fat (which includes meat, cream, eggs, butter, poultry, chocolate, coconut, palm oil and lard) boosts your blood cholesterol level more than anything else in your diet. Eating less saturated fat is the best way to lower your blood cholesterol level.

The Hindrances 18

Christians, who had formerly taken part in idolatrous ceremonies where they committed fornication and drank blood.

What is interesting, though, is what God is saying here – in the part of the Bible that is supposed to do away with the laws of Hebrew Scripture. He says that even Gentiles under the New Covenant should abstain "from blood and from things strangled." If the food laws against eating blood and eating even clean animals that were strangled are still valid for all under the New Covenant, so are the laws about unclean meats!

These verses from the pen of meticulous Luke are clear. Peter said that people often misunderstood Paul. And in the question of unclean meats, this is also the case. If Peter continued to refrain from unclean meats after conversion, it is certain that Paul did as well. It is beyond the scope of this book to examine the verses from Paul that people cite to justify eating pork. Suffice it to say that the context of Romans 14 involves not judging others about days of fasting.

Some of Paul's statements may seem unclear to some. He is quite clear, however, when he states that we are the temple of God (I Cor. 3:17). The connection with the tabernacle is unmistakable. God did not allow unclean animals into the tabernacle. So why would we – as God's temple today – allow the meat of unclean animals into our temple? The priests were never allowed to eat the sacrificial meat of unclean beasts. Why would God demand any less of us – His New Covenant priests? Have human stomachs been miraculously changed under the New Covenant and in this twenty-first century?

No, and end-time prophecy proves it. Jesus never changes, and His judgment is coming against those who "eat swine's flesh, detestable things and mice" (Isa. 66:15-17).

Again in an end-time context, Malachi 4:4 tells us to remember the laws God gave Moses – all that "Old Testament stuff." That includes laws of health.

As I am doing last minute editing, I am watching on Trinity Broadcasting TV Dr. Ted Broer, internationally known nutritionist, who is respected by top political and religious leaders. He is preaching from Isaiah, where God calls those who eat pork and rat "smoke in His nostrils" (65:4-5). As he warns against the dangers of sugar replacements, he lambastes lobster lovers, calling these scavengers (the shellfish – not the people!) "giant cockroaches."

On a preaching circuit in 1987 my family was eating at a gourmet restaurant in the French Caribbean when my seven-year-old daughter Lisa spied a giant cockroach on the ceiling. In French she blurted out to the waitress, "What is that animal up there?" It seemed almost as big as a lobster. But had it fallen in my plate, I don't think it would have been worth $25 a pound!

Taste deceives. The forbidden fruit looked and tasted good. When we let God show us from His Word the knowledge of discerning between good and evil, we walk in spiritual and physical health. When we eat that which God says is unclean, we open the door for the master of the unclean to attack us with sickness.

Hindrances to All of God's Blessings

61. Stealing from God by not tithing (Mal. 3:1-12; Mat. 23:23). God requires a minimum amount under both the Old and New Covenants to teach us to be givers like our Father. Abraham tithed long before the Old Covenant. And Hebrews 7, carefully studied, shows clearly the tithing principle stays under the New Covenant, only not with the same national administration and not with the Levites as recipients.

God does not specify an amount for the *offerings*, which are voluntary as to the sum given. That is where New Covenant free-will generosity and joyful giving come into play. God promises to bless the tithe-payer and meet all his needs. Those who don't tithe are stealing God's money and bring His curse upon them.

Stealing from God Himself is one of the most serious of sins. Such thieves are saying, in effect, "I don't care about God's message of salvation going out as a witness to the world."[37]

The parable of the sower shows degrees of blessings in the laws of sowing and reaping. Miserly tight-fistedness brings a curse and allows the spirit of stinginess to influence you. Basic tithing is good, yet paying only the tithe amounts to being an unprofitable servant, doing only what is required. Giving out of coercion because of a manipulative minister robs you of all blessings. Giving begrudgingly gives you a thirty-fold return on your offering. Giving for giving's sake but with no feeling of joy gives a sixty-fold harvest. Giving with a joyful heart produces a one-hundred-fold harvest and allows God to bless you from every direction, in any way *He* can imagine.

Malachi 3 shows the blessings that come when we give tithes and offerings. God promises to "open the windows of heaven" in financial blessings. He even promises to take away the curse on the land and rebuke Satan the devourer. All nations will call Israel (the believers) blessed. That blessing also implies that the curse of sickness, which goes along with the curses in Genesis and Deuteronomy, will be removed, all things being equal.

62. Involvement with demons. God does not coexist with evil. When we are playing around with demons, He can withhold healing. Ignorance need not be an excuse. God does not want us to be ignorant of Satan's devices, and may allow the lack of healing to incite us to stop questionable practices.

Here are some examples of problem areas: witchcraft, séances, contact with

---

[37] Matthew 24:14 says that in the last days the gospel of the Kingdom of God will be preached as a powerful witness to the world. As we saw in Chapter 2, God's plan of salvation honors Adam's and the world's free will as swayed by Satan. Jesus did indeed come to save all mankind, but He chooses only a few first fruits now. He will resurrect all the unsaved after the Millennium. Although God has prophesied a great end-time harvest as His Spirit is poured out (Acts 2:17), His main purpose is to proclaim the message of hope that Jesus is returning to save the world. That gospel being preached is what is central in God's mind. When we don't tithe, we are saying that what is most important to Jesus is not important to us.

mediums, fortune tellers and fortune-telling, games such as "Dungeons and Dragons," books and movies glorifying witchcraft, Pokémon cards, satanic jewelry, psychic telephone lines, ouija boards, horoscopes, transcendental meditation and hypnotism.

Any activity where you enter into the realm of the supernatural, but where God is not involved, is to be avoided. You don't have to be attending the church of Satan and worshipping demons openly to be guilty. Some things may seem harmless, but are entering subtly the demonic realm. The New Age movement is a good example. We should not be getting anywhere close to worshipping demons or lifting them up in any way.

Most people – even surprising numbers of Christians – think it is harmless to let their children dress up like demonic ghosts and goblins on Halloween night. There is no question about the pagan and demonic origins of this overtly satanic feast. Why should we Christians be a part of exalting demons and then doing harm to those who don't participate in their demonic feast? Doing harm to others is no more Christian than dressing up like demons. God wants us to have no part with the evil of this world, especially when the evil ones are directly involved.

Deuteronomy 18:10 and 11 are clear: "There shall not be found among you ... one who uses divination, one who practices witchcraft, or one who interprets omens, or a sorcerer, or one who casts a spell, or a medium, or one who calls up the dead." Christians who think popular movies encouraging witchcraft are harmless are harming their children.

God spells it out in Ephesians 5:11-12: "And have *no fellowship* with the unfruitful works of darkness, but rather expose them. For it is shameful even to speak of those things which are done by them in secret" (NKJV). Not exposing the works of darkness is as bad as involvement in them. Dabbling with demons is playing with fire.

63. Not providing for the needs of one's family (I Tim. 5:8). Since this verse says a man who does not do this is "worse than an unbeliever," he obviously will not be able to receive the promises reserved for believers.

64. Not interceding in prayer for someone when God shows us we should (I Sam. 12:23). A hostile social worker forbade a teenage Christian friend of mine from going to church and gave him no money for food. My friend used his knowledge of spiritual warfare to bind the demons affecting the social worker and interceded in prayer for her, asking God to forgive and bless her. Only 30 minutes after his prayer, she called and said *she* wanted to go to church! When God leads us to intercede, the results can be dramatic. When we don't follow His lead, He may withhold blessings.

65. Attempting to bear fruit apart from Jesus – "dead works." Jesus tells us to abide in Him, not simply to drop in for an occasional visit. We can do nothing without Him (John 15:4-5). The first foundational doctrine of Hebrews 6:1 is

Why Doesn't God Heal Me?

"repentance from dead works." Any work, even a great work for God, is a *dead work* if we do it on our own strength. Anything we do for God is not truly of God unless we do it by the power of the *living* Jesus in us. "Abide in me" should be more than a song for us. Trusting in ourselves brings a curse from God (Jer. 17:5).

66. Putting traditions of men before the Word of God (Mat. 15:3). (Hindrance No. 8 deals only with traditions relating to healing. Before you read this controversial hindrance, I suggest you pray aloud the prayers on self-examination and coming to terms with sin, found under "Prayers" in the Appendix.) The Pharisees put all kinds of traditions ahead of God. We do the same thing today. So much of what we call religion is "pure" tradition – not the uncompromisingly pure Word of God. The truth may shock you, and yet once you understand it, not accepting it could hinder your healing.

We have muddied the waters of the originally pure stream of Christianity with tradition. Ever see "Easter" in the Bible? It's only there in an old King James mistranslation.

Easter comes from the name of the pagan goddess Ishtar, not from the Bible. What do pagan sexual fertility rites have to do with Jesus?

And what about December 25?

Shepherds would never have been out with their flocks in the middle of the winter rainy season. And Rome would never have called for a census in the middle of winter. Yet we observe the birth of our Savior on December 25. Read the seasonal Christmas articles in your local newspaper. Even witches can tell you that this period of the winter solstice was the time the pagans kept their feast. Satanists still attach importance to that time in which the sun is at its lowest and darkness rules.The Holy Spirit has confirmed what Jewish calendar calculations have given strong evidence to support: Jesus was born on the Feast of Trumpets in the fall.[38] It's not that complicated. The Bible says Jesus started His ministry at the age of 30 (Luke 3:23) and died in the spring at Passover at the end of a three and one-half year period of ministry. Since He died in the spring, He would logically have been born six months earlier – in the fall.

The Feast of Trumpets, followed by a great harvest feast, celebrates the coming of the King – His birth and His return. The first Adam came to life at harvest time. How interesting that the last Adam – Jesus – also came to life during the fall harvest time. And Jesus will return as well at harvest time to reap a great harvest.

Why blindly follow tradition as if it were our god? Why celebrate Jesus' birth at a time of pagan revelry? Why not do it God's way instead of the pagan way? Why go out of our way to disobey a clear command of God (Deut. 12:30-32)? Why do we put so much stock in tradition?

---

[38] This author obtained confirmation of the above in the article "Consider the 24th of Kislev," December 2000, that was available at that time on the website www.yacovrambsel.com. Not all the opinions expressed in articles on this website necessarily represent the views of this author.

The Hindrances **18**

God's time has come to restore and reveal important truths to His church so Jesus' Bride can be ready for His coming.

What God has revealed is shocking: at this writing over 9,000 "doctrines of demons" pollute the teaching of our modern churches. Many come from the traditions of that "good 'ole time religion," the "faith of our fathers." Biblical fathers? No. Church fathers who often traded the Word of God for tradition. Shocking, but true.

"Teaching as doctrines the precepts of men" in Matthew 15:9 is a bit different from verse 3, transgressing "the commandment of God for the sake of your tradition …" Some gay churches teach that Jesus was gay and that we should have the gay experience to be Christian. That is a precept of men and an outright lie. We can't walk in lies and expect to receive God's blessings.

67. Being a "tare" (Mat. 15:13). If you are not God's "wheat" but a "tare" or weed planted by Satan and your job is the destruction of God's people, you may not be healed. God will mercifully decide your eternal destiny. You may be sincerely deceived. Wolves in sheep's clothing, however, cannot expect God's blessings.

68. Being spiritually blind (Mat.15:14; II Cor. 4:3-4). If a person has no understanding of what God is doing, how can he or she receive what God has to offer? Also, a spiritual leader and potential healing servant whose eyes are blinded by a "beam" cannot remove a "speck" of sickness from anyone (Matt. 7:3).

69. Not having our hearts right with God (Mat. 12:34-37; 15:18-20). Our words reveal what is in our hearts. Jesus emphasizes the importance of both the words we speak and the thoughts revealed by those words. Even the man after God's heart had a heart problem in Psalm 32. He went through a terrible time of physical and mental suffering until he drew near to God to have his heart cleansed. God couldn't bless or heal Simon Magus in Acts 8 because his heart was not right before God. Blasphemous words or dirty language reveal a sad state of the heart. God doesn't focus on our face or our body like the world does; He looks on the heart (I Sam. 16:7). If our heart is right with God, we can expect His blessings.

70. Not accepting God's forgiveness of our sins (Mat. 9:2; I John 3:19-22). We must accept God's forgiveness. Some do not admit that in their minds and hearts. For whatever reason, they are not accepting Jesus' gracious sacrifice.

Jesus died for your sins. Believe it! Paul says to forget those things that are past, even if they happened yesterday or even today. Washed by Jesus' blood, you *have* no past! You don't feel dirty when you step out of a cleansing shower, do you? Guilt does not come from God. Rebuke it! Christians are not under condemnation (Rom. 8:1).

71. "Playing footsy" with the Devil (Mat. 10:5; I John 2:15). Jesus said not to go into the "way of the Gentiles." We should not flirt with false religions or false gods. Do we go 18 blocks out of our way to pass "casually" by the porn shop?

The Gentile Samaritans had a false religion. They claimed to be of God

Why Doesn't God Heal Me?

but did not follow the ways of God. If we want to do things the pagan way – the rebellious way – God cannot bless us.

72. Not trusting in God for our needs (Mat. 10:9; 6:11, 25-34). Although this was a specific command for a special mission, the principle is true. God can't heal us or prosper us if we can't trust Him for our needs.

73. "Cramming religion down people's throats" (Mat. 10:13-14; I Pet. 3:15). In ministry, we are to bestow a peaceful greeting and blessing upon a house that receives us. If people refuse to hear us, we are not to try to force them.

Jesus tells us to "shake the dust off [our] feet," sometimes in a literal gesture, in order to avoid partaking of their sins. The Passover foot-washing (John 13) washes us clean. Jesus told Peter that if his feet were clean, all of him was clean. When we "shake the dust off [our] feet [or sometimes the snow, if we live in Canada]" we renounce the sins of the belligerent party. We also acknowledge that they are not worthy of the blessing, and God will then bring that blessing back upon us.

74. Not being "wise as serpents and harmless as doves" (Mat. 10:16, NKJV). We need to be innocent as little children in regards to sin and yet mature and wise in our relationships, especially with unbelievers. We mustn't create stumbling blocks for potential believers.

75. Not enduring in the face of persecution (Mat. 10:22). Not enduring to the end in a time of persecution is tantamount to denying Jesus.

76. Not obeying God in a time of persecution (Mat.10:23). The time will come for some of God's people in the future when He will instruct them to flee to another city when persecuted severely in one area.

77. Trying to be "better than Jesus" (Mat. 10:24-25). We cannot be better than our Teacher. Yet some try. Super and self-righteous, "holier-than-thou" types – intoxicated with the spirit of religiosity and churchianity – try to be more "righteous" than Jesus.

Too many churches have false standards of legalistic righteousness. God's empowering grace goes much further, exceeding the fake righteousness of modern Pharisees (Mat. 5:20). The real thing is powerful – not picky.

So many professing Christians don't know the real Jesus! They major on minors Jesus never mentioned.

For instance, He obviously drank wine in moderation. He didn't turn water into grape juice! The custom was to save the worst wine for the last – when everybody was too drunk to tell. Jewish weddings were great celebrations. Jesus obviously didn't save the best grape juice for last! The religious crowd would not have labeled Jesus a "winebibber" and "friend of sinners" if He never touched alcohol or showed love to sinners.

It is neither sin to drink moderately or not to drink at all. It is a sin, on the other hand, to be judgmental and self-righteous about anything.

In over 30 years as a pastor I have seen members and ministers emphasize phys-

The Hindrances 18

ical standards of righteousness that border on stupidity. Picky legalism is not God's way.

Movies and playing cards and women's hair in a bun are not addressed in the Bible. God does believe in His Children having good, clean fun. He wants us to be modest in dress and demeanor. Cultures and individual circumstances and motivations, however, are different. God tells us not to judge or compare.

Some Christians judge gays more severely than Jesus did. Homosexual acts are indeed condemned throughout the Bible. But God condemns sins of the heart like religious hypocrisy much more severely than sexual sins of any kind.

All sin, of course, leads to death and should be confessed and reversed. God does, however, emphasize some things more than others. Jesus spoke of "weightier provisions of the law" (Mat. 23:23) and God says He especially hates certain sins (Prov. 6:16-19).

78. Not transmitting messages from God He wants us to pass on (Mat. 10:27). God wants us to preach the gospel freely and boldly without fear of men. At times He may tell us things in the "dark," such as in dreams, that He may want us to share. We must be willing to share what God wants us to share when He shows us it is His will to do so. Wisdom sometimes dictates that we refrain from speaking all we know, yet the context here involves preaching the gospel even when men want to shut us up. In Acts 5:29 the apostles preached Jesus, obeying God rather than a human edict.

79. Fearing men rather than God (Mat. 10:28). We must not fear puny man, but rather stand in awe of the God who has the power of eternal life and death. The French call it the "what will others say?"(syndrome) as a noun-form expression. Americans say, "What will the neighbors say?" Christians should ask, "What does God say?" The Bible says that the fear of man brings a snare (Prov. 29:25), while the reverential awe of God brings boldness and inner peace.

80. Not being willing to endure persecution from even within our physical family (Mat.10:34-37). Many have the false idea that Jesus came to bring peace at His first coming. His siblings deemed even Jesus Himself crazy. He warned that even family members would persecute Christians, at least initially. Prayer for enemies within our own household can be effective, and yet some may have to pay the price of family persecution in the last days. Our love for our family must *seem* like hatred, as the Greek implies in a parallel passage, in comparison to our love for God. He must come first.

81. Not being willing to "bear our cross" and follow Jesus (Mat. 10:38). The context is forsaking family if need be for Jesus. There are other burdens we are called to bear in the Christian life. One of the 25 divine graces is the burden-bearing grace (see "Grace" in the Appendix). Sometimes we are tempted to swap burdens with someone else whose grass looks easier to mow. Surprisingly, the yoke we sometimes feel uncomfortably chafing our necks is exactly what we need individually to grow more like Jesus.

Why Doesn't God Heal Me?

82. Not being willing to "lose our lives" for Jesus' sake (Mat. 10:39; II Tim. 3; Titus 1:7; II Pet. 2). The popular notion is to "get a life." God condemns our selfish society. Self-help, self-glorification and personal success are society's shrines in our me-first generation.

God shocks us by demanding the exact opposite. "Crucify yourself [your old, sinful ways]!" He says. "Lay down your life!" "Deny yourself!" When we die to ourselves, Jesus can live in us His resurrected life. If you've done it, you know the joy worshippers of self cannot enjoy. Solomon tried it all and came up empty.

Selfishness is the greatest addiction. It is also the root to which all other addictions cling. It can open the door to unforgiveness, stinginess and rebellion. It can make you a thief, a coward and a traitor. You can't walk in faith, love or peace. A spirit of legalism comes in to judge and condemn others, thus helping you to justify your own sins. You cling selfishly to those sins, making you feel unworthy to be the righteousness of God.

Selfishness blocks your blessings and your ability to walk in your anointing. A lack of satisfaction ensues, increasing the need to satisfy the flesh. Obedience becomes only an outward show or a position-seeking method.

The way of self is the way of curses and death. It destroys your walls of protection. It blocks all workings of the spirit of humility and brings a judgment from God.

As you walk in selfishness, you feel more and more depressed and you can feel God resisting you. Addictions that destroy the flesh and the mind multiply until Satan takes over your life.

Genesis 6 describes the selfishness of society in Noah's day. This sickness of selfishness was prophesied for this age and permeates our world today (Mat. 24:37-38). That selfish attitude – the root of the violence that ensued – was the reason Jesus was grieved with mankind and chose to destroy all but Noah's family. Selfishness blocked mankind's repentance.

If God destroyed the world because of selfishness, it must be a grievous sickness of the soul. But you can be free of this modern plague.

Accepting the righteousness of God gives power to break selfishness. One of the reasons our wise God gave us the tithing system was to break selfishness. If you don't learn to lay down your money, you can't learn to lay down your life.

Only when we lay down our lives in submission to the Master and in service to others do we find true freedom, deep joy and real life – abundant life here and now and an eternal life of unending accomplishment and joy.

For some God may require a literal laying down of their lives. Prophet Rick Joyner of Morningstar Ministries recounted a vision he had of an unknown, unsung Christian who God said would have a higher position in the Kingdom than a certain well-known evangelist. The famous Christian leader was a power-hungry individual. The other man, not highly considered in the church at all, was found lying on top of a "useless" drunkard who lay on the frigid street of a large city. The

The Hindrances 18

loving soul who lay on top of this ne'er-do-well to cover him was dead. The drunken man was alive because of this Christian's selfless act. Great was his reward in heaven.

83. Not receiving the servant Jesus sends to heal us (Mat. 10:40). If God sends someone to us to be His tool of healing, we should accept him, whoever he may be.

"I will not get healing from anybody but Benny Hinn!" some may say. The Holy Spirit has inspired many to seek healing at Benny Hinn crusades. But what if God sends someone else to you? Beware of this "Hinn-drance."

84. Not being willing to receive revelation and correction from God as a "babe" (Mat. 11:25). We can become so wise in our eyes that we are not willing to be corrected by God or His servants. The insidious "pride of power" of many a pastor has blocked God's correction and thus His blessings. If we think we know more than the Holy Spirit, He will not "teach [us] all things ..." (John 14:26).

85. Not believing the Father has given Jesus authority over all things (Mat. 11:27; Eph. 1:20-21). We must accept the truth that Jesus has the authority over all and the keys to every good thing for us.

86. Not accepting "rest" in Jesus (Mat. 11:28-30). The Bible says that Noah found grace in God's eyes. Did you know his name means "rest"? Because he found a quiet resting-place in God – an intimate, quiet place of total trust – he found grace. Rest in God precedes grace. The Word speaks of "quiet confidence." Rest and faith are related and both enable God to lavish upon us His manifold grace (Isa. 30:15).

Resting in Jesus includes the weekly "Sabbath rest" which pictures our eternal rest (Heb. 4:9). This major key to righteousness and healing is the subject of another hindrance, yet it deserves a whole book (already in process).

87. Rejecting mercy and condemning the innocent. Matthew 12:7 deals with these related hindrances. Jesus was accused of breaking the Sabbath by healing on that day. Healing is an act of compassion and a part of Jesus' priestly ministry that exempted Him, as with the Old Covenant priests, from obligation to keep the literal letter of always resting physically on the Sabbath. Doing good and showing mercy by healing may require some physical exertion yet fit the spirit of the day, which prefigures a time of healing and restoration during the millennial reign of Jesus on earth.

The Pharisees did not understand mercy and even condemned the perfect Son of God. We must not condemn the guiltless. Jesus erases our past guilt by His blood and by the Passover foot-washing. If we bring up a brother's past sin that God has removed "as far as the east is from the west" (Ps. 103:12), we show unforgiveness and condemnation.

Let's not criticize Christians, even leaders, for a past that does not exist in God's eyes. As humans we cannot forget. We can, however, lovingly refuse to bring up in a negative way any past sin of a brother. Would we want others to mention our past blunders? Let's see our brothers the way God sees them – pure and clean and new – every day! Make forgiveness a daily habit.

88. Not realizing the value of every human being (Mat. 12:12). The Pharisees seemed to love sheep more than people! God wants us be kind to every living creature within the bounds of common sense. Today, however, some almost worship animals. Some of the same people will kill precious human beings by abortion. Baby seals seem more important than baby humans. Some even murder people who do animal testing! (Professing Christians who use violence against abortionists are equally guilty.) People will spend money on bird sanctuaries but won't help the poor. Some rich animal lovers have left millions to their pets! We kid ourselves that we love God when we don't value man made in His image.

89. Attributing the works of Jesus' servants to Satan (Mat. 12:24). Although a small percentage of supernatural manifestations in Christian groups may be demonic, accusing God's servants of the works of Satan is dangerous, bordering on the blasphemy of the Holy Spirit. We are really saying that Jesus is doing the work of the Devil. That is saying that Jesus is under Satan.

If you have no proof a manifestation is demonic when a Christian is involved, you better hold your peace. If the Holy Spirit did it, you are blaspheming Him. If you are sincerely deceived, God may extend His mercy to you, but it's better to refrain from judging what you may not understand.

The apostle Paul said he spoke in tongues more than all the mostly carnal Corinthian tongues-speakers. Satan counterfeits everything, but that is no excuse to blaspheme the work of the Holy Spirit. Instead, admit your ignorance. God can work in any way He chooses, and He does. Don't judge. You may be judging God Himself!

90. Not being "with Jesus" and not "gathering with Him" (Mat. 12:30). "He who is not with Me is against Me …" If your paradigm is not Christ's, are you "with Him"? If you are walking contrary to Him, you are being hypocritical.

"… he who does not gather with Me scatters." We must not have our own agendas but do it His way. Otherwise, we will cause a destruction of the harvest and will be cursed by God.

91. Not keeping the commandments of God (Mat. 19:17). Life refers in a general sense to abundant life – wholeness, healing and health. Break one law and you break them all (James 2:10). The Ten Commandments may be out of vogue in our nations today – but not in God's book.

Knowingly breaking God's law is one of the possible roots of *cancer*. Breaking natural laws can also cause this disease. When we break God's law and know full well we are doing so, the guilt causes such stress on our body that the immune system is weakened and cancer results. When praying for a cancer patient, it is necessary to curse the root of the cancer.

92. Not being willing to follow Jesus fully (Mat. 19:2; II Chron. 16:9; Jer. 29:13). We must search Him out, really seek Him as they did here. Caleb

The Hindrances 18

entered the Promised Land because he "followed [God] fully" (Num. 14:24).

93. Rebellion. The Bible says that rebellion is as the sin of witchcraft (I Sam. 15:23). God would not heal a witch, and He will not bless someone who is blatantly rebelling against Him or His will. If a person publicly states that he or she doesn't trust God for healing but asks for it anyway to see what will happen, God has every right not to honor this open rebellion.

94. Denying Jesus (Mat. 10:33). Jesus said that if we denied Him before men, He would deny us before the Father. Those are strong words.

Jesus told His disciples – and that includes us – to preach the gospel and be the salt of the earth and the light of the world. If we lose our savor or put our light under a bushel, woe unto us!

St. Francis of Assisi said we should preach the gospel, "and use words if necessary." Our light – not our trumpet – is the main means of witnessing. He who toots his horn may blow his reward!

We must glorify Jesus by our shining example! We must not be ashamed of His name. We're not secretive spies – we're ambassadors! Undercover Christians will not be wrapped with God's approval. If we are not willing to take the "wrap" of being a Christian, God will not "unwrap" His blessings for us. We are not bona fide members of the Kingdom if we are not busy advancing it. The sheepfold of the Kingdom is not made up only of the five-fold (Eph. 4:11). Every Christian is an evangelist! That is our job description. Our name doesn't have to be Billy Graham to bring in the lost. God wants all lay members to preach the gospel where they are in their own unique way.

One of the most effective methods is "friendship evangelism." Befriend the lost. Ask God for wisdom to properly time the sharing of your story and preaching the gospel. We don't have to sound like a preacher. Friendship is more powerful than a preachy, self-righteous, condescending air. The stench of the latter will drive people away.

Don't give them religion. Give them Jesus. You may be surprised how receptive they are to your words if relayed naturally and unashamedly. Be real – like Jesus was. Don't preach – reach! Reach out to them and reflect the light of Jesus' love.

From a safe distance, some Christians timidly shine a flashlight into the darkness, afraid of getting too close to the sinners that need them. Jesus Christ was a "friend of sinners." Shining for all to see, he "ran" into the darkness.

You too can at least plant a seed for those who remain in the dark. God may not be calling them in this life (John 6:44). We have already seen the good news for those who never hear or never really get it. Jesus died to offer **all** men His righteousness and eternal life (Rom. 5:12-21). All means all! But the comforting truth of the post-millennial resurrection for the unsaved is no excuse for us to be timid little Christians. God wants unashamed, card-carrying, cross-bearing, caring, sharing Christians. People desperately need Jesus, and multitudes will come to Him in the end-time harvest. Let's share our light, by deed and when appropriate by word.

95. Receiving an accusation against someone without at least two witnesses (I Tim. 5:19; Deut. 19:15). The Scriptures in Hebrew apply this principle to more than spiritual elders. We must not make judgments that only God can make.

96. Offense. We must avoid offending and being offended. Offenses destroy faith. They can block the anointing. And yet Jesus said they were inevitable (Mat. 18:6-7). When He says "woe," He means business. Offending unnecessarily is serious. If we offend, as the "Stone of Stumbling" himself sometimes did (I Pet. 2:8; Luke 20:17-18; Isa. 8:14), it must not be because of sin or unwise procedure.

Those who love God's law are not easily offended (Ps. 119:165). The love chapter (I Cor. 13) confirms this.

Yet alas, love is not yet perfected in us. We do get offended. We must resolve the offense quickly by reconciliation and/or forgiveness. If we let it fester, powerful demonic spirits, especially the spirit of betrayal, have access.

As a pastor, I know that offenses are a major cause of people leaving church fellowship. These can be real offenses by pastors and others who sin against us. We can even be offended by the Word as well as by correction, especially from a superior.

Conservative Christians are often offended by the manifestations of the Holy Spirit in healing crusades. People thought the early Christians on Pentecost were drunk. Some may be offended by teaching about demonic involvement in sickness, even though it is Biblical as well as tested by experienced men of God. Why not fast and pray and ask for the Holy Spirit's guidance? Prove all things.

97. Refusing to do the work of God by "burying the dead" (Luke 9:60). Putting the affairs of spiritually dead family or friends ahead of God is definitely setting the wrong priorities. The man in this passage wanted to cater to the needs of his father until his dad died, instead of obeying the command of Jesus. Jesus knew the situation with his father should not be put ahead of his calling. It was simply an excuse.

98. Looking back longingly to our life of sin. God judges harshly those who long for the "onion and garlic" of Egypt, those who look back at Sodom as did Lot's wife. We may not be turned into pillars of salt, but God will not bless us. We must not live in a past that does not exist for us as new creations. We must not see them as "the good 'ole days."

99. Not getting rid of spiritual stumbling blocks (Heb. 12:13). The Greek words for "make straight paths for your feet" imply removing the stumbling blocks in our path. Most of the time we are aware of these obstacles, but we are not willing to do anything about them. This general hindrance explains that we must have an attitude that is willing to eliminate hindrances.

100. Committing blasphemy against the Holy Spirit (Mat. 12:31-32). This hindrance addresses this blasphemy in a general sense. This is speaking of making

The Hindrances 18

a declaration against the Holy Spirit, such as: "I will not allow the Holy Spirit to work in my life. I give myself to Satan and His ways." Lucifer became Satan by setting his will against God and speaking that self-will and independence of God in a permanent decision.

God is extremely merciful to backsliders, but we have a choice. We can always come back to God in repentance, unless we set our will permanently against God and refuse to allow the Holy Spirit to work in us. Jesus is the perfect Judge who will discern when a Christian has made such a choice. Only Christians who return permanently to their "vomit" (II Pet. 2:22) will be sent upon their death to the lower levels of hell.

In rare cases a non-believer may so set his will to give himself completely and knowingly to demonic possession that he could also be condemned eternally for such a choice. Jesus, the Judge, did warn the Pharisees about blaspheming the Holy Spirit, so it is possible in rare cases for non-believers to commit the unpardonable sin. In these cases, they would simply be resurrected physically at the third resurrection to be thrown in the lake of fire and cease to exist rather than live eternally in "the black darkness" (II Pet. 2:17). Remember, their spirits are dead in Adam and they never accepted Life Himself, so only their souls and bodies can be destroyed (Mat. 10:28).

101. "Your silver has become dross, Your drink diluted with water" (Isa. 1:22). Isaiah 1 is the introduction to end-time prophecy. Although it refers initially to the city of Jerusalem, it expands to include the whole world. It is God's powerful declaration that He will set His mighty hand to clean up the mess this world has made. Especially when linked to Ephesians 5:1-27, it is a stark warning to the end-time church, a bride full of spots and hindrances – a number of which are covered in these Scriptures.

This verse has multiple meanings. Silver signifies the righteousness Jesus has given to man. Dross is the impure ore material that has polluted that righteousness. The truth of God's Word has been twisted and tainted by deceptive doctrines of demons. The dross of theft, demoralization and cowardice has entered the church. That is part of the reason that Christians cannot stand firm in the Word – and in its healing promise. As the good has been removed, only the dross of sickness remains. By claiming God does not love them, many have betrayed Him and thus become as dross to Jesus. Christians become as dross when they betray their mates, thus inviting Satan into the marriage. Christians are weakened with dead works, not willing to rest in Jesus' strength. This dross makes them feel worthless – unworthy of healing. The dross of habitual sin and addictions has become the identity of many. The pride of personal opinions has risen above the Word of God. And finally, Christians have defiled their bodies by abusing them in sexual sin and eating unhealthy foods.

"Your drink" can apply to the wine or blood of Jesus. Christians have mocked the blood of Jesus by their disobedience. Their religion, polluted by false doctrine,

199

Why Doesn't God Heal Me?

has become as worthless as sewer water. The church has mixed sewer water with wine and called it the blood of Jesus. They have thus lost the protective shield of Jesus' blood. The result is a worthless, confused and powerless church. The world laughs at a hypocritical church that has exchanged the Father of Love for the Father of Lies.

102. Demanding a "sign" or miracle from God (Mat. 12:38-42). Faithless, evil men require signs from God, a common practice under the Old Covenant, since the Holy Spirit was not generally given. Today the only time a Christian would ask for a "sign" is possibly as he is sincerely seeking God's will in an uncertain area of his life.

The problem mentioned in Matthew was the attitude of the Pharisees. They had no faith and wanted to be entertained by signs and wonders. Many have the same approach today. "I'm not going to believe God unless I see a sign or miracle!" Healing and/or blessings from God are unlikely with such a mindset. If you want entertainment, don't go to a healing meeting. Go bowling!

103. Taunting God or His servants (Mat. 12:38). In this same passage we see the Pharisees taunting Jesus, pressing Him for a sign. Though not as serious as mocking God, it is a lack of respect toward God or His servants. The Pharisees were disrespectful, constantly trying to trap Jesus. As with their trick question about taxes, He always turned it around and made them look silly. Taunting God is akin to tempting or wrongly testing Him (Mat. 4:7).

104. Denying the only sign Jesus gave that He was the Messiah (Mat. 12:40). Many are sincerely deceived on this important issue. If you are among them, once you are faced with the Biblical proof, you will be responsible for accepting this truth. It was the only sign Jesus gave that He was the Christ – the Messiah.

He said he would be "three days and three nights" in the grave just as Jonah was that length of time in the belly of the fish. Although the Bible uses the general term "after three days" and similar expressions, this passage is specific.

It is true that there is some leeway in the meaning of this phrase in Greek. Matthew wrote in Greek, but Jesus refers to the Hebrew of Jonah 1:17, which can mean nothing else but three full days of 24 hours each, not parts of days.

There is absolutely no way to fit 72 hours between a Good Friday and Sunday morning, neither of which is correct. Even a child can figure that one out!

If you know the Holy Days Jesus kept, it is easy to understand the chronology of the week He died. With the aid of the sacred lunar calendar based on the 19-year time cycle, the Jews know exactly when the Passover fell the year Jesus died. It was on *Wednesday* – not Friday!

The Passover was called the "day of preparation" for the first day of Unleavened Bread, an annual "high Sabbath" which began Wednesday night at sunset and ended Thursday night at sunset. Jesus died about 3 P.M. on Wednesday and was buried just before that annual Sabbath or first day of Unleavened Bread. Luke 23:54 describes clearly the moment of burial: "It was the preparation day,

The Hindrances 18

and the Sabbath was about to begin." Jesus was put in the tomb before sunset on Wednesday (see also John 19:42).

Three days and three nights later is *Saturday* afternoon before sunset. He was resurrected just before sunset on the weekly Sabbath or Saturday during the days of Unleavened Bread. Since it was dark, Jesus' followers did not see Him until early Sunday morning. They found an empty tomb for He *had* already *risen* about twelve hours before (Mat. 28:6). Nowhere does it say He *rose* on Sunday morning. The faithful women followers who were to prepare Him for burial could not have had time to do so before sunset on Wednesday, the beginning of the high Sabbath or annual Sabbath.

When you compare the accounts, it becomes evident that they bought spices when the shops were open on Friday, made the lengthy preparations, then rested on the weekly Sabbath "according to the [fourth] commandment" (Luke 23:56). There had to be two Sabbaths that week, for Mark says they saw Jesus' burial, and then "when the Sabbath [obviously the annual Sabbath on Thursday] was over ..." they bought spices (Mark 15:47-16:1). After preparing the spices on Friday and then resting on the weekly Sabbath on Saturday, they went to anoint Jesus' body on Sunday morning, but He was already risen (Mark 16:2-6). They couldn't have bought and prepared spices "when the Sabbath was over" and then rested on the same Sabbath *after* buying and preparing the spices.

It only makes sense when you realize there were two Sabbaths that week, and three days (Thursday, Friday, Saturday) and three nights (Wednesday, Thursday, Friday) during which Jesus' body lay in the tomb. Just like He said!

Those who cling to tradition and believe the Good Friday to Sunday lie will have a serious hindrance to receiving blessings from God once they see it in God's Word. If we don't believe the only proof Jesus gave that He is our Savior, something is seriously wrong. The fact that "everybody" believes it doesn't make it true. Prove all things (I Thes. 5:21)!

105. Not seeking God and His ways after having been delivered from demons (Mat. 12:43-45). If you do not fill your mind with the things of God after being delivered from demonic strongholds, influence, infestation or possession, demons have the right to return with reinforcement. Not declaring the Word over ourselves after deliverance allows demonic backlash to occur. If delivered from a spirit of infirmity, the illness often comes back worse than before. Critics take delight in exposing healings that didn't last. The fault lies with the person healed who chose to surrenders his or her healing to Satan, not with the healing evangelist.

106. Not being willing to pray in agreement for another person's needs (Mat. 18:19). When two or three agree in prayer for another, the results are powerful. When others ask us to pray for them, or when God directs us to pray for someone, we need to heed.

107. Declaring deception and suffering from the Devil to be from God.

201

Much of the suffering and deception we experience is either self-inflicted or comes from Satan. We must not blame these on God. God never deceives. Hebrews 12 shows that He does discipline us for our good, although most of our suffering comes from the consequences of our sins or is the Devil's doing. If you "blew it" or the Devil made you do it, don't blame God.

108. Blocking others from praising God because of a spirit of religiosity. The religious spirit hates true worship. We must not stifle the enthusiasm of Christians who want to be expressive in their worship. Whatever the reason, stopping someone from praising God with all his being is a serious offense to the One being worshipped.

109. Cursing others (James 3:9-10; I Pet. 3:9-12). We can't expect God to bless us if we are cursing others. Cursing is speaking bad things over people. "He's a stupid idiot!" "You're gonna be a lazy bum like your dad!" "She's a real witch!" Cursing others will bring backlash. Bless others and God can bless you!

110. Not having a sense of vision about the things of God (Heb. 11; Rom. 4:16-21). We must see the promises of God as a reality in our lives. We cannot believe what we cannot envision, whether it be healing or any of God's blessings. We must come to see the awesome truth of what it means to be a part of God's own Family and inheritor of all His blessings. Without vision, the people perish – even physically.

111. Not receiving information from God as a little child (Mat.18:3). A little child is trusting, having an honest expectation and belief his parents are going to give him what he needs. He expects to be fed. He expects to get hugs. His spirit soars in wonder over the smallest of God's miracles. He is in ecstasy before a butterfly.

Our Father wants us excited about what He gives us and teaches us, as little children are. He wants us to stand in awe of Him and trust Him expectantly.

At a conference I attended, praise and worship leader Chris Bowater said he wanted to write a song that contained only one word: **wow**! We need more "wows" and "hallelujahs" pouring from the mouths of God's Children. The Word says that out of the mouths of babes and infants God has ordained praise. When it comes to open-mouthed wonder, which is the French way of expressing the idea of awe, we need to be more like children. God does awesome works for those who stand in awe of Him.

He wants us to have childlike simplicity. Famous Swiss Reformed theologian Karl Barth is quoted as saying to someone who asked him to explain the most important concept in theology: "Jesus loves me this I know, for the Bible tells me so."

112. Not seeking God's Kingdom first (Mat. 6:33). God promises to meet our physical needs if we seek Him and His righteousness above everything else. This is a principle that applies as well to His blessings and includes tithing our money and our time. God even says He will give us the desires of our heart if we delight in Him (Ps. 37:4).

113. Knowingly rejecting part of God's Word (Mat. 4:4). Jesus says we are to live by every word of God. In order to be accountable before God for breaking His law, however, we must know that we are sinning (James 4:17; John 9:41). Yet just as the law of gravity exerts influence on us whether we know it or not, so God's law will exact penalties upon us regardless of our knowledge. If we reject the Word knowingly, the results are more serious. Rejecting God's Word is the same as rejecting **God.**

114. Not speaking God's Word over ourselves (I Tim. 4:13; Josh. 1:8). We have seen the awesome power of our words, especially in relation to healing. Let's practice it! That includes reading the Bible *aloud*, allowing the words to penetrate the words into our heart, mind and will. Reading the Word out loud brings almost all the senses into play and affects the psyche in a way simply reading doesn't do.

Those who hasten to finish their Bible study to get it over with are not hungering after God and could be hindering their healing.

The righteousness of God *speaks* (Rom. 10:6). In our righteousness, we must speak out God's Word and His promises. Simply believing them is not enough.

115. Comparing ourselves with others (in a general sense) (II Cor. 10:12). God deals with us as individuals. Let's not be overly concerned about what happens to others, no matter what their position may be. We must guard against jealousy. Peter expressed to Jesus that he was concerned about what was going to happen to John. Jesus said to him, "If I want him to live until I come again, what's that to you? You – follow me" (John 21:22, NIV). God has a unique plan for each of our lives. Our circumstances or position of honor in this life have little to do with our eternal reward. It's what we *do* with our situation, no matter how humble it may be, that matters.

116. Not knowing how to respond to a "backlash" from Satan (see "Curses, general" in the Appendix). When we do damage to Satan's kingdom or eliminate a demonic stronghold, that makes the demons angry. They often come back to attack in vengeance. We can prevent that by asking our Father to cover us with the blood of Jesus as a protective shield. Communion is often necessary. When we realize a backlash has begun, we can counterattack by prayer and praise. The Devil is clever and persistent, so we need to be alert and persevering. Remember what Jesus said about demons returning seven times worse if we have not planted the Word in our minds after being delivered (Luke 11:24-26). Let's not lose our healing or our blessing by either allowing or not responding to a demonic backlash.

117. Not accepting our anointing. Our first anointing is that of the Anointed One, Jesus Christ, who lives in us after we accept Him. Most Christians do not grasp the awesome reality of that anointing – who we are in Christ.

We all have, however, a unique anointing – a calling, function, purpose, role or authority – in our Christian lives. The Holy Spirit gives us His empowerment to do what no one else can do exactly like we can. We need to discover that special anointing, accept it, and learn to walk in it.

118. Not receiving "a prophet in the name of a prophet" (Mat. 10:41). When a servant God is working through to heal comes to us, we should receive him. Those who received Biblical prophets were blessed. Those who did not were cursed. Those who refuse to accept God's servants are speaking a curse over themselves and will not receive God's blessings. This is a significant hindrance.

119. Carnality. There are some that profess to be Christian who walk at enmity with the Spirit. They may be justified or saved but have not begun the process of sanctification. They have the Holy Spirit in them but refuse to be led by Him. They have not really died to their old nature.

The healing verse of I Peter 2:24 is preceded by the verse that says Jesus entrusted or committed Himself to the Father. He gave Himself completely to His Father. We are supposed to "die to sin and live to righteousness" (verse 24).

Some are not healed because they have not died to their carnality. God is waiting on them to make their move toward Him before He can release His blessings (see "Prayer of Identity in the Crucifixion" in the Appendix).

120. Being hypocritical or two-faced (to God) (Mat. 15:7-9). We can fool some of the people some of the time – but we can't fool God. He hates hypocrisy. Cowardice and bigotry often accompany this evil. Bigots hate being "upstaged" and any infringement of their sphere of influence. They didn't like Jesus because He was more popular with the people than they were, and somehow He was always right. If He came a second time the way He did the first, religious bigots would kill Him again. Why? Because they want to make Him in their image, to fit into their false doctrines. They hate anyone who comes with fresh revelation that uncovers the falseness of their teachings.

121. Not worshipping God in truth (Mat. 15:7-9; Ps. 145:18). God does not bless those who obey *their* way. Those who worship Him according to the precepts of men are doing it in vain.

122. Not being aware of the leaven of the Pharisees and Sadducees (Mat. 16:6,12). They were condemning others for not meeting the standard they themselves were not reaching. They were puffed up because they were comparing themselves with others whose sins seemed more grievous to them. Their heady self-righteousness blocked their repentance, while those they condemned repented.

123. Rejecting the keys of the Kingdom (Mat. 16:19). If we reject these keys, which include Jesus' name, God's love and the Holy Spirit, we are rejecting the way to receive all the promises of God. We are denying our authority in Jesus.

124. Discouraging another Christian from doing the will of God (Mat. 16:22). Peter's effort to deter Jesus from dying sounded righteous, but it was against God's will. Even when we mean well, we can be keeping others from doing God's will. "Oh, a little white lie never hurts!" "If I was married to a witch like that, I'd divorce her too!" "Oh, poor you. You don't deserve that!" Actually,

The Hindrances **18**

they may be undergoing their loving Father's discipline to bring them back on track. That misplaced sympathy, "sloppy *agape*" or "unsanctified mercy" as Rick Joyner at Morningstar Ministries calls it, is the subject of another hindrance.

125. Reflecting the views of an unbelieving and perverted generation (Mat. 17:17; Acts 2:40). We live in a generation of mockers who don't believe God can heal and who don't even believe it when they see it. As God foretold, we call evil good and good evil. Even in the jargon of our youth, on a lighter note, "bad" and "wicked" mean good and really good. God wants us to be separate from this faithless, twisted generation.

126. Doing things we know are offensive to others (Mat. 17:27). When it came to obedience to God, neither Jesus nor Paul compromised (Acts 5:29). But if it involved something they had a right to do, they were careful not to offend (I Cor. 8:13). I have found to my surprise that even my presence can be offensive to some people, so I try to lovingly avoid them for their and my sake.

127. Being a stumbling block for a believer (especially a new one) (Mat. 18:7). If your humble obedience is a problem for them – well, that's their problem. You can't please everybody. Nevertheless, God's love makes us extra-careful not to offend. Let's not flaunt our freedom (Rom. 14; I Cor. 8 and 10). I know that Jesus was a moderate alcohol user. But drinking around someone with a drinking problem can be a problem. Before I discovered the balance Jesus exemplified, the only alcohol I consumed was the sherry fruitcake and tipsy cake my grandmother made. Although I admit I did drink a beer at a Montreal Expos baseball game, I wouldn't do so at the widows' tea party at the corner church.

128. Despising new believers ("babes in Christ") (Mat. 18:10). Pastors sometimes won't listen to new believers God is speaking through – especially if they have identified one of his sins. They may think you have to prove yourself before they listen to you. Jesus may well be speaking through a new believer. He loves to work through the humble. If we reject them, we are rejecting Jesus.

This verse can also apply to those dreaded dandies loosed from the lips of little ones. As Art Linkletter and Bill Cosby can confirm, kids say the "truest" things. They have a way of cutting through the deceptive haze and saying the naïve yet unadulterated truth. One young Chicago boy wrote a national leader and said a truth many others wanted to gloss over. "My daddy punishes me for lying. How come you get away with it?" "Out of the mouth of babes. ..."

As God's sheep, we need to remember God once spoke through a donkey. He also speaks through lambs and kids.

129. Not searching for the sheep that has gone astray (Mat. 18:12). We're not talking about goats! And we're not talking about wandering sheep arriving from some other pasture seeking to hear some "sweet thing." Whether we are pastors or not, however, we need to go after a sheep that has gone temporarily astray. A wayward Christian needs prayer as well as real encouragement. We are indeed

Why Doesn't God Heal Me?

our brother's keepers. And though we don't tend to, we *must* tend to – and tend – our fellow sheep (Gal. 6:1).

130. Not having the Father's desire that none of these "little ones" (new believers) perish (Mat. 18:14). It seems some Christians, even pastors, desire the downfall of some new Christians. They don't accept them in their little clique. They even curse them, speaking evil of them, gossiping about their problems. These little ones are precious to God – and should be precious to us.

131. Not going to a brother when we should (Mat. 18:15). This may be one of the most unpracticed verses in the Bible. It doesn't mean we're always taking other Christians aside because of our super sensitivity. It is a loving favor to point out a sin so a brother can grow. We must, of course, use wisdom.

132. Not going to a brother in private (Mat. 18:15). I have had my share of public "crucifixions." They hurt. And they are unloving and unnecessary. Remember the golden rule.

133. Refusing to hear a brother who comes to point out a sin (Mat. 18:15). David said, "Let the righteous smite me in kindness and reprove me; It is oil upon the head; Do not let my head refuse it ..." (Ps. 141:5). Some of us treat it like that "greasy kid stuff." We want no part of it. We should humbly and prayerfully consider it. If our brother is wrong, we can simply point it out to him from the facts and from the Word. Remember this too: maybe only a part of it is true. If so, let's not reject the part with the whole.

134. Putting a limit on forgiveness (Mat. 18:22). Seventy times seven is God's number of infinite perfection. Peter thought he was being generous with seven times, and it *was* generous compared to rabbinical teaching. This doesn't mean we must submit ourselves to endless abuse. Yet we must always be willing to forgive. Believe me. The price for not forgiving is much worse than the cost of forgiving. It almost cost me my eternity. You may be tempted to say, "That's too much." Remember how much Jesus took – and forgave. Thank God He never says to us, "That's the last straw!" We only become straw to burn (Mal. 4:1) when we turn permanently from God and refuse His forgiveness. That's the only "last straw" God knows. Through every cruel and unjust act committed against Him in the last day of His life, Jesus kept saying, "Father, forgive them, for they know not what they do."

135. Not showing mercy on a fellow Christian in need (Mat.18:33; 25:40). In view of God's mercy to us, we should show mercy to others. If a brother comes to us and asks for prayer and encouragement, we should not deny him help – even when it's inconvenient.

136. Divorcing without Biblical grounds (referring to Christians) (Mat. 19:9; I Cor. 7:1-15; Jer. 3:8, 20). When I studied problems of the American democracy in high school, one of the grounds for divorce in South Carolina was "crackers in bed." Many Christians today are lookers for loopholes to escape from the covenant they made with the wife of their youth. Speaking of divorce and not annulment, the

The Hindrances 18

Bible only gives two escape clauses to the marriage covenant for a Christian. In this verse Jesus only cites marital infidelity, the reason He divorced Israel (Jer. 3:8). Paul adds to that, showing that if an unbelieving mate refuses to live in peace with the Christian mate, he or she is not bound and thus free to divorce (I Cor. 7:15). There are cases that require guidance from the Holy Spirit and/or from enlightened servants of God, but these are the two Biblical guidelines. In either case, reconciliation, while not impossible, is not always feasible or advisable. God hates divorce (Mal. 2:16). If we don't keep one of the most important promises in our lives, we prevent Him from keeping His promises to us. Divorce without Biblical grounds is sin. When we confess and repent of sin, however, we are cleansed from all unrighteousness by the blood of Jesus (I John 1:9). Those who judge should ask themselves which one of *their* sins the blood of Jesus has not washed away.

137. Not being willing to give to the poor (Mat. 19:21). God can't bless us if we are not willing to bless others. Jesus told the man in this passage to sell all because his possessions were an idol. He does not necessarily ask us to give all we have. Nor does He want us to give money to those who will use it to destroy themselves or others. I have often taken men who asked for food money at their word. When I have the time and money, I invite them for a meal. Some accept. Some don't. They show their true motivation. We must be givers – but wise ones. Advantage has been taken of my generosity, but I would rather err on the side of mercy, for it triumphs over judgment. God shows mercy to the merciful.

138. Desiring possessions on earth more than the heavenly ones (Mat. 19:21-22). In our materialistic culture, we need to be on guard against this kind of idolatry. "Who has the most toys in the end wins" is not God's game plan. You can't take it with you. On the other hand, if we don't worship money and physical things, God will bless us with them. He wants us blessed so we can be givers like Him.

139. Trying to manipulate God to get what we want (Mat. 19:22; James 4:3; Mal. 2:13). It's one thing to claim a promise. It's quite another to wheel and deal with God. "If You take vengeance on this person, then I'll obey You." Trying to twist God's arm is dirty spiritual arm wrestling. It's a twisted version of covenanting with God.

140. Not accepting God's call (Mat. 22:3). "I'm having so much fun sinning, I'm gonna wait." If we know God is calling, and we wait, we will also wait on His blessings.

141. Not realizing the importance of communion and its practice. This is an important and all-too-common hindrance today. It is such an important subject that I dedicated part of Chapter 4 to stress the need for daily communion. We can claim no Biblical covenant promise outside of the body and blood of Jesus. We must claim the healing promise in the body of Jesus in communion and seal it in His blood.

142. Taking God's name in vain (Ex. 20:7). How can a Christian curse God

207

Why Doesn't God Heal Me?

with his mouth and expect to receive His blessings? How can a person who professes falsely to be a Christian receive the promised blessing of healing?

God reserves His blessings for His own Children. Healing is "the children's bread." John 3 says we must be "born again" to enter the Kingdom of God. We must accept Jesus as our Savior and have a relationship with Him. Otherwise we are not His and cannot therefore claim blessings reserved for a Christian. Excluding exceptions the sovereign God makes, we must accept Jesus as our Savior and our Healer if we want to be healed. His beaten body and His blood are the two elements of His sacrifice.

We can even take God's name in vain by using it to make a declaration when we do not really believe God.

143. Not acknowledging God's right to call and reward as He pleases (Mat. 20:11-12). God is God. Let Him be God. His ways and thoughts are higher than ours. He says He shows mercy on whom He decides to show mercy. He decides whom to bless and reward here and now and for eternity. He does not want us to be jealous of others, but happy for them and confident of His perfect wisdom – even when it doesn't make sense in our limited logic.

144. Grumbling against God's generosity to others (Mat. 20:15). Only a shade of difference from the previous hindrance, the same principles apply. When God blesses another Christian, do we rejoice for him and praise God? Or do we lament: "How come I didn't get that blessing? I'm a better Christian than he is!" We thus limit God and ourselves and invite the spirit of limitations and all his agents to hinder our walk in righteousness. Such was the case with the brother in the parable of the prodigal son. It's not always easy when we're in a valley and others are enjoying a mountaintop view from their penthouse suite. We should, nevertheless, learn to rejoice with those who rejoice.

145. Wanting to be served instead of being a servant (Mat. 20:26). When there is a need, no task is too menial for a true servant. Jesus washed feet. That was the duty of the lowliest house slave. Whatever our position, we should have His foot-washing attitude. God will bring the high and mighty down to size. The offices of the five-fold ministry are not positions of glory. They are positions of humble service.

146. Using the temple of God the wrong way (Mat. 21:12). "… your body is a temple of the Holy Spirit …" (I Cor. 6:19). We are not to defile these temples of God in any way. That includes eating wrong foods as well as any kind of sexual sin.

Sexual sin has become rampant in our hedonistic, "Hefneresque" society. Pleasure at any price is the byword. "As long as it doesn't hurt anybody" – which it always does. The price is exorbitant – even though the monetary price has gone down due to the infernal Internet. Now you can have sex chat and even explicit simulated sex via computer camera. I have seen cases where marriages have dissolved because of the Internet.

The Hindrances 18

Auto-eroticism in the form of masturbation must be recognized as sin, since it may involve lust, self-gratification and idol worship. We are to be vessels of honor, "sanctified, useful to the Master" (II Tim. 2:21).

Whatever the sin that defiles your body, don't claim it as a pet sin. A pet sin is one you feel you must conquer in your own strength before you can finally be righteous. You are already the righteousness of God! Fight any sin in your righteousness, not feeling condemned and guilty. The sin you committed yesterday has been erased from God's memory. Upon confession, you are back to being the righteousness of God – with no sense of guilt or shame. Don't condemn yourself. You are one with Jesus.

If a sin is habitual and persists, be sure you lay it down at the foot of the cross. Turn it over to Jesus. Ask for the mercy of God to be rid of stubborn habits. This applies to any addiction that tears down the temple of your body. Make positive declarations daily. Thank God for your deliverance.

147. Resisting the servants whom God sends to teach us or correct our ways (Mat. 21:35). This might apply to anyone, but it is specifically directed to the religious hierarchy of Jesus' day, and thus to their equivalent today – pastors. These "vinedressers" often demean God's servants among the flock. How dare God speak through anyone but the almighty pastor! God may be working through a humble sheep to correct a pastor or teach some important truth. Woe be unto those who are not willing to listen when it truly is of God. Those who revel in "pastor worship" may wake up some day to find their flocks departed for greener pastures and purer pastors.

148. Refusing to answer the invitation to the wedding feast of the Lamb (Mat. 22:3). This can refer to those who find excuses to delay their calling to come to Jesus. It can also apply to those who do not progress past the point of accepting Him. They may have given their heart to Jesus but are not willing to bury the old nature and submit their mind and will to God. "Greasy grace" replaces anointed oil and gets you singing "Slip, slidin' away" all the way to the land down under – and I don't mean Australia.

149. Putting carnal concerns above spiritual ones (Mat. 22:5). Some pursuits are not wrong in themselves. When we put them before God, however, they can become idols. Examples: too much TV, too much Internet (even the good stuff!), too much gabbing on the phone, too much work and too little God and family, too much sports (golf, bowling, boating, fitness center workouts), too much housework, too much reading books other than the Bible, too many courses, too much Bible college (where you don't have time for intimacy with God), too many commitments, too much stuff (hoarding things you don't need that clutter your space and time), too much food, and even too much church (when your intimate life with Jesus and family are neglected). But you can't have too much of Jesus!

150. Honoring our own self-righteousness instead of the righteousness of God (Mat. 22:11). The wedding garment in this verse is Jesus' righteousness in us.

209

Why Doesn't God Heal Me?

When we try to perform and do things in our own strength, God calls our works "filthy rags" (Isa. 64:6). When we yield to the Holy Spirit, He does the work as we rest in Jesus and let His grace empower us to obey (Eph. 2:10; Titus 2:11-12).

Many misunderstand grace, not realizing that our loving Father bestows 25 different graces – one of which gives us the Godly strength to obey (see "Grace" in the Appendix). The "luvvy-duvvy," "sloppy *agape*" Christians who think that love is the only thing, close their eyes to plain verses like Romans 13:10 and I John 5:3. These verses clearly teach that love is the fulfilling or accomplishing of the law. Love obeys the law of God, which is simply the definition of perfect love. John defines love as keeping the commandments and says that the law is not a burden. It is the way to peace and happiness – to eternal life and abundant life now (Deut. 5:29; Mat. 19:17; John 10:10).

The false "under grace" teaching makes God boil! Read Romans 6:14. Sin, which is breaking the law of God, will not master you because you are not under the law but under grace. That's Pauline theology!

In the flesh – without the Holy Spirit – the law is indeed a burden. It is impossible to keep it and it leads to death. But Jesus' righteousness in us keeps the law God's way. Abolish the holy law of the holy God, which David loved and Jesus observed perfectly, and you abolish as well the blessings of obedience to it. Grace pardons us for disobedience to the moral law of God (we're not talking about rituals and sacrifices!) But New Covenant grace and love do not do away with the Ten Commandments!

On the contrary, grace and love empower us to keep them in a way Israel could not begin to imagine. Read Matthew 5, 6 and 7. The Ten Commandments are even stricter under the New Covenant. That's because we have Jesus' righteousness in us. And we're not only talking about imparted righteousness – but actual obedience to the law – by the grace of God!

"Be holy," He says, "for I am holy." He has made us "the righteousness of God," but He wants us to walk in His righteousness. In so doing, we honor His righteousness – not our own.

God is Love. His law is love (I John 5:3). Do away with the law and you do away with love. You do away with God!

151. Rejecting God's truth in favor of man's opinion, showing partiality to man instead of God (Mat. 22:16). "… Teacher … [You] defer to no one; for You are not partial to any." Jesus did not bow before or court the favor of religious leaders. And He did not make a habit of quoting men. He quoted the Word of God.

"It must be true because so-and-so said it." It doesn't matter how many letters follow a man's name, or how many sermons he has preached. If what he says does not agree with God's Word, then, as the Word says, "Let God be true, and every man a liar" (Rom. 3:4, KJV).

In the early church, if a pastor taught an untruth, a lay member could correct him by quoting the Word. In some circles, if someone tried that, he would be

The Hindrances 18

severely corrected – if not excommunicated – for daring to insinuate that the pastor could be wrong. As a pastor I can say for sure that pastors aren't perfect. We must be willing to be corrected by the Word of God – whether it comes out of the mouth of a prominent elder, an elderly widow, or a six-year-old child.

152. Not rendering "unto Caesar that which is Caesar's" (Mat. 22:21, KJV). Not paying our taxes will get us into trouble with the taxman – and with God! He can withhold His blessings from those who steal from the government, even if we think they're the ones who are stealing from us by exorbitant taxes (self-justification is also a hindrance).

Once I got a bad surprise when Revenue Canada told me I owed over $300. I asked God for a miracle, following Jesus' example of the coin in the mouth of the fish. During my colleague's sermon, I received $350 in miracle money in my Bible! God gave me enough to pay the tax and the tithe! All things are possible – even paying taxes when the money isn't there.

We should also cooperate with government directives, such as restricting the use of power. If asked to serve the government, we should comply. If the government asks us to do something that is not against God's will, we should make every effort to obey.

153. Doing our deeds to be noticed by men (Mat. 23:5). Most of us golfers agree with the saying, "Drive for show and putt for dough." But in the game of life, some people do everything for show. We "play religion" every Sunday so we can be *seen* – seen as respectable members of our community, seen as good, righteous people. If our religion – our righteousness – is for show, we're full of dough – the leavened kind. So until our "puff-pastry" has been turned into nice flat bread, God has every right to deprive us of His blessings.

154. Seeking out places of honor (Mat. 23:6). It's better to be summoned to the king's table than to assume that honor (Prov. 25:6-7). The Pharisees wanted the chief seats so they would be seen by men as important. It is not a sin to sit in the first row at church, but we must be careful to guard against the *attitude* of the Pharisees.

155. Giving oneself vain, grandiose titles of honor (Mat. 23:7). The Pharisees loved their titles – as do their equivalents today. "The Most High Reverend Bishop Borumuch" is more than vain. It's blasphemous. That's trying to take God's glory and authority – not giving glory to God.

156. Allowing oneself to be called "Rabbi" (Mat. 23:8). *Rabboni* signifies "my master," or literally, in the Hebrew from which it is derived, "my great one." The term "Rabbi" was not known in Jewish society until Hillel and Shammai, which was around the time that Jesus lived. Jesus was pointing out a common human tendency – that of wanting to show everyone else that one is better/greater than the others in every respect. Without being judgmental, we do need to take seriously these words of Jesus. Our society, without fully realizing it, has based its religious traditions on human ideas that seem right, rather than on the Word of

211

18   Why Doesn't God Heal Me?

God. Although God will judge the offenders with mercy, it is important for us to know the truth.

Actually, the implication is *the* rabbi or teacher, as if no one else in the congregation could teach.

Since this is so close to the "pastor worship" concept, allow me to expand on this pervasive problem in the church today. Pastors, I hope you will read this, since the members you serve will take note of it.

In the early church the pastor was just what the word implies – an overseer. He was a mentor, training others with the gift of teaching to share that role. He spent time in prayer and the Word so he could correct any error in the teaching of the many who taught (Acts 6:1-4) Being close to God, he was able to discern gifts in the people, encourage them and even send them out elsewhere to minister in their calling or anointing.

He was not a candidate for burnout like many pastors today. They have an inflated conception of what a pastor is supposed to be. Today's ubiquitous pastor has his hands in every pot. Those who have the gifts to make a great stew are instead in a stew of frustration – and it's the church that's going to pot! Fellow pastors, we're not the Most High! If we think so, God will bring us low. He's about to close the curtain on the one-man show.

Puffed-up pastors seemed to have overlooked Ephesians 4:11-12. First of all, they are only one fifth of the five-fold ministry. In addition, those in the five-fold ministry are not there for their own glory, but to train the saints for the service of the ministry. That's the motto of Morningstar Church in Charlotte, NC. When will it dawn on the rest of the body that we are indeed a body? Self-exaltation stinks. Synergy saves. The big toe is essential to body balance.

157. Putting oneself on a pedestal above the other brothers in the faith (Mat. 23:8b). Jesus was *the* Teacher and now the Holy Spirit fulfils that role. Those who have the occasion or the calling to be teachers simply teach what *the* Teacher teaches them. They share it with their brothers. You may be *a* teacher, but you are not *the* Teacher. If we think that we as pastors or teachers are the only ones in the church who can teach, we need to get off our pious pedestals.

We are all brothers – and sisters – in Christ. And its too bad male leaders have squelched the gifts of our women. The first ones commanded to preach the good news of the resurrection were women! Did Jesus make a mistake in telling these women to evangelize? Female servants of God in the Bible, in both the Hebrew and Greek Scriptures, weren't limited to evangelizing. In Bible history five women are denoted as prophetesses, with Deborah listed as both a prophetess and judge (Judges 4-5). Later we find Anna (Luke 2:36) and Philip the evangelist's four daughters (Acts 21:8-9) mentioned as prophetesses, with Acts 2:17-18 removing the differentiation between sexes regarding prophetic gifts.

Paul made apostolic decisions that were specific to certain circumstances, cities and cultures. They were based on Biblical principles but were not meant to be a standard for all time. He forbade certain clothing to be worn by women because that is what prostitutes wore at the time (I Tim. 2:9). By the same token, he commanded women to be silent in the churches in Corinth, especially women under the authority of their husbands. That's because only prostitutes spoke out in public in that city at the time.

Rightly dividing the Word of truth involves distinguishing doctrinal dogma from cultural considerations. If one or two Scriptures contradict the rest of the Word, choose the Word. Ask for God's light to clear up foggy verses. It's too bad we have deprived the body of Christ of the essential and precious input of our feminine helpmeets. They are indeed helpmeets to the male and helpmeets to the body of Christ. Thank God for Gloria Copeland, Paula White, Taffi Dollar, Cindy Jacobs, Mary Glazier – and Joyce Meyer, who says it like no man can!

158. Using "Father" as a religious title (Mat. 23:9). Jesus said it! It is obvious here that Jesus is not referring to calling a physical or adoptive father by that term. He's referring to a religious title. Not many people seem to have read the Book. Otherwise, why would they do the exact opposite of what Jesus said?

159. Exalting oneself as a leader. Mat. 23:10 – As is often the case, the NASB gives the more correct translation: "Do not be called leaders; for One is your Leader, that is, Christ." The Greek *kathegetes* contains a form of the word *hegeomai*, from which comes the English "hegemony," referring to the authority of one nation over others. God did put leaders over God's physical nation Israel. And even then God's desire was to make the whole nation "a kingdom of priests." In Ephesians, God calls the husband head over his wife. He is her leader, as Jesus is the Leader of the church (Eph. 5:23). Those in five-fold ministry do indeed exercise leadership as they serve and mentor their brothers (Heb. 13:7). Jesus said, however, not to call them "leaders," since He is the Leader or Head of the church, His body.

Self-exaltation and "hero worship" are all too common in the church today. Instead of lifting up "stars" that may fall by pride like Lucifer, let's lift up the true Morningstar (Rev. 22:16) and give Jesus the glory!

The main thrust of this hindrance is what could be called the "Nebuchadnezzar syndrome" (Dan. 4:29-37). He gloated, "… 'Is this not Babylon the great, which *I myself* have built as a royal residence by the might of *my* power and for the glory of *my* majesty?'" Jesus cut his pompous speech short to tell him that "his royal highness" would be brought low and be like a beast for seven years until he learned that the Most High God is the real Ruler or Leader. He would be "Nebuchadnever" unless he gave glory to the God who rules forever.

160. "Shutting off" the Kingdom of God from men (Mat. 23:13). The Pharisees had their own doctrines and were not willing to be corrected by God or by man. We have our modern Pharisees in pulpits today. They curse saints by calling them sinners. They encourage negative songs that curse the people and take them back to the Kingdom of Darkness. They teach a sleazy grace that does not allow people to attain to the stature of the fullness of Christ. They condone sins that God condemns. In so doing they shut off God's Kingdom from people.

161. Devouring widows' houses and for a pretense making long prayers (Mat. 23:14). These are mentioned together, and sometimes do accompany one another. Too many poor parishioners must pay the pastor to pray and bury their loved ones. That's "devouring widows' houses." Jesus said we were to "freely give" because we have freely received. Making long prayers and charging by the hour is the opposite of a spirit of service. Salaried ministers are a Biblical concept. Charging for services is not. Jesus denounced teachers who preached for a price (Micah 3:11).

162. "Straining out a gnat and swallowing a camel" (Mat. 23:23-24). Jesus leveled this attack at the religious leaders. They made a big deal of small matters and yet ignored the things that were important to God. We have seen modern examples of legalistic church leaders who major on minor things and then commit flagrant sins like adultery. Some preach picky rules, judging others for not being as rigorous as they are, thus ignoring the more important principles of mercy and love.

163. Allowing ourselves to be deceived (Mat. 24:4). We have a responsibility for not being deceived by false doctrine. We must be studying the Word, enlightened by the Holy Spirit.

164. Denying Jesus' name by not being willing to stand persecution (Mat. 24:9-10). If we have a nature that sneaks out of standing up for Jesus for fear of persecution, we won't be ready when persecution really does hit.

165. Allowing our love to grow cold (Mat. 24:12). Many Christians have become callous by the lawlessness in this end-time world of wickedness. They become hardened by what they see around them and on their "hellevision" sets. "The tube" has become instead a sewer pipe pouring out filthy fare – polluting our minds and numbing our senses. A "what's the use?" approach often results in a detached, selfish attitude that does not love other Christians enough to even pray for them. French singer Gibert Becaud said it well with his song years ago entitled "L'indifference." An indifferent, apathetic frame of mind plagues our society, including too many Christians. The attitude the song describes that "kills you little by little" also kills the sensitivity of how a Christian should live, as well as your blessings.

166. Changing God's Word to following man-made paradigms. Too many alter God's Word and instead teach their pet paradigm as if it were God's Word. It is indeed possible to sin by dancing or playing cards. The Bible nowhere, however, condemns such activities. Whether we sin by dancing, of course, depends on how we do it (see Hindrance No. 177). Murder is wrong no matter how you commit it.

167. Willingness to take every opportunity to backslide. Jumping at every

The Hindrances 18

opportunity to go on a drinking or carousing binge with the wrong crowd – not even fighting it – is deplorable. It mocks God. Until they fully repent, He doesn't bless backsliders.

168. Abusing one's fellow servants in Christ (Mat. 24:48-51). Verbal, physical, mental or spiritual abuse of a fellow Christian is serious. Showing favoritism and putting down the lowly is a common example. Pastors have their special seats and special treatment, but the newly converted skid row dweller with his dirty jeans gets dirty looks. Some Christians look at him judgmentally and with a condescending air. That is out-and-out self-righteousness, and bordering on subtle but sure abuse.

169. Not being spiritually alert to the signs of the times (Mat. 25:13). We must be watchful in prayer. And we should not be oblivious to the prophetic signs of Jesus' coming.

170. "Hiding your talent" (Mat. 25:25). God is a God of increase. He expects us to work with what He has given us. We all have a special calling or anointing that the Holy Spirit desires to lead us in. We must be walking in our anointing, the area where the Holy Spirit supernaturally empowers us to serve.

171. Not desiring to let Jesus live His life in us (Luke 9:23). We must deeply desire to let Jesus live in us by denying ourselves, taking up our cross or burden and following Jesus. As we read in Titus 1:16: "They claim to know God, but by their actions they deny him. They are detestable, disobedient and unfit for doing anything good" (NIV).

172. Hindering someone who is doing God's work (Luke 9:50). It is easy to judge someone who is not doing God's work as perfectly as we are. We might be able to help him do the work more effectively. We should not, however, curse or hinder him. Jesus is the One who will ultimately judge. He is the only One who may say one day, "You cast out demons in My Name, but I never knew you."

173. Not keeping God's day of rest holy can limit God's blessing in our lives. Some say it's Sunday, some Saturday, some any day of the week. God will soon give special revelation about the importance of this weekly day of rest. God is merciful and will judge us according to our conscience and understanding. And He does command us to fellowship with other Christians, "not forsaking the assembling of ourselves together ..." (Heb. 10:25).

Isaiah 58 shows the importance to God of His day of rest. Verses 13 and 14 strongly warn against profaning or ignoring that day. The blessings promised are colossal. It's a gateway to greater intimacy with God. That intimacy with Jesus brings us into the realm of the supernatural to know the blessing of physical healing as well as spiritual healing.

Although not a requirement for salvation at the present time, not keeping it can deprive a Christian of the blessings of this day in which God's special presence resides. If we knowingly refuse to keep it once we see it *is* required in order to be

215

perfect, God may withhold healing and other blessings.

God is not talking about the picky legalism of the Pharisees of Jesus' day or the more familiar Sunday "blue laws," but a day of rest and celebration of our Creator. What a joy to bask in that special weekly intimacy with Him! It is a rejuvenating time of fellowship and worship, so God does not like His people infringing on that precious period of time. It shows a lack of reverence for God.

The day of rest is God's joyful time of fellowshipping with His Children. As He communed with Adam and Eve on that day, so He deeply desires to enjoy us and allow us to enjoy Him and His special presence on a weekly basis.

174. Listening to a pastor or being involved in a church that is directly opposed to God's Word (especially regarding healing). A young Edmonton man was afflicted with arthritis and deterioration of the lower back. He went in faith to a healing crusade and was healed beyond any shadow of doubt. His pastor was one who did not believe in divine healing and thought "faith healers" used demonic powers. When the man came to share the good news, the pastor had several church officials gather around him. They detained him and harassed him for hours until he renounced his healing as from Satan. He relented. The sickness returned in greater force. From then on he even had to use a wheelchair.

If you want healing and your church doesn't believe in it, you better find another church!

175. Idolatry. Although this may fit in the hindrance on disobeying the commandments of God, it is important enough to mention separately. An idol is anything or anyone we put ahead of God. It may be something we cherish in our hearts above God or something that crowds out our time with God. It may be the television, or the Internet, a hobby or a habit. If we allow something to push God to second place in our lives, He has every right to withhold His blessings until we repent.

176. Preventing Christians from expressing themselves in the praise and worship of God, especially in the dance. While praise and the dances of praise express our joy, the dances of worship supernaturally generate a special, deep-down joy. When someone criticizes and/or prevents such free expression of worship to God, they hinder the worshippers and they hinder their own blessings and healing. Look what happened to David's critical wife (II Sam. 6:23).

177. Sensual dancing. This hindrance is not referring to private romantic dances between mates. It refers to the lewd dances glorified by such movies as *Dirty Dancing* – lustful dances that God calls fornication and/or adultery. If Jesus says a lustful look is adultery, how much more, then, actual touching in a dance. Physical contact, on the other hand, does not necessarily mean lust is involved. The dance the Israelites engaged in at the foot of Mount Sinai was both idolatrous and sensual.

Dancing itself is not a sin, as some think. It is only sinful when it causes us

The Hindrances 18

to disobey God. David danced before the Eternal. And guess what? God Himself dances over us with shouts of joy! That's the meaning of the KJV "singing" in Zephaniah 3:17 in Hebrew.[39] Are you holier than the Holy One?

178. Praying controlling prayers of "witchcraft." The essence of witchcraft is to try to control the will of another person. The demon spirit of witchcraft comes under the major demon of control. When our prayers reflect our desire to control the will of another person, even if it is for his or her good, we are praying a witchcraft prayer. Sometimes we can do so without realizing it. Here are some examples: "God, make him be nicer to me." "Make him love me, 'cause I want to marry him." You may never sweep him off his feet unless you throw away your broomstick!

Witchcraft prayers are more common than you may think. Jesus told us to watch and pray. I add this: watch *how* you pray – and *what* you pray. Even better, ask God to activate the gift of tongues or prayer language He has already given you. The Holy Spirit always prays perfectly. Speaking in tongues isn't charismatic chaos. Yet in delicate, personal matters, not praying that way can cause chaos in the lives of those for whom you pray. If you do pray for people in your native tongue, be sure to pray *for* them – not *at* them.

179. Not practicing the "give" way of life. Luke 6:38 is quite clear on this. "Give, and it will be given to you." God will "pour into our lap a good measure (of blessings)" if we are givers.

180. Not blessing others. The morning that I wrote these words, I had a divine appointment with Joe, a Christian brother. He was excited about I Peter 3:9, which shows that blessing others is an important part of our calling. The NIV says it this way: "Do not repay ... insult with insult, but with blessing, because to this you were called so that you may inherit a blessing." How can we expect to receive God's blessings if we do not bless others?

The Jewish people are a blessed people – with finances, success and good health. That's because they bless their children and bless each other every time they greet one another.

My friend and I prayed blessings upon each other on his front lawn. And I shared an important truth that the Holy Spirit had revealed: curses can be revoked, but blessings can never be taken back! As we bless others, God can pour out His

---

[39] Excerpt from *The Spirit-Filled Life® Bible*, General Editor, Jack W. Hayford, Thomas Nelson Publishers, Nashville, 1991 "Word Wealth" note on Psalm 30:5: "**joy**, *rinnah* (ree-nah); Strong's #7440: A shout of rejoicing; shouting; loud cheering in triumph; singing. *Rinnah* describes the kind of joyful shouting at the time of a great victory ... Zeph. 3:17 literally says that God will dance over His beloved people with singing or a shout of joy ..." Note on Zeph. 3:17: "His satisfaction with His people will be expressed through loud, demonstrative singing ..." The idea in Hebrew is that of God the Father and Jesus spinning around in a dance of celebration over each of us, those special ones redeemed by Jesus' blood. God is pleased when we rejoice over Him in the same way in exuberant praise and worship. A Hebrew scholar and university professor I consulted in Charlotte, NC, at a conference there, confirmed that this Hebrew word could easily include the celebrative twirl in a praise dance.

217

18   Why Doesn't God Heal Me?

blessings upon us, including finances, healing and health.

181. Stopping others from walking in their anointing. The Biblical concept of anointing is multifaceted. It is the enabling power and grace of the Holy Spirit to perform the job God has called us to do. That calling or vocation or activity is also termed our anointing. When we block others from walking in their anointing, we disqualify ourselves from receiving God's blessings.

Here are some of the symptoms we may experience if we are blocking someone's anointing: frustration (especially with the person whose anointing we are blocking); anxiety; a combination of anger, stress and rage; judgment; critical spirit; an attack of the mind and heart by the spirit of betrayal; loss of security; major resentment; seclusion and withdrawal; burnout; *illness* in ourselves or our family; need to control; absence of miracles in our lives; confusion and disorientation; fatigue; tendency to say false prayers (of control or witchcraft); blaming; increasing denial; rejection and loneliness; the spirit of death; attention-getting devices; manipulation; nagging, harping; coldness; heart and mind in turmoil and ready to explode.

Sounds like the warnings of side effects on drug packaging! As with prescription drugs, ask yourself: is it worth it?

If we find ourselves in this trap, nothing seems to satisfy us. We hear more easily from demons than from God.

Here are some of the roots of this problem: unwillingness to reconcile or be reconciled with another; wanting it "my way"; high evidence of false love; pride; need to control another to fulfil your needs instead of looking to Jesus; listening to and creating gossip, including gossip in the form of prayer; not trusting God, taking things into your own hands; frustrating people by putting them in the wrong jobs (common problem of church leaders); focusing on the other individual's problems and thus unwilling to change yourself; unforgiveness and expecting a Jesus-like perfection in the other person; strong need to set boundaries for others (e.g. pastors forbidding people to pray for others in church, or forbidding "hallelujahs" and "amens"); worship of self-designed rights; emotionally susceptible and easily offended.

The person whose anointing we are blocking experiences the following symptoms: loss of purpose; inability to pray; pressured feeling; disorientation; inability to give and serve; trouble hearing from God; blocking of provision and prosperity; no miracles; stopping of the flow of love; feeling of defeat. That's not loving your neighbor, is it?

God says that if we destroy the temple of God, He will destroy us (I Cor. 3:17). We cannot expect to be healed and blessed if we are destroying a brother in Christ by blocking his anointing.

Following is the prayer you should say, with communion to seal it, if you have been guilty of blocking another's anointing. *"Father, I am sorry I have judged another. I rejected their anointing because I was caught up in the flesh, trying to get my needs, desires and expectations fulfilled by a person or a group – not by Jesus Christ and the Holy Spirit. I took on the spirits of intolerance, anxiety, anger, betrayal, resentment, blockage, denial and rejection so that my will could be done in their life and not Your will. My prayers became full of false love and witchcraft in my attempts to control, manipulate and destroy another person's free will. I became full of rottenness, fatigue, coldness, stress, illness and confusion, which have ruled my day because of my error. I have let pride and unforgiveness bring in the tormentors instead of acknowledging my sins before now.*

"I see how my curses and false prayers have destroyed my brother in Jesus. Help me be reconciled to You and to him/her. I hereby rescind, reject and break off all curses that I have placed upon anyone and I repent of and revoke any false prayers I have said over anyone. I bind all demons involved in these curses in chains of confusion and send them back to the pit in Jesus' name.

"Thank You, Father, for Your love, healing and forgiveness. May all power, glory and honor be Yours forever and ever. It is in Your name, Father, that I pray blessings on all I have cursed. Let them walk fully in Your love, peace, joy, anointing and Your will for their life. I thank You in Jesus' name. Amen."

182. Worshipping the spirit of betrayal. This is a long subject that cannot be sufficiently covered in this book. Here is a brief summary.

Betrayal, also known as Beelzebub or lord of the flies, is the demon directly under Satan, the one who inspired Judas to betray Jesus. When we feel betrayed by someone and refuse to forgive them, we fall under this demon spirit with his many agents. They include control, under whom come cruelty and stinginess, with their multiple agents (Satan's system of hierarchy is a counterfeit of God's and looks like a pyramid). Betrayal's other right-hand man is unforgiveness, under whom fall rejection and infirmity. The spirits of mental and physical disability come under infirmity.

This connection with infirmity is why betrayal is so important when it comes to healing. The roots of these demonic strongholds must be discovered and repented of before healing can occur. God may sometimes sovereignly heal in His mercy, yet He would prefer that we get rid of the sin that is blocking our healing.

Any sin, recognized or not, that falls under the umbrella of betrayal and his agents and that we refuse to repent of can bring us under betrayal and allow him to bring his other agents to affect us, even infirmity. To name only a very few, that could include rebellion, worthlessness, witchcraft, occult, sexual lust, addiction, manipulation, anxiety, fear and self-pity.

Those who refuse to believe in demonic involvement in illness may seem to represent a balanced approach. On the contrary, these individuals are grossly naïve about the power and work of demons. Following their deceptive philosophy may gain you the favor of the religious world, but it won't get you healed.

As a part of end-time revival, the Holy Spirit has graciously revealed to us at

Why Doesn't God Heal Me?

Freedom Church of God the demonic connection to illness. Doing as Jesus did, we often use demonic deliverance to effect physical healing. Our ministry has been blessed with multiple healings. Many who have been prayed for over and over without success have found healing here when the Holy Spirit revealed the demonic roots.

183. Refusing to be baptized. Although many modern evangelists overlook it, God *commands* baptism for those who receive Jesus. He commanded His disciples to baptize believers (Mat. 28:19). Jesus even said, "He who has believed *and has been baptized* shall be saved" (Mark 16:16).

It is up to God to decide when there may be exceptions. I counted about 50 Greek scriptural allusions to baptism in an abridged concordance. Even our perfect Savior was baptized as an example for us. If evil Simon Magus in Acts 8 knew it was a requirement, why can't we see its importance?

Seeds cannot bear fruit unless they germinate. We receive the seed of the Holy Spirit when we accept Jesus. Baptism, when properly understood and practiced, allows the seed to germinate – to sprout into eternal life.

This supernaturally empowered physical rite confirms and symbolizes the circumcision of the heart (Rom. 2:28-29) and the burial of the old nature (Rom. 6). It is a basic doctrine of Hebrews 6.

184. Unwillingness to submit to the Word of God. When we are not willing to obey the Word, we can't be loyal to God.

185. Accepting and/or preaching a lie when we know it's a lie. This is the basic root of *Parkinson's* disease. The demons have manifested physical symptoms because of the sin of flouting conscience to teach a lie.

186. Saying "forget it" instead of "I forgive you." God wants us to forgive from the heart, not tell those who have sinned against us to forget it. This is the root cause of *Alzheimer's* disease. If you know someone who has these last two illnesses, you can "stand in the gap" and intercede for them. You declare that you are standing in place of them before God and ask Him to forgive you for the sins involved. Be sure to declare after the prayer that you cease standing in the gap for them. This prayer will open doors to allow them to proceed toward healing. In this last case, as a family member you may need to take authority over the person who is incapacitated. It would be helpful to have a few Christians come together with a prayer of agreement and even communion.

187. Not repenting in the time God allotted for our repentance (Rev. 2:21-23). God sometimes gives us a certain space in which to repent. He expects us to change in that time period.

188. Not submitting to God's chastening. Hebrews 12 shows God as a loving Father who chastens those He loves. That chastening does not have to be that painful, but our resistance sometimes requires God to bring severe measures to get us back into the way of blessings. He proceeds in different degrees of severity of chastisement:

220

The Hindrances 18

1) By His Word;

2) The conviction of the Holy Spirit;

3) Chastened by God Himself – He allows pains for course correction;

4) Rebuked by God and His agents – verbal correction;

5) Reproved by God and His agents – action taken;

6) Disciplined by God – He takes away a reward or gain made by sin (e.g. David's child from Bathsheba dies);

7) Scourged by God – this is like a public flogging, a severe and public embarrassment and correction;

8) Meeting God's direct wrath – (e.g. famine, depression);

9) Being punished in God's wrath (e.g. loved ones not healed; children die);

10) Being consumed in the hot wrath of God – He allows everything to be taken away from us and diseases to come upon us that eat us up from the inside out. Remember what Jesus said about rebellious mankind before the flood: "'My Spirit shall not strive with man forever ...' " (Gen. 6:3).

189. Cursing unsaved people to hell. Satan, working through religious leaders, has twisted the Word of God to say that those who have not accepted Jesus in their lifetime are condemned to a fiery hell forever (see Chapter 2). That damnable lie is straight from hell. Those who condemn the unsaved to go to hell make it hard on them when they are called to Jesus. These unjust judges also bring backlash upon themselves as the curse they spoke comes back on them, often in the form of sickness.

190. Not accepting that we are the righteousness of God. Accepting this truth is the key to unlocking all blessings, including healing. Not accepting it, therefore, is a sure way to invite sickness in.

191. Gambling. God is not a God of chance. When we accept Jesus, we are to come out of the idea of luck ruled by Satan and into the concept of blessings from God. Gambling is asking Satan to bless us. That includes buying lottery tickets. God wants to bless us, and He is quite able. Turning to Satan's world of chance and luck is a lack of trust in God to bless us, as well as often a show of greed and lust for money. It is a denial of Jesus' name of Provider. At a healing banquet I attended, one lady was not healed because she insisted on going to play bingo for money. I'm sure that when that hindrance was corrected, "Bingo!" – she was healed. It may sound trite, yet God wants us to be upright and walk in honesty and integrity. When we take care of the small stuff, we will surely take care of the major sins in our lives.

192. Seeking sympathy and pity. Nowhere are these words mentioned in the original Bible languages as being encouraged for believers. As He does, God wants us to show compassion – not sympathy and pity. Instead of sighing "poor you," we should speak God's Word into the situation and show the person the way

221

Why Doesn't God Heal Me?

out of his or her problem. When the Devil invites you to a pity party, take Joyce Meyer's advice, "No, Devil! I've attended before. I was all by myself and it was no fun!"

193. Beating up on ourselves. Not accepting and walking in our righteousness has dire consequences. Fear and doubt cause us to say we're no good. We're actually beating up on Jesus, since He's in us. And He can't be crucified twice. Beating up on ourselves is the last step before we reach the point of the unpardonable sin. At some point the spirit of blasphemy enters. We see ourselves only as sinners. We're walking in sin and we're too scared to read the Word. We seek out other sins to bring comfort. Sin and fear replace faith as we run cowardly away from God.

194. Not using the name of Jesus – using almost exclusively the title "Lord." Television preacher John Hagee recounts the story of three young boys who found themselves trapped in a refrigerated locker. They screamed for help to no avail. Then one of the boys, an eight-year-old, said, "Let's call out for Jesus to get us out. He'll hear us!" They did. And He heard. The door miraculously swung open and they scurried to safety. There is power in that name.

As we saw in Chapter 12, the derogatory title "Lord" has no power when not used in context with Jesus. When translated back into Hebrew, it refers to Baal, and to the sexual prowess of the leaders who were worshipped in antiquity as Baals. The word translated "Lord" in both Hebrew and Greek means "Divine Master." And the frequent King James "LORD" in the Hebrew Scriptures was simply the name *Yahweh*, who actually was the One who became Jesus. Declaring healing in the name of the Lord rather than in the name of Jesus will be no declaration at all. There is only power in the name of Jesus. The Holy Spirit has actually revealed that a demon called "quagmire" calls himself "Lord." He loves to hear people say "Lord" instead of Jesus, or Father, or Holy Spirit, or God. He gets the pleasure of pushing them from one quagmire or ditch to the other, including the ditch of sickness. That's his job. "Lord" may be in the Bible, but it's a wrong translation. Use the name of Jesus and see how things go better.

195. Not delighting in Jesus (Ps. 37:4). When we don't delight in Jesus and become like putty in His hands, we forfeit blessings, including healing.

196. Harboring a complaining, negative spirit (Phil. 2:14). This may be a difficult verse to practice perfectly, yet nothing will steal our blessings faster than a down-in-the-mouth, complaining spirit. How can God bless us if we're constantly cursing the blessings we already have and the blessings He's planning to give us? A complaining attitude stops all blessings. The sickness that comes upon us as a result will simply give us more to complain about until we renew our mind and our mouth.

197. Cursing ourselves as sinners and specifically saying "The Sinner's Prayer." Declaring that we are sinners and not saints is a dangerous curse that afflicts many. When we curse ourselves back into the Kingdom of Darkness, we open ourselves up to all that darkness has to offer, including sickness. If you have ever said this prayer, here is another prayer you need to say instead:

"Father, please forgive me for having cursed myself as a sinner. I forgive those who encouraged me to do this. I forgive myself for having spoken it. I bind up all the demons and their agents enforcing this curse in chains of confusion. I cut them off from all support. I take the sword of Jesus with my right hand of authority [as you lift your arm] *and I destroy* [as you bring your arm down] *all their weapons, artillery and armaments. I burn up their slime and command them to go back to the pit in Jesus' name. I rip off the sinner label from my forehead* [with your right hand] *in Jesus' name. I declare that I am a saint – a Child of the Kingdom of Light. Thank You Father, for the freedom from this curse. In Jesus' name. Amen."*

198. Limiting God and ourselves. Putting limits on God and ourselves gives an open door to the spirit of limitations with his many agents to keep us from walking in the righteousness of God. One of the effects of limitations is the onset of spiritual and physical paralysis. The chief agent of limitations is infirmity. Other effects of this spirit and/or curse are achy bones and joints and disability.

199. Trauma. Traumatic experiences, if not dealt with by proper teaching and communion, can seriously affect our health. The Holy Spirit has given us at Freedom Church of God breakthrough revelation on release from trauma by the blood of Jesus. However, a comprehensive explanation of this information would be too long to share in this book.

200. Not surrendering our pains and concerns to Jesus (I Pet. 5:7; Mat. 11:28-30; Isa. 53). Jesus came to bear our sorrows. If we don't lay them down at the foot of the cross, He can't. This is a hindrance to both health and healing. God did not intend for us to bear the pain of family tragedy, betrayal by a trusted friend, sexual abuse or rape. He tells us to cast our cares and burdens on Him. In our ministry we often have emotionally hurt people to act out the laying down of their pain at the foot of the cross, placing their hands on their chest and then lowering them to an imaginary foot of the cross at their feet. As they do so, they declare what they are doing and that they choose to leave their pain with Jesus. It's hard to forgive colossal wrongs when we refuse to acknowledge the hurt we feel and turn it over to Jesus.

201. Pride (James 4:6). This major hindrance is touched on throughout this book and is thoroughly examined in the Appendix, under "Pride." Pride is the result of using a gift from God without thankfulness and thus claiming success and blessings as our own instead of acknowledging God's hand in our lives.

202. Not accepting new Christians (Luke 9:48). This verse refers not only to children but also to children in the faith. Different from the concept of despising them, this hindrance refers to not accepting new believers. They may not be dressed like you or fit into your little group, so you give them the brush-off instead of a loving, Christ-like welcome. Since Jesus said it was Him you are rejecting, don't expect Him to welcome you into His healing arms. If they don't qualify for your love, you don't qualify for Jesus' healing.

Why Doesn't God Heal Me?

203. Not bearing one another's burdens (Gal. 6:2). We must not follow the way of Cain, who claimed he was not his brother's keeper. The "law of Christ" is the law of love summed up in the Ten Commandments. Loving our brothers as ourselves means we are willing to help them with their burdens – sins, sicknesses, cares, concerns. They may need assistance in seeking God's grace to forgive someone who hurt them. Jesus bore our burdens, and He is the ultimate Burden-bearer, but He wants to help others bear their burdens through us.

204. Mocking God (Gal. 6:7). We can mock God and His blessings a number of ways, some of which we have briefly covered. The greatest miracle that God does in our life is to take us out of the Kingdom of Darkness and put us into the Kingdom of Light, declaring us to be His saints or holy ones.

When we declare that we are sinners after accepting Jesus as our Savior, we mock God's most important blessing of love that He can bestow on us. We are sayings that we are still held in the Kingdom of Darkness, that Jesus' sacrifice, His blood, is not worthy of us and that our heart is still for the Kingdom of Darkness. We must confess this error and start declaring what God says about us (see Hindrance No. 197).

God says that He has given us a sound, "well-balanced mind" (II Tim. 1:7, AMP). If we make such declarations as "I'm manic-depressive, A.D.D. (attention deficit disorder), paranoid, schizo …" or "I just can't remember things," or "I'm no good at figuring things out," we're saying that God's gift to us is faulty or a failure. That's mocking God.

Jesus says that we have access to all His authority in heaven and on earth. Our Father says, however, that vengeance is His. If we decide to take vengeance into our own hands, or to bind someone up with a curse, or tell God what sort of vengeance we want, we are usurping God's authority. We are telling God that His blessing of forgiveness in our life is not good enough to allow us to forgive others. When we bind someone in vengeance, we are also binding ourselves. We are forfeiting all of God's blessings for us until we confess our error, unbind that person and speak blessings over him or her and his or her life. Blessing those who curse us allows God to bless us.

As we saw in Chapter 2 and in Hindrance No. 61, it is the Father's prerogative to draw people to Jesus (John 6:44). Jesus gave us His authority to preach the gospel to all nations and to make disciples of them. Jesus did not give us authority to use fear tactics, intimidation, nagging, cursing, guns, or incantations to get another to repent and believe. We are not to abuse another's free will. We mock God every time we move outside His boundaries in trying to get someone to come to Jesus. We are literally telling God by our actions that we think that He is incompetent at His job and that we know better than He does when someone should commit themselves to Jesus.

So how do we approach unconverted mates, relatives, and children? Subject to their free will, we can claim them in the Passover covenant – the New Covenant

The Hindrances 18

(see "Communion" in the Appendix). Our prayers and unconditional love for them open the door, but when they see our walk with God, they will also seek Jesus.

If we want someone outside our family to be called, we should use Isaiah 58:6 as our guide. To speed up the process of the calling, find two or three others to pray in one accord. We are to intercede for them, daily binding the demons afflicting them and declaring blessings on them.

We can also mock God in money matters. Let's say we receive $1,000 as an unexpected blessing. If we exclaim, "Wow, what luck I've got!" or "I thank my lucky stars," we are mocking God by claiming that Satan has blessed us. We also mock God if we don't ask Him how He wants us to use the money, or even if He wants us to give some or all of it to bless someone else.

Carnal thinking grieves, blocks and rejects the Holy Spirit. It prevents Him from showing us God's will for us and thus mocks God and His blessings (II Cor. 1:12-20).

205. Not realizing the importance of acknowledging the forgiveness of sins in the context of healing (Mat. 9:2-8; John 20:23). This book has expounded this important hindrance and it cannot be overemphasized. Jesus mandates His disciples to declare to people that their sins are forgiven, especially in the context of healing (James 5:14-16). The sick need that assurance. And healing servants of God need to use their God-plane authority on earth to forgive sins. Doubting the certainty of Jesus' sacrifice for us and not recognizing in our minds and hearts that we are washed clean in the blood of Jesus can be a serious obstacle to our healing. One of the main themes of this book is that we must let Jesus lift our burden of sin before He can lift our burden of sickness.

The Hindrances of the Sermon on the Mount

206. Insulting and labeling others (Mat. 5:22). The key here is anger. Angrily pouring forth insults can result in being brought before "the council" if there is no repentance for this. The Greek *raca* (KJV) from the Aramaic *reqa* literally means "empty-head." How can we expect God to bless us when we are insulting others? What follows in the same verse is much more serious and is a more important hindrance. Both can be classified as curses. If someone has labeled us, we need to reject and break it off in Jesus' name. Using our right hand of authority, we need to rip the imaginary label off our forehead and send it back to the pit. Then we should declare the corresponding positive truth about ourselves.

207. Angrily cursing and condemning someone as a "worthless one" whom even God cannot redeem (Mat. 5:22). That is the meaning of the word "fool." The real meaning is this: "You are a worthless human being – past, present and future. I publicly condemn you and even God can't change you." You are actually condemning the person to the lake of fire, which is where you deserve to go for such a public condemnation. You must publicly repent for such a declaration

225

18 Why Doesn't God Heal Me?

before God and man, or God has every right to condemn you to *gehenna*, the final lake of fire. Such a condemning judgment is almost like an incantation spoken by a witch to bring someone down.

208. Refusing to reconcile with our brother (Mat. 5:23-24). This is probably the only time in the Bible God says to *stop praying*, except for the time God told Jeremiah not to pray for rebellious Israel. "Your offering at the altar" can include a financial gift or a prayer presented before God's heavenly altar. God is saying: "I don't want your gift – or your prayer – if you're not right with your brother!"

Notice an important practice some have overlooked. Verse 23 says not to present your offering at the altar if you "remember that your *brother* has something against *you*. ..."

Now your brother in Christ may not be in the best of attitudes and may not be ready to reconcile. But you must make the effort to reconcile if he clearly has something against you and you know about it.

The implication, combined with chapter 6:15, is that you must forgive and seek reconciliation.

Sin, especially unforgiveness, causes God to turn a deaf ear to our prayers (Isa. 59:1-2). The only prayer He will hear is the one in which we ask Him for the grace to forgive. Forgiveness is always possible, while reconciliation may never occur. Even when reconciliation is possible, circumstances do not always allow us to reconcile immediately, but our heart and our prayers must be toward reconciliation.

Dr. Michael Murray of Cincinnati recounted a poignant example of the effects of a lack of reconciliation. On a Christian television show he admitted that he and his wife had an argument about whether to buy small or large light bulbs for their Christmas tree. They were not on speaking terms for the good part of a day. The next day they both fell sick and remained so for two weeks. The lack of reconciliation caused the sickness and became a hindrance to God healing them.

209. Not "agree[ing] with your adversary quickly ..." (Mat. 5:25-26, NKJV). This can apply to debts, a word interchangeable with sin, as some versions of the model prayer of Matthew 6 indicate, or to court cases in which someone sues you. If you have done something to cause someone to take you to court, you should try to amend the situation before the court date (I'm not referring to ridiculous suits all-too-common in our litigation-happy society).

In a real sense, by your sin you have bound someone in pain, and what is bound on earth is bound in heaven. You must share that pain ("the last penny") until you have rectified the situation. Otherwise, you may go to literal prison. In any case, God will allow you to be delivered to the demonic tormentors in a spiritual prison in order to lead you to repentance.

210. Not applying the "cutting off your right hand" principle (Mat. 5:29-30). This phrase has multiple meanings in Greek. In Hebrew thinking the right hand was the symbol of authority and will. We should be radical in our approach for banish-

The Hindrances 18

ing sin from our lives. We will to lust and we will to steal. We must declare God's will, not ours, over our lives.

"With Jesus in me, I will not lust after that woman." "I will not let my hand steal someone else's property." Positive verbal declarations on a daily basis marshal our will to agree with God's will and submit our "hand," "eye" or will to the will of God. This permits our will to "listen" to our spirit and our heart and thus submit to God's Spirit in us.

Some use their wills in a legalistic "pride of power" system. If they don't submit to God's humility, the law they tout will judge them.

211. Making false vows or oaths (Mat. 5:33-37). What comes out of our mouths is serious to God. As Christians we should be careful of any promises or commitments we make, being sure they are in the will of God. We are to be people of our word. A simple yes or no is sufficient.

We are not to swear at all, even on a Bible in court. Haven't they ever read the Bible?

Yet even our yes and no must be carefully weighed so we know we can meet our commitments. Sometimes we may have to literally say, as James 4:15 teaches us, "God willing, I will do this or that." If we actually promise to do something, that is akin to a vow said in God's presence. He expects us to come through. God expects Christians to make and respect their marriage vows, but to make any other promises or vows sparingly.

The Jews would swear by their hair or beard. That tradition has been perpetuated in such children's story phrases as "not by the hair of my chinny chin chin." Jews would actually rip out the beard of one they perceived had not fulfilled his promise or vow. That's what they did to Jesus.

Oaths call God to witness that we are telling the truth. Phrases such as "I swear to God" or "I swear on a stack of Bibles" are sin. "God will be my judge in this matter" is a better way to say it.

212. Seeking revenge instead of suffering loss, persecution or injury for Jesus' sake (Mat. 5:38-41). This is an often-misunderstood passage and a verse some use to make Christians look silly. Jesus was stating a principle that does not have to be taken literally. The "eye-for-an-eye" Old Covenant law was God's justice or "revenge," i.e. just retribution for wrong done. Under this covenant you could be "revenged" and not have to suffer loss.

On the other hand, under the New Covenant, a stricter agreement with Spirit-led Christians, at times we must be willing to suffer loss, to accept evil, unjust treatment from people.

But there is a time for everything. When falsely accused during His ministry by self-righteous hypocrites, Jesus did not bow to their insults, but plainly told them they were a band of snakes. When businessmen invaded His Father's house, He took a whip and drove them out.

Such boldness gave way to silent courage at other times. When His time had

227

18 Why Doesn't God Heal Me?

come for martyrdom, He was as silent as a lamb, not justifying Himself or seeking any revenge. We cannot be sure that He literally turned His right cheek to the abusing soldiers when they struck Him on the left. The point is this: He humbly submitted to mistreatment for the gospel's sake in the spirit of a martyr. Though we are not all called to be martyrs, His spirit of humility and self-sacrifice must guide us.

If we take this verse literally, as devil's advocates admonish us, it could be absurd. "Okay, you've raped and beat my wife. Now here is my daughter." We must walk in the wisdom of Jesus, taking every verse in its own context as well as the whole context of the Bible.

We should have faith in God's promise of protection. We can command demons and people to take their hands off our loved ones in Jesus' name and let them know we mean business. We don't have to be Christian doormats. We are warriors, spiritually speaking. We must not be vengeful, however, but willing to give up certain rights for the sake of the gospel and a shining Christian example.

Remember also the context is one of Jews being under Roman occupation. "Wisdom is the better part of valor," and God does tell us to submit to governmental authorities, unless there is a conflict with His law (Rom. 13:1-7; Acts 5:29).

Ecclesiastes 3 must balance this principle. There is a time for everything – a time to tell the Pharisees bluntly their problem and a time to submit to mistreatment and suffer loss for the cause of Christ. Jesus is both Lamb and Lion, Peacemaker and Warrior. Our real war, of course, is with the spirit world. We are to love and bless those who spitefully use us and curse us, thus " heaping coals of fire on their heads" (Prov. 25:21-22), letting God provide any vengeance He judges they deserve.

"I'll defend myself!" is not the Christian cry. We are not to be vengeful resisters, blabbermouths, or self-justifying instruments of condemnation, but gentle, humble, loving servants who are lights to a cruel world, overcoming evil with good, not with more evil. God will not bless us unless we are "blessers" ourselves, even in the face of persecution and martyrdom.

213. Being stingy (Mat. 5:40-42). God may be stingy with His blessings if we are stingy with others. While we need discernment in choosing to whom we give or lend, Proverbs teaches us that when it is in our power to do good, we should (Prov. 3:27-28). We must not worship money or things more than God.

If an emergency comes up, and we have the money, we should lend without interest, especially to a brother in Christ. God's nature is to give, to bless others with everything He has. He has everything, of course, and yet He does not give indiscriminately. We have our limits, and yet we are often unjustifiably stingy.

God does not want us to be victimized by con artists, but sometimes we should give people the benefit of the doubt.

There is a time to say, in effect: "Gold and silver I have not, but what I have I give you …" We should not be embarrassed to pray for people, even publicly. We must not be ashamed of Jesus. You will be surprised to find that about 80% of peo-

228

The Hindrances 18

ple will respond positively to the question: "May I pray for you?" People usually welcome a brief prayer of blessing if not done in a syrupy, religious way. Let's not be stingy with our physical or spiritual possessions.

214. Not blessing our enemies who curse us (Mat. 5:44-45). If we do not respond to our enemies with forgiveness, blessings and prayer, God enjoins us to seriously ask ourselves if we are in reality Sons and Daughters of our Father. If we are not acting like Jesus, do we truly have fellowship with the Father? And if we are not acting as His Children in regards to those who hate, curse and persecute us, can we claim God's promises? If we only love and bless those who love us, what reward, such as healing, can we claim? Apart from the exceptions we have seen, we must be Children of God to claim His blessings.

215. Not seeking perfection (Mat. 5:48). God commands us to seek perfection, to grow daily towards it. God says in many ways throughout the Bible: "Be perfect!" He means what He says. Some have the attitude that says, "God accepts me as I am, warts and all. I don't have to do anything. I'll just coast my way to glory."

"God knows my heart" may be true, but it can often be an excuse to continue in sin. In His letters to the churches at the beginning of Revelation, Jesus didn't mention their hearts. He repeatedly said, "I know your *deeds*!" Faith without works is dead.

216. A Pharisaical, self-righteous, glory-seeking, people-pleasing attitude (Mat. 6:1). The "look how righteous I am!" attitude stinks to highest heaven. It is earthly and carnal. If people's praise is what we seek, we better enjoy it. That's all we'll get.

217. Doing charitable deeds publicly for vainglory (Mat. 6:2). Although some alms may be public, we mustn't do it for show. If we give to be admired or to have our name on a plaque, God sees our motives. He blesses only those who give Him the glory.

218. Praying publicly for attention only (Mat. 6:5-6). Vain, posturing, super-righteous, or whining diatribes in public prayer do not please God. Are we trying to sound righteous or religious or are we simply talking to God? If some religious people talked to their friends the way they talked to God, their honest friends might say, "Get real!" If we come boldly before the throne we will receive what we request. If we seek only attention, that's all we'll get.

219. Needless repetition in prayer (Mat, 6:7). God does not want meaningless mantras or empty, repetitive phrases – including even mentioning His name repetitively. He wants effective prayers from the heart.

220. Ostentatious fasting (Mat. 6:16-18). If we fast for show, we will not grow – and God won't bless us. We may not always be able to hide it, but we should not go out of our way to publicize our fasting. Tooting horns blow rewards.

221. Not trusting God with your treasure (Mat. 6:19-21). Money is not a sin. It is the love of money that is wrong. When we don't love it, but invest in the work of preaching the gospel, our Father loves to prosper us so we can be blessed and

Why Doesn't God Heal Me?

bless others. If we love money more than God, God will withhold blessings from us until we change. If we don't trust God to take care of us financially, we put ourselves under Satan's umbrella instead. If we don't make God our financial partner by tithing and generous giving, the Devil takes His place to steal, plunder and destroy our finances.

222. Worry (Mat. 6:25-34). When we are anxious about things in our physical lives, we can't pray properly. Panic and doubt lead us to listen to Satan. Fear cancels our faith. When worry about today and tomorrow inhibits our trust in God, we prohibit Him from blessing us. When we seek God's Kingdom first, including tithing, we need have no worry about Him meeting our needs today, and we need take no anxious thought about the possibility that our needs may not be met tomorrow and next month. "Let go and let God." (See "Prayers, Ten Steps to Heartfelt Prayer" in the Appendix.)

223. Judging or condemning (Mat. 7:1-5). Being overly critical of our brothers in Christ is an all-too-common problem in the church today. It is true God wants us to be discerning and He does say we will know others by their fruits. Nevertheless, wrongly judging our brothers, categorizing them or condemning them is tantamount to judging Jesus Himself, for we are all a part of His body. And if we are not truly yet a part of His church, He will take care of that – He who judges perfectly the hearts of men.

Pride often keeps us from seeing that mercy is indeed better than judgment. As one man said, "If you are looking for the perfect church, just realize that when *you* become a part of it, it ceases to be the perfect church." Give your brothers a break. You were at their point once, and probably still are without realizing it. Your problem may not be their problem. Focus more on your need to change. Allow your brothers to be themselves, and even forgive them for not allowing you to be yourself.

God is a God of mercy and judgment. But He only *delights* in mercy!

224. Giving that which "is holy to dogs …" (Mat. 7:6a). The dogs Jesus is referring to are wild dogs who will rip you apart, even from behind. If we give holy things to "dogs" – viscous mockers and persecutors – God may withhold blessings until we walk more in the wisdom of Jesus. Sometimes we do everything right and still get persecuted. At other times we pay the price for our stupidity. Handing a whip to someone we know is going to lash out at us is not wise.

225. "Cast[ing] your pearls before swine …" (Mat. 7:6b, NKJV). In Hebrew terms, a pearl is a secret between you and God. "Swine" refers to people who "eat" anything and everything. They "suck you dry," leaving nothing for anyone else. As swine see no value in a pearl, so these people despise your spiritual secret, and will probably curse you for it. If we want God's blessing, we must be careful with whom we share certain pearls of wisdom. And it takes wisdom to know what to share with whom.

226. Not "asking, seeking and knocking" (Mat. 7:7-11). Some feel, "God

The Hindrances **18**

knows what I need, so I don't need to ask." Yes, your Father knows, but He wants you to humbly ask Him. "For everyone who asks receives …" (verse 8). Asking shows trust and faith, which give joy to the Father's heart. Don't you love to hear your children ask for things you know they need?

227. Not following the golden rule (Mat. 7:12). If we are not concerned about others, will God be concerned enough about us to give us His blessings? We reap what we sow.

228. Not being aware of false pastors (Mat. 7:15-20). Some pastors or others in full-time ministry may have wrong motives. They may want to devour us, desiring our money more than us. They will not lead us to God or His blessings. God says we will know them by their fruits. As we get in harmony with God, He will show us which "trees" are rotten and produce bad, negative fruit, so we can go to the trees that produce good fruits and healing.

229. Saying "Lord, Lord" but not doing the Father's will (Mat. 7:21-23). This hindrance is a shocker, especially to those who will hear these ominous words. There will be a surprising number of ministers who use the name of Jesus to do even mighty wonders, but Jesus will say, "I never knew you!" These people "know" Jesus but are not necessarily Christians. They go by their own strength, using all the right words – but they refuse to submit to the will of the Father. God gives His Spirit to those who *obey* Him (Acts 5:32). Even Satan can do miracles. Miraculous works do accompany true servants of God, but we know they are Christians by their love and obedience – the evidence of the Holy Spirit in them.

230. Not acting on the Word (Mat. 7:24-27). Some have not built their spiritual houses on the right priorities, the rock of Christ. "All other ground is sinking sand." Jesus' brother James also drives home the importance of hearing and doing. The Hebrew idea of faith and belief is being founded on solid rock. Both Hebrew and Greek, in their words expressing the idea of faith, imply action as an integral part of faith. In Greek, you can't "just b'lieve!" If your faith is in the Rock, you will automatically *act* on what you believe. Those who give only lip service and no action will get no action from God.

N.B. These hindrances are not a Talmudic burden but only a reminder of what God's Word says and that He expects us to obey it. I have tried to explain them in an understandable, non-threatening manner so you feel encouraged and energized for determining and dealing with any personal hindrance you might have at this time.

I believe you will see by the fruits that these are indeed divine revelations. The Holy Spirit has revealed that there are about 600 hindrances to healing. He has chosen to reveal 200 or so in this book to give us the idea. He can reveal others to us if we ask Him.

18 Why Doesn't God Heal Me?

It is written...

Be diligent to present yourself approved to God as a workman who does not need to be ashamed, accurately handling the word of truth ... if anyone cleanses himself from these things, he will be a vessel for honor, sanctified, useful to the Master, prepared for every good work.

II Tim. 2:15, 21

CHAPTER 19
Hindrances Checklist

Hindrances Relating More Specifically to Healing

1. Lack of faith.
2. Hoping or wishing instead of believing.
3. Not accepting God's promise.
4. Not confessing faith.
5. Insufficient instruction.
6. Lack of unity in the Spirit.
7. Community unbelief.
8. Traditions of men regarding healing deny God and preach Satan's lies.
9. Healing fails when natural laws continue to be broken.
10. Unbelief of the elders who pray and/or anoint for healing.
11. Not dealing first with the evil spirit causing the affliction.
12. Unrepented sins.
13. Lukewarmness.
14. The "halter" hindrance.

Why Doesn't God Heal Me?

15. An unforgiving spirit, holding a grudge, seeking your own vengeance or gossip.
16. Wrongs not righted hinder the faith of some to receive healing.
17. Lack of diligence, wholeheartedness or intense desire.
18. Accepting no less than an instant, miraculous healing as a sign or wonder, as opposed to a progressive yet still divine healing.
19. Watching the symptoms (Satan's lies), which Satan uses to convince us God will not heal us.
20. Not acting on our faith (which without works is dead).
21. Failing when faith is tested.
22. Substituting personal faith for belief in the doctrine of divine healing.
23. Believing God's Word is not directed to us.
24. Waiting until we see the healing before we believe.
25. Denial of sin.
26. Tempting God.
27. Guilt.
28. Curses.
29. Trying to play games with God and His promises.
30. "God can cure some diseases, but not mine."
31. The belief that sickness is time and chance and that God cannot alter the results of time and chance.
32. Not discerning the Body of Christ at the Passover and/or communion.
33. Partaking of the Passover and/or communion and then partaking of the table of demons.
34. The medical profession.
35. Fear.
36. If we don't really want to be healed, God will not heal us.
37. Self-image.
38. Believing our illness is too small for God to heal.
39. Having no hope.
40. Allowing evil influences to destroy our health.
41. Not being joyful.
42. Religious thinking (as opposed to godly thinking).
43. Refusing to believe in demonic involvement in sickness.
44. Comparing ourselves with others (in regard to healing).
45. Wanting healing to the exclusion of accepting our calling as a Christian.
46. Not giving God the glory for our healing (this can apply either to the person who is the instrument of healing or to the person who is healed).
47. Lack of respect for God's authority and sovereignty.
48. Wrong motives.
49. Misplaced faith.
50. Trusting in merit.

Hindrance Checklist **19**

51. Lack of prayer and fasting.
52. Putting even natural remedies ahead of God's healing.
53. Lack of praise and thankfulness to the Healer, God.
54. Speaking evil of our father or mother.
55. Not dealing with problems that must be dealt with before laying on hands for healing.
56. Abuse.
57. Not confessing our sins.
58. Not developing our spirit, or "spirit man".
59. Anger.
60. Eating foods God says not to eat.

Hindrances to All of God's Blessings

61. Stealing from God by not tithing.
62. Involvement with demons.
63. Not providing for the needs of one's family.
64. Not interceding in prayer for someone when God shows us we should.
65. Attempting to bear fruit apart from Jesus – "dead works."
66. Putting traditions of men before the Word of God.
67. Being a "tare."
68. Being spiritually blind.
69. Not having our hearts right with God.
70. Not accepting God's forgiveness of our sins.
71. "Playing footsy" with the Devil.
72. Not trusting in God for our needs.
73. "Cramming religion down people's throats."
74. Not being "wise as serpents and harmless as doves."
75. Not enduring in the face of persecution.
76. Not obeying God in a time of persecution.
77. Trying to be "better than Jesus."
78. Not transmitting messages from God He wants us to pass on.
79. Fearing men rather than God.
80. Not being willing to endure persecution from even within our physical family.
81. Not being willing to "bear our cross" and follow Jesus.
82. Not being willing to "lose our lives" for Jesus' sake.
83. Not receiving the servant Jesus sends to heal us.
84. Not being willing to receive revelation and correction from God as a "babe."
85. Not believing the Father has given Jesus authority over all things.
86. Not accepting "rest" in Jesus.
87. Rejecting mercy and condemning the innocent.

Why Doesn't God Heal Me?

88. Not realizing the value of every human being.
89. Attributing the works of Jesus' servants to Satan.
90. Not being "with Jesus" and not "gathering with Him."
91. Not keeping the commandments of God.
92. Not being willing to follow Jesus fully.
93. Rebellion.
94. Denying Jesus.
95. Receiving an accusation against someone without at least two witnesses.
96. Offense.
97. Refusing to do the work of God by "burying the dead."
98. Looking back longingly to our life of sin.
99. Not getting rid of spiritual stumbling blocks.
100. Committing blasphemy against the Holy Spirit.
101. "Your silver has become dross, Your drink diluted with water."
102. Demanding a "sign" or miracle from God.
103. Taunting God or His servants.
104. Denying the only sign Jesus gave that He was the Messiah.
105. Not seeking God and His ways after having been delivered from demons.
106. Not being willing to pray in agreement for another person's needs.
107. Declaring deception and suffering from the Devil to be from God.
108. Blocking others from praising God because of a spirit of religiosity.
109. Cursing others.
110. Not having a sense of vision about the things of God.
111. Not receiving information from God as a little child.
112. Not seeking God's Kingdom first.
113. Knowingly rejecting part of God's Word.
114. Not speaking God's Word over ourselves.
115. Comparing ourselves with others (in a general sense).
116. Not knowing how to respond to a "backlash" from Satan.
117. Not accepting our anointing.
118. Not receiving "a prophet in the name of a prophet."
119. Carnality.
120. Being hypocritical or two-faced (to God).
121. Not worshipping God in truth.
122. Not being aware of the leaven of the Pharisees and Sadducees.
123. Rejecting the keys of the Kingdom.
124. Discouraging another Christian from doing the will of God.
125. Reflecting the views of an unbelieving and perverted generation.
126. Doing things we know are offensive to others.
127. Being a stumbling block for a believer (especially a new one).
128. Despising new believers ("babes in Christ").
129. Not searching for the sheep that has gone astray.

Hindrance Checklist

130. Not having the Father's desire that none of these "little ones" (new believers) perish.
131. Not going to a brother when we should.
132. Not going to a brother in private.
133. Refusing to hear a brother who comes to point out a sin.
134. Putting a limit on forgiveness.
135. Not showing mercy on a fellow Christian in need.
136. Divorcing without Biblical grounds (referring to Christians).
137. Not being willing to give to the poor.
138. Desiring possessions on earth more than the heavenly ones.
139. Trying to manipulate God to get what we want.
140. Not accepting God's call.
141. Not realizing the importance of communion and its practice.
142. Taking God's name in vain.
143. Not acknowledging God's right to call and reward as He pleases.
144. Grumbling against God's generosity to others.
145. Wanting to be served instead of being a servant.
146. Using the temple of God the wrong way.
147. Resisting the servants whom God sends to teach us or correct our ways.
148. Refusing to answer the invitation to the wedding feast of the Lamb.
149. Putting carnal concerns above spiritual ones.
150. Honoring our own self-righteousness instead of the righteousness of God.
151. Rejecting God's truth in favor of man's opinion, showing partiality to man instead of God.
152. Not rendering "unto Caesar that which is Caesar's."
153. Doing our deeds to be noticed by men.
154. Seeking out places of honor.
155. Giving oneself vain, grandiose titles of honor.
156. Allowing oneself to be called "Rabbi."
157. Putting oneself on a pedestal above the other brothers in the faith.
158. Using "Father" as a religious title.
159. Exalting oneself as a leader.
160. "Shutting off" the Kingdom of God from men.
161. Devouring widows' houses and for a pretense making long prayers.
162. "Straining out a gnat and swallowing a camel."
163. Allowing ourselves to be deceived.
164. Denying Jesus' name by not being willing to stand persecution.
165. Allowing our love to grow cold.
166. Changing God's Word to following man-made paradigms.
167. Willingness to take every opportunity to backslide.
168. Abusing one's fellow servants in Christ.
169. Not being spiritually alert to the signs of the times.

Why Doesn't God Heal Me?

170. "Hiding your talent."
171. Not desiring to let Jesus live His life in us.
172. Hindering someone who is doing God's work.
173. Not keeping God's day of rest holy can limit God's blessing in our lives.
174. Listening to a pastor or being involved in a church that is directly opposed to God's word (especially regarding healing).
175. Idolatry.
176. Preventing Christians from expressing themselves in the praise and worship God, especially in the dance.
177. Sensual dancing.
178. Praying controlling prayers of "witchcraft."
179. Not practicing the "give" way of life.
180. Not blessing others.
181. Stopping others from walking in their anointing.
182. Worshipping the spirit of betrayal.
183. Refusing to be baptized.
184. Unwillingness to submit to the Word of God.
185. Accepting and/or preaching a lie when we know it's a lie.
186. Saying "forget it" instead of "I forgive you."
187. Not repenting in the time God allotted for our repentance.
188. Not submitting to God's chastening.
189. Cursing unsaved people to hell.
190. Not accepting that we are the righteousness of God.
191. Gambling.
192. Seeking sympathy and pity.
193. Beating up on ourselves.
194. Not using the name of Jesus – using almost exclusively the title "Lord."
195. Not delighting in Jesus.
196. Harboring a complaining, negative spirit.
197. Cursing ourselves as sinners and specifically saying "The Sinner's Prayer."
198. Limiting God and ourselves.
199. Trauma.
200. Not surrendering our pains and concerns to Jesus.
201. Pride.
202. Not accepting new Christians.
203. Not bearing one another's burdens.
204. Mocking God.
205. Not realizing the importance of acknowledging the forgiveness of sins in the context of healing

Hindrance Checklist

The Hindrances of the Sermon on the Mount

206. Insulting and labeling others.
207. Angrily cursing and condemning someone as a "worthless one" whom even God cannot redeem.
208. Refusing to reconcile with our brother.
209. Not "agree[ing] with your adversary quickly ..."
210. Not applying the "cutting off your right hand" principle.
211. Making false vows or oaths.
212. Seeking revenge instead of suffering loss, persecution or injury for Jesus' sake.
213. Being stingy.
214. Not blessing our enemies who curse us.
215. Not seeking perfection.
216. A Pharisaical, self-righteous, glory-seeking, people-pleasing attitude.
217. Doing charitable deeds publicly for vainglory.
218. Praying publicly for attention only.
219. Needless repetition in prayer.
220. Ostentatious fasting.
221. Not trusting God with your treasure.
222. Worry.
223. Judging or condemning.
224. Giving that which "is holy to the dogs ..."
225. "Cast[ing] your pearls before swine ..."
226. Not "asking, seeking and knocking."
227. Not following the golden rule.
228. Not being aware of false pastors.
229. Saying "Lord, Lord" but not doing the Father's will.
230. Not acting on the Word.

19   Why Doesn't God Heal Me?

It is written...

If you do these things, your salvation will come like the dawn. Yes, your healing will come quickly. Your godliness will lead you forward, and the glory of [Jesus] will protect you from behind ... [Jesus] will guide you continually, watering your life when you are dry and keeping you healthy, too. You will be like a well-watered garden, like an ever-flowing spring.

Isa. 58:8, 11 – NLT

PART III
SHALOM! To Your Health!

CHAPTER 20
Walking in Divine Health

Isn't there something better than getting sick and then getting healed? Yes, there is. Not many Christians, however, have yet arrived at this place of bliss. I'm speaking of divine *health*.

Obeying God, taking care of our bodies by exercising and eating right are certainly necessary for the enjoyment of divine health. But there's more to it.

John G. Lake, powerful healing evangelist in the nineteenth century, tells of an experience he had on a boat full of sailors. A horrible plague broke out on the vessel, and everyone was affected – except Lake.

An 82-year-old Christian lady appeared on a religious television program. No one guessed she was that old. She looked like a voluptuous 35-year-old model. Her secret?

When she accepted Jesus at 65, she was all shriveled up – in her body and her face. She had to use a cane to walk. She began to declare daily over herself positive scriptural promises – especially Psalm 103:5: "Who satisfies your mouth with good things, so that your youth is renewed like the eagle's" (NKJV).

It worked! Her hair turned to its natural color, her wrinkles disappeared – and

241

Why Doesn't God Heal Me?

she threw away her cane! At evangelistic meetings, hundreds came forward – not to date her, but to accept Jesus!

She is a testimony to the power of our words. The words of Christians and non-Christians alike pack power! They can give life or death. They can kill or heal. But the words of Christians are more powerful.

Negative words or curses of unbelievers over themselves or others invite the evil spiritual world to enforce those words. Just ask black Africans. They know the power of a word curse.

Christians, on the other hand, have the authority of Jesus Christ and His Word behind their words. We have seen that when we speak the Word of God in faith, what we speak happens. God sends angels to enforce what we say – over ourselves and others. It is even more powerful when we use our authority in Jesus to release the appropriate angels (warring, ministering, messenger, etc.) to fulfill the specific covenant promise we are claiming and seal it in communion.

The Word of God is more powerful than a two-edged sword (Heb. 4:12). And what a power when it's in our *mouth* (Josh. 1:8)!

Speaking the Word can give wealth – and health! Proverbs 12:18 says: "… the tongue of the wise promotes health" (NKJV). The King James simply says a wise tongue *is* health.

Proverbs 4:20-22 says that God's words treasured in our hearts are life and health to our flesh. How much more if we speak them! Death and sickness and life and health are indeed in the power of the tongue (Prov. 18:21).

Speak It!

Speaking the words, "By His stripes I was healed," promotes rapid disappearance of Satan's symptoms of sickness. There are other words that could even keep the Devil from getting us sick in the first place. Let's look at a few.

One of the main ones is a passage we have referred to repeatedly, Exodus 15:26. Although this verse does indeed refer to healing, with God identifying Himself as our Healer, its primary emphasis is on health. Not only is God our Healer and our Health, He gives a conditional promise we can claim. If physical Israel could claim it, how much more can we who are God's Children by His Spirit?

He said if they obeyed Him, He would bring none of the diseases on them that He brought on Egypt. Egypt is a type of this world of sin and sickness. If we obey God, we can claim the promise of divine health. None of these diseases that affect this sinful world will come upon us. Jesus even promised to remove all sickness from Israel – the believers (Deut. 7:15; Ex. 23:25). Speak it – over yourselves and your family.

I will quote the following verses in the first person. Psalm 91:3: "For it is He who delivers me from the snare of the trapper and from the deadly pestilence [plague or sickness]." Verses 10-11: "No evil will befall me, nor will any plague

Walking in Divine Health

come near my tent. For He will give His angels charge concerning me, to guard me in all my ways."

Want to have a long life? Speak Psalm 91:16 over yourself: "With a long life He will satisfy me and let me see His salvation." And if you've begun honoring your parents since accepting Jesus, and you honor your heavenly Father, why not claim out loud the promise of the fifth commandment in Exodus 20 – long life?

Declare over yourself the condition of the men of God in the Bible. Take Moses for an example: he died at 120, and "his eye was not dim, nor his vigor abated" (Deut. 34:7b).

Remember the old commercial for the iron elixir? "Are you tired? Do you have iron-poor blood? Take G_____!" Well, there's a better solution.

Here's God's prescription – the best from the Best. He is our Healer and our *Health*. Take one tablespoonful – in the morning or whenever you're too tired to do what God wants you to do – of Isaiah 40:29-31: "He gives strength to the weary, and to him who lacks might He increases power. Though youths grow weary and tired, and vigorous young men stumble badly, Yet those who wait for the [Eternal] will gain new strength; they will mount up with wings like eagles, they will run and not get tired, they will walk and not become weary."

That's great medicine. Take it. Declare it! Declare it in prayer over your mate, your children – your employees! Speak it in faith – and you will have more energy than you thought possible.

Don't confess tiredness (unless it's bedtime). Don't confess sickness. That's Satan's permission to weaken you further.

Do you confess memory loss and absent-mindedness? I know a wonderful lady who, when forgetting something, declared as her mother before her, "I haven't got bitty brains!" That curse began to come true. And it wasn't her age that caused it. When she rescinded it in Jesus' name, things began to change.

If we confess bad mental health, that's what we'll get. Confess that you have the mind of Christ! Confess that you have the spirit of a sound, disciplined mind. Confess that your youth is renewed like the eagle. And that includes your brain.

Confess health! Declare God's Word! That pleases God. And He will back it up.

Remember what God inspired the apostle of love to say: "Beloved, I pray that in all respects you may prosper and be in good health just as your soul prospers" (III John 2). The principle applies to healing, but the word John uses is *health*.

In the next few verses John says he rejoices to see us walking in the truth. In verse 2 he made it clear that God desires for us to walk in divine health.

God's Part

God has a part in the sanctification of our bodies. "Now may the God of peace Himself sanctify you completely; and may your whole spirit, soul, and *body* be preserved blameless at the coming of our Lord Jesus Christ. He who calls you is

Why Doesn't God Heal Me?

faithful, who also will *do it*" (I Thes. 5:23-24, NKJV).

God has revealed the role of the Trinity in the sanctification or rendering holy and blameless of our spirits, souls and bodies.

The Old Covenant tabernacle or temple is a type of our sanctification. Aaron, who represented our High Priest Jesus, entered the Holy of Holies once a year. The Father wants us to enter the very Holy of Holies in heaven one day – not only now in our prayers. But we must be holy – in spirit, soul and body.

Those who preach "sloppy agape" or "greasy grace" don't realize that God is a holy God. He has made our spirits holy and perfect, but He wants to sanctify our souls and bodies as well. Each member of the Trinity does His part.

The door of the tabernacle was adorned with four colors representing the four gospels, which revealed Jesus. Jesus said He was the *door* to the Father (John 10:7). That first door was also called "the way."

Gentiles could not enter the tabernacle, into the part called the "outer court," until they went through that first door or gate. We cannot be a part of spiritual Israel, the church, until we accept Jesus as our Savior. When we accept Him, Jesus begins to live in us through the Holy Spirit. The presence of Jesus in our spirits brings the seed of eternal life into our dead spirits. And by His death to blot out our sins and by His life in us our spirits are made perfect. Yes, God says we are holy.

And yet God tells us to *be* holy. This "progressive sanctification" means He wants us to allow Him to make our souls and bodies holy also.

To enter the inner court by the gate called "the truth," a series of washings was necessary. Jesus, "the truth," is involved in every step. The Holy Spirit, however, is more specifically involved in this second step. He is compared, as is the Word, to water.

The Holy Spirit does, of course, impregnate us when we receive Jesus. He does not, however, begin to work on our souls – our hearts, minds and wills – until we allow Him to do so in obedience to the baptism command.

Baptism is our outward proof to God that we are ready to bury our old selves or souls and allow the resurrected Jesus to live His life in us through the Holy Spirit. Yet it is more than a symbol. It is a supernaturally anointed ceremony. The Holy Spirit begins His work in our souls with our hearts or emotions.

As we allow the Holy Spirit to work in us, studying and reading the Bible aloud, we speak to our heart, mind and will and begin to get them in line with our spirit, which is perfect. We yield to God – the Holy Spirit – so He can renew our minds, hearts and wills to be conformed to Him.

The first disciples had received Jesus as their Savior. He had breathed on them to impart the Holy Spirit to them. And it is probable that John had baptized them with the baptism of repentance during the same period in which he baptized Jesus (Mat. 3:5-6).

And yet Jesus told them to wait for a period of time before they would be baptized – not in or with water – but in or with the Holy Spirit. The baptism or immersion or being filled full with the Holy Spirit was necessary to allow them to be operative in His gifts so as to be witnesses of Jesus. It was a complete yielding of themselves to His power in their lives – so He could change their hearts, minds and wills in the fullest sense.

So, as Jesus works with our spirits, the Holy Spirit works with our souls.

In addition, each member of the Trinity imparts gifts to us. Jesus gives us brotherly love, the Holy Spirit gives us His gifts (over 200), summarized only in brief in I Corinthians 12, and the Father gives us His special *agape* love and His *zoe* life.

Many think we need only receive the gifts of the Father and the Son. The Holy Spirit does not want us to miss out on His all-important gifts – both to edify ourselves spiritually with a special prayer language from Him and to edify the whole body with His precious gifts. Paul was flowing in those gifts (I Cor. 14). It is not a badge of superiority. It simply makes the Christian life so much easier and exciting. Just because some, like the Corinthians, have misused or even counterfeited the gifts, does not mean that we don't need them.

Charismatics may seem like "crazimatics" to some, but they are reaping blessings many have not wanted – for various reasons. Until you open yourself up to receive all the Holy Spirit wants to give you, you're missing out on a joy and a fullness God wants for you – even though you may be a wonderful Christian and a mighty servant of God.

Though it may seem like favoritism, baptism in water and the baptism in the Holy Spirit are necessary to come into the "inner court." It is only then that the Father can begin to impart His *zoe* life and begin to work on sanctifying our bodies.

That work can begin before we enter one day the heavenly Holy of Holies. Yes, we can begin here below to walk in divine health – free of sickness and disease. What an exciting possibility!

For that process to be complete, though, we must be *ready* to enter the Holy of Holies. Once again, Jesus is the gate of entry.

The way to the Holy of Holies was called "the life." And, of course, Jesus said He was all three gates, "the way, the truth and the life."

When they pierced Him with a spear, He shed the blood that releases us from all curses. It is only when those curses are acknowledged, rejected in Jesus' name and, in the case of blood curses, broken by communion that we can be ready to enter the Holy of Holies in heaven.

God is a holy God. He cannot sit in the presence of demons. If there are curses we have not recognized and rejected, demons are present enforcing those curses. We must be rid of those curses and those demons before we can approach a Holy Father God. Jesus paved the way.

Born again Christians can still be under curses. Jesus did become a curse for us, but as with salvation and healing, we must recognize our sin, sickness or curse, reject it, and accept Jesus' sacrifice for it.

God said even His people could be destroyed for lack of knowledge. But God

20 Why Doesn't God Heal Me?

is good, and He is about to reveal heretofore hidden knowledge that will release God's end-time people from curses.

Thankfully, death annuls all curses. But for those who are alive when Jesus comes to seek His blameless Bride – sanctified in spirit, soul and body – God will prepare them to enter the Holy of Holies. They will begin to walk in divine health.

It is written…

"Oh, that you had listened to my commands! Then you would have had peace flowing like a gentle river … Peace and prosperity [*shalom*] will overflow Jerusalem like a river," says the [Eternal] … When you see these things, your heart will rejoice. Vigorous health will be yours! Everyone will see the good hand of the [Eternal] on his people …

Isa. 48:18a; 66:12a, 14a — NLT

CHAPTER 21
Shalom – Receive It! And Share It!

In the mid-1970's at the Sorbonne in Paris I enjoyed greeting people in my Hebrew class. We would say, *"Shalom! Ma Shalom(cha)?"* Literally, that means, "Peace to you. What is your peace?"

Having worked in French Europe and Quebec for 15 years of my life, I know firsthand that some things just don't translate. As a native South Carolinian, I would have to translate the above phrase, "Hey, how 'ya doin'?" Or, as I learned to say while living in Texas, simply "Howdy!" A more revealing translation would be the familiar "Salut!" in French. The word can also mean "salvation" but no one really thinks of that when they say "salut." And modern Jews are also missing the full etymological meaning of *shalom*. It is my favorite Hebrew word. Here's why.

In Hebrew roots are extremely important. *Shalom* comes from *shâlêm* (*"be complete, sound, whole"*). *Shalom* is translated in various ways: "Health, prosperity, welfare, peace, rest, salute, be well, whole." The idea is that of "nothing missing, nothing wanting, nothing broken." Together with the *shêlâm* of Daniel 4:1, these two words have over 100 meanings! That's too much to cover here. Our linear languages can't convey the conceptual richness of *Biblical* Hebrew. Let's simply say that *shalom* refers to physical, spiritual, mental, emotional and even financial well-being.

I love the story my father told me of the man who finds a Jewish man lying on the street after a car accident. He says to the injured man, "Are you comfortable?" The Jew replies, "I make a living." God's people descended from Judah are known for financial prowess.

This book is not only about healing. It reveals why many Christians have not been blessed in every way, including financially. Many believers are only "half there" in all these areas of life. God wants us to have the peace that comes from being *whole*, which is the best way to summarize *shalom*.

All of the above meanings of *shalom* are a part of Jesus' atonement, the sacrifice of His body and blood – except finances. Spiritual as well as physical, mental and emotional healing and health are provided for in His sacrifice, as we have seen in a previous chapter.

As we have also seen, however, poverty is a curse and not a blessing. God's perfect will is that His people prosper. "Health and wealth" is not just some religious fad. It's God's perfect will.

That does not mean that all Christians will be millionaires. He promises to meet our needs – and then some – so we can be givers like He is (Mat. 6:33; II Cor. 9:6-13; Mal. 3:8-12; Job 1:3; 42:10; Prov. 21:20). As we walk in our identity in Christ and learn to obey certain laws of prosperity, including tithing, God will bless us in every way – which is what *shalom* is all about.

God wants peace or wholeness and wellness for His people. He wants the end-time body of Christ to be whole, "without spot or wrinkle" (Eph. 5:27), united as one (Eph. 4:3-6,12-13). He wants "nothing missing, nothing broken" – in our spirits, souls and bodies – and in His body, the church.

Share It!

God's perfect will for Israel was that they be a shining light of God's way of *shalom* – peace, health, happiness, obedience to His laws, prosperity – and that they would share that with the world.

And today He wants His people to be a "city on a hill" – "the light of the world" – to be ablaze with His light and to let that light shine for the world to see.

And yet, alas, we see instead a church that is sick – spiritually, physically and financially. We need to see and repent of the hindrances and sins that have kept us from *shalom*. How can we share it if we don't have it?

This is the Holy Spirit's book. He wants to use it to open the way to healing and health in every area of our Christian lives. As we repent of the sins that have hindered our blessings, as we walk in our newfound and awesome identity in Christ, we can receive *shalom*.

God and His true people grieve over a world that is becoming darker and darker as we head toward end-time cataclysms. Some of us have read the end of the

Shalom – *Receive It! And Share It!*

Book. We know Jesus Christ is soon going to take over this world and shine His light of truth and freedom that will transform our world.

Nevertheless, this dark world needs to begin to see that light now. They need to see a people who have been healed in every way – a people who by their actions and words will show them the way to peace – *shalom*.

Mark 16:15-18 shows what believers – not only full-time ministers – will be able to do. One of those things is to "lay hands on the sick, and they will recover."

One popular running shoe, whose name comes from a Greek word meaning victory, had an ad that simply says: "Just do it!" That is what God is telling us Christians about healing the sick. Our prayer should be: "Make us instruments of Your peace – *shalom!*"

We are supposed to be doing what Jesus did – and even greater works! You don't have to be a Billy Graham, Bob Larson or Benny Hinn to preach the gospel, cast out demons and heal the sick! You have Jesus' authority and He expects you to use it. Just do it!

I believe the time is coming soon when Christians who know who they are in Christ will do what Jesus did – heal the incurable sick, cast out demons and raise the dead! They will powerfully preach the gospel by the Light they have finally realized lives within – with their lips and lives.

My hope and prayer is that many will be set free from the burdens that hinder them and go out and share Jesus' healing love with the sick of this world. This book is not about theological arguments. It's not about cold doctrine. It's about the warmth of God's love – His healing love.

God is waiting on *you* to be aflame with the fire of His healing love and power. He wants to work through *you* to heal the sick.

If you have not accepted Jesus as your Master and Savior, please read the Epilogue. If the Father is drawing you at this time, it's for you. God loves you and wants the best for you – *shalom*.

He wants for all people to know the peace that comes from being whole in every way. He wants them to know Him – the Prince of Peace – and share Him and His way with others.

Do you know why the Dead Sea is dead or stagnant? And do you know why the Sea of Galilee is fresh and alive?

The Dead Sea is dead because it gives nothing out. No waters flow from it. The Sea of Galilee is alive and beautiful and thriving with life because it gives out its waters. It doesn't bottle them up like the Dead Sea. It gives. It lives. When we cease to give, we die. Love is not love until we give it away.

We're not truly living until we're *giving*.

You do indeed need to receive God's living Word and His healing waters. You and your loved ones need healing. You need healing in every area of your lives.

I lost my Southern accent 35 years ago, but I sometimes use that excellent, all-inclusive "y'all." But I want to bless all y'all who have read this far with two

Why Doesn't God Heal Me?

words from the conceptual, Biblical Hebrew that far surpass the "Southern" language. I give you over 100 blessings in Biblical Hebrew (and Aramaic) by these two words expounded earlier: *shêlâm* and *shalom*! Be blessed! And "y'all come back now, y'heah," for the next book. In this, His book, God is saying, "Y'all come!" He beckons to you, "Come and drink of My healing waters." But those living waters are not just for you!

God is also saying, "Y'all go! Y'all go into all the world and preach the gospel and heal the sick. Y'all need to get free. But I want you to be like Me and set others free!"

Shalom! Receive it. Thank God for it. And above all – share it!

Epilogue

What many call "the Sinner's Prayer" is a terrible misnomer. What follows should be called "the *Salvation* Prayer." The moment you accept Jesus as Savior, you cease being a sinner and become a saint. You may acknowledge your sin, but don't curse yourself by calling yourself a sinner. You have been called out of the Kingdom of Darkness into the Kingdom of Light and life. From this day forward you are a holy Child of God, not a sinner. If you agree, say out loud the following prayer:

"Dear Father in Heaven,

"I have sinned and fallen short of Your glory. I believe Your Son Jesus Christ, Whom You sent and anointed as Savior of all mankind, was born of a virgin, lived a sinless life, was crucified and died for me, was buried and after three days and three nights, was resurrected and ascended to heaven. I believe He now sits with You as my High Priest, soon to return as King over all the earth.

"Jesus, thank You for dying for me. I now accept You into my heart and into my life. I give myself to You, so that You may live Your life in and through me. I accept You as my Savior and Master, and as my Brother and Friend.

Why Doesn't God Heal Me?

"Every sin I have ever committed is now blotted out – erased from Your memory – by Your precious blood shed on the cross for me. From this moment forward, I am a new creation – clean and holy in Your sight. In Your eyes, I have no past. I am one with You, the Eternal God. I am Your special, beloved Child. Thank You for giving me the precious Holy Spirit. I now have eternal life. I choose to spend eternity with You in Your glorious Kingdom.

"Fill me with Your brotherly love for my fellowman. I choose to pray and study Your Word on a regular basis so I may grow up to be just like You. Please lead me to a church fellowship where I may grow to walk in the special calling You have for me, and where I may help others to grow.

"I choose to learn my new identity in You and follow the Biblical command to be baptized by immersion to show You I want to bury the old me for good and have the Holy Spirit work in a special way in my heart, mind and will. I desire to be filled to overflowing with the Holy Spirit, and I want to receive all He has to offer me."

Signed: _____

Date: _____

Begin reading aloud the declarations in the Appendix until you become familiar with your new identity in Christ. Then ask a spiritual leader to baptize you by immersion. Be sure to read Chapter 6 in Romans regarding baptism. Seek out those who can lead you into receiving the gifts of the Holy Spirit.

Appendix
(in Alphabetical Order according to Subject)

Some have claimed that tonsils and the human appendix are vestigial organs – useless leftovers from evolution. On the contrary, scientific research has shown the tonsils fight infection and the appendix prevents problems in the lower bowel. You may have had your appendix removed surgically, but please don't remove this one from your reading assignment. It is a treasure chest of jewels from the Holy Spirit.

Organizationally, the information found here fits better in this context. This appendix, however, is a vital key to your health – physically, financially and especially spiritually. It will help unlock the heretofore hidden treasure of all God's blessings. Enjoy!

Adversity

Adversity is a spirit that often works with infirmity. The purpose of adversity is to steal your joy and success. Be determined not to let that happen. Adversity always hurts. Turn the pain over to Jesus and begin using the tools below. Focus on Jesus, not on the problem. Trouble your trouble! When you rejoice in adversity, you qualify for special blessings as a bonus.

As you praise God, rejoicing in Jesus and in His Word, you discourage the spirit of adversity. He flees. Speak the Word that applies to your situation. Let redemption become a reality for you by declaring you are redeemed by the blood of Jesus. When trouble strikes, trouble it by using the following tools to be victorious in adversity:

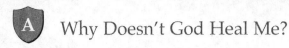
Why Doesn't God Heal Me?

Tools for defeating adversity
1. Sing
2. Dance
3. Shout
4. Listen to praise and worship music
5. Praise and thank God
6. Scripture (read aloud and speak out the Word.)
7. Prayer partners
8. Support of the church congregation
9. The Holy Spirit
10. Wisdom
11. Declaration of redemption in Jesus' blood (because our Father loves us)
12. Laughter

Communion, meaning and practice of

Guidelines for Communion

The Holy Spirit has revealed that there is more to communion than what is explained in Matthew 26 and I Corinthians 11. (These verses are good guides for your personal communion.)

If you have activated your gift of tongues, pray in the spirit briefly before beginning. Then, ask God to bless the unleavened bread and wine to be (in a very real spiritual sense) the body and blood of Jesus. (Bread and wine of themselves have no power).

Ask that God bless the bread and wine to be the body and blood of Jesus. Partaking of the body of Jesus has many meanings which may be incorporated into your communion prayer. The bread (body) binds us to Jesus, to our Brothers throughout all time, into the Father's love, commits us to follow Jesus, allows the Holy Spirit access to our soul and our mind to accept eternity, gives us access to Jesus' nature and helps it grow in us. It shows we belong and that we accept our destiny with God, our change and growth, our freedom in Jesus, our authority in Him, our identity and self-worth in Him and our position as joint-heirs.

It also demonstrates that we discern the body of Christ, that we are betrothed to Him, inseparably joined to God, and that we are blood brothers. We acknowledge, confess and repent of sin, stand fast in Jesus, follow Him, break free of curses, ask to be filled with the Spirit, partake in the bread of life, accept His call to be resurrected into life, have power to move all things in Him, and we show we are Sons who have the ear of our Father.

Almost every communion should include the words, before we break the body, "I reject any curses said against me or by me, in Jesus' name, and I forgive those

Appendix **A**

who have cursed." (I strongly recommend the general or composite curse release prayer in the Appendix, under "Curses.") We can also claim any of the many Bible promises. It is vitally important that we claim the covenant(s) as a basis of claiming the promises of the Word. It is also a good idea to call on the name of God that applies in the promise we are claiming as well as to release angels to perform the covenant by speaking out the Word.

When combining covenants and the names, an example would be a request for provision for a desired purpose. Both the covenant with Abraham and the Old and New Covenants contain the promise of prosperity, and the appropriate name would be *Yehovah Yireh* (or *Jireh*) in Genesis 22. When needing victory over an attack from the enemy, we can call on *Yehovah* or *Yeshua Nissi*, Jesus our Banner or Victory, and dispatch warring angels to fight.

We can even hold the two parts of the bread (body) in our hands, as representing the Alpha and Omega who lives in us. In our right hand we can claim the Alpha promises and in our left hand pledge by God's power to follow Jesus as He leads us in His righteousness through the figure eight of infinity (Jesus walked in that way through the two parts of the sacrifice with Abraham in Genesis 15).

The blood gives a seal of protection from Satan's attacks. The early church took the cup in two sips. We should ask (and this can be done in the first sip) for a shield against backlash from Satan or blacklash (a whip-like, sudden attack on our bodies) and a seal over all that we have claimed in the body since the last communion. (Daily communion is a powerful weapon Satan hates.) The blood breaks curses, blood curses, soul ties and bondings, purifies the heart and body, heals the mind, binds and looses, unifies us with other saints, heals wounds, including emotional hurts between brothers and mates, past scars and sins, heals infirmities (Ps. 118:17), opens gates, revives and opens doors to miracles.

The blood is our declaration activator, the healer, the renewal of body and soul, the thirst-quencher, our joy that makes the heart merry, life to us, our seal of hope and of protection against curses, our calling card for growth in Jesus. The blood is a sign of our acceptance of grace, of Jesus' sacrifice for our sins and salvation, a celebration of our unity with God, of the removal of the veil between us and our Father, of our commission, our authority in Jesus, a celebration in the love of God. It is a call on the Holy Spirit to change us, a washing away of our sins, the seal of our salvation and of brotherhood with Jesus.

I Corinthians 10:16 calls it the "cup of blessing." Here are examples of some blessings we can declare at each drink of the small communion glass: freedom; *shalom*; life – abundant and eternal; the joy of Jesus is our strength; victory over Satan; unity; prosperity; love; "To the Kingdom!"

Important Note:. In communion and/or prayers that involve taking authority over demons or demonic blockages, it is extremely important to state at the beginning of the prayer, "I take my place in the heavenlies with Jesus" (Eph. 2:6).

255

Why Doesn't God Heal Me?

Curses, general, release from

Release from Curses

Curses have been an unknown factor in the church. That's why we emphasize the subject. If you are limited by curses, you can't enjoy the many blessings God explains throughout the Bible (e.g. Deuteronomy 28) and in the prayer of blessing in the Appendix. Understanding curses will open the door for all the covenant blessings of God.

But first we must understand what constitutes a curse. Satan makes people hostile to us and agitated against us until they curse us. They may say such things as these: "You're stupid." "You're a bad Christian." "You're a bad parent." "You're demon-possessed." "God hates you." "May Satan destroy you." They may say a large number of other vulgarities with sexual connotations. The curse word beginning with f, for instance, is a curse of sexual perversion. Any gossip, judgmental statement, put-down, satirical quip or any non-edifying phrase that someone says to us or about us is, in fact, a curse.

We need to seek God to find out why the person issued the curse and what sin we may need to confess. Most curses are issued because of our attitude, manner or demands that we have put upon another. Repenting of the sin, if sin is involved, and asking God for grace to overcome it, is important.

One of Satan's favorite tactics is to get us to curse ourselves. He encourages us to sin so we will issue a curse against ourselves. He tries to make us feel guilty and rejected so we will say negative things over ourselves. That's why being established in our righteousness and speaking it out are so important. When we let words cursing ourselves slip out, we need to say aloud as soon as possible, "I rescind that curse in Jesus' name," and state the truth.

When we reject blood curses and witchcraft curses, we must do communion within 24 hours after rejecting them. In the case of generational and authority figure curses, we should reject and break them off as we take the body of Jesus in communion.

Curse Release Prayer

"Father God, I reject and break off this curse (or these curses) in Jesus' name [name the curses]. I forgive all those who have cursed me and I forgive myself for having accepted these curses. I bind up all the demons and their agents enforcing these curses in chains of confusion. I cut them off from all support. I take the sword of Jesus [lifting your right hand of authority] and I destroy [lowering arm in cutting motion for each item] all their weapons, armaments, and artillery. I burn up their slime and command them to go back to the pit in Jesus' name. Thank You, Father, for the freedom."

Then declare over yourself the positive counterpart to the negative curse. For example, if you were cursed with being crazy, you could make the following decla-

Appendix **A**

rations: "I have the mind of Christ. I have the spirit of power, love and a sound, disciplined mind. I have the spirit of counsel and might and of quick understanding."

Curses from Authoritative Curses

These are curses issued by those in authority over us (parents, husbands, employers, pastors, doctors, etc.) or by two or more people coming into agreement). In Exodus 21:6, a master pierced the ear of a servant, making a blood bond between employer and servant or slave. Due to that precedent and to the fact that authority figure curses are often from blood relatives, it is necessary to break these curses off with the blood of Jesus in communion. The demonic agents of control are always involved, so they must be dealt with as well.

Here is a sample prayer: *"Father, I reject and break off this curse of _____ in Jesus' name. I forgive the person(s) that spoke it over me and pray blessings upon him or her. I ask Your forgiveness, Father, for the sins* [state them if the Holy Spirit reveals them to you] *and/or offenses that caused this person to curse me. I bind up all the demons and their agents enforcing this curse, especially control and his agents of cruelty and shame, in chains of confusion. I cut them off from all support. I take the sword of Jesus and I destroy all their weapons, armaments and artillery, burn up their slime and command them to go back to the pit in Jesus' name.*

"Father, may that which was taken from me by this curse be fully replaced and may Jesus heal me of all effects of this curse and bless me abundantly.

"Thank You, Father. In Jesus' name. Amen."

Actions that Bring Curses from God
- ◆ Misuse of free will
- ◆ Taking of innocent blood
- ◆ Unforgiveness and seeking our vengeance
- ◆ Blasphemy of the Holy Spirit
- ◆ Claiming God spoke when He did not
- ◆ Worshipping an idol in defiance of God
- ◆ Seeking advice from demons
- ◆ Not remembering to keep God's day of rest holy

Curses from Christians, release from
1. Call on Jesus to be the judge in the situation.
2. Ask Jesus to show you if there is any guilt on your part.
3. Confess and repent of any guilt shown.
4. Repent and reject and break off the curse of _____.
5. Forgive the person [name] who cursed you and release them to Jesus so the Father's will may be done in their lives.
6. "I bind up all the demons enforcing these curses, binding them in chains of confusion, cut them off from all demonic support [if physical symptoms

257

Why Doesn't God Heal Me?

involved, add "command them to take all their demonic slime with them"], and send them back to the pit in Jesus' Name."

7. Put the cross between the law of sowing and reaping (the effects of the curses) and yourself, your family and those who cursed you.
8. Pray for blessings, reconciliation and unity in Jesus for all involved in the curse.
9. Thank Jesus for your freedom.
10. If people in authority, blood relatives or witchcraft are involved in the issuing of the curses, take communion to seal it in the blood of Jesus. Be sure in any case to plead the blood of Jesus against any backlash or blacklash (sudden, unexplainable pain) from Satan as a result of the action taken against him.

General Release Prayer from Curses*

The curses from Satanists and witches against Christians have intensified so dramatically in this end-time that Christians would be wise to pray this prayer with daily communion – and at least on a weekly basis. It may be new to you and sound strange, but it works!

"Father God, I reject and break off in Jesus' name all curses spoken against me and my family, including any authoritative curses, witchcraft curses, spells, hexes or incantations, as well as curses from all those who gather with Satanists and witches to curse Christians. [Name the curses. They have volumes of curses, but the principal ones are sickness, death and seduction.] *I forgive all those who have cursed me, releasing them to You for Your blessing and repentance. I forgive myself for having accepted these curses and I ask You to forgive me for any sins or offenses that may have caused people to curse me.*

"I cancel all demonic assignments that have been issued against me. No weapon formed against me shall prosper. I condemn every tongue that rises against me in judgment, curse, criticism, gossip, revenge, vengeance or accusation. This is my inheritance and right as your brother (sister) and servant, Lord Jesus, and my righteousness is from You, my Savior.

"Grant me discernment of curses in the future. I bind up all the demons and their agents [include control with his agents of cruelty and shame if an authoritative curse is involved] *enforcing these curses in chains of confusion. I cut them off from all support. I take the sword of Jesus* [lifting your right hand of authority] *and I destroy* [lowering arm in cutting motion for each item] *all their weapons, armaments, and artillery and destroy their nets. I burn up their slime and command them to go back to the pit in Jesus' name.*

"I claim total restoration and Jesus' healing of all damage done to my soul and body by these curses. I put the cross of Jesus between me, as well as those who have cursed me, and the law of sowing and reaping.

"Thank You, Father, for the freedom. In Jesus' name. Amen."

Appendix **A**

[Then declare over yourself the positive counterpart to the negative curse. For example, if you were cursed with being crazy, you can state that you have the mind of Christ. For Satanist and witch curses, declare the following: "I walk in divine health. I will live and not die. I belong to Jesus."]

* Be on the lookout for signs of curses. For instance, if you are having frequent accidents, someone may be cursing you with the words, "Drop dead," "Break a leg," or even behind your back, "He's an accident waiting to happen."

Generational Curses, release from

God sends generational curses when serious sin is involved, but only for three or four generations. Sin may or may not be the root of generational witchcraft curses. Most often sin is involved. You must repent of the sin that brought on the curse, preferably standing in the gap for those ancestors that sinned and confessing the sin in their stead, asking to be cleansed by Jesus' blood. Remember to say, *"I cease standing in the gap for _____, and I'm back to being myself."*

Ask the Holy Spirit to reveal to you the sin that brought on the curse. If a number of curses are involved, and some time may be required to deal with all of them, you may bind the demons enforcing the curses daily, saying, *"I bind all you demons enforcing these curses. You cannot influence my family or myself in any way, shape or form, in Jesus' name. Amen."* The prayer and procedure for breaking generational curses should be altered according to the instruction for witchcraft curses if they are involved.

After standing in the gap, you should include the following in your prayer to break off these curses. *"Father, I confess that I have activated these generational curses by my words or by accepting words spoken over me. These curses came about because of sin and (in the case of curses from God) You are righteous and just in bringing on these curses so they would bring us into repentance and blessing. I forgive myself for activating these curses by my words and/or others who have spoken words over me to activate these curses and I release them to Your will. I bind up all the demons and their agents enforcing these curses in chains of confusion. I cut them off from all support. I take the sword of Jesus and I destroy all their weapons, armaments and artillery. I burn up their slime and command them to go back to the pit, in Jesus' name. I ask for complete cleansing for my family by the blood of Jesus and His healing of all problems caused to my family and me by these curses. I pray the blessings of* shêlâm *and* shalom *upon my family. Thank You, Father, for the freedom from these curses. In Jesus' name. Amen."*

Signs of Curses from God
- ◆ No healing
- ◆ Blessings and answers to prayer limited
- ◆ No peace of mind
- ◆ Poor sleep

259

Why Doesn't God Heal Me?

- Loss (of finances, health, family, etc.)
- Feeling cut off from God, having to run on carnal strength
- Frustration
- Dragged down by many burdens

Voodoo Curses, release from

The breaking of these curses may seem like mumbo-jumbo to some, yet the following is what the Holy Spirit has revealed. The procedure is the same as for other witchcraft curses, except for the baths that must be taken before communion.

Bathe in plain water first. Then pour some salt into the same bath water and bathe a second time. Then pour a few drops of hyssop oil or tincture (available at some natural food pharmacies and stores) into the same water and bathe a third time.

Jesus broke all curses when, after His death, soldiers thrust a spear into his side. Out flowed blood and salt water from His body to cleanse us from all curses. The reason for the hyssop is expressed in Psalm 51 where David asks to be purged with hyssop so he would be clean.

Witchcraft Curses

Readers in Africa and places like Haiti have greater need of this revelation, but witchcraft is becoming more and more common in our Western world as well. Surprisingly, much illness comes from witches cursing Christians.

- Death – Witches often put these curses on jewelry. And don't think unsuspecting Christians can't die because of death curses! God says, "My people are destroyed for lack of knowledge."
- Coldness – This common curse creates both a physical sense of coldness and a circle of spiritual coldness and rejection, since the demon of coldness is a servant of rejection.
- Neglect – Those you expect to love you will reject you.
- Depression
- Failure – You won't succeed at anything.
- Lack
- Pain on pain
- Abandonment
- "Soulishness" – This is the condition where you refuse to listen to your spirit man or to the Holy Spirit, insisting on doing your will while relying on your soul – your emotions, mind and will.
- Transformation – You will get warts, cancer, etc., or you will be led into role changing or even a sex change. Believe it or not, humans have even been transformed temporarily into hyenas. (This may sound ridiculous to North Americans, but it has happened in Africa. My colleague attended a church

Appendix **A**

where he actually saw a woman beginning to take the form of a hyena. He bound the demons and the process stopped. Demons are usually more subtle in the Western world. We mustn't underestimate their power, nor the much greater power of Jesus' name.)

- Backlash, Blacklash – Backlash can be any attack from demons. Blacklash can be a negative blackness that hits you or a sharp, sudden, unexplainable pain, usually in the back, that feels like a whip lashing at you.
- Deception
- Dumping – This curse causes you to unload your troubles to friends so they will "dump" you.
- Evil eye – This curse is mainly issued to children. It makes their eyes look evil in order to scare others.
- Two-facedness
- Fragmenting – Things in your life become disjointed (families are fragmented).
- Self-pity
- Darkness – This curse steals your joy. You see darkness everywhere, even in the fun times.
- Nonfulfillment

Prayer for Breaking Witchcraft Curses

Because witches use blood sacrifices, communion must accompany this prayer. Take Jesus' body to break the curse and as you take the blood of Jesus, seal all that has been claimed in the blood and put a blood shield against backlash and black-lash from the enemy.

Because the evil blood seal has affected mind, heart and will, have someone anoint you and pray for God's seal to be upon you. The anointing prayer should include a request that you be able to walk with God, your will in line with His will. Note that hexes specifically target the physical condition.

Curses attack your character, emotions and prosperity, but they often affect the body. Incantations attack your heart so that you cave into temptation. They invoke the spirit of seduction. Spells focus on controlling the will of people and governments.

"Father, we (or I) ask You to send the Holy Spirit to shed the light of God upon this situation where the witches have invoked the powers of darkness in our lives. We reject and break off these curses, spells, hexes and/or incantations and we forgive those who have cursed us. We turn the instigators over to You, Father, and to Your authority. We ask you to bless them with full repentance.

"We declare Isaiah 54:17 in our righteousness: No weapon formed against us shall prosper. Every tongue that rises against us in judgment, curse, criticism, gossip, revenge, vengeance, accusation, we do now condemn. This is our inheritance, our right as brothers and sisters and servants of Jesus Christ, and our righteousness is from You, Lord Jesus, our Savior.

Why Doesn't God Heal Me?

*"We ask for discernment to be able in the future to know when we are under a witchcraft curse. (*The second time you pray this prayer, simply give thanks for the discernment.) *We bind up all the demons and their agents enforcing these curses in chains of confusion. We cut them off from all support, burn up their slime and command them to go back to the pit in Jesus' name.*

"We pray for the healing of the damage done to our mind, heart, will, brain and body by these curses. Jesus shed His blood for the breaking of witchcraft curses and for our healing from their effects, and we claim that healing now.

"Thank You, Father, for the release from these curses. In Jesus' name. Amen."

You can use this prayer to break off the effects of witchcraft prayers as well. Simply mention the prayers and omit spells and hexes. Witchcraft or controlling prayers may involves curses and/or incantations, depending on the words used. Witchcraft prayers are surprisingly common. Well-meaning people pray "at" us by praying their will rather than God's will in our lives. Since Christians are involved, add this prayer: "Father, we put the cross of Jesus between the Christians who prayed these prayers and the law of sowing and reaping, in Jesus' name."

Debt, ending
(supernatural debt cancellation)

Ending Debt God's Way

God has a simple formula for debt cancellation. It's written in red – in the blood of Jesus. In the Bible, debt and sin are synonymous. Jesus "canceled out the certificate of debt consisting of decrees against us, which was hostile to us; and He has taken it out of the way, nailing it to the cross" (Col. 2:14). As the righteousness of God, you have a right to claim that powerful verse. Jesus wiped out your debt of sin and your financial debt. Claim it! Claim it in communion, sealing it in Jesus' blood.

To make your request even more emphatic, sow a financial seed offering and make your claim the cancellation of your debt. Whatever you do, don't claim your debt. You've given it to Jesus. He's already paid it in full. Do like Gloria Copeland. As she has shared on television, she told the bill collector at the door, "Jesus paid my debt!" He returned to his office to find the records showing the debt was paid in full!

Debt is sin. But you have been pardoned. Don't let doubt enter. Simply keep thanking and praising Jesus for paying your debt. He can't lie. Trust God to lead you in His time to live in His perfect will for you. It's not His perfect will for you to have any debt – and that includes mortgages. He is capable of erasing it. He is also capable of providing you the money to buy your own home and even your car outright. He meets us where we are.

Appendix

But remember this: the only thing that limits God is our capacity to believe Him and to receive all the blessings He has promised us. The more persistent the bill collectors get, the more frequent should be your declarations of God's Word over the situation. Here are two prayers to help you in speaking God's truth instead of Satan's loud lies about your financial situation.

Prayers for the Release from Debts

"In you, O Jesus, I have taken refuge; let me never be ashamed. In Your righteousness deliver me from the power of sin and from my creditors and accusers. Incline Your ear to me. Rescue me quickly from the clutches of debt and the ways of the world, for You are my Rock and my Fortress. For Your namesake, Jesus, You will lead me and guide me. You will pull me out of the net they have secretly laid for me, for You are my Strength, my Savior, my Deliverer, my Redeemer and my God.

"Into Your hand I commit my spirit, my soul and my body. None can take me from Your hand. You have ransomed me, my Jesus. You are my Provider who shelters me in a safe place.

"I will speak boldly of Your miracles and in Your name. For You, Jesus, have heard my voice, forgiven my sins, set me free from debts and stopped the mouth of my accusers. Let the love of the saints pour forth in song and dance, for You have preserved the faithful, made strong the weak, given strength to the faint – and joy to all who love You.

"Thank You, Jesus, for the freedom from debts."

(Based on Psalm 43, combined with other Psalms)

"Vindicate me, O my God. Plead my case against ungodly creditors. Deliver me from the deceitful and unjust men, for I have forgiven the debts of those who owe me. Why should I go in mourning because of the oppression of the creditors? Has not Jesus already paid my debts? Am I not the righteousness of my God? Is Jesus not my Savior? Is His arm cut short? I know that I am redeemed by the blood of Jesus and that I am righteous. Therefore I am already saved from the hands of the creditor and my debt is paid.

"Therefore, I will rejoice and call for Your light and Your truth to lead me to Your holy hill, to Your dwelling place. And there I will go to the altar of my God with exceeding joy and I will praise You. For You, Jesus, are my Strength, my Joy, my Purpose and my Destiny. In You, Jesus, I have freedom from all debt, all torment, all imprisonment.

"Thank You, Father, for all that I have in Jesus. Amen and Amen."

Why Doesn't God Heal Me?

Daily Declarations

Daily declarations first thing in the morning are extremely important. We need to renew our minds every day to choose anew the godly way to which we have committed ourselves at conversion. Here is a sample to help you.

1. I choose life and blessings today – not death and curses.
2. I choose to be renewed in my mind.
3. I choose to walk in the Spirit – not in the flesh.
4. Change my heart to be more like You – in everything I think, say and do.
5. I give myself and every part of my body to You today – as a living sacrifice.
6. I want, allow, ask You, Jesus, to live Your life in me today.
7. I choose to rejoice in You and in Your way today.
8. I choose to seek Your face today.
9. I bind myself to Your will and Your way today.
10. Add your own personal declarations, guided by the Holy Spirit.

Daily Declarations of "My Identity in Christ"

The following is a sampling of declarations we should make daily. This is not to say we will necessarily make all of them every day. They are guidelines to use to speak over ourselves and to meditate upon.

1. I am free! Free from sin's slavery. Free from condemnation, guilt, shame. Free from people-pleasing and flesh-pleasing – Rom. 8:1-2; 6:7, 18; Gal. 1:10.
2. I am dead to sin, crucified with Christ – the old me is dead! He died __ years ago. The resurrected Jesus lives in me now – I am alive in Him! Gal. 2:20; Rom. 6:2, 8, 11; Eph. 2:5.
3. I am "the righteousness of God." I stand before God as if I had never sinned. It is Jesus' righteousness in me – not my own – II Cor. 5:21; Phil. 1:11.
4. I am unique and extra-special to God. No one has ever looked exactly like me and had my personality and gifts. I am "the apple of His eye" (Zech. 2:8; Ps. 17:8), His special treasure or treasured possession (Deut. 7:6; Mal. 3:17). He sings and dances over me with shouts of joy (Zeph. 3:17). God called me to a unique ministry at a special time in my life, and my growth is following a unique course designed by God just for me.
5. I am God's Child – His very Son (Daughter) – John 1:12; I John 3:1-3. I have been born into the Kingdom or Family of God, a younger Brother (Sister) of Jesus Christ – John 3:5; Rom. 8:29. I am far above the angel kind, for I am of the God kind, in the God realm or class – on the God plane! Heb. 1 and 2; John 10:34-35; Ps. 82:6; Rev. 3:9; John 20:23. Thanks to Jesus, I am now fully "in His image and likeness," the "spitting image" of my Father. Although not yet glorified, I am growing up to be just like my Daddy in character, power, glory and plane or quality of existence.

Appendix **A**

My birthright is to share God's glory.

6. I am forgiven of all my sins, justified, made right with God – Col. 2:13-14; Rom. 5:1. Since God forgives me, I forgive myself.

7. I am an enemy of the Devil and a demon-defeater – Satan's worst nightmare. I use my authority in Jesus to bind and cast out demons. No weapon formed against me will prosper – Mark 16:17; John 14:12; James 4:7; Isa. 54:17.

8. I ask for and receive angelic protection daily – Ps. 91:7, 11-12.

9. I walk in the supernatural because of Jesus in me. I can do miracles, heal the sick, raise the dead, rebuke the wind and storms, move mountains, walk on water, translate myself by God's power from place to place when necessary (Satanists do it. Why can't I?) – Mark. 16:15; John 14:12.

10. I am strong in Jesus, bold as a lion, blessed with power, love and a sound, disciplined mind, of quick understanding. I can do all things through Jesus who strengthens me – II Tim. 1:6-7; Phil. 4:13; Prov. 28:1; Isa. 11:2. I walk in the awesome anointing of Jesus Christ! – Isa. 61:1-3.

11. I am confident all things in my life – "the good, the bad and the ugly" – are working out for good according to God's plans – plans to give me a future and a hope – Rom. 8:28; Jer. 29:11.

12. I'm a winner! A victor! More than a conqueror! An overcomer! I'm a "never-give-upper." I'm a survivor of trials that refine me as gold tried in the fire – Rev. 12:11; Rom. 8:37; I Pet.1:7.

13. I am rich – in every way! I am prosperous and able to be a giver like my generous Father. I walk in divine health and prosperity – III John 2; Ex. 15:26; II Cor. 9:8-13; Ps. 112:3.

14. I am a joint-heir with my elder Brother Jesus to inherit all He has inherited – glory, honor, and the grace to be highly exalted as a co-heir with Him to rule over the earth during the coming Millenium of peace – Rom. 8:17, 29; John 17:22; Rev. 3:9; 5:10; Heb. 1 and 2.

15. I am graced with God's love – able to love even my enemies. I am able to overlook the past and present, and see people for who they will be in Christ – John 13:35; Phil. 4:8.

16. I am God's temple – His property. My body is used only for His glory – I Cor. 6:19-20. I have found where I belong. I belong to God.

17. I am God's workmanship – and He isn't finished with me yet! – Eph. 2:10; Phil. 1:6; I John 3:2.

18. I am a servant – to God first, to my siblings in Christ, especially widows and orphans, and to all. No task is too menial for Jesus in me – John 13:5-17; Gal. 6:10; Mat. 25:35-45; James 1:27.

19. I am an ambassador of God's Kingdom, a spreader of the gospel – II Cor. 5:20; Mat. 28:19.

20. I am a saint – a "holy one," pure and blameless in God's sight, washed in Jesus' blood. I am not a sinner! I'm a saint who occasionally sins – but I

Why Doesn't God Heal Me?

am sinning less and less and enjoying life more and more – Eph. 1:1, 4; II Cor. 3:18.

21. I am the salt of the earth (preserving and flavoring it) and the light of the world – Mat. 5:13-14.

22. I am sitting in heavenly places with Jesus – above sinful earthly pursuits – Eph. 2:6.

23. I am the Bride of Christ – Eph. 5:23-32. He gave His life for me, His Beloved, and would have done so had I been the only person on the earth. I am in love with Him – deeply passionate, more intimate than husband and wife – Ps. 42 and 63; Song of Solomon.

24. I am one with the Eternal – so I am eternal (I Cor. 6:17; I John 5:11-13). He chose me before time began – Eph. 1:4. I have no past! (If you bring it up, that's your problem.) – Phil. 3:13-14; Rom. 6:4; Gal. 2:20. I am new every day – II Cor. 4:16; Mat. 6:34; Gal. 6:14-15; Eph. 4:22-24.

25. I am Jesus' witness or representative on earth (and He mine in heaven!) – Acts 1:8; I Tim. 2:5

26. I am a king and a priest – I Pet. 2:9; Rev. 1:6.

27. I am a minister of reconciliation – a peacemaker – II Cor. 5:17-20; Mat. 5:9.

28. I am a Christian soldier – a spiritual warrior against unseen forces of evil – Eph. 6:10-18.

29. I am God's friend – John 15:15. We share everything – Deut. 29:29; Amos 3:7; Ps. 62:8; I Pet. 5:7.

30. I am the recipient of God's boundless, unconditional love. There is nothing I can do to make Him love me more – or less. Absolutely nothing can separate me from His mercy, comfort, encouragement – His amazing love – Rom. 8:38-39; John 3:16; I John 3:1-3; II Cor. 1:3-4.

In short, I am accepted, secure and special – a precious Child of the Eternal God. I choose today to walk in the awesome anointing of the Anointed One in me. I put on the armor of God (refer to Ephesians 6). I choose today to give a tithe of my time to my God and to walk in my special and unique anointing. I yield today to God so that He, by His empowering grace, may fulfill His plans and purposes in my life as I minister to others in my daily walk. Good morning, Father. Good morning, Jesus. Good morning, Holy Spirit. Please fill me. Jesus, shine through me today, as my youth and vigor are renewed like the eagle (Ps. 103:5; Isa. 40:28-31).

Faith, levels of

Common faith – Rom. 12:3 – "… according as God hath dealt to every man the measure of faith" (KJV). It takes faith to take an elevator, fly on a plane, even walk out of our house in the morning. And atheists have no excuse, even though they will not be condemned eternally for their professed unbelief. God would not call them fools if they didn't have an innate faith in the unseen Creator God.

Weak faith – Rom. 4:19 – "Without becoming weak in faith, he [Abraham] contemplated his own body, now as good as dead since he was about a hundred years old. ..." Weak faith implies being untrained in the Word.

Little faith – Mat. 6:30 – "...will He not much more clothe you? You of little faith!" Implies they are in the beginning stages of learning to walk in the Word.

Temporary faith – Lk. 8:13 – "... [those on rocky soil] believe for a while, and in time of temptation fall away."

Mental faith – James 2:14-26 – The Word has entered the brain, but not the heart. They accept the facts of the Bible, but are not able to move on with the Word as a driving force in their lives. (95% of Christians are presently in this category!)

Active faith – James 2:14-26 – Able to start moving with the Word in their heart and mouth, producing works of faith (e.g. pray for sick, personal evangelism).

Strong faith – Rom. 4:20 – "yet, with respect to the promise of God, he did not waver in unbelief but grew strong in faith, giving glory to God." Trusts, refuses defeat, persists in speaking God's Word.

Great faith – Mat. 8:10 – Speaking of the centurion who knew His words would be carried out, Jesus said, "... I have not found such faith with anyone in Israel." Simply speaking the Word and awaiting the sure results. Moving in Jesus' authority, expecting results.

Unfeigned faith – II Tim. 1:5 – "When I call to remembrance the unfeigned faith that is in thee ..." (KJV). A faith based in the mind, will and heart. Sincere faith, at peace with God. Total reliance on God, turning everything over to Him.

Divine or perfect faith – Gal. 2:20 – "I have been put to death on the cross with Christ; still I am living; no longer I, but Christ is living in me; and that life which I now am living in the flesh I am living by faith, the faith of the Son of God ..." (*The New Testament in Basic English*). God's faith within you. Christ's faith inside of you. Jesus lives actively in you. Powerful miracles, martyrdom, etc. No wavering in following God's will.

Fear, general

Fear is a major hindrance to healing. And since September 11, 2001, fear has become a plague in our western world – even among Christians. Satan has 288 agents of fear. Fear is the unconditional acceptance of what Satan says about us. Fear demoralizes and causes us to crave sin and addictions. Fear inhibits our walk in faith and righteousness. The Holy Spirit has given the following revelation to help us be free from this sin.

A Why Doesn't God Heal Me?

Why Do We Hold onto and Cherish Fear?
1. It creates a slave mentality.
2. It's easier to trust in the power of evil than the power of God.
3. People want to suffer as penance for their sins.
4. It's an escape mechanism.
5. We fear when we have no identity in Christ.
6. We fear when we have no understanding of righteousness and are afflicted with a sin consciousness.
7. We fear because of rebellion against the Word of God.
8. We fear because of worshipping the wrong god.
9. We fear because of a defiant spirit that picks and chooses what we believe.
10. We fear because of practicing sin willfully and claiming grace to continue in it.

How Does Fear Enter?
Following are 20 of 100 possible entry points:
1. TV and movies – Shows designed to scare us or cause adrenaline rushes are big sellers and can hypnotize.
2. Horror books
3. Bad reports from doctors or medical documentaries, speaking futility at fighting killer diseases
4. News reports about terrorists, catastrophes, economic collapses
5. Words we speak over ourselves (e.g. "I'm afraid God won't answer my prayers." "That scares me." Words of fear amount to curses that give demons of fear legal grounds in our life.)
6. Words we hear others say. The warning "Be careful" from a concerned mother conditions a child to accept fear. "Make sure you look both ways before crossing the street" is a wiser way to say it. Mothers who go out screaming at a boy climbing a tree scares the boy and enforces fear. It's better to pray over a child and say, "I'm releasing angels to protect you today."
7. Traumas with which Satan conditions us
8. Looking at the waves Satan makes to scare us. Peter walked on water until he began to look at the waves.
9. Sin makes us cowardly and causes us to speak out words of fear.
10. Sin steals our confidence, trust and faith.
11. Fear makes it impossible for us to rest.
12. Lost hopes
13. Broken promises
14. Lack, loss or poverty
15. Acting the part of a fearful character in a play
16. When we see a catastrophe come upon a family member or friend, we tend to speak fear over ourselves and others.
17. Relying on drugs (legal or illegal)

Appendix **A**

18. Loneliness. No Christian should be lonely. Jesus promised to never leave us.
19. Seeking to get – not give
20. Trying to eat at God's table and Satan's at the same time

Sources of Fear

Of the total of 150 sources of fear, change is the most common root. Even the fear of death is based on this fear of change. Here is a sampling of the sources of fear:

♦ **Exposure** (of sin, our past, both of which have been washed away by Jesus' blood, shortcomings, body shape, failures, loss, emptiness, loneliness)

♦ **Entrapment** (e.g. mortgage, credit card debt, partnering in business with an unbeliever, caught in a no-love marriage, poisoning, bankruptcy, jail and inescapable, certain death)

♦ **Falling** – We fear falling down so we can't complete what we started. We fear falling out of grace with those in positions of authority, and those in authority often fear falling from their positions. Pastors in churches under the spirit of betrayal revel in pastor worship and are fearful of members taking their place. They fear anyone who is walking with God, and they use the spirit of undermining and limitations to keep members from walking in their anointing. We fear falling from a position or being fired from our job. This fear causes us to do things that will get us fired. We fear falling into debt.

♦ **Entombment** – This can also be a curse. We feel boxed in and unable to move, as if buried alive. Some examples are phobias about being locked in a small room, cornered by enemies, all escape routes blocked, as in a mine shaft, and being caught in past mistakes.

♦ **Death** – Christians should never fear death, yet that's how all are trained from childhood. We have the promise of long life and no weapon formed against us can prosper if we believe and declare it. Following are examples of "deaths" and fears of death: death of a child (the hardest to take), of a mate, of a friend, of a pet, when a job comes to an end, death of a way of life, death of self.

♦ **Change** – This is the greatest fear. People fear to change their habits because that involves effort. Change is unsettling.

♦ **Travel**

♦ **Being left behind**

♦ **Technology** – There have been times when I have had to repent of this fear. The old computer on which I began to write this book gave me many stressful problems and caused many delays. One virus only came out by prayer. I have even wondered at times if I should change the title of this book to "Why Doesn't God Heal My Computer?"

♦ **Cancer** – As Job said, what we fear comes upon us. Fearing cancer can cause it.

♦ **A controlling spirit** – When we walk under a spirit of control, we surrender our rights and our blessings. We speak fearful words like "I'm anxious." "I'm terrified." "That's a fearful thing. It paralyzes me with fear." "What would

269

Why Doesn't God Heal Me?

happen if ...?" "What would people say if ...?"

- ◆ **Traumas** establish roots of fear.
- ◆ Often we won't ask God for help, because "**what if** it doesn't work"? "What if God doesn't come through?" With such questions, we deny the power of Jesus' blood and the righteousness He gave us. If we do ask God, we often set time limits on Him. Fear replaces faith.
- ◆ Much fear is rooted in **words of fear**. "That scares me silly." "The Book of Revelation is scary." Words of fear invite doubt. When we express fear, we doubt God and His promises. We're saying that Satan is more powerful than God! All words of fear are sin and encourage attack from demons. Fear is a powerful root of sickness. When we fear, we shut down our immune system. Over and over again God's Word says "Do not fear." Fear can lead us into the full gamut of sins faster than any source. Fear that encourages other sins leads to all forms of sickness and disease. And the more sickness we have, the more we fear. It's a vicious circle.

Fear spoken over an unborn child can cause many sicknesses in the child. "I'm afraid he'll have Down's syndrome." Satan has permission to enforce a condition when we speak it. Words of fear about possible unfaithfulness to a mate can push a mate who has never been unfaithful to commit adultery. A parent who speaks out fear to a child about premarital sex, drugs, etc. can actually drive them to follow such a course. Let's speak love and righteousness – not fear! Speaking out blessing and righteousness can conquer sin and sickness. Knowing what not to do is never enough to stop fear and sin. Knowing what to say and do changes everything.

Prayer for Release from Fear

"Father, I turn all my fears over to Jesus. Help me recognize when I am speaking fear or acting in fear, that I may stand against it and be of the mindset that I am clean by the blood of Jesus. I know all of Your Word is righteousness and right for my life and that I have no right to fear.

"I trust You, Father, to meet all my needs, to bring peace to my soul by Your lovingkindness and the words You have given me to say. As Your Child, Father, I reject all fears and cowardly approaches that it encourages. I have all confidence in You that I am more than a conqueror. I am a complete victor over all things in Jesus.

"Thank You for Your anointing in overcoming all fears. In Jesus' name. Amen."

Finances

Seven Keys to Financial Prosperity

1. Stand in the Word (do not let Satan sway you to speak concerning what you lack, because doing so invites the spirit of lack).
2. Pray in confidence (expect answers).
3. Be transfigured into the image of Jesus (accept your identity and learn

Appendix **A**

to walk in it).

4. See yourself as free from financial distress and free to walk in financial freedom, speaking out words of renewal.
5. Willingly come into the fullness of where Jesus wants you.
6. Seek God first in everything so "all these things" can be added to you.
7. Do not be satisfied with the minimum when God wants to give you His maximum.

Seven Steps to Financial Success

1. Go with Jesus. See Him as Provider. Hold Him to His promise.
2. Trust in Jesus, not money, to be your Savior, no matter how much or little you have now.
3. Do not think or act like a beggar.
4. Receive your wealth and blessing. Declare you receive it now.
5. Become a partner to sow financial seed where you are fed.
6. Speak out the Word. Nothing can happen unless you speak it out.
7. Seek out the supernatural – God's purpose in your life. You must know that divine design if you are to walk in it.

Activators: Remember that although the bulk of world wealth is presently in the hands of the wicked, it is our destiny as the righteous to receive it (Prov. 13:22; Isa. 45:1-4 and 60:1-7). Thank Jesus for the wealth and keep giving Him thanks. The more we thank Him, the faster will be the manifestation of the promise. All wealth belongs to God. And since we belong to Him, that wealth is ours too.

Key Declaration: I am alive in Jesus.
I have it (wealth) now because I have Jesus!

Hindrances to Receiving Hidden Treasures

God promises to release the wealth of the wicked to His chosen, righteous ones (Prov. 13:22; Isa. 45:3). Following are 21 hindrances to receiving that wealth. Confession of and repentance for these hindrances are essential.

1. Not knowing or thirsting after Jesus
2. Not accepting Jesus' definition of right and wrong (eating from tree of knowledge of good and evil)
3. Not seeking righteousness with a true heart
4. Not letting salvation bear fruit in us
5. Quarrelling with God and how He does things
6. Not asking God what to do
7. Not submitting to the correction of God's Word
8. Not letting Jesus make our way smooth
9. Not leaving vengeance to God
10. Not allowing Jesus to be God in our life

Why Doesn't God Heal Me?

11. Letting our hearts be lifted up in pride and arrogance
12. Not acknowledging God in all provision and blessing
13. Planning and doing things in our own strength
14. Not showing ourselves trustworthy in all things
15. Gathering treasure for ourselves without God's okay
16. Not planting and watering and expecting to receive a harvest
17. Not honoring a pledge or keeping a vow
18. Not stimulating our minds and hearts by the words of God and faith
19. Running to Satan for money
20. Not seeking first the Kingdom of God
21. Not rejecting money that God did not give us as a blessing

God, harmony or unity with

What Brings You into Harmony with God?

In Matthew 25:10, Jesus shut the door to the wedding feast for some. What opens the door?

1. Giving for the joy of giving
2. Taking communion and binding ourselves to Jesus by the blood
3. Accepting Jesus as Divine Master in our life
4. Accepting in our heart our identity as Children of God
5. Fasting to set people free
6. Obeying God's voice (written or spoken word)
7. Praying in the Spirit (in tongues); shows we want our spirit man to rule over the flesh
8. Using the name of Jesus
9. Being a witness of the gospel, people seeing Jesus in us
10. Declaring God's Word over our life
11. Resisting Satan (e.g. quoting the Word correctly to him)
12. Walking in integrity
13. Having a serving heart
14. Willingness to stand in the gap for someone else
15. Issuing blessings over people
16. Walking in righteousness and love
17. Praising Jesus
18. Worshipping Jesus
19. Accepting God's leadership in our life
20. Walking by faith
21. Waiting on God
22. Praying together in one accord
23. Asking God for direction and waiting for His answer before we act

Appendix **A**

24. Not accepting a gift from Satan (physical symptom or temptation to satisfy the flesh)
25. Yielding our will to God

> These actions cause our Father to exclaim with pride,
> "That's My Son!" – "That's My Daughter!"

Things That Please God
- Setting priorities
- Spending time in prayer praising Him
- Sounds of joy
- Songs of joy
- Bringing sinners to Jesus
- Hearing us speak His words back to Him
- Hearing us speak His words over others
- Binding Satan (and his demons) and casting him out
- Seeing His Children walk in His will
- Joining together to take back dominion from Satan
- Standing fast against Satan, the flesh and the world
- Giving cheerfully
- Relying on Him for our daily needs
- Seeking God's face – not only His hand (i.e. His blessings)
- Speaking blessings over others
- Receiving His blessings with thankfulness
- Walking in humility, love and righteousness
- Showing love to Him and His Children
- Putting faith and hope into action
- Showing patience in waiting on God
- Listening to His voice
- Listening for His voice
- Seeking intimacy and quiet time with Him
- Studying His Word
- Asking the Holy Spirit to guide us
- Gathering together in His name

Grace, the manifold grace of God, 25 divine graces

1. **God's glory**
2. **God's power in us**
3. Supplication
4. Fearing God
5. Saving grace

Why Doesn't God Heal Me?

6. **Serving grace**
7. Standing grace (standing firm, even in trials)
8. **Speaking grace**
9. Giving grace
10. Pruning grace
11. Grace of identity – knowing who we are in Christ
12. Grace for relationships
13. Grace of inheritance
14. Grace of empowering ("Go ye into all the world" – empowerment to know the truth)
15. Ministering grace
16. Strengthening grace
17. Grace of forgiveness
18. Intercession, caring, watching out for others
19. Grace to walk in faith, trusting, relying on God, coming into harmony with Him
20. Favor with God
21. Grace to be able to walk in our anointing or calling
22. **Grace to praise and worship God**
23. Grace to have hope (and be consoled and encouraged)
24. Overcoming grace, deliverance from sin
25. Grace to walk in miracle-working power

N.B. The number 5 is the Biblical number of grace. The 25 graces represent 5 x 5 or perfect grace. All 25 graces combine to grant us the grace to walk toward perfection. I Peter 4:10-11 shows that there are five principal aspects (in **bold type** above) to the multi-faceted grace of God: speaking, serving, praise (NIV), power ("strength" and "dominion" [NASB]) and glory. These five major graces, which are among the 25 listed above, can be broken down into subdivisions from this same list, each major grace having three to seven accompanying graces. Faith and grace work together to enable us to walk in our identity in Christ. God grants us the faith to believe He will empower us with these graces, which allow us to live up to who we are in Christ.

Identity in Christ

Resumé of Our Identity in Christ
What follows is an alphabetical summary of our identity – encouraging material for meditation.

I am … (or: I am a / an / the …)

Accepted, adopted, appointed, anointed, apple of God's eye, alive in Jesus – eternally, alien or stranger in this world, ambassador of God's Kingdom, author-

Appendix **A**

ized by Jesus to forgive sin, bind and cast out demons, perform miracles;

Blood-bought, beloved, blameless, bold, Bride of Jesus, bringer of salvation, blessed and a blesser, breaker of yokes, born of God, brother of Jesus Christ;

Child of God with all the rights, privileges, power, authority, nature and level of existence of the God Family, called, chosen by God before the foundation of the world, citizen of heaven, confident of who I am, confident that all things work for my good, confident I can do all things through Christ, clean in God's sight, crucified with Christ to my old nature, cherished one, clay in the Potter's hands shaping me into an exquisite vessel, conqueror and more, complete, conformed to His image;

Delivered, deliverer, defender, determined, dedicated, dead to sin and my old self, Daughter of God, demon-defeater, disciplined, dependent upon God to meet all my needs – physical, financial, emotional and spiritual;

Elect of God, encouraged and an encourager, enemy of Satan and the demons, example, epistle for all to read, evangelist of the good news, eternal due to the Eternal dwelling in me;

Free from sin and condemnation, freedom fighter, forgiven, forgiver, faithful, fearless, friend of God, friend of sinners;

Gate-opener, godly, giver;

Heir of God, holy, helper of widows, orphans and the helpless, "the least of these my brethren," healer (by God's power) of the sick and brokenhearted, humble heart of a child;

Intercessor, image and glory of God, inseparable from God's love, imbued with God's power;

Jewel, justified, judge, joint-heir with Jesus;

King, kindhearted, kin of the Eternal God;

Laborer, loved unconditionally by God, light of the world;

Minister of reconciliation, messenger, member of Christ's body, mover of mountains (strongholds, governments, obstacles and literal mountains), made in God's image and likeness, married to Jesus;

New creation, never forsaken by God, "name and a praise among all peoples of the earth";

One with the Eternal God, thus having no past, overcomer, obedient;

Pure, peacemaker, pillar in God's house, possessor of all God has promised me, partaker of the heavenly calling and of the divine nature, prosperous, protected,

Why Doesn't God Heal Me?

provided for, perfect in my spirit, preserver, pilgrim here below, partaker of divine graces, including the grace of God's forgiveness, grace to forgive, to obey God's laws, to share eternity with God on the God plane in His own Family;

Queen, quick understanding, quiet and peaceable;

Redeemed, ransomed, renewed, rescuer, righteousness of Jesus, repairer of the breach, restorer of paths to dwell in, reborn, recipient of all of God's promises, refined (not destroyed) by trials, rejoicing always, resting in God's grace, rich in every way;

Salt of the earth, sheep of His pasture, Son of God, sanctified, seated in heavenly places with Jesus, soldier in God's army wearing spiritual armor engaging in spiritual warfare, Satan's worst nightmare, secure, significant, satisfied in all circumstances, saved by grace, strong, slave of righteousness, speaker of God's Word over myself and others, spokesperson for the Kingdom, servant, sound-minded, sweet fragrance of God to others;

Temple of God, treasure (special, of God), tender-hearted, tither and generous offerer of my money and time to God (the other nine tenths going farther than ever before), thankful in everything, transformed by the renewing of my mind, from glory to glory;

Under the blood of Jesus, unfazed by criticism, unafraid, understanding and wise, useful to the Master;

Victor, valued and valuable; valorous, vessel of honor to serve God;

Watchman, winner, witness of Jesus, workmanship of God, worshipper, wise;

X-tra special;

Young, my youth being renewed like the eagle, yielded to God, yoke-fellow;

Zealous for God, *zoe* life of God the Father. I am one with the Alpha and Omega, the beginning and the end, and from A to Z, I am one with Him. From A to Z, I know who I am in Jesus.

The next page has a poem to help us remember who we are in Jesus.

Appendix **A**

I AM

I am one with the Alpha and Omega
Forgiven. Without past.
I am one with my Savior
One way, one mould, one cast.

The old me is dead to sin
The new man is risen
I am now alive in Him
I live for all I'm given.

I have all power
In Jesus' name
We raise the dead
We heal the lame.

I am accepted in the Beloved
Comfortable and secure
The precious object of His love
Comforted and reassured.

I am the righteousness of God
A captive set completely free
Brother to Him who walked this earth
Who died, arose and lives in me.

I am one with Yahweh
I am His very Son
I am in His Family
Nurtured by His Love.

When all is said and all is done
I know my God-identity
I am my reborn Father's Son
And share with Him eternity.

– Robert Scott

Why Doesn't God Heal Me?

Jesus

Jesus – God of the "Old" Testament

Yahweh or *Yehovah* (the Eternal) refers to every member of the Godhead. This Hebrew YHVH, however, is used almost exclusively in the Hebrew Scriptures to mean the One who became Jesus. Compare the following pairs of verses with each other (Isa. 8:13 and I Pet. 2:7; Isa. 48:12 and Rev. 22:13; Ps. 23:1 and John 10:11; Isa. 43:1 and Mat. 1:21; Isa. 40:3 and Mat. 3:3.)

Jesus was the spiritual Rock who was Israel's Rearguard (I Cor. 10:4; Deut. 32:4). The clincher is John 1:1-18. Jesus was the Word who created all things by His spoken words (Gen. 1:3, 26; Heb. 1:2; Col. 1:16) and who spoke to men in the period from Adam to the birth of Jesus as a human. He later became flesh. He declared that no one had ever seen or heard the Father, whom He came to reveal (John 1:18; 5:37; 6:46; 14:7; 17:25-26), and yet men did see and hear *Yahweh* as a human (Gen. 3:8-9; 18:1-3; Gen. 32:24-28; Josh. 5:13-14; Judges 2:1-5; 6:11-24; 13:3, 21-22) and in glorified form from the back (Ex. 3:1-6; 33:18-23). The Father will only come down to live on the earth when it has been purified from all sin (Rev. 21:4; I Cor. 15:24).

God's intimate ones in the period recorded by the Hebrew Scriptures knew of the Father (Dan. 7:13; Ps. 2; Prov. 30:4). David refers to the Father ("the Eternal") who tells David's *Adonai* or Divine Master to sit at His right hand (Ps. 110:1; Mat. 22:44). The Eternal who was on the earth at that moment (Jesus) and the Eternal in heaven (the Father) are even contrasted in Gen. 19:24. And the Trinity is revealed in the Hebrew section of God's Instruction Book (Gen. 1:26; Isa. 48:16). In John 8:52-59, Jesus tells His critics they did not know the Father, and they picked up stones to kill Him when He said, "… before Abraham was born, I am."

Jesus – Who He is and What He Expects from Us

Jesus is our … God, High Tower, Support, Rock of defense and stability, Light, Path, Bridegroom, Burden-bearer, Hope, Eternal Life, Substitute, Fullness, Delight, Anointing, Sustainer, Partner, Friend, Power, Sabbath, Vindication, Helper, Claim (like a claim check or title deed to the promises), Blessing, Promise, Teacher of skills, Jealousy (as a father for his child), Contender, Jerusalem (King of peace for all our affairs), High Priest forever and Priestly King worthy of worship, the living Word of God, Creator, Redeemer-Avenger who moves in like a whirlwind to protect His own, destroying the enemy, paying the price to buy us back and all stolen from us – and also Master who wants total surrender of all sins, burdens, bad habits and addictions so He can give us total favor. The following prayerful declarations, if said sincerely and followed, can open the door to freedom and a full life dedicated and submitted to Jesus:

"Without Jesus I can do nothing. My Father loves me and wants me free. I confess my specific sins, bad habits and addictions. I declare my willingness to change and be led by the Holy Spirit. God made me a commander under Jesus – not a vic-

Appendix **A**

tim. I have a rod of authority (my mouth) over every demon, sin and addiction. I make my will and heart speak the truth of God's Word. My enemy will not triumph over me ... I will overcome because I have Jesus in and with me. Father, I choose to be someone you can trust, choosing to obey and walk in integrity. I will set boundaries and keep them. I am expecting strength, power and enlightenment, not looking to my own strength. I'm expecting back all that Satan stole from me. My days of defeat, frustration and failure are over forever. I have Jesus; therefore I have His joy and strength. I choose to grow in the divine way. I will allow and call on Jesus to shut the doors to all wrong addictions. Today starts the time of favor for me and my family. All fears, pain, lies and wrong circumstances have to bow to my Father's will for my life. I own my choices and will not be a victim of circumstances, chance or fears, having made my choice to stay with Jesus. I choose to learn love and its ways, for love conquers all."

Jesus' Name, meanings of

Ability to praise God
Ability to prophesy and understand prophecy
Access
Anointing
Authority
Belief in the virgin birth
Believing
Belonging
Deliverer
Devotion
Direction
Grace
Jesus came only from God
Kingdom of God
Light of Jesus
Love
Obeying power
Opportunity
Our identity
Power to change yourself, others and the world
Protection from injury, disease and illness
Receiving

Reconciliation of a family
Redeemer
Release of all glory
Release of all the power of heaven
Rewards
Right to be a follower of Jesus
Right to be acknowledged as a Son of God
Right to be an overcomer
Right to be employable by God
Right to cast out demons
Right to claim a giving heart
Right to claim eternal life
Right to claim Jesus' sacrifice
Right to claim the power of His blood
Right to come before God's throne and to speak from a heavenly position

Right to forgiveness of sins
Right to get answers to prayer
Right to have the Holy Spirit be with you
Right to speak in tongues (heavenly and earthly).
Right to the benefits of baptism
Right to walk with compassion
Righteousness
Savior
Sonship
Submission
Teachability
Thankfulness
Trust
Understanding
Unity in Jesus and the Trinity
Victory
Yoke-destroyer

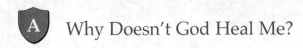

Why Doesn't God Heal Me?

Jesus' Substitutionary Sacrifice (What He went through to set us free)

Since this book is about healing and healing begins in the soul, it is important that we understand what Jesus did for us. The Holy Spirit has revealed 80 experiences Jesus went through in His lifetime as a substitution for us. He went through all these pains so we would be spared from them. Below are listed 31 of those experiences, followed by what He intended us to experience because of His sacrifice.

Jesus took or endured ...... so we could have ......

1. Temptation .... Victory
2. Accusation .... Purpose in our lives
3. Criticism .... Identity
4. Mocking .... Confidence
5. Dread (foreknowing suffering ... Became our High Tower of Strength
6. Fear .... Peace
7. Infirmity (beatings) .... Healing
8. Guilt .... Innocence
9. Sin's curse .... His righteousness
10. Sickness .... Wellness
11. Curse of the law .... Blessing and freedom
12. Poverty (only on His last day) ... Wealth
13. Death .... Eternal life
14. Captivity .... Release
15. Wrath of God .... Forgiveness
16. Rejection .... Acceptance as a Child of God
17. Abandonment .... Belonging (wrapped in God's arms)
18. Martyrdom .... Brotherhood
19. Abuse .... Glorification
20. Humiliation .... Exaltation
21. Tears of pain .... Joy and unity
22. Sweating blood .... Justification
23. Agony .... Joy
24. Corruption of our old nature .... Control and free will
25. Being an outcast .... Adoption
26. Criticism .... Ability to walk in boldness
27. Betrayal .... So He could show Himself loyal to us
28. Loss (those He loved left him) ... Fullness
29. Spat upon .... Gift of prophecy (spit = negative prophecy for Jewish people at the time)
30. Exposure .... Protection
31. Pains of birth .... Brotherhood

Appendix **A**

Life, choosing

Many Christians are not healed and blessed because they do not understand what it means to choose life. God sets life and blessings and death and curses before us and challenges us to choose life. But what does that mean?

Life is Jesus. Choosing Him is choosing life. Choosing to read, study, speak and obey God's Word is choosing life. Choosing to be led by the Holy Spirit is choosing life. Choosing life is seeking Him with all our heart, mind and strength. It is surrendering to God to receive all His blessings. It is choosing to live the abundant life in Jesus.

The Hebrew section of Scripture tells us something important: life is in the blood. That is not merely a physical fact. It is also referring to the precious blood of Jesus. Some Christians find the concept of the blood of Jesus distasteful for reasons I do not fully understand They avoid it. They water down the blood.

In so doing they water down life. Life is in the blood. Eternal life is in the blood of Jesus. It both saves us from death and gives us life. Every time we partake of communion, we have a fresh "transfusion" of the life-giving, life-sustaining blood of Jesus. The blood of Jesus quenches our spiritual thirst and renews us body and soul. If we don't partake of His blood, we have no part with Him. His blood is our life. It is only through His blood that we have continual access to the Father. His blood is our lifeblood.

Choosing life means drinking His blood in communion and eating of Him – the Bread of Life. (Remember, unless the bread and wine actually become in a spiritual sense the body and blood of Jesus, they have no power.) The unleavened bread of communion is the perfect, sinless Jesus. We eat and drink of Him. He is our Life. We eat of Him in communion and we eat of Him as we read His Word. To paraphrase John 6:63, "These words that I speak to you, these words that are written in the Bible, these words are spirit – and they are life."

If we don't understand and embrace the concept of choosing life, we will by default opt for death. That means sickness, poverty and a life of limitations. If we don't want disease and death, let's make a daily commitment to choose life – in all its fullness.

Prayers

Ten Steps to Heartfelt Prayer
1. You must have cast your cares upon Jesus (I Pet. 5:7).
2. Find Scriptures relating to your prayer, sowing the seed of the Word (Isa. 55:11) as well as a monetary seed offering claiming what you have requested. *
3. Meditate on the related Scriptures, settling the Word in your heart (Ps. 1:2;

Why Doesn't God Heal Me?

Josh. 1:8; Isa. 51:7; Jer. 15:16). This will fire you up and make you fervent in your prayer (Jer. 5:14; 23:29).

4. Pray a fervent prayer (James 5:16).

5. Quote back to God the covenant promise He has made relating to your request (Neh. 1:5). God's covenants are sealed in Jesus' blood, and He cannot break His Word (Isa. 45:23; 46:11; Jer. 1:12).

6. Remind God of what He said in His Word (Neh. 1:8-11). For example: "Father, You cannot lie, and Your Word says ..."

7. Precede your prayer in your native language by praying in the Spirit (in tongues) in your heavenly language to your Father. When the Holy Spirit prays through you, He prays the perfect prayer – a prayer that releases miracle-working power (Jude 20; Rom. 8:26-27; I Cor. 14:4, 18).

8. Start praising God for the answer (II Chron. 20:18-21).

9. Give thanks (Col. 4:2; Phil. 4:6).

10. Keep staying steadfast in expecting results, avoiding thoughts and words of fear, doubt and undermining (Rom. 4:16-21; Isa. 64:4.)

Note: Don't repeat a specific prayer as a request. Faith in our Father of Love leads us to simply give Him thanks and praise. Asking the same thing again is a doubting, double-minded prayer (James 1:6-8).

* For example, if you are praying for the salvation of your children, use Isa. 49:25; 44:3; 48:19; 61:9; Gen. 18:19. For family salvation, use Exodus 12:3 (they took a lamb for each household, showing that Jesus' sacrifice is for the whole family) and Acts 10:1-2; 11:13-14; 16:15, 31-34; 18:8). For release from a sin, surrender it to Jesus and claim: "I am redeemed from _____ by Jesus' blood because my Father loves me."

Identity in the Crucifixion Prayer

"Father, God of the covenant with men. How great and awesome are Your ways! You never fail nor do You slumber. All peace and blessings come from You.

"We are your Children in Jesus Christ, and we want Your help in understanding and claiming our crucifixion so that we may walk fully in our new identity as Your Children.

"We surrender our past, our pain, our sins, our old identity in Adam, our ways of thinking, our old ways of speaking and our will to the cross.

"We want the life that Jesus gives us to be fully shown, fully understood and fully accepted in us. Let Your glory shine in us and on us, Father. We want Your plans for our life to be fully manifested so the world will come to know You and love You.

"You are our prosperity and our peace.

"We pray that all Glory, Honor and Power be Yours forever and ever. And thank

You for all that You have given us in Jesus' name. Amen."

Prayer against Prayers Said Not according to God's Will

"Father, I hereby reject and nullify all prayers [and/or prophecies] that have been said on my behalf that are not according to Your will for my life or my family's. I break off all the effects and plans of the enemy that were thus authorized."

The following should be added if you know you are under attack from this kind of prayers (communion is highly recommended):

"I cancel all assignments that demons have been given in relation to these prayers [and/or prophecies]. I choose to walk in Your will [and prophesied future for me], in Jesus' name. I forgive all those who have issued prayers [and/or prophecies] that are not according to Your will, Father, and I put the cross between them and the law of sowing and reaping, in Jesus' name.

"Thank You, Father, for this freedom, in Jesus' name. Amen and Amen."

This prayer should be said on a regular basis and sealed in communion.

Prayer for Blessing

One of the hindrances involves not blessing others. Here is a sample prayer of blessing to pray over other Christians. When we joyfully bless others from the heart, we receive back one hundredfold the same blessings. The following blessing is based on Psalm 37 and Matthew 5.

"In Jesus' name, I bless you with humility, gentleness, empathy and with a hunger and thirst for righteousness. May God bless you with mercy and purity. May you be a peacemaker. May you be patient and generous like your Father in heaven. May God give you the grace to rejoice always and count your blessings.

"May you be a teacher and keeper of the law of God, and may it be written on the tables of your heart. May God bless you with a desire to bless others. May He bless you with discernment and growth in righteousness.

"May you know in your heart that you are the righteousness of God and be established in the righteousness Jesus bought for you. May you see your growth and be encouraged by what God is doing in you. May you understand the purpose of persecution, even rejoicing and accepting it without reviling. May you be growing strong and prospering in every way next year, the year after that – and for all eternity.

"May you and yours receive the hundredfold blessings of the Biblical words shêlâm *and* shalom. *May you prosper and be in health, as your soul prospers. May God free you from fretting and worry, filling you with His peace that passes all understanding. May God bless you indeed and enlarge your border. May His hand be with you. May He keep you from harm and may you not cause pain.*

"May you hear clearly the voice of God. May your eyes and ears be open to the spirit realm. May you experience and express God's love. May you be filled to overflowing with the joy of Jesus.

Why Doesn't God Heal Me?

"May your youth be renewed like the eagle. May you walk in God's perfect will for your life. May He give you a future and a hope. May God bless you and keep you, make His face shine upon you, and be gracious unto you. May He lift up His countenance upon you and give you peace. May you come into intimate fellowship with your Father in heaven, your Brother Jesus and your precious Teacher, Encourager and Friend, the Holy Spirit.

"May your heart always be open to receive the extravagant love and overflowing blessings your Father wants to lavish upon you, the apple of His eye. May God grant you long and vigorous life and may He preserve your going out and your coming in from this time forth and forevermore. Amen."

Prayers for Healing

Following are the prayers that were actually said over this author for the healing of his soul and then for the physical healing. They have been only slightly edited to preserve their integrity. Although they are good guidelines for those who are new to prayers for healing, every situation is different and requires special guidance from the Holy Spirit. I also remind the reader that Jesus never prayed a prayer in which He said, "Father, heal this person if it is Your will." We must pray the prayer of faith, realizing it is always God's will to heal and it is our covenant right.

Prayers for Soul Healing

Opening Prayer

"Father, we have come together in Jesus Christ's name to present our brother Bob Scott to You.

"He has followed Your instructions and called upon the elders to pray over him and with him for the healing of his soul. We therefore call upon Jesus Christ to be here with us and before You to plead his case.

"We pray that Your Holy Spirit unify us so that we can be guided by Your love, Your discernment and Your understanding of the importance of what we are claiming.

"Therefore, we hereby bind all evil spirits that are currently afflicting our brother (and those spirits whom Satan may send against us during this ceremony) to total silence and inactivity in their ability to afflict anyone present. We bind and rebuke them by the authority of Jesus Christ.

"Father, we thank You for hearing our prayer. In Jesus name. Amen."

Second Prayer

"Father, we open ourselves to You as Your Children to do Your will and to be led by Your Holy Spirit in our request for Bob Scott's soul to be healed.

"And now as we lay hands on our brother (elders place their hands on Bob Scott's head), *we pray that Jesus who suffered so much for us, will now intercede and plead Bob Scott's case before You, for the pain he has carried has troubled him greatly. Our brother dedicated himself to You and to serving You. He was then not*

Appendix **A**

only persecuted for Your name's sake but also rejected. He was told that he was unwanted by You, unloved by You, and a burden to the church. He has endured in the faith as he has understood it, but has found that he has been unable to forgive his supervisor.

"We now ask You to remember what You asked Jesus to go through on the cross, especially when the demons were possessing the leaders of Judah that came before Him to mock Christ. And then the ultimate pain was directed at Jesus by You turning Your back on Him in those last moments before His death. Our Savior felt that pain of Your loss more than all the pain He had ever suffered. We therefore ask that You allow Jesus to heal Bob Scott of all the hurts and bad memories that plague him, that Jesus will walk back through Bob's life and not only heal but give our brother the true spirit of forgiveness so that only praise for You, Father, will be in his heart, with Your peace and Your joy."

(All hands are then removed from Bob and he is asked these questions:)

"Bob Scott, are you willing to repent of your sins? Bob Scott, are you willing to obey every word of God? Bob Scott, will you let Jesus into your heart? Bob Scott, will you let Jesus heal you? Bob Scott, are you willing to exercise your authority in Jesus over the demons that Satan sent at you?

"Bob Scott, are you willing to forgive your tormentors before God and man?"

(Hands are then returned to Bob Scott.)

"Then, our dear brother, by the authority of Jesus Christ, we now give God's message to you: Your sins are forgiven; your soul is now healed."

(Then all say: "We give thanks and give our praises to God.")

"Father, we thank You for hearing our prayer. In Jesus name. Amen."

[I was asked to refer to a list of major and minor demons, some of which had legal right to affect me because unforgiveness had opened the door for them to enter.]

For each one that is found that applies to you, you must say out loud:

"Spirit of _____ , you are now bound, rejected and cast out never to return, in Jesus' name."

(When the list is completed, Bob Scott is to offer up a prayer of thanksgiving for God's help in seeking the forgiveness of those he may have injured and for wisdom on knowing how to forgive himself.)

Then comes the closing prayers for healing of the body and the blessings.

(Optional: Taking of the bread and the wine.)

Conclusion

"Father, we thank You for restoring our brother Bob to full fellowship with You, for stirring up his spirit to full repentance and for opening his mind to Your glory. You have filled all of us with Your joy, Your peace and, most of all, Your love, for

Why Doesn't God Heal Me?

You have shared Your very nature with us.

"Now as we conclude this ceremony of soul healing, we say this with all our soul: we love You, Father, and we give ourselves in love to You. Thank You again, Father, for all that You have given us, in Jesus' name. Amen."

Prayer for Healing, Health, Security and Peace

(Personalized paraphrase of Psalm 91, the psalm whose miraculous power has been demonstrated on the "It's Supernatural" TV program on the Church Channel of Trinity Broadcasting Network – www.sidroth.org; 1-800-548-1918 in U.S. and Canada)

I am he (or she) who dwells in the shelter of the most High. I will abide in the shadow of the Almighty forever.

I will say to Jesus, "My Refuge and my Fortress, my God in whom I trust."

For it is You, Jesus, who delivers me from the snares of Satan, and from all his deadly pestilences.

Christ will cover me with His feathers and under His wings I will seek my refuge, for Jesus is always faithful to be my Shield and defensive Rampart.

I will not be afraid of the terrors by night, nor of the arrows of Satan that fly by day,

Nor of the pestilences that Satan brings to stalk me from the depths of his darkness, nor from the destruction that lays everything waste at noon.

For I may see a thousand fall by my left side, and ten thousand die at my right hand, but this I know: Jesus' promises will stand – it will never approach me.

I will only observe with my eyes, protected in Christ, as I watch the recompense of the wicked,

For I have Jesus as my ever faithful Refuge. Even with the Most High I will dwell.

No evil, no sickness, no curse, no enemy shall be a plague to me because of my God and Savior,

For Jesus has given His angels orders concerning me, to guard me in all the ways of my walk with Him.

His angels will bear me up in their protective hands, in case I may strike my foot against a stone.

I will tread underfoot all the agents of Satan, whether it be lions, cobras, scorpions or serpents.

Because my heart and my love is in Jesus, He has delivered me to the Father Who has set me securely on high, and since I am in Christ, He knows my name.

I am His lamb. I know His voice. When Jesus calls, I answer Him. When trouble comes, I run to Him. He rescues me and gives me much love, honor and authority in Him.

I am satisfied with a long life in Jesus, and I have beheld the salvation of my Divine Master.

Appendix **A**

I live only to bring glory to You, my God, to give praise and thanks for Your lov-ingkindness. Amen.

Prayer for Protection and Long Life

(Psalm 26 – Declaring our Stand with Jesus and His Protection)

Vindicate me, O righteous Judge, for I have walked in my integrity; and I have trusted with my whole heart in Jesus, and have not wavered.

Examine me, most righteous God; try me, test my soul; look into my mind and my heart.

For Your lovingkindness is before my eyes, and I have walked with You in Your truth.

I do not entertain nor sit with deceitful men. Nor do I go about with those who are pretenders, false-hearted, worthless, or men of false holiness.

I hate the assembly of evildoers, schemers and secret societies. And I will not sit with the wicked, those who worship the Evil One and those who make incantations.

I will wash my hands in innocence. What I say and what I do will be pure in Your eyes. And I will go about Your altar, lifting up the name of Jesus,

That I may proclaim in praise and thanksgiving and give to all a testimony of Your miracles and purposes.

O Jesus, I love the tabernacles of Your glory and the places where You send Your glory to dwell.

Do not allow my soul to be taken away with sinners, nor my life to be blotted out in the bloodshed of men.

Protect me from the hands of wicked men and their schemes, and from the lust for money that perverts truth for bribes.

But this I declare, I shall walk in my integrity that comes from obeying Your Word. Redeem me and be gracious in favor to me,

So that my foot stands firm on a level place, and in the congregations of God I shall bless my Savior, Jesus.

Prayer for Release from Frustration

"Father, I come before You to reject and break off frustration in Jesus' name. I forgive myself for speaking the frustration into law in my life by my words. I forgive those who have provoked or added to my frustration.

"I take the sword of Jesus and destroy the box of frustration that has hemmed me in. In Jesus' name I bind up the demons who are causing and enforcing these frustrations in chains of confusion, cutting them off from all support, commanding them to take all their weapons and go back to the pit. I turn all the pain and frus-tration over to You, Jesus, at the cross.

"I thank You, Father, for the freedom from these frustrations. I pray blessings into my life (or into the life of another if praying for another). *I put the cross*

Why Doesn't God Heal Me?

between me and the law of sowing and reaping. I seal all this in the blood of Jesus and ask for the blood of Jesus to shield against any backlash or blacklash from Satan." (Be sure to seal all this by these last words in communion.)

Prayer for Release from Satan's Hands

"How blessed am I, Father, to have all my transgressions forgiven, to have my sins covered in the blood, to be clean in Your eyes because of Jesus. Father, I place myself upon Your altar so that whatever is not of You can be removed. I want more of Jesus and less of me.

"Let all Your saints pray to You in a time when You may be found. Let them seek release from the curses over their lives, release from the power of sin, from debts and from the pollution that Satan has implanted in their mind.

"Let all Your saints pray in unity for Jesus to come to Jerusalem as the King of Peace. Let Your holy ones be strong in claiming back all that Satan has stolen. Let Your Children cause fear and trembling in the camp of the enemy at the sound of their praise and worship. Let the heavens shake and the earth tremble at the sound of Your loved ones singing out the name of Jesus.

"By the word of Jesus the heavens were made, and by the breath of His mouth all the hosts. Let all the earth bow in fear and respect of Jesus.

"Let Satan know we declare that You are our God whom we trust, and in Jesus' name we declare that Satan must restore seven times all that he has stolen from Your saints. We declare this day a day of breakthrough. We call forth this day as the day of release. We stand on Your Word, Jesus, and call for renewal in our lives. We call forth reformation to Your church. We call forth revival in Your saints to the understanding of Your Word. We call forth the saving of our loved ones.

"Father, let the whole earth stand in awe of Jesus and give thanks to You for all that He has done. For when Jesus spoke, it was done. And all that He has commanded has stood fast. Jesus, at Your Word all the plans of Satan are nullified, all his yokes broken, all Satan's traps destroyed and all his bondages released. Your brethren, Jesus, call for release. Let Your Word confirm it. For our hope and strength is in You.

"Thank You, Father, for our Redeemer, Jesus. In Jesus' name. Amen."

Prayer for Release from Sympathy and Pity

"Father, I confess the sin of seeking sympathy and pity and/or expressing them to others. They are demonic forces that prevent Your love from flowing through my heart to others. They block business ventures, family relations and prosperity. I will to change my heart and mind to speak Your Word into every situation. I declare that I will change and stop seeking and expressing sympathy and pity. I choose instead to express empathy and compassion. I forgive myself for having spoken and sought words of pity and sympathy. I forgive those who have expressed sympathy and pity to me. I reject and break off these words, whether spoken by others or myself.

Appendix **A**

"I bind up all the demons and their agents encouraging sympathy and pity, namely lust, selfishness, self-gratification, sexual perversion, control, manipulation, cruelty, stinginess, anxiety, fear, paralysis, standardization, agony, sorrow, people-pleasing, devouring, blockage, poverty, seduction, bitterness, wallowing, defeat, misuse, distraction, hiding, dead works, quagmire, fantasy, discontentment, emotional theorizing, possessiveness, greed, hoarding, complaining, imposing, addiction, festering, exaggeration, hypochondria, contempt and infirmity.

"I bind them all in chains of confusion, cutting them off from all support. I take the sword of Jesus and I destroy all their weapons, armaments, artillery and nets. I command the pits they dug for me to be filled up. I burn up their slime and command them to go back to the pit in Jesus' name.

"I claim Your blessing back into my life and restoration of all the Devil has stolen from me because of sympathy, pity and their agents. Thank You, Father and thank You, Jesus, for the freedom. In Jesus' name. Amen."

Prayer for Restoration

(Church, Personal, Life, Home, Family Life, Years)

"Father, I will bless You always. The name of Jesus shall forever be upon my lips. My soul shall make its boast in Jesus. Father, magnify Jesus in me. And let all the saints exalt the name of Jesus in unity.

"I sought You, Jesus, and You answered me and delivered me from all my fears. I called out to You, Jesus, 'Restore, restore,' and You opened the pathway of my mind to receive You. I call out to You, Jesus, now and say, 'Restore Your church and let Your body be unified in truth, love, wholeness, with nothing missing and nothing broken. Restore my life to the fullness You had with Adam in the garden of Eden and restore all the years that Satan has stolen. Restore and cause breakthrough for all my family line and all my friends.

" 'Restore all that Satan has stolen from my wealth and increase. Restore all my heritage lands and estates that have been stolen over the years and generations.' And Jesus, I call forth the restoration of Your Kingdom on this earth. Let Your Word be proven true, that those who call upon Your name, Jesus, shall suffer no want, no lack, no hunger, no emptiness and be in want of no good thing. Thank You, Jesus, for the restoration of all things. In Jesus' name. Amen."

Prayer for Self-Examination and Removal of Hindrances

"Father, I hereby declare that I submit to You and Your will. If my words are wrong, show me my error and help me speak Your words. If my thoughts are wrong, correct me in mercy. If I am stubborn, show me where I have blocked myself from learning and growing in Jesus.

"If I am not obeying Your Word, correct me and teach me again. If I am not changing, show me and I will repent. If I am not submitting to those You have given as authorities over me, show me. Humble and renew me. If I am blocking or griev-

Why Doesn't God Heal Me?

ing the Holy Spirit, forgive me and let my spiritual ears and eyes be open to Him. If I am so caught up in watching Satan's attacks on me that I fail to pray for others, I repent. Give me a heart for prayer.

"If I am not a blessing to others, correct me. Show me how to be a blessing. If I have become stingy or begun to worship money and things, teach me to give and use my assets as a help to others. Father, I surrender to You, now and forever, for You alone are God.

"Thank You. In Jesus' name. Amen."

Prayer for Coming to Terms with Sin

"Father, Your ways are awesome. Your truths are beauties within beauties and Your patient love is beyond our abilities to measure. Therefore, Father, we come before You to confess and acknowledge our sins. Where we have had hidden sins, open our eyes to see them, to acknowledge them, confess them and let them go to Jesus at the cross.

"Where we have presumptuous sins, let us see them, acknowledge them, acknowledge the cause and effect of them and confess them to You.

"You are always right in Your judgments and we submit to You, Father, for the correction of presumptuous sins. We turn them over to the cross.

"Where we have sins of omissions, Father, let our eyes be open to these short-comings. In Your grace, let us no longer omit doing what is right in Your sight, what is right by Your Word.

"And Father, where false doctrine or doctrines of demons have filled our minds with misconceptions, misperceptions of You, of Jesus, of the Holy Spirit, of Your plans for us, or of our understanding of Your Word that You have written as our guide, let our minds be open to Your truth.

"Let us have a willing heart to present, to acknowledge and to confess these truths. Let Your Word be true and every man a liar.

"And Father, where there are sins of commission, we confess these errors and ask that we be forgiven for them, that we be washed in the blood and that the cross be put between us and the law of sowing and reaping for all these sins.

"We thank You, Father, for Jesus, the cross and for Your forgiveness for these sins. We are blessed in Your mercy. Thank You. In Jesus' name. Amen."

Pride

Pride – Its Subtle and Not-So-Subtle Manifestations

God warns us not be friends with this world and its ways (James 4:4; Acts 2:40). Pride leads us to do just that. Pride makes God resist us and eventually destroys us as it did Lucifer. It is a substitute for our identity in Christ and our righteousness in Him. Self-righteousness is pride.

Appendix **A**

Following are some of the manifestations of pride:

Pride of doctrine – "I'm right and you're wrong."
Pride of past accomplishments (even of sins)
Pride of ideas – inventions, songs, poems, solution to a problem, etc.
Pride in knowing the mistakes of others (gloating over failures)
Pride of knowledge
Pride of contention – annoying and quarreling with others
Pride in open-mindedness – tolerating things God doesn't (gay life style, false religion), worshipping relativism ("no right or wrong")
Pride in religious legalism – Pharisees who use the rules to judge others but can't even keep them themselves
Pride in competition
Pride of possession – obsessed with material goods and collecting things (antiques, stamps, sports cards, etc.)
Pride of life
Pride of seduction – using and abusing people as valueless, seducing and deceiving them
Pride of seeing lawless deeds
Pride of having done a lawless act and gotten way with it ("I'll sleep around all I want and won't get AIDS.")
Pride of control
Pride of expectancy – expecting everything but not thankful for anything
Pride of self-will
Pride of temper – using a weakness as our identity
Pride of addiction – "I smoke two packs a day." You can't be released from the spirit of addiction until you repent of the pride of addiction.
Pride of shrewd dealing
Pride of fast gain
Pride of laziness
Pride of gluttony – "I can down five cheeseburgers at a time."
Pride in worthless activities and stupidity – One man ground up a Volkswagen and ate it to make the Guinness Book of World Records.
Pride that enslaves to various lusts and pleasures
Pride that blocks from seeing and meeting others' needs
Pride in the use of vulgarity – "Everybody does it, and you can't fight the world."
Pride of uninhibited sexual conduct (orgies, sexual conquests, etc.)
Pride of drunkenness
Pride in rejecting God's day of rest to fit in with the world
Pride in keeping the world's feast days
Pride in judging by worldly standards

Why Doesn't God Heal Me?

Pride in no time to be with God

Pride in keeping idols – giving priority to anything over God (e.g. clothes, cars, knowledge, etc.)

Pride in going all the way your way, being a self-made man

Pride in letting mammon rule your actions – "Money makes the world go 'round."

Pride in giving (to be seen by men)

Pride in having parties only for your friends

Pride in showing kindness to those who can repay you

Pride in seeking a position, rank or title to look good in the eyes of men

Pride in putting on a show by doing something good or bad

Pride in hating the underdog, the outsider, the loser

Pride in not standing up for righteousness

Pride in submitting to abuse (running to the coward's chair because of pride)

Pride in teaching a false doctrine

Pride in looking for loopholes in God's Word

Pride in sickness – "Look how righteous I am to endure this illness."

Pride of a broken or bad marriage – "You wouldn't believe what I endured with my husband!"

Pride that encourages lazy work habits – "Don't work too hard!"

Pride Specifically Related to Friendship with the World

Pride of popularity – Many teens will do anything to be popular, even torment others.

Pride of gambling – Wheelers and dealers get respect.

Pride in astrology – It's cute and trendy to know your sign and discuss horoscopes with others.

Pride in pornography

Pride in griping and murmuring

Pride in exotic vacations – "We're going to Hawaii."

Pride in debt – "I owe more than you."

Pride in tax evasion

Pride in theft (bringing friendship with other thieves)

Pride in adultery – bragging to the guys about hidden liaisons

Pride in being a hypocrite – The world respects that.

Pride in watching sitcoms and soap operas

Pride in watching violent shows

Pride in reading cheap romance novels

Pride in fast cars – showing off so people will idolize you

Pride in authority bashing – Cursing the president or prime minister is a popular activity.

Pride in trends and fads

Pride in loud, harsh music

Appendix **A**

Pride in criticizing leadership and destroying people – It's the "in" thing today to destroy the reputation of leaders by gossip and slander. Tearing others down lifts us up in pride.

Pride in name-dropping – "I have power because I know somebody who has power."

Pride in hearing gossip and spreading it – If you walk away from gossip you will be the object of it.

Pride in bragging about the operation you've had – I'll never forget the elderly lady in France who constantly spoke of her 26 operations and reminded me that it was all because of the Americans who bombed her city in the war.

Satan, why he doesn't have to listen to our rebukes

Can Satan withstand a rebuke from a Christian? The answer is yes! For the following reasons, Satan and his demons have a legal right to stay and continue attacking us.

1. When God removes a protective hedge around us for a special reason, as with Job (Although an exceptional measure, when God gives Satan permission to test us, no rebuke will work.)
2. When it serves as a test of our character or will, and enables us to grow
3. When we have unconfessed sin (Satan can then resist in a big way)
4. When there is a curse over our lives we have not rejected
5. When we look back longingly to our old life (one foot in church and one out)
6. When our knowledge of the Word and speaking it out are being tested. God may allow Satan to test us until we persist in speaking the Word over ourselves in a bad situation.
7. When our identity in Christ or in our anointing is challenged. Satan may say, "Don't move forward," when an opportunity arises to powerfully fulfil our calling.
8. When we have lingering doubts or fears (Job 3:24-26 – "what I fear comes upon me")
9. When God allows the test to bring us to repentance and accept Him as our Master
10. When we accept an error, such as a doctrinal error or idol worship
11. Lack of thankfulness
12. Taking the credit for what God has done
13. A cursing tongue
14. Unforgiving, critical attitude
15. Blasphemy against the Holy Spirit
16. Bringing false witness against a brother
17. Eating at God's table and the table of demons (e.g. taking communion and

293

Why Doesn't God Heal Me?

then going to a pagan feast)
18. Rebuking improperly (e.g. not using Jesus' name or going against a principality alone)
19. Rebuking Satan or demons without binding them in chains of confusion (Mark 3:27)
20. When God withdraws His Spirit from you because of serious and repeated disobedience (e.g. Saul in I Sam. 16:14 – "Now the Spirit of the [Eternal] departed from Saul, and an evil spirit from the [Eternal] terrorized him." Also, the man who slept with his father's wife in I Cor. 5 was delivered to Satan to wake him up.)
21. When you are wearing Satanic ornaments that invite demons
22. When we fear Satan more than God (90% of the churches today don't teach about Satan, the enemy we are supposed to know. They thus show their fear of Satan.)
23. When trauma in our lives opens the door to Satan and gives him legal claim

*All of these reasons can be hindrances to healing as well.

Ten Things Satan Hates
1. When we consciously stop what we're doing and listen to/wait to hear from God and expect an answer (Satan can't deceive you because you're not moving in his way)
2. When we take time to be intimate with God (and not rushing about in a pressured, driven state)
3. When we exercise our authority in Jesus' name (casting out demons, healing the sick, etc.)
4. When we give joyfully (expressing the nature of the Father), which blocks Satan from stealing our blessings
5. When we expect to receive from God
6. When we declare the Word faithfully in love
7. When we free brothers from Satan's strongholds
8. When we claim the promises of God for ourselves
9. When we demand return of stolen money or property back from Satan
10. When we confess sins quickly (loosing Satan's hold and legal claim on us)

Healing Scriptures

Healing Scriptures

It is extremely important to read aloud and speak out what God says about healing. The following list is not exhaustive (especially in regards to the many healings in the gospels), but includes some important verses to meditate upon and read aloud. They are part of our covenant with God of which we need to remind Him.

Gen. 20:17 – Abraham prayed to God, and God healed Abimelech and his wife and maids, so that they bore children.

Ex. 15:26 – … I will put none of the diseases on you which I have put on the Egyptians; for I, [Jesus], am your Healer.

Ex. 23:25-26 – … I will remove sickness from your midst. There will be no one miscarrying or barren in your land; I will fulfill the number of your days.

Num. 11:23 – The [Eternal] said to Moses, "Is the [Eternal's] power limited? … "

Num. 23:19 – "God is not a man, that He should lie, Nor a son of man, that He should repent; Has He said, and will He not do it? Or has He spoken, and will He not make it good?"

Deut. 7:15 – [Jesus] will remove from you all sickness …

Deut. 32:39 – "… there is no god besides Me; It is I who put to death and give life. I have wounded and it is I who heal …"

Deut. 34:7 – Although Moses was one hundred and twenty years old when he died, his eye was not dim, nor his vigor abated.

Job 22:28 – You will also decree a thing, and it will be established for you …

Ps. 91:3, 5-6a – For it is He who delivers [me] … from the deadly pestilence … I will not be afraid of the terror by night, Or of the arrow that flies by day; Of the pestilence that stalks in darkness …

Ps. 103:2-4a, 5 – Bless the [Eternal], O my soul, And forget none of His benefits; Who pardons all your iniquities, Who heals all your diseases; Who redeems your life from the pit … Who satisfies your years with good things, So that your youth is renewed like the eagle …

Ps. 107:20 – He sent His word and healed them, And delivered them from their destructions.

Why Doesn't God Heal Me?

Ps. 110:4 – The [Eternal] has sworn and will not change His mind …

Ps. 112:7 – He [the righteous] will not fear evil tidings; His heart is steadfast, trusting in [Jesus].

Ps. 118:17 – I will not die, but live, And tell of the works of [Jesus].

Prov. 3:7b-8 – [Revere Jesus] and turn away from evil. It will be healing to your body And refreshment to your bones.

Prov. 4:20a, 21b-22 – My son, give attention to my words … keep them in the midst of your heart. For they are life to those who find them And health to all their body.

Prov. 17:22 – A joyful heart is good medicine, But a broken spirit dries up the bones.

Prov. 18:21 – Death and life are in the power of the tongue, And those who love it will eat its fruit.

Isa. 40:31 – Yet those who wait for [Jesus] will gain new strength; They will mount up with wings like eagles, They will run and not get tired, They will walk and not become weary.

Isa. 53:5b – … by His scourging we are healed.

Isa. 54:14b, 17a – … the well-being of your sons will be great … No weapon formed against you will prosper…

Isa. 55:11 – So will My Word be which goes forth from My mouth; It will not return to me empty, Without accomplishing what I desire, And without succeeding in the matter for which I sent it.

Jer. 30:17 – 'For I will restore to you health And I will heal your of our wounds,' declares [Jesus] …

Isa. 58:8a, 11a – … your recovery will speedily spring forth … [Jesus] will … give strength to your bones …

Isa. 66:14 – … your bones will flourish like the new grass …

Jer. 1:12 – … I am watching over My word to perform it.

Jer. 17:14 – Heal me, O [Jesus], and I will be healed … For You are my praise.

Jer. 32:17b – Nothing is too difficult for You …

Jer. 33:6 – Behold, I will bring to [Israel] health and healing, and I will heal them …

Ezek. 34:16 – … I will … bind up the broken and strengthen the sick …

Mal. 3:6 – "For I, the [Eternal], do not change…

Mal. 4:2 – But for you who [revere] My name, the sun of righteousness will rise with healing in its wings; and you will go forth and skip like calves from the stall.

Mat. 8:16b-17 – [Jesus] cast out the spirits with a word, and healed all who were ill. This was to fulfill what was spoken through Isaiah the prophet: "HE HIM-SELF TOOK OUR INFIRMITIES AND CARRIED AWAY OUR DISEASES."

Mat. 9:5 – "Which is easier, to say, 'Your sins are forgiven,' or to say, 'Get up and walk'?"

Mat. 9:29 – … "It shall be done to you according to your faith."

Mat. 9:35 – Jesus was going through all the cities and villages … healing every kind of disease and every kind of sickness.

Healing Scriptures

Mat. 10:1 – Jesus summoned His twelve disciples and gave them authority over unclean spirits, to cast them out, and to heal every kind of disease and every kind of sickness.

Mark 11:24 – "… all things for which you pray and ask, believe that you have received them, and they will be granted you."

Mark 16:18 – …They will lay hands on the sick, and they will recover.

Luke 13:16 – "And this woman … whom Satan has bound for eighteen long years, should she not have been released from this bond on the Sabbath day?"

John 10:10 – "The thief comes only to steal and kill and destroy; I came that they may have life, and have it abundantly."

John 20:23 – "If you forgive the sins of any, their sins have been forgiven them …"

Acts 3:16 – "And on the basis of faith in His name, it is the name of Jesus which has strengthened this man … and … has given him this perfect health …

Acts 10:38 – "You know of Jesus … how He went about healing all who were oppressed by the devil …"

Rom. 8:11 – … He who raised Christ from the dead will also give life to your mortal bodies through His Spirit who dwells in you.

I Cor. 6:19-20 – Or do you not know that your body is a temple of the Holy Spirit …? … glorify God in your body.

I Cor. 11:29-30 – For he who eats and drinks, eats and drinks judgment to himself if he does not judge the body rightly. For this reason many among you are weak and sick, and a number sleep.

I Thes. 5:23 – Now may the God of peace Himself sanctify you entirely; and may your spirit and soul and body be preserved complete, without blame at the coming of our Lord Jesus Christ.

Heb. 13:8 – Jesus Christ is the same yesterday and today and forever.

James 5:15-16 – and the prayer offered in faith will restore the one who is sick, and the [Divine Master] will raise him up, and if he has committed sins, they will be forgiven him. Therefore, confess your sins to one another, and pray for one another so that you may be healed …

I John 3:8 – … The Son of God appeared for this purpose, to destroy the works of the devil.

I John 3:21-22 – Beloved, if our heart does not condemn us, we have confidence before God; and whatever we ask we receive from Him, because we keep His commandments and do the things that are pleasing in His sight.

I John 4:4 – … greater is He who is in you than he who is in the world.

I John 4:18 – There is no fear in love; but perfect love casts out fear …

I John 5:14-15 – This is the confidence which we have before Him, that, if we ask anything according to His will, He hears us. And if we know that He hears us in whatever we ask, we know that we have the requests which we have asked from Him.

III John 2 – Beloved, I pray that in all respects you may prosper and be in good health, just as your soul prospers.

Why Doesn't God Heal Me?

Index

A

Adam and Eve 7, 9, 12, 103, 215
Adversity 78, 133, 253
  is a spirit 78
  see also "Prayer" in Appendix
Alpha and Omega 30-34
Anointing 23-24, 32, 44-45, 48, 68, 84,
  86, 93-94, 102, 118, 123-124, 132,
  144, 160, 164 178 181-182, 194,
  198, 203-204, 212, 215, 218
  anointing or calling to walk in 154
  supernatural enabling power and
    presence of the Holy Spirit 166
Atonement 25-26
  see Chapter 4
  types of 35

B

Baal 40, 74, 120-121, 221
  see also "Lord" – 117-126
Backlash/Blacklash 43, 201-203, 221,
  236, 255, 258, 261
Baptism 83, 136, 138, 219, 244
  fuller life, a resurrection occurs 139
  in the Holy Spirit 245
  in water 245
  obedience to baptism command 244
  of the Holy Spirit 139
  water baptism by immersion 83-84
Book of Love (God's Instruction Book)
  1, 4-5, 21, 26-27, 35, 87, 126, 146,
  164, 186
Bride of Jesus or Jesus' Bride 6, 11,
  15, 86, 106, 123, 115, 117, 152, 190
  see Chapter 12
Bridegroom 117, 152
  name is Jesus 118
  see Chapter 12

C

Christ's Bride, see Bride of Jesus
Christian 26, 52, 56, 60-61, 64, 66, 68,
  72, 74-75, 81-83, 97-98, 109, 111,
  113, 115, 117,125, 129, 131, 133,
  136, 139- 140, 144, 164, 173, 175,
  181, 185, 191, 243
  God tells us to be holy 244
  has Jesus' nature 137
  key to victorious Christian living 160
  living sacrifice 26
  new identity. 141
  obedience 151
  see Chapter 11
Christianity 60, 63, 110
  all about confession 110
  Baptist 64
  Christian battle 64
  mainstream 63
  self-esteem 82
  self-worth 82
  spiritual warfare 64
  walking with Jesus 115
Communion 29-35, 83, 112-115, 130-
  131, 171, 175, 186, 203, 207, 218,
  220, 223, 225, 254
  healing and salvation represented 48
  Passover 28
  see also "Jesus, Bread of Life" in
    Appendix
  sign of the New Covenant 47
Conversion 82, 138
  see also "Baptism" in Appendix
Covenant(s) 4, 21, 25, 30-35, 40, 47-
48, 144, 148-149, 154, 167
  blessings are conditional 149
  God expects us to make demands
    according to the covenants 149

Why Doesn't God Heal Me?

Curse(s) 3, 9, 11, 24, 30, 35, 39, 48, 52, 56, 60, 67, 69, 100, 109-110, 112, 132, 137, 161, 164, 166-167, 171, 173-176, 178, 184, 188, 190, 194, 196, 203-207, 213, 215, 217, 219, 221-230, 242-245, 251, 254
  actions bringing curses from God 257
  curse release prayer 256
  curses, authoritative 257
  curses from Christians, release from 257
  curses from God 112
    signs of 259
  general release prayer 258
  generational curses, release from 259
  major hindrance to healing 111
  reject curses in communion 115
    see also "Communion" in Appendix
  release from 256
  see Chapter 2 and Chapter 11
  see also "Curses" in Appendix
  sickness and death 10
  voodoo curses, release from 260
  witchcraft curses, prayer for breaking 260–261

D

Daily declarations 88, 157, 161,177, 209, 227, 264
  identity in Christ 264
  most important listed in Appendix
Debt, ending 130, 226, 262
  prayers for release from debts 263
Demon(s) 23, 29-30, 42-44, 48, 50, 52, 55-57, 67, 73, 85, 98, 100, 104, 109, 111, 114, 117, 119,121, 140, 144-145, 156, 160, 170, 172, 178, 180, 183, 188-189, 191, 196, 198-203, 217, 219-220, 222, 228, 245, 285, 293

crippling spirit called "bent" 63
quagmire – pushes you from one ditch to another 121
see Chapter 7
see "Curses" in Appendix
see also "Satan" in Appendix
Devil, see "Satan" in Appendix
Divine healing xi, 1, 19-20, 37, 131, 166, 173-174, 216

E

eternal life 9, 14-16, 21, 83, 90, 131, 136, 138-139, 149, 162, 193-194, 197, 209, 220, 244, 281
  see "Identity in Christ" in Appendix

F

Faith 2, 22, 24, 27, 39-40, 42, 45-46, 52, 65, 69, 74, 76, 78, 100-101, 108, 131, 160, 162-166, 242-243, 268-274, 282. 284
  condition to God's promise of healing x
  gift from God 174, 182
  intensified and activated by faith 34
  lack of 169
  levels of 266
  misplaced faith 181
  obedience implied as well 162
  persevering faith 27
  see Chapter 18
  without works, without fulfilling the conditions 163
Fear 5, 11-12, 45, 67, 78, 100, 125, 144-146, 149-150, 154, 170-172, 176, 193, 222, 224, 230, 282, 293-294
  cancels our faith 230
  fear of God 146
    directly related to health and healing 147
    means obeying Him out of loving, reverential awe 145

Index

general 267-270
godly fear leads to obedience 147
important hindrance 176
praise sweeps Satan and fear away 73
prayer for release from fear 270
Satan instills fear in us when we are
   passive 73
see "Fear" in Appendix
sin brings fear 145
Finances 130, 217-218, 230, 248, 260
hindrances to receiving hidden
   treasures 271
Jesus is our Provision 28
see "Debt, ending" in Appendix
see "Finances" in Appendix
Seven Keys to Financial Prosperity
   270
Seven Steps to Financial Success
   271

G

God 51, 154, 272
blessings 97
Children of God 92
   "You are gods" 92
harmony or unity with 272
His names reveal who He is 88
intimacy with God 155
main purpose for us: loving relationship with our Father 154
poem: "I AM" 277
things that please God 273
God kind, God plane 54
"after their kind" 89
called to be in the God Family 90
Grace 10, 26, 28, 32, 43-44, 47, 53, 56,
   84, 89-94, 100, 114, 141, 162-163,
   170, 183, 192-193, 195, 210, 218,
   224, 226, 255-256, 266, 273, 276
empowerment, most important
   meaning 43
gives us Godly strength to obey 210

grace to forgive 56
saved by 162
see "Grace" in Appendix
twenty-five (25) divine graces 273
unmerited, enabling power God
   freely gives us to overcome sin 141

H

Healing 12, 25-27, 31, 33, 38-41, 44-
   45, 47-48, 68, 72, 99, 111, 113, 131,
   134,146-147, 155, 161, 163, 165,
   169, 284
a process 51
already healed 2,000 years ago 52
by Jesus' stripes 52
emotional healing 29
health 134
hindrances to healing 34, 98, 161
in Jesus' atonement 25
lying symptoms 65
our right 134
part of covenant promises 78
part of salvation 5
poem: "Saved By His Stripes" vi
promise 134
   based on condition of obedience 52
prosperity 134
Scriptures, healing 295
see Chapter 3 and Chapter 4
see Chapter 18
see "Prayers for Healing" in Appendix
sickness, don't tolerate 152
soul 284
victory 134
Healing Scriptures 295
Hindrance(s) xii, 3, 20-21, 24, 34, 44-
   46, 49, 52, 65, 68, 72, 81, 98, 115,
   159-162, 166, 169, 283, 289
accepting identity in Christ 99
Biblical concept of hindrances 165
breaching details and conditions of
   covenants 148

301

Why Doesn't God Heal Me?

curses, major hindrance 111
introduction to hindrances 165
key to elimination of 160
godly fear, lack of 147
guidelines 166
often occur by disobedience 52
praying and fasting, only way to
  override all hindrances 160
removal of, prayer for 289
see Chapter 18
to healing 147
to receiving hidden treasure 271
unforgiving heart 147
Holy Spirit 2-3, 14, 16-17, 24. 47, 53,
  56, 91, 139-140, 160, 244
actions of 138
Spirit of humility 93
teaches us the Word 120

I

Identity in Christ 43, 81, 264
basis of our Christian walk 81
change our present by showing us
  who we are 83
Daily Declarations of 264
freedom from hindrances to healing
  81
knowing our identity is a process 87
most important truth we can know 88
precedes behavior 81
resumé of 274
Satan's lies block maturity and
  growth 83
see "Crucifixion Prayer" in Appendix
see kings and priests 84
see also Who We Are in Christ 84

J

Jesus 28, 117, 278
Bread of Life 31
Bridegroom 119
God of the "Old" Testament 4, 278
King of kings, and Lord of lords 118

living Word 2
our Salvation 130
see "Jesus" in the Appendix
see "Jesus' Substitionary Sacrifice"
  in the Appendix
see also "Jesus – God of the 'Old'
  Testament" in Appendix
see also "Jesus' Name, meanings of"
  in Appendix
see also "Jesus: Who He Is and
  What He Expects from Us" in
  Appendix

K

Kingdom of Darkness 10, 100, 137,
  213, 222, 224, 251
Kingdom of God 2, 75, 125, 133, 188,
  208, 213
  keys of the Kingdom 97-98, 103,
  107, 204
Kingdom of Light 10, 100, 137, 223-
  224, 251
Kings and priests 84
  royal priesthood 84
  see "Identity in Christ" in Appendix
Knowledge xii, 5-6, 12-14, 53, 60-61,
  64, 81-82, 86, 88, 95, 115, 120-121,
  136, 160, 187
  destroyed for lack of 6, 114, 149,
  159, 245
  restore knowledge 115

L

Life 159
  see "Life, choosing" in Appendix
Lord 117-127, 219, 222
  Adonai, only 4% of the time 120
  derives from the concept of breadwinner 126
  meaning of 122
  mistranslation 123
Lucifer, see "Satan

Index

M
Millennium 13-15, 92, 132, 183, 188

N
Name(s) 10, 88, 130
Jesus, His exciting names 130
mistranslation 4
Yahweh's redemptive names 27-28
New Covenant 4, 21, 26, 33-34, 47-48,
53, 112, 145-149, 161, 163, 186-188,
210, 224, 227, 255
New Testament 4, 13, 99
Nimrod 182

O
Oil 24, 32, 145, 170, 206, 260
anointing 48, 122, 181, 209,
Old Covenant 21, 26, 47, 53, 112, 184,
188, 195, 200, 227, 244
Old Testament 3-4, 21, 47, 99, 187

P
Poem(s) vi, 176, 277
I AM 277
Ode to a Hypo C 176
Saved By His Stripes vi
Power of the tongue 108
claim the healing Jesus paid for you
with your mouth 110
God's power is in His words, so is
ours 108
power to bless or to curse 110
reject curses with our mouth in
Jesus' name 110
speaking good things over people
has power to promote blessings 112
Praise 21, 73, 133
activates all aspects of your inheritance 74
activates and intensifies faith 34
allows you to walk in the righteousness of God 74
benefits of praise are enormous 72

brings answers from Holy Spirit 74
can single-handedly defeat enemy 73
celebrating something that hasn't yet
happened 72
contains explosive power 73
establishes God's dominion 74
lack of praise 133
most important part of a church
service 73
not always easy 77
out of mouths of little children 72
persistent praise can eliminate hindrances to healing 72
praise test 77
praising God in the spirit 72
rejoice 76
releases your hope and joy 74
see "Adversity" in Appendix
see steps to heartfelt prayer under
"Prayers" in Appendix
should be a way of life 73
song of praise after communion 34
unleashes power 73, 134
Prayer(s) 41, 74, 157, 281
bathe in thanksgiving 75
for blessing 283
for coming to terms with sin 290
for healing 30, 284
for healing, health, security and
peace 286
for protection and long life 287
for release from frustration 287
for release from Satan's hands 288
for release from sympathy and pity
288
for restoration 289
for self-examination and removal of
hindrances 289
for soul healing 284
identity in crucifixion prayer 282
prayer against ones not said according to God's will 283

Why Doesn't God Heal Me?

quality time 156
ten steps to heartfelt prayer 281
Prayer and fasting 183
 lack of 183
Pride 44, 69, 73, 76, 92-93, 122, 164,
 172, 195, 199, 213, 218, 223, 227,
 230, 272
 Lucifer's principal sin 92
 see "Pride" in Appendix
 some manifestations of 290-293
 specifically related to friendship
  with world 292
Prosperity 33, 78, 86, 129, 137, 167,
 218, 247-248, 255, 261, 270

R

Resurrection 13-15, 28, 36, 66, 90, 93,
 97, 103, 107, 139, 145, 170, 197,
 199, 212
Right(s) 24, 36, 78, 82, 98, 101, 104,
 109, 123, 132, 135-137, 184, 205,
 208, 211, 216, 226, 228, 262, 275
 as citizens of Kingdom of God 133
 blessings of salvation 132-134
 covenant promises 149
 legal rights of Satan and demons 54,
  109, 136, 172, 180, 201
 to be cleansed from sin 101
 to be healed 104, 134
 to be like God 105
 to be protected 12
 to become Children of God 124
 to call down God's blessings 104
 to claim freedom from debt 262
Righteousness 3, 23, 52, 101-107, 160,
 174, 195, 199, 267
 righteousness consciousness 100, 174
 righteousness of God xii, 12, 21, 24,
  28, 36, 74, 86, 98-101, 104-106,
  108, 151, 176. 178-179, 184, 194,
  203, 209-210, 221, 223, 262, 264,
  277

righteousness, a gift 100
speak out in righteousness 107, 152,
 203, 256, 270
walk in Jesus' righteousness 85, 110,
 124, 210

S

Salvation 15, 20, 25-26, 28, 45, 48,
 108, 114, 129, 132,138, 145, 149,
 183, 215, 245, 247, 251
 a gift 162
 become new creations 130
 cannot accept salvation unless you
  accept Jesus 133
 healing part of salvation 5, 110
 in name Jesus 129
 in no other name 13, 119
 rights of salvation 133-134
 see Chapter 13
Satan 6, 9-11, 24, 27, 35, 43-44, 52,
 57, 60, 66, 71-73, 83, 86, 92, 97,
 103-104, 109, 114, 119, 135, 137,
 141, 156, 170, 173, 179,180, 188,
 190, 203, 219, 221, 255, 293
 demons 60
 god of this age/world 12, 60
 power of sin 135
 principal sin: pride 92
 rebellion caused loss of authority 92
 see also Chapter 7
 see "Satan" in Appendix
 ten things Satan hates 294
 why he doesn't have to listen to our
  rebukes 293
 works miracles 61, 231
Semiramis 182
Septuagint 29 130
Sermon on the Mount 105, 225
 hindrances of 225
seven "Power Passages" on healing 20
shalom viii, xii, 20, 27, 36, 45, 130, 247
 refers to physical, spiritual, mental,

Index

emotional and even financial well-being 248

Sin 10, 16, 35, 52-53, 85, 92, 98, 135
breaking God's law of love 160
brings death 85
brings fear and cowardice 144
defeating the power of sin 135
forgiveness of sin a promise 22
hinders healing 161
living force, an evil power 135
often a factor in illness 52
power of sin 138-141
sin and healing 165
sin consciousness 100
"Sinner's Prayer" 100

Soul 3, 5, 28, 46, 54, 57, 83, 85,104, 110, 130, 166, 199, 243, 245, 254, 260, 280

Soul healing 284

Speaking the Word 242, 267, 293

Spiritual warfare 64-66, 68-69, 140, 156, 180, 276
part of healing 180
praise, most powerful form of spiritual warfare 73

T

Ten Commandments 5, 114, 125, 196, 210
"law of Christ" is law of love summed up in them 224
Third Commandment – protection and right use of Jesus' name 125

Ten Reasons Why EVERYONE Needs This Book viii

Tithe, tithing 75, 156-157, 188, 211

Tongues 120, 140, 196, 217
speaking in 140
three kinds 140

Tradition 49, 57, 115, 190-191, 201, 227

Tree of life 9, 16

Tree of the knowledge of good and

evil 3, 9

Trinity 54, 90, 141, 244-245, 278
members all called God 91

Twenty-five (25) graces 43, 193, 210, 273-274, 276

V

Voodoo 35, 112
voodoo curses, release from 260

W

Who we are in Christ 52, 61, 82, 84, 88-89, 95, 177, 203, 274

Witchcraft 24, 131, 189, 217, 258, 260
medication 131
pharmacy 131

Witchcraft curses 35, 256, 258-262

Y

Yahweh 20-21, 27-28, 40, 47, 89, 120-121, 176, 222, 277-278
redemptive names 27

Yeshua 35, 104, 108, 119, 121, 125, 129, 132, 155, 255

YHVH 11, 27, 120, 123, 147, 278

305

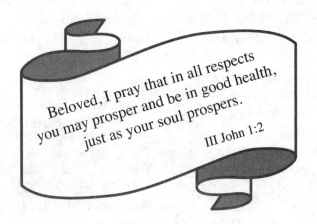

332 Leffingwell Ave., Suite 101
Kirkwood, MO 63122

AVAILABLE AT YOUR LOCAL BOOKSTORE, OR YOU MAY ORDER DIRECTLY. Toll-Free, order-line only M/C, DISC, or VISA 1-800-451-2708.

Visit our Website at *www.impactchristianbooks.com*

Write for *FREE* Catalog.